The publisher gratefully acknowledges the generous
support of the Humanities Endowment Fund of the
University of California Press Foundation.

Migra!

AMERICAN CROSSROADS

Edited by Earl Lewis, George Lipsitz, Peggy Pascoe, George Sánchez, and Dana Takagi

Migra!

A History of the U.S. Border Patrol

———

Kelly Lytle Hernández

UNIVERSITY OF CALIFORNIA PRESS

Berkeley   Los Angeles   London

University of California Press, one of the most distinguished university presses in the United States, enriches lives around the world by advancing scholarship in the humanities, social sciences, and natural sciences. Its activities are supported by the UC Press Foundation and by philanthropic contributions from individuals and institutions. For more information, visit www.ucpress.edu.

University of California Press
Berkeley and Los Angeles, California

University of California Press, Ltd.
London, England

© 2010 by The Regents of the University of California

Library of Congress Cataloging-in-Publication Data

Hernandez, Kelly Lytle.
   Migra! : a history of the U.S. Border Patrol / Kelly Lytle Hernandez.
      p.   cm. — (American crossroads ; 29)
   Includes bibliographical references and index.
   ISBN 978-0-520-25769-6 (cloth : alk. paper) — ISBN 978-0-520-26641-4 (pbk. : alk. paper)
   1. United States. Immigration Border Patrol—History.   2. Mexican-American Border Region—History.   3. Illegal aliens—Mexican-American Border Region.   4. United States—Emigration and immigration.   I. Title.
   JV6483.H45   2010
   363.28'50973—dc22   2009039563

Manufactured in the United States of America

19 18 17 16 15 14 13 12 11
10 9 8 7 6 5 4 3 2

This book is printed on Cascades Enviro 100, a 100% post consumer waste, recycled, de-inked fiber. FSC recycled certified and processed chlorine free. It is acid free, Ecologo certified, and manufactured by BioGas energy.

For my mother
because you taught me to write

For my father
because you inspire me to take on the world

For my brother
because you teach me that change is possible

For my husband
because you are beautiful

For my children
because I love you

[Spoken] It's a bird!
It's a plane!
No man, it's a wetback.
[Sung] He came from the sky, but he is not a plane.
He came in his spaceship from Krypton,
And by the looks of him, he's not American.
He's someone like me—undocumented.
So the migrant should not work
Because even though it hurts, Superman is an illegal.
He's a journalist, and I am too;
He didn't serve in the army (what a bum!)
He is white, has blue eyes and is well-formed;
I'm dark-skinned, chubby, and short.
But in my homeland I already marched
With the coyote I paid when I crossed.

He didn't serve in the military
He doesn't pay taxes and he wants to pass judgment
He doesn't have diamonds or a license to fly.
I'll bet he doesn't even have a social security card.

We need to kick Superman out of here
And if it's possible, send him back to Krypton.
Where is the emigration authority?
What's the news, Mr. Racism, in the nation?
For all I know they don't fine him for flying
But on the contrary, they declare he's Superman.

JORGE LERMA, "SUPERMAN IS AN ILLEGAL ALIEN"

CONTENTS

ILLUSTRATIONS

FIGURES

TABLES

ACKNOWLEDGMENTS

It was only with the love, support, and generosity of a community of scholars, activists, archivists, friends, and family that I was able to conduct the research and develop the ideas at the heart of this book. To do my best to thank them all, I must start with this book's origins in the years that I spent volunteering in the migrant camps of Northern San Diego County. I was just a teenager then, but Reverend Roberto Martínez and Osvaldo Vencor of La Casa de los Hermanos allowed me to participate in their work with undocumented families and laborers living in the canyons. Representing La Casa, I did a little bit of everything. Year after year, Roberto, Osvaldo, the staff of La Casa, and camp residents created space for me to continue contributing in whatever way I could. I thank them for the opportunity that they afforded me to participate in the lives, struggles, and occasional triumphs that were often overlooked as the State of California slid toward the passage of Proposition 187 in November of 1994.

As I worked in the camps, I took courses from George Lipsitz at the University of California–San Diego. George made me want to be a scholar, and in the past fifteen years I have looked to him as a model of intellectual excellence and dexterity matched by a deep reservoir of personal commitment to the pursuit of a life better lived and a world better made. George asked all the right questions, he allowed me to stumble, and he always pushed me to do just a little bit better because the inquiries at the heart of our work demand and deserve it. Thank you, George.

As a graduate student, I had the pleasure to work with Eric Monkkonen. It was Eric's passion for "cop history" that pushed me to see the Border Patrol from a new perspective, to search in unexpected places for evidence of the past, and to test new methods. And it was Eric's incredible sense of humor that made me look forward to a life in academia.

This project never would have left the ground without Marian L. Smith, the historian of the Immigration and Customs Enforcement Service. Marian brokered a rare collaborative agreement between what was then Immigration and Naturalization Service (INS) Historical Reference Library, the National Archives and Records Administration, and myself, by which I assisted with an ongoing indexing project of all INS files held at NARA. I thank David Brown and Cynthia Fox, who were overseeing the INS indexing project, for graciously allowing me to work in the stacks. The opportunity to participate in an indexing project was an invaluable experience. All of the staff and archivists of NARA were helpful during my summer at the archives, but I worked most closely with Suzanne Harris. Like Marian, Suzanne had an extraordinary knowledge of Record Group 85; her assistance was invaluable, and her generous guidance was a constant support.

Another crucial resource for this book was the National Border Patrol Museum (NBPM). The NBPM staff was kind, open, and supportive upon learning that I was writing a history of the U.S. Border Patrol. I thank Brenda Tisdale and Kristi Rasura, in particular, for all of their assistance and conversation. I thank Mike Kirkwood, who was then director of the NBPM, for allowing me full and unrestricted access to all of the museum's records, photos, and files. I am sure that we tell very different stories of the Border Patrol's past, but the staff of the NBPM exemplified a level of openness and transparency that is uncommon for a police historical society. Also I thank the many Border Patrol officers with whom I spoke during my trips to INS Headquarters in Washington, D.C., the NBPM, and the Public Information Officers who have taken me on tours of the U.S.-Mexico border in Texas and California. Gus de la Viña and Bill Carter took time out of their busy schedules to sit down and share their thoughts with me about the history of the U.S. Border Patrol and their experiences as Border Patrol officers and administrators.

My initial research in Mexico was facilitated by Antonio Ibarra, Ariel Rodríguez de Kuri, and Jaime Vélez Storey, who so generously introduced me to the Archivo General de México (AGN) and the Archivo Histórico de la Secretaría de Relaciones Exteriores (AHSRE). A fortuitous partnership with Pablo Yankelevich made it possible to enter and explore the resources of Mexico's Instituto Nacional de Migración. I cannot express enough gratitude to Antonio, Ariel, Jaime, and, most of all, Pablo, whose critical support allowed me to conduct research in Mexico and opened new avenues for my professional and intellectual development.

Numerous colleagues and mentors have generously read and offered their comments on chapters or articles derived from the manuscript. They include Ellen DuBois, Deborah Cohen, Michael Meranze, Erika Lee, Mae Ngai, Eric Avila, Scot Brown, John Laslett, Teresa Alfaro Velkamp, Roger Waldinger, Ruben Hernández-Leon, Kitty Calavita, Benjamin Johnson, Gilbert González, Roger Lane, and Wilbur Miller. Robert Alvarez, George Lipsitz, Steve Aron, Naomi Lamoreaux, Natalia Molina, Geraldine Moyle, George Sánchez, and Vicki Ruiz each read entire drafts of the manuscript. Their comments along with the readers' reports secured by the University of California Press have strengthened my writing and analysis.

I want to acknowledge and thank the following institutions for the financial support that they have provided to move this project from an idea to a book: The Mary M. Hughes Research Fellowship in Texas History of the Texas State Historical Association, the Institute of Global Conflict and Cooperation's Graduate Internship in International Affairs, UC MEXUS, UC MEXUS/CONACYT, the Chicano Studies Research Center at the University of California–Los Angeles, the Center for U.S.-Mexican Studies, the Center for Comparative Immigration Studies at UC–San Diego, the John and Dora Randolph Haynes Faculty Fellowship, the UCLA Institute on American Cultures, the UCLA Academic Senate, UCLA Institute for Research on Labor and Employment Mini-Grant, UCLA International Institute Faculty Fellowship, UCLA Career Enhancement Award, and the UCLA Department of History.

Remarkable graduate and undergraduate student researchers helped with the completion of this book: Carlos Niera, Anahí Parra Sandoval, Paola Chenillo Alazraki, Jennifer Sonen, Morelia Portillo, Monika Gosin, Adriana Flores, Alfred Flores, Amin Eshaiker, Angela Boyce, Rachel Sarabia, and Liliana Ballario.

Finally, I thank my friends who have listened to far more than their fair share of Border Patrol stories. My good friend, Angela Boyce, conducted "emergency research" on my behalf in San Diego. My father, Cecil, and my Aunt Alice each accompanied me on research trips to watch over my sons while I worked in the archives. They, along with all of my father's brothers and sisters, have also been a constant inspiration in their personal courage, devotion to family, and commitment to social justice. My mother taught me to write. She told me to listen to the preacher—not just what he says but how he says it—to read more James Baldwin, and to practice the art form of clearly arranging my thoughts. Then, "Be fierce," she said. She is no longer here, but until the very end she read each and every draft of my school papers. In the hours she spent lovingly and enthusiastically revising my writing, she gave me an enduring gift. And I thank my husband, Sebastian, and our two sons, Isaiah and Solomon. Isaiah and Solomon are the remarkable force that, literally, get me up in the morning; Sebastian carries me through.

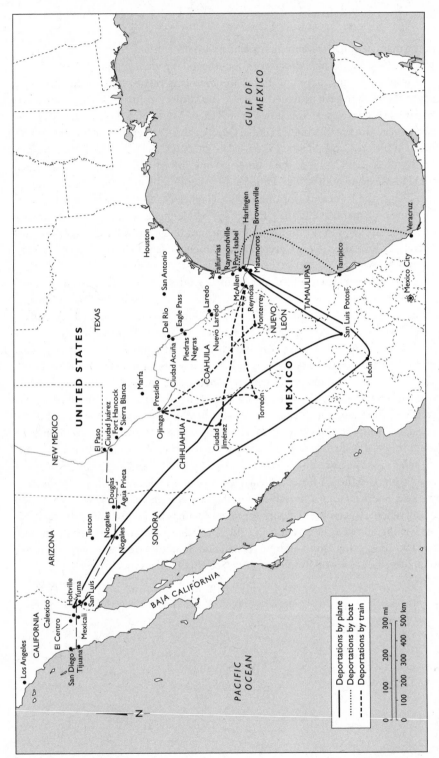

U.S.-Mexico border region, showing selected cities, towns, and deportation routes

Introduction

Toward the end of the Great Depression, DC Comics launched its fantastic tale of an orphaned infant alien who grew up to become an American hero named Superman. The Superman saga begins with the young superhero's dramatic arrival on earth. Just moments before the destruction of his home planet, Krypton, Superman's parents rocket their infant son toward salvation in Kansas. Adopted by a childless but moral and God-fearing couple, Superman spends his early years as nothing more than an average Anglo-American boy coming of age in rural America. But beneath his external appearance, he is different. Unlike his neighbors, Superman can fly, melt steel, and see through walls. And, unlike his neighbors, Superman is an illegal alien.

Thirty-one years before Superman landed in American folklore, the United States Congress passed the Immigration Act of 1907. This law required all immigrants entering the United States to pass through an official port of entry, submit themselves to inspection, and receive official authorization to legally enter the United States. Dropping from the sky and failing to register with the U.S. immigration authorities, Superman entered the United States without authorization. According to U.S. immigration law, the incorruptible leader of the Justice League of America was an illegal immigrant. Yet the tale of Superman evolved free of any hint or consideration of his illegal status. Surely, Superman was just a fantasy and, as such, the character and the narrative were not subject to the basic realities of U.S. immigration restrictions. But in the same years that Superman's popularity soared, the United States became a nation deeply divided over the issue of illegal immigration. From Congress to school boards, Americans decried what many described as an "immigrant invasion" and a loss of control over the country's borders. These debates swirled around the issue of unsanctioned Mexican immigration at the U.S.-Mexico border. By the mid-1970s, vigilantes were patrolling the border, and Congress was hosting explosive debates about how to resolve the so-called wetback problem. As the issue of unauthorized Mexican immigration rippled across the American political landscape, Chicano activist and songwriter Jorge Lerma asked his listeners to consider the irony of Superman's enormous popularity. "It's a bird. It's a plane. No man, it's a wetback!" shouted Lerma. But few people took note that the iconic Man of Steel was an illegal immigrant.

Lerma's provocative interrogation of Superman as America's forgotten illegal immigrant was a critique of the U.S. Border Patrol's nearly exclusive focus on policing Mexican immigrant workers despite many other possible subjects and methods of immigration law enforcement. Established in May 1924, the Border Patrol was created to enforce U.S. immigration restrictions comprehensively by preventing unauthorized border crossings and policing borderland regions to detect and arrest persons defined as unauthorized immigrants. With Asians, prostitutes, anarchists, and many others categorically prohibited from entering the United States and with a massive territory to police, Border Patrol officers struggled to translate their broad mandate into a practical course of law enforcement. Soon, however, in the U.S.-Mexico border region, the officers began to focus almost exclusively on apprehending and deporting undocumented Mexican nationals. Then, during the early 1940s, the entire national emphasis of the U.S. Border Patrol shifted to the southern border. Since the end of World War II, the national police force, which had been established to enforce U.S. immigration restrictions broadly, has been almost entirely dedicated to policing unsanctioned Mexican immigration in the U.S.-Mexico borderlands. With his song, Jorge Lerma offered a sharp criticism of the racialization and regionalization of U.S. immigration law enforcement. Superman was an undocumented immigrant who flew across the cultural landscape but, cloaked in whiteness, he escaped capture, while Mexicans in the borderlands, regardless of immigration or citizenship status, were subject to high levels of suspicion, surveillance, and state violence as Border Patrol officers aggressively policed not only the U.S.-Mexico border but also Mexican communities and work-sites.

This book tells how Mexican immigrant workers emerged as the primary targets of the U.S. Border Patrol and how, in the process, the U.S. Border Patrol shaped the story of race in the United States. It is, in other words, a story of how an American icon lost his illegality and how Mexicans emerged as the "iconic illegal aliens."[1] Framing the contours of this story are the dynamics of Anglo-American nativism, the power of national security, the problems of sovereignty, and the labor-control interests of capitalist economic development in the American southwest. But this book unfolds at the ground level, presenting a lesser-known history of Border Patrol officers struggling to translate the mandates and abstractions of U.S. immigration law into everyday immigration law-enforcement practices. When the working lives of U.S. Border Patrol officers are considered, and when the chatter of big men in big debates in faraway places is taken as the context rather than the content of U.S. immigration law enforcement, the Border Patrol's turn toward policing unsanctioned Mexican immigration emerges as a process that evolved in far more complex and contingent ways than indicated by the master narratives that typically frame our understanding of U.S. immigration control. In particular, this book explores U.S. immigration law enforcement as a matter of state violence in community life, unearths the cross-border dimensions of migration control, and explains the U.S. Border Patrol's growth in the U.S.-Mexico borderlands as intrinsically embedded in the expansion of federal law enforcement in twentieth-century American life. The community, cross-border, and crime-control dimensions of the Border Patrol's development offer new precision to the analysis of how immigration law enforcement evolved as a site of racialization and inequity in the United States. This book, therefore, digs deep into the expansive social world of U.S. immigration law enforcement to chronicle the making and meaning of the Border Patrol's rise in the U.S.-Mexico borderlands.

Although this is the first book dedicated to the history of the U.S. Border Patrol, many scholars have perceptively written about the politics of immigration control that shape Border Patrol practice. The work of Peter Andreas, Joseph Nevins, and Timothy Dunn in particular makes clear that Anglo-American nativism, rising concerns with sovereignty in an era of economic integration, and the labor interests of capitalist economic development play pivotal roles in the shaping of contemporary U.S. immigration law and law enforcement.[2] Daniel Tichenor, David Montejano, Kitty Calavita, Mae Ngai, Gilbert González, and George Sánchez have pushed this analysis back in time and have confirmed the influence of nativism, sovereignty, and labor control in the design of U.S. immigration control.[3] In particular, these scholars emphasize the significant impact of agribusiness in the American southwest upon the early formation of U.S. immigration law-enforcement practices in the U.S.-Mexico borderlands. The Border Patrol, they explain, was established at a moment of a dramatic expansion in agricultural production in the southwestern United States. To plant, pick, and harvest the rapidly expanding acres of crops, agribusinessmen recruited seasonal labor from Mexico and rarely hesitated to demand immigration control practices that promoted their desire for unrestricted Mexican labor migration to the United States. But many employers also appreciated what Nicholas De Genova describes as the emergent "deportability" of undocumented workers, because the threat of deportation disciplined and marginalized the Mexican immigrant labor force.[4] Agribusinessmen kicked, screamed, winked, lobbied, and cajoled for Border Patrol practices that allowed unrestricted access to Mexican workers while promoting effective discipline over the region's Mexicano workforce.[5]

This book shores up the notion that agribusinessmen and the overall demands of labor control within the vortex of capitalist economic development, especially in the American southwest, significantly influenced the development of the U.S. Border Patrol. Established to manage human migration across the nation's borders, the Border Patrol policed the corridor of international labor migration between the United States and Mexico.[6] But a close look at the Border Patrol's everyday efforts to enforce U.S. immigration restrictions reveals that the Border Patrol's project in the U.S.-Mexico borderlands was far from an inevitable and unmitigated expression of the interests of capitalist economic development. Rather, Border Patrol practice was a site of constant struggle. Employers, immigrants, Border Patrol officers, bureaucrats, Mexican politicians, nativists, Mexican American activists, and many others battled over the translation of U.S. immigration restrictions into a social reality in the U.S.-Mexico borderlands. This book foregrounds the constant struggle involved with the Border Patrol's enforcement of immigration restrictions.

To tell this story of struggle required many years of digging through boxes stored in garages, closets, back rooms and, in one case, an abandoned factory where the records authored by and written about the U.S. Border Patrol have sat undisturbed for decades. Gaining access to records that had yet to be officially archived and/or properly indexed required the generosity of a wide range of people who supported my requests to literally unlock and unpack the history of the Border Patrol. For example, when I began this study, the vast majority of the Border Patrol correspondence records remained lost in the stacks of the National Archives and Records Administration (NARA), unseen since first archived in 1957. With the expert guidance of the U.S. Immigration and Naturalization Service (INS) historian, Marian L. Smith, and the support of NARA archivists, David Brown and Cynthia Fox, I was able to move out of the research room and into the NARA stacks to sift through the archival goldmine of Border Patrol memos, personnel files, field activity reports, and internal investigations.[7] Similarly, the National Border Patrol Museum in El Paso, Texas, provided full access to the stacks and suitcases of material that retired Border Patrol officers have donated to the museum over the years. Out of these boxes, stacks, and suitcases emerged reams of records that had yet to enter the official historical record. The detailed and candid documents of the officers of the U.S. Border Patrol—their poetry, their memos, their letters, their memories, their reports, and their handwritten notes—are at the center of this book's narrative and present a complicated portrait of the Border Patrol's rise in the U.S.-Mexico borderlands.

First, Border Patrol correspondence records and oral histories offer new insight into the many ways that Border Patrol officers and the border communities in which they lived shaped the development of U.S. immigration-control practices. Revealing the community histories embedded within the making of federal law enforcement offers a crucially important perspective upon the complicated process of translating U.S. immigration law into law enforcement because, although higher authorities barked mandates and established a broad context for immigration control, Border Patrol officers typically worked on back roads and in small towns. There, they made discretionary decisions, compromises, and innovations that intimately bound Border Patrol work to community life while profoundly shaping the organization's overall development. Most important, Border Patrol officers negotiated how to use the authority invested in them as U.S. immigration law-enforcement officers, engaging in daily struggles over their unique police function to distribute state violence in the pursuit of migration control. At the intersection of their lives in the borderlands and their authority as federal police officers, Border Patrol officers rationalized and prioritized their mandate for immigration law enforcement with regard to the social anxieties, political tensions, and economic interests invested in the overall police project of using state violence to establish and maintain social order through migration control. The development of the Border Patrol, in other words, is best understood as an intrinsically social and political process revolving around questions of violence and social order rather than as a system of unmitigated responses to criminalized activity.

This book concentrates on the negotiations and contests over the use of violence as it became embedded within the Border Patrol's evolving practices. I explore this story at its most basic level of the uneven struggle among officers, immigrants, and community members over the violence implicit to the project of controlling human mobility not only across the U.S.-Mexico border but also within the greater U.S.-Mexico borderlands. This approach to the history of the Border Patrol forwards a textured understanding of how Mexican immigrants emerged as the primary targets of U.S. immigration law enforcement. For example, during the Border Patrol's early years in the U.S.-Mexico borderlands, a region where the deeply rooted divisions between Mexican migrant laborers and Anglo-American landowners dominated social organization and interactions, Border Patrol officers—often landless, working-class white men—gained unique entry into the region's principal system of social and economic relations by directing the violence of immigration law enforcement against the region's primary labor force, Mexican migrant laborers. Still for the men who worked as Border Patrol officers, the authority vested in them as federal immigration law-enforcement officers did not simply mean servicing the needs of agribusiness. Rather, it also functioned as a means of commanding the respect of local elites, demanding social deference from Mexicans in general, achieving upward social mobility for their families, and concealing racial violence within the framework of police work. In this social history of Border Patrol practice—a history of the violence emerging from the everyday politics of enforcing U.S. immigration restrictions—I argue that the U.S. Border Patrol's rise in the U.S.-Mexico borderlands not only evolved according to economic demands and nativist anxieties but also operated according to the individual interests and community investments of the men who worked as Border Patrol officers.[8]

At the same time that the officers of the U.S. Border Patrol shaped the enforcement of federal immigration restrictions, they also pursued their specific mandate for U.S. immigration law enforcement by policing foreign nationals for crimes committed along a shared boundary. Border Patrol work, therefore, emanated from national mandates and pivoted on local conditions, but it also unfolded within an international framework that established cross-border politics and possibilities for U.S. migration-control efforts. This book details how the Border Patrol took shape within a bi-national context of the politics and practices of controlling unsanctioned Mexican migration along the U.S.-Mexico border.

When I began research on this project, I did not fully appreciate the importance of the bi-national dimensions of migration control upon the development of the U.S. Border Patrol. The patrol is a national police force dedicated to enforcing federal immigration law, and I proceeded with the assumption that its work, the enforcement of national law against unwanted and excluded outsiders, was the ultimate expression of national sovereignty and nation-bound interests.[9] Further, its authority as a national police force stopped at the international border. The analytical implication of my early assumptions about the bounded nature of U.S. Border Patrol work was that, while I could examine the translation of national law and federal police power within the local contexts of the borderlands, the final and outer limit of the development and deployment of Border Patrol practice would be defined by the territorial limits of the nation-state. But the more dusty records I read, the more I came to realize that the Border Patrol's rise took shape within a cross-border context of migration control along the U.S.-Mexico border.

The first traces I found of the cross-border influences upon U.S. Border Patrol practices and priorities surfaced in the U.S. Border Patrol and U.S. State Department correspondence records. Here and there, memos from U.S. attachés in Mexico and Border Patrol officers working along the border referenced a Mexican Border Patrol within the Mexican Department of Migration that worked with its U.S. Border Patrol counterpart to police unauthorized border crossings along the U.S.-Mexico border. I had never before heard of a Mexican Border Patrol (nor had any of the scholars and archivists with whom I spoke) and was intrigued by the possibility that U.S. Border Patrol practices in the U.S.-Mexico borderlands developed in conjunction with efforts south of the border.[10] To learn more, I headed to the archives in Mexico City, where I conducted research at Mexico's Archivo General de la Nación, Archivo de la Secretaría de Relaciones Exteriores, and the Hermenoteca Nacional. While extraordinarily helpful in terms of understanding the Mexican politics of emigration control, these archives did not hold what I was hoping to find—the records of the Mexican Department of Migration.

Established in 1926 and known as the Mexican Department of Migration (MDM) until 1993, the Instituto Nacional de Migración (INM) in the Secretaría de Gobernación is responsible for enforcing Mexican immigration law by managing, facilitating, regulating, and policing human migration into and out of Mexico. The officers of the INM spend their days enforcing immigration restrictions against foreign nationals and managing the exit and return of Mexican citizens. Much of the history of migration to and from Mexico during the twentieth century is thus held in the records of the INM. When I first began my research in Mexico, the historical records of the INM, namely, the records of the Mexican Department of Migration, had yet to be officially archived, systematically indexed, or publicly released, much like the records of the U.S. Border Patrol. But in collaboration with the INM and Professor Pablo Yankelevich of Mexico's Instituto Nacional de Antropología e Historia, we launched the first indexing and research project at the Archivo Histórico del Instituto Nacional de Migración (AHINM). The archive was housed in an abandoned factory in Mexico City. Many of the boxes contained papers that had literally disintegrated into slush, but about four thousand boxes containing an estimated four hundred thousand files had survived the years of disregard in a forgotten and leaky warehouse.[11]

The surviving records of the Mexican Department of Migration speak against the tendency to frame U.S. immigration control and border enforcement exclusively in terms of U.S.-based concerns regarding sovereignty, labor control, and unwanted migration. South of the border, Mexican officers attempted to prevent Mexican workers from illegally crossing into the United States and, when politically possible, pushed and prodded representatives of the U.S. Department of State, the U.S. Immigration and Naturalization Service (INS), and the U.S. Border Patrol to improve border control and to deport Mexican nationals who broke both U.S. and Mexican law by surreptitiously crossing into the United States.[12] Further, a constellation of records pulled from U.S. and Mexican archives trace how the rise of the U.S. Border Patrol in the U.S.-Mexico borderlands developed in partnership with the establishment and expansion of cross-border systems of migration control during the 1940s and early 1950s. The Border Patrol's deepening focus on the southern border and on persons of Mexican origin evolved during the 1940s, in great part, in response to Mexican demands and in coordination with Mexican emigration-control efforts. This book, therefore, complicates notions that the rise of the U.S. Border Patrol is the product of exclusively U.S.-based interests and makes Mexico a crucial partner in the development of modern migration-control and border-enforcement practices in the U.S.-Mexico borderlands.

To incorporate Mexican interests in and influences upon the U.S. Border Patrol, I tell the history of the patrol within the bi-national context of migration control between the United States and Mexico. I narrate the U.S.-Mexico encounter implicit within this bi-national history according to the career of U.S. imperialism in Mexico. Between 1848 and World War II, U.S. economic imperialism in Mexico was aggressive, uncompromising, and punctuated by threats of military invasion. But World War II shifts in U.S. global power and claims by the Mexican political and economic elite forced U.S. imperialism in Mexico to operate with the support and collaboration of Mexican economic and political elites.[13] John Mason Hart describes the new era of U.S. imperialism in Mexico as one defined by "cooperation and accommodation."[14] Under the new conditions of U.S. imperialism in Mexico, migration control operated as a site of cross-border cooperation and accommodation. Understanding U.S. Border Patrol practice as a site of cross-border negotiation and cooperation (although still shadowed by an imbalanced relationship between the United States and Mexico) opens space for exploring the pivotal role that Mexico played in deepening the Border Patrol's focus upon the southern border and policing undocumented Mexican immigration, particularly during World War II.

While unearthing such community and cross-border influences, this book stretches the domain of the U.S. Border Patrol from its familiar home within U.S. immigration history to write immigration control into the history of crime and punishment in the United States. The history of the U.S. Border Patrol is much more than a chapter in the story of Mexican labor migration to the United States. As such, this book centers upon examining the entanglement of Mexican labor migration and Border Patrol practice, but it enters this story from the perspective of a police force coming of age in twentieth-century America. In particular, this book charts the history of the Border Patrol within the context of the expansion of U.S. federal law enforcement in the twentieth century.

When Congress first established the U.S. Border Patrol, it joined a small and relatively weak collection of federal law-enforcement agencies.[15] Not until the New Deal did Congress and executive authorities begin to part with the American tradition of local law enforcement by strengthening federal crime-control bureaucracies and expanding federal crime-control powers. In its first decades, the U.S. Border Patrol, like its federal counterparts, was a small outfit of officers working on the periphery of law enforcement and crime control in the United States. In these days, the mandate for migration control may have come from Washington, D.C., but Border Patrol practices and priorities were primarily local creations.

During World War II and in the decades to come, federal initiatives, resources, and, at times, directives dramatically altered the balance of law enforcement and criminal justice in the United States. While municipal police forces continued to dominate patrol activities, World War II internment and border-security efforts, Cold War concerns regarding saboteurs, the demands of civil rights workers for federal protection from local political violence in the American south, and, most important, the ascent of drug control as a national program all pushed a hard turn toward nationalized systems, discourses, and projects of crime control in the second half of the twentieth century. The U.S. Border Patrol benefited enormously from new investments in and concerns about federal law enforcement. Overall funding increased, payroll expanded, technologies improved, and, most important, immigration control was more tightly linked to federal objectives ranging from domestic security to drug interdiction, namely, those concerning the U.S.-Mexico border. Throughout the second half of the twentieth century, there would be expansions and contractions in Border Patrol budgets, but the organization never returned to its origins as a decentralized outfit of local men enforcing federal law. In many ways, the rise of the U.S. Border Patrol in the U.S.-Mexico borderlands is a story about the expansion and consolidation of federal law-enforcement capacities in the twentieth century.

In detailing these many dimensions of the patrol's turn toward policing unsanctioned Mexican immigration, this book sharpens our understanding of how U.S. Border Patrol practice evolved as a very specific site of racial inequity. Immigration control, as legal scholars Linda Bosniak, Kevin Johnson, and others argue, is not simply matter of keeping immigrants out or letting immigrants in. Rather, the U.S. immigration regime operates as a formal system of inequity within the United States because, beyond questions of basic political enfranchisement, various social welfare benefits are distributed according to immigrant status, and individual protections such as those against indefinite detention are categorically denied to excludable aliens. The U.S. immigration regime, in other words, operates as a deeply consequential system that manages, shapes, and participates in the inequitable distribution of rights, protections, and benefits between citizens and immigrants and among the various immigrant-status groups within the United States.[16]

For unauthorized immigrants, the formal tiers of inequity embedded within the U.S. immigration regime are compounded by the fear of deportation that encourages unauthorized migrants to attempt to evade detection by finding safety in zones of social, political, and economic marginalization. Susan Bibler Coutin describes these zones of marginalization as "spaces of nonexistence" that function as "sites of subjugation" and "loci of repression" by both formally and informally "limiting rights, restricting services, and erasing personhood."[17] Similarly Mae Ngai defines illegal immigrants as "a caste, unambiguously situated outside the boundaries of formal membership and social legitimacy."[18] Whether understood as a manifestation of nonexistence or caste, the relentless marginalizations of illegal status, formal and informal, transform persons guilty of the act of illegal immigration into persons living within the condition of being illegal.[19]

Yet being illegal is highly abstract in everyday life. Not only are there countless ways of becoming illegal—entry without authorization, overstaying a visa, or violating the conditions of legal residency—but, as Coutin explains, "The undocumented get jobs, rent apartments, buy property, go to school, get married, have children, join churches, found organizations, and develop friendships. . . . Much of the time, they are undifferentiated from those around them."[20] Without any precise indicators of the condition of illegality, it is difficult to identify unauthorized immigrants. However, with the mandate to detect, detain, interrogate, and apprehend persons for violating U.S. immigration restrictions, officers of the U.S. Border Patrol spend their working hours bringing bodies to the abstract political caste of illegality. Border Patrol officers, therefore, literally embody this site of political disenfranchisement, economic inequity, and social suspicion within the United States. The patrol's focus upon policing unsanctioned Mexican immigration assigned the inequities, disenfranchisements, suspicions, and violences of being illegal to persons of Mexican origin.[21] In other words, as Jorge Lerma and many scholars and activists have noted, the rise of the U.S. Border Patrol in the U.S.-Mexico borderlands effectively Mexicanized the set of inherently and lawfully unequal social relations emerging from the legal/illegal divide.[22]

U.S. immigration control is widely recognized as a site of racial inequity, but this book's social history of Border Patrol practice allows for more precision in identifying the targets of immigration enforcement while calling for a more expansive understanding of how migration control in the borderlands evolved as of the story of race in the United States. Border Patrol correspondence records, complaint files, and cultural artifacts—cartoons, humor, autobiographies, and so forth—reveal tacit distinctions of gender, class, and complexion that Border Patrol officers policed. As one officer liked to joke, the Border Patrol's primary target was a "Mexican male; about 5'5" to 5'8"; dark brown hair; brown eyes; dark complexion; wearing huaraches . . . and so on."[23] In the 1940s, Border Patrol officers expanded the gender profile of the undocumented immigrant to encompass women and families, but their commitment to class, complexion, and national origins remained firm. Tracing the nuances of the Border Patrol's targeted enforcement of U.S. immigration restrictions clarifies dimensions of gender, class, and complexion that were rendered invisible when officers simply referred to their targets as "Mexican." Class and complexion are undeniably slippery social categories, but this book's focus upon the unarticulated discretions of Border Patrol practices reveals crucial intersections of class and complexion that shaped the Border Patrol's policing of Mexicans. To capture the complexion-inflected class specificity of these practices, I introduce the term *Mexican Brown* as a conceptual and rhetorical tool because, regardless of immigration or citizenship status, it was Mexican Browns rather than abstract Mexicans who lived within the Border Patrol's sphere of suspicion.

Further, the nuances of policing Mexicans unfolded in conversation with questions, discourses, and structures dedicated to upholding distinctions between blackness and whiteness in twentieth-century American life. From the days of Jim Crow racial segregation to the expansion of the prison system, the Border Patrol's policing of Mexicans always drew degrees of logic, support, and legitimacy from black/white racial stratification. There is, in other words, no "beyond black and white" in the story of U.S. immigration control, and it is precisely the black-and-white dimensions of policing Mexicans for unsanctioned migration that clarify how U.S. immigration law enforcement evolved as a story of race in the United States. This book therefore charts how the black/white divide shaped the Border Patrol's Mexicanization of the legal/illegal divide.[24]

Finally, the Border Patrol's racialization of the legal/illegal divide also evolved as a bi-national formation of migration-control efforts across the U.S.-Mexico border. The participation of Mexican officials in the U.S. Border Patrol's rise in the U.S.-Mexico borderlands reveals the bi-national dynamics of policing Mexicans in the United States. This story runs contrary to the tendency to interpret the transnational and international impact upon U.S. race relations, particularly in the post–World War II era, as a turn toward progressive reform and liberation politics.[25] This book, therefore, provides one example of how anxieties and interests from beyond U.S. borders contributed to the hardening rather than the dismantling of racialized social and political inequities within United States after World War II.[26]

By the time that Jorge Lerma sang his song, "Superman Is an Illegal Alien," a song about race, illegality, and inequality in America, the Border Patrol's turn toward policing unsanctioned Mexican immigration in the U.S.-Mexico borderlands was already complete. The consequences of the Border Patrol's uneven enforcement of U.S. immigration restrictions were significant, but the reasons for it seemed simple and unalterable: Mexicans crossed the border without sanction, and the Border Patrol, in response, concentrated on policing unsanctioned Mexican immigration in the U.S.-Mexico borderlands. Yet, all told, the making of the U.S. Border Patrol in the U.S.-Mexico borderlands turned upon much more than the unsanctioned border crossings of Mexican nationals. From the interests and concerns of individual officers to the demands of policing the corridor of international labor migration, the patrol's turn toward policing Mexican immigrants quite often had less to do with the men, women, and children who crossed the border and more to do with the communities they entered, the countries they crossed between, and the men they confronted along the way.[27] From Mexico City to Washington, D.C., down to the sister cities of Brownsville, Texas, and Reynosa, Tamaulipas, the U.S. Border Patrol created the practices of U.S. immigration law enforcement at the vexing crossroads of community life, regional interests, national politics, and international relations in the U.S.-Mexico borderlands. And from the expansion of federal police powers in the twentieth century to the shifts in the black/white divide in modern America, the U.S. Border Patrol's steady rise is a history that unfolded in conversation with far more than the laws that the institution was founded to enforce. Therefore, by carefully examining the dusty and scattered record of the U.S. Border Patrol, this book provides what Antonio Gramsci once described as an "inventory" of the many "traces," that is, a catalogue and analysis of the many histories that shaped the making and the meaning of the U.S. Border Patrol in the U.S.-Mexico borderlands.[28]

This book is arranged into three chronological parts. Each part represents one of three generations in the U.S. Border Patrol's first fifty years on patrol between 1924 and 1974. Part 1 addresses the highly regional and local period of Border Patrol operations from the establishment of the U.S. Border Patrol on May 28, 1924, to the entrance of the United States into World War II in 1941. Chapter 1 provides a foundation for understanding Border Patrol work in these years by outlining the mandate, the men, and the bureaucracy of the U.S. Border Patrol during the 1920s and 1930s. Chapter 2 tells the story of the greater Texas-Mexico borderlands, where a concentration of local men hired as U.S. Border Patrol officers directed the development of U.S. immigration law enforcement. Here, the patrol's narrow enforcement of U.S. immigration restrictions was deeply connected to the social world in which the officers came of age before they became officers of the state. Chapter 3 focuses on the development of Border Patrol practices and priorities along the California and western Arizona border regions, where Border Patrol officers tended to be outsiders struggling to rationalize the many possibilities for U.S. immigration law enforcement. Here, the shifting political economy of Mexican labor migration and the fiscal limitations of policing European and Asian immigration tilted the Border Patrol's focus toward policing Mexican immigrants. Together, chapters 1, 2, and 3 argue that, while immigration restriction was a national phenomenon, U.S. Border Patrol practice in the 1920s and 1930s was a deeply social project that was defined by highly regionalized interpretations of the possibilities and limitations of U.S. immigration law enforcement. Chapter 4 heads south of the U.S.-Mexico border to explore how the 1924 consolidation in U.S. immigration control sparked Mexican efforts to prevent Mexican workers from committing the crime of illegal entry into the United States.

Part 2 opens with the nationalization of the U.S. Border Patrol during World War II, continues with an exploration of the impact of cross-border systems of managing Mexican labor migration upon U.S. Border Patrol practice, and closes with an examination of the opposition of agribusiness in South Texas to the delocalization of Border Patrol personnel, practices, and priorities during the 1940s. Chapters 5 and 6 address how the establishment of the Bracero Program as a cross-border program for managing U.S.-Mexico labor migration transformed migration control along the U.S.-Mexico border: bilaterally managing the importation of legal Mexican labor into the United States provided new possibilities and demands for the bilateral management of deporting illegal Mexican labor out of the United States. Chapter 7 examines how bilateral migration control upset Border Patrol relations with old friends and neighbors, namely, South Texas agribusinessmen accustomed to familiar Border Patrol officers enforcing federal law according to local customs and interests. Together, Chapters 5, 6, and 7 demonstrate how the dramatic and contested delocalization of U.S. Border Patrol operations actually intensified the patrol's concentration upon policing unsanctioned Mexican immigration.

By the early 1950s, the U.S. Border Patrol was embroiled in crisis. The South Texas farmers were in rebellion, and a constant upward tick in U.S. Border Patrol apprehension statistics suggested that the patrol had lost all control along the U.S.-Mexico border. Part 3 opens by examining how the U.S. Border Patrol triumphed over the crises of consent and control in the U.S.-Mexico borderlands and closes with an analysis of how the patrol proceeded in the quiet years that followed. In particular, Chapter 8 demonstrates that while Border Patrol officials declared that an unprecedented show of force during the summer of 1954 had ended the crises of control and consent in the U.S.-Mexico borderlands, it was actually compromise with farmers and a retreat from aggressive migration control that closed the so-called "wetback decade" of 1944 to 1954. Chapter 9 offers an examination of the dramatic reimagination of U.S. migration control after the triumphs of 1954. In particular, subtle changes in U.S. Border Patrol rhetoric, propaganda, and strategies along the U.S.-Mexico border reframed the patrol's mission from controlling unsanctioned labor migration to preventing cross-border criminal activities, such as prostitution and drug trafficking. In these years, the policing of the unsanctioned migrations of poor Mexican-born workers increasingly intersected with the policing of the cross-border trafficking of marijuana and narcotics such as Mexican-grown heroin, a.k.a. Mexican Brown. My use of the term *Mexican Brown*, therefore, is not only a conceptual and rhetorical tool that captures the shades of class and color of the people that Border Patrol officers policed but also an intentional indication of the entanglements of migration control with crime control and drug enforcement during the 1960s, 1970s, and beyond.

This book closes at the dawning of the embattled decades of the late twentieth century, when the U.S. Border Patrol's management of the problems of race, crime, and migration became almost impossible to disentangle. These years were marked by a steady escalation of border enforcement and a dramatic intensification of the raids upon Mexican communities in the borderlands region. In song and litigation, Jorge Lerma and a growing number of Chicano/a activists and immigrant rights advocates protested the impact of U.S. Border Patrol practices upon Mexicans crossing into the United States and Mexicans living north of Mexico. Superman took to the skies and floated right on by, Lerma complained, but Mexicans had to carry identification and, if illegal, be detained or deported. Lerma identified "Mr. Racism" as the root of Border Patrol prejudices and discretions. While the legal/illegal divide functioned as a racial divide through the Border Patrol's uneven enforcement of U.S. immigration restrictions, the racialization and regionalization of U.S. immigration law enforcement was far more complicated than Lerma imagined, and reducing U.S. Border Patrol practices to Anglo-American racism masks the strange but powerful nexus of men, interests, choices, and chances that, despite a world of other possibilities, ultimately delivered the U.S. Border Patrol to the project of policing Mexicans in the U.S.-Mexico borderlands. Over the years, farmers, U.S. and Mexican government officials, U.S. Border Patrolmen, influential members of the Mexican American middle-class, and even undocumented Mexican immigrants themselves all played roles in the regionalization and racialization of migration control within the United States. Their participation, unequal and often contradictory, pushed the Border Patrol toward its rise in the U.S.-Mexico borderlands while giving nuanced formation to the problem of race that emerges from the patrol's uneven policing of the legal/illegal divide.

PART ONE

Formation

U.S. Border Patrol officers near the California-Mexico border, 1926. Courtesy of the Security Pacific Collection, Los Angeles Public Library.

ESTABLISHED IN MAY OF 1924, the United States Border Patrol's broad police powers rested in its mandate to protect the national interest by enforcing federal immigration laws. Yet, throughout the 1920s and 1930s, poor national coordination effectively regionalized the development of U.S. immigration law enforcement. Part 1 of this book examines the complexity of the U.S. Border Patrol's turn toward policing unsanctioned Mexican immigration in the U.S.-Mexico borderlands. In the greater Texas-Mexico borderlands, defined by the two Texas-based Border Patrol districts with jurisdiction extending from the Gulf of Mexico to southeastern Arizona, the first officers were local boys who had come of age in the borderlands before they became officers of the Border Patrol. These men allowed their work as federal law-enforcement officers to unfold in intimate conversation with the social world of the borderlands. They quickly focused the violence of U.S. immigration law enforcement on policing poor Mexicans and thereby racialized the caste of illegals in the greater Texas-Mexico border region. Along the California and western Arizona borders with Mexico, the Border Patrol's turn toward policing unsanctioned Mexican immigration accompanied a slow turn away from policing unsanctioned European and Asian immigration as policing Mexicans emerged as an expedient and cost-effective strategy for U.S. immigration law enforcement. Finally, part 1 also tells a story that Border Patrol officers of the 1920s and 1930s never would have imagined as part of their own. During this period, conflict was far more common than cooperation between U.S. and Mexican immigration officers working along the U.S.-Mexico border. U.S. Border Patrol officers working during the 1920s and 1930s, therefore, would not have recognized the politics and practices of emigration control south of the U.S.-Mexico border as relevant to the story of U.S. Border Patrol development. These officers had no idea of the massive changes that World War II would bring to U.S. Border Patrol and the practices of migration control along the U.S.-Mexico border. After 1942, U.S. and Mexican officers would often join forces to prevent the unsanctioned border crossings of Mexican nationals and to coordinate mass deportation campaigns not only out of the United States, but reaching deep into the interior of Mexico. Chapter 4, therefore, lays the foundation for U.S.-Mexican collaboration in the 1940s by exploring the politics and practices of emigration control in Mexico during the 1920s and 1930s.

1

The Early Years

Hired in El Paso, Texas, in September 1924, Emmanuel Avant "Dogie" Wright was one of the first officers of the United States Border Patrol. Born and raised in the Texas-Mexico borderlands, Dogie had deep roots in the region where he worked for twenty-seven years as a U.S. Border Patrol officer. Dogie's great-grandparents, Elizabeth and John Jackson Tumlinson, had joined Stephen Austin's 1822 expedition into the northern Mexican province of Coahuila y Tejas (Texas).[1] Dogie's great-grandparents were among the original Anglo-American colonists, commonly known as the "Old Three Hundred," in Austin's Texas project. Although many in the Austin expedition were southern slaveholders hoping to rebuild their prosperous plantations in Texas, the Tumlinsons were simply modest farmers: when they arrived in Texas, their property consisted of some cattle, hogs, horses, and farming utensils.[2] Troubles began soon after the Tumlinsons settled in a district along the Colorado River. The Colorado District was offered to the settlers by the Mexican government but claimed by the Comanches, Tonkawas, Apaches, and Karankawas, who dominated the region along with an assortment of smugglers and frontiersmen. Several months after the colonists arrived, three men guarding a shipload of the colonists' provisions disappeared. Their disappearance frightened the settlers, and, to better protect themselves they formed a government and elected John Jackson Tumlinson as mayor (*alcalde*).[3] John Jackson had yet to take office when two more settlers were found dead. In defense of the colonists and their interests in the region, John Jackson proposed the establishment of a permanent roving patrol. He was killed soon after by a group of Karankawa and Huaco Indians, but the roving patrol that he founded lived on to become the Texas Rangers.

The Texas Rangers shaped and protected Anglo-American settlement in Texas.[4]

They battled indigenous groups for dominance in the region, chased down runaway slaves who struck for freedom deep within Mexico, and settled scores with anyone who challenged the Anglo-American project in Texas. The Rangers proved particularly useful in helping Anglo-American landholders win favorable settlements of land and labor disputes with Texas Mexicans. Whatever the task, however, raw physical violence was the Rangers' principal strategy. As the years unfolded, the stories of the Tumlinson family, Anglo-American settlement in Texas, and the Texas Rangers remained closely intertwined: no fewer than sixteen of John Jackson's descendants protected the interests of Anglo-Americans in Texas in the service of the Texas Rangers.[5] Among them were Dogie Wright and his father, Captain William L. Wright, each of whom served as Rangers in southern Texas.

Anglo-American settlement was slow to develop in south Texas. A few ranchers had pushed southward in the mid-nineteenth century, but most Anglo-American farmers saw little value in the dry and distant lands near the U.S.-Mexico border. Not until the late nineteenth century, when new irrigation techniques and refrigerated rail cars promised to transform the arid border region into a profitable agricultural zone, did Anglo-American farmers begin to imagine and seek their fortune in south Texas. When they arrived, Anglo-American farmers confronted a well-established Mexicano ranching population that did not easily acquiesce to the changes the Anglos envisioned. The violence of the Texas Rangers played a pivotal role in transforming south Texas into a region dominated by Anglo-American farmers.

Born at the dawn of the Anglo-American push into south Texas, Dogie Wright came of age during one of the most brutal periods of the Texas Rangers' history. Walter Prescott Webb, a sympathetic chronicler of the Texas Rangers, described these years as peppered with "revenge by proxy," a strategy by which Rangers indiscriminately killed Mexicanos to avenge the transgressions of others.[6] One of the Rangers' most notorious episodes of bloodshed took place just two months after Dogie was born.

On June 12, 1901, a Mexicano rancher named Gregorio Cortez stood at the gate of his home in Karnes County, Texas. There, he resisted arrest for a crime that he did not commit. The sheriff persisted, drew his gun, and shot Gregorio's brother in the mouth when he charged at the sheriff to protect Gregorio. Gregorio shot back and killed the sheriff, an act that was sure to bring the Texas Rangers to his doorstep. When they came, Gregorio and his family (including his wounded brother) were gone: all that remained was the dead body of the sheriff. The news of Gregorio's deadly defiance quickly spread across southern Texas, and Dogie's father, Captain William Wright of the Texas Rangers, joined the search for Gregorio Cortez. For ten days, the Texas Rangers and posses numbering up to three hundred men hunted for him. When they could not find him, they sought revenge by proxy, arresting, brutalizing, and murdering an unknown number of Mexicanos.

These were the days when Dogie Wright took his first breaths in the U.S.-Mexico borderlands. In the years to come, he helped his father and the Rangers take care of their horses, and as a young adult, Dogie himself became a Ranger. At the age of twenty-three, Dogie joined the U.S. Border Patrol. Descended from the Old Three Hundred, embedded in the history of the Texas Rangers, and born in the shadow of one of the borderland's most brutal battles between Anglos and Mexicanos, Dogie carried a long and complicated history into his work as a Border Patrolman. He was joined by hundreds of other borderlanders hired as Border Patrol officers during the 1920s and 1930s. Like Dogie, they had grown up and lived in the U.S.-Mexico borderlands before they became Border Patrol officers. Their pedigree was not that of the landholding elite but of the Anglo-American working class, who often used law enforcement as a strategy of economic survival and social uplift in the agriculture-based societies of the borderlands. And they had grown up with white violence toward Mexicanos. The broad congressional mandate for migration control provided the outer contours for their work, but the decentralized structure of the early U.S. Border Patrol granted Dogie and the others significant control over the development of U.S. immigration law-enforcement practices. Far from the halls of Congress, the early officers of the Border Patrol enforced U.S. immigration restrictions according to the customs, interests, and histories of the borderland communities where they lived and worked. Therefore, the story of the early years of the U.S. Border Patrol begins in the U.S.-Mexico borderlands.

THE U.S.-MEXICO BORDERLANDS

When the Old Three Hundred first entered Texas in 1822, what would later become the southwestern United States was still part of northern Mexico. From Alta California's Pacific Coast to the Texas plains, many Anglo-Americans coveted the rich natural landscape of the Mexican northwest. The most covetous argued that it was the duty and "manifest destiny" of Anglo-Americans to rule the North American continent from sea to sea.[7] Their imaginings drew strength from the triumph of the Anglo-American colonists in Texas who, in 1836, successfully fought a war for independence against Mexico. Nine years later, the United States annexed the Republic of Texas, but President James Polk (1845–49) wanted more. Inspired by the theory of Manifest Destiny, Polk in January 1846 sent troops into disputed territory below the newly acquired state of Texas. The Mexican army engaged the U.S. troops, but the battle quickly turned into a war that the debt-ridden Mexican government could not afford to fight. United States armed forces occupied Mexico City in 1848 and declared victory over Mexico in the U.S.-Mexico War of 1846–48.

The U.S.-Mexico War was a war of conquest that forced Mexico to cede nearly 50 percent of its northern territory to the United States. The new U.S.-Mexico border was drawn down the belly of the Rio Grande between the Gulf of Mexico and

El Paso, Texas, and from there the border pushed west across the deserts and mountains to the Pacific Ocean. Above this line, an estimated one hundred and fifty thousand Mexicans and one hundred and eighty thousand members of free, indigenous tribes lived in the newly declared American territory. Transferring land ownership from their hands to those of Anglo-Americans would be the final element of conquest in the new American West.

Anglo-American settlers used a variety of techniques to acquire land rights from Mexican and indigenous landholders. While violence, the reservation system, and genocide were popular methods of dispossessing indigenous populations, Anglo-Americans most often gained access to Mexican land rights through marriage, debt payment, fraud, or purchase. By the late nineteenth century, the transfer of ownership from Indians and Mexicans to Anglo-Americans was nearly complete.[8]

The new landholders tended to own large tracts of land. The small, family-owned farm never took root in the American West.[9] Instead, the land barons of the West held tracts averaging tens of thousands of acres, and their visions of agriculture in the region centered upon building massive enterprises that Carey McWilliams described as "factories in the fields."[10] The factory floor was land enriched by eons of geologic shifts. For example, millions of years before the U.S.-Mexico War opened California to Anglo-American farmers, the Pacific Ocean and its many tributaries had washed across the alluvial plains of the San Joaquin Valley in central California, depositing a rich silt of minerals and organic matter. Several hundred miles to the south, much of the Imperial Valley ranked as one of the hottest and driest deserts in all of North America, but the long natural history of the region had buried enormous potential in the dust. The Gulf of California once stretched north and covered much of the Colorado Desert. In time the gulf receded, but the Colorado River spilled into the region and formed Lake Cahuilla, a massive lake a hundred miles long, thirty-five miles wide, and three hundred feet deep. Lake Cahuilla is estimated to have existed for several thousand years before drying up and leaving behind dry but fertile land. Similarly, natural migrations by the Rio Grande, its tributaries, and the Gulf of Mexico left rich silt deposits in the region later divided by the U.S.-Mexico border.[11]

Millions of years of geologic history may have enriched the land barons' land and kindled dreams of agricultural empires in the American West, but water was uncontrolled in the region. Erratic climatic shifts from floods to droughts created unpredictable and thus unsustainable conditions for the development of capitalist agricultural production. The land barons' dreams of industrial farming in the American West depended upon controlling the flow of water through the region.

Congress passed the Newlands Reclamation Act of 1902 to fund large irrigation projects in the West.[12] As dams, canals, and reservoirs controlled the waters, landholders quickly transformed the rich but arid lands into fields of grains, fruits, vegetables, and cotton. By 1920, the southwest served as an orchard and winter garden to the world. With almost thirty-one million acres of crops valued at more than $1.7 billion in California and Texas alone, the southwest was the nation's most productive and profitable agricultural region.[13] During the 1920s, the fortunes reaped from the southwestern soil swelled to new heights as acres of crops boomed to a combined total of more than thirty-nine million in Texas, New Mexico, Arizona, and California.[14]

The rapid expansion of the factories in the fields depended upon an ever-increasing number of migrant workers to seasonally plant and harvest the crops.[15] In California, agribusinesses had once had access to various sources of labor. In the late nineteenth century, landholders had hired California Indians and Chinese immigrants to harvest everything from wheat to fruit and sugar beets.[16] The near success of a genocidal campaign against California Indians, however, had reduced their total population to fewer than nineteen thousand by the turn of the twentieth century, and a violent wave of anti-Chinese politics pushed through the passage of the Chinese Exclusion Act of 1882, which severely limited the availability of Chinese laborers. Some of the Chinese workers fled south into Mexico, where they worked on U.S.- and Mexican-owned farms in the Mexicali Valley just below the California-Mexico border, but the Chinese presence in California agriculture declined significantly in the following years.[17]

Some landowners attempted to replace Chinese immigrants and Indian workers with black migrants from the southern states, but there was significant popular resistance to black settlement in California, and the state's agribusinessmen searched elsewhere for a labor supply.[18] Next they experimented with Japanese laborers, encouraging slightly more than twenty-seven thousand Japanese nationals to enter the United States between 1891 and 1900.[19] Japanese immigrants upset the expectations of agribusinessmen by quickly organizing themselves in the fields to demand higher wages and by making inroads into the business of farming as small landowners and tenants. As agribusinessmen negotiated in the fields, Anglo-American communities, primarily, San Francisco, strongly protested the arrival of Japanese immigrants and created an international incident between the U.S. and Japanese governments by prohibiting Japanese children from attending white schools.[20] In 1907, the U.S. and Japanese governments addressed the mounting tensions between Anglo-Americans and Japanese immigrants in San Francisco by signing the Gentleman's Agreement of 1907, an international treaty by which the Japanese government agreed to significantly curtail Japanese immigration to the United States.[21] Restrictions upon Japanese immigration effectively ended the experiment with Japanese field-workers, while the passage of California's 1913 and 1920 Alien Land Laws significantly curtailed the remaining Japanese presence in California agriculture by prohibiting "aliens ineligible for citizenship"—that is, Asians—from owning or renting farmland.[22] Pushed out of California farming, some of the Japanese followed the Chinese to Mexico and became tenant farmers on U.S.-owned farms in the Mexicali Valley. North of the border, however, labor unrest, immigration restrictions, international treaties, community prejudice, and state law effectively ended the short experiment with Japanese farm laborers.

The end of the Spanish-American War in 1898 launched an era of empire that established new migration corridors between the Philippines and California. Whereas only five Filipinos lived in California in 1900, an estimated thirty thousand Filipinos resided in the state by 1930.[23] Most were male sojourners who came to work. They took jobs as farmworkers and domestic servants, but Filipino migrants proved to be skilled labor organizers who constantly upset the agribusinessmen's search for a docile labor force.[24] California's agribusinessmen barely said a word when Congress effectively ended Filipino migration to the United States with the passage of the Tydings-McDuffie Act of 1934.

All told, as California agribusiness developed, the California Indian population was plummeting to its nadir; Chinese, Japanese, and Filipino workers were prohibited from entering the United States, and black settlement was unwanted. A few experiments with white farm collectives had been tried throughout the state but, by and large, agribusinessmen were looking for temporary, cheap, and marginalized workers who would come and go with the harvests. It was within this context that California's agribusinessmen developed a dependence upon Mexican laborers migrating across the U.S.-Mexico border. By the mid-1920s, Mexicans comprised the vast majority of agricultural workers in the Golden State. Of the estimated eighty thousand workers migrating across the state picking alfalfa, melons, and cotton in the Imperial Valley, peas, cotton and asparagus in the San Joaquin Valley, and citrus in Los Angeles County and the Inland Empire, between 80 and 95 percent were Mexicans by the mid 1920s.[25]

Some agribusinessmen described their turn to Mexican immigrant workers as a result of the "docile" nature of Mexican workers. Mexican workers, they argued, were quiet, diligent, docile, and therefore ideal farm workers. This characterization of Mexican workers disregarded the robust activity of Mexican labor organizing in the United States—the 1903 strike in Oxnard, California; the 1904 railroad strike in the Rio Grande Valley of Texas; and, the 1922 strike in Imperial, California, for example—and ignored the role of Mexican workers in the making of the Mexican Revolution of 1910, but it was a comforting thought for agribusinessmen, who realized that U.S. immigration restrictions had left them with few options by the 1920s.[26] As one of California's many agribusiness lobbyists admitted, "We have gone east, west, and north, and south and he is the only man power available to us."[27]

In south Texas, the story of labor, migration, and agribusiness was different. With a history of black slavery, Texans had fewer hesitations about encouraging black settlement, but while cotton cultivation and fruit production expanded during the 1910s and 1920s, World War I had drawn black southerners north. Texans were unable to attract enough black farm laborers away from their northern destinations. Texans, particularly those in the U.S.-Mexico borderlands, quickly turned to and depended upon Mexican labor.[28] By the 1920s, local farmers estimated that Mexican workers comprised almost 98 percent of the agricultural workforce in south Texas and 80 percent of the state's annual "army" of migrant laborers.[29] They began their work, twenty-five thousand members strong, picking fruits, vegetables, sugarcane, and cotton in the Lower Rio Grande Valley and grew to a migrating army of three hundred thousand workers throughout the state of Texas at the height of the cotton-picking season.

To encourage Mexicans to cross into the United States, U.S. agribusinessmen sent labor contractors into Mexico.[30] Disruptions in the Mexican countryside made their job relatively easy. Until the late nineteenth century, the majority of Mexican laborers were locked in debt peonage and isolated in rural areas that lacked the railroads or other transportation systems that facilitated massive migrations. But the presidency of Porfirio Díaz (1876–1911), a period popularly known as "el Porfiriato," changed the history of Mexican immobility. Díaz pursued a program of modernizing Mexico in the image of nations such as Argentina and the United States. He dramatically expanded Mexico's railroad system (with significant investments from U.S. and English financiers), sparked massive land accumulation (land most often purchased by foreign investors), and encouraged a switch to wage labor. His campaign for "order and progress" released an estimated five million Mexican campesinos from debt peonage and laid tens of thousands of miles of track as economic production increased at a relatively robust rate of 2.7 percent annually, exports in general rose by 6.1 percent per year, with agricultural exports, in particular, expanding by 200 percent between 1876 and 1910. These marks of modernity were followed by a dramatic population increase from nine million in 1876 to more than fifteen million in 1910. In addition, literacy was on the rise. Yet, Díaz's world of "order and progress" was forged at a tremendous price of dispossession and poverty for Mexico's overwhelmingly rural population.[31]

Unabated poverty was the consequence of Díaz's program. More Mexicans were free wage laborers, but more Mexicans were also dangerously poor. Therefore, Mexico's newly mobile wage-labor force migrated in search of work and higher wages.[32] In 1884, the completion of the railroad at El Paso, Texas, directly linked Mexican workers in the populous central regions of Mexico to jobs north of the U.S.-Mexico border.[33] The expansion of U.S. capital in Mexico created corridors of migration that brought Mexican workers north when the southwestern agribusiness boom began in the early twentieth century.

Lawrence Cardoso estimates that Mexican nationals made at least five hundred thousand border crossings into the United States between 1900 and 1910.[34] Migration continued during the 1910s, when the violence of the Mexican Revolution of 1910, combined with disease and the ongoing entreaties of U.S. labor contractors, encouraged Mexican labor migration to the United States. It was during the

1920s, however, that Mexican labor emigration surged with the massive expansion in southwestern agribusiness. Cardoso estimates that the total number of border crossings undertaken by Mexican nationals skyrocketed to more than one million during the 1920s.[35] Amid the convergent booms in southwestern agriculture and Mexican labor migration, the United States Congress launched a new era of work, labor, and migration in the U.S.-Mexico borderlands by tightening U.S. immigration laws and establishing the U.S. Border Patrol. Although Mexico's emigrant workers were not the primary targets of U.S. immigration restrictions, in time and according to a collision of dynamics, they would become the primary targets of U.S. immigration law enforcement.

U.S. IMMIGRATION LAW: THE GENEALOGY OF A MANDATE

The United States Congress established the U.S. Border Patrol on May 28, 1924, by discreetly setting aside one million dollars for "additional land-border patrol" in the Department of Labor Appropriations Act of that year, but the congressional effort of migration control began many years earlier and carried many ambitious projects within it. Beginning with the passage of the 1862 Act to Prohibit the "Coolie Trade," Congress launched an era of increasingly restrictive immigration laws that climaxed with the passage of the National Origins Act of 1924. Passed during the Civil War and driven by the notion that Chinese immigrants were unfree workers, that is, "coolies," the 1862 act functioned, argues historian Moon-Ho Jung, as both the "last slave-trade law" and "the first immigration law."[36] In the era of black emancipation, Jung explains, the turbulent and contested intersection of race, labor, and freedom in the United States framed the origins of U.S. immigration control.

After the passage of the 1862 coolie labor law, Congress spent the next several decades deeply shaping the course of American history by placing a series of limits on immigration to the United States.[37] In 1875, Congress prohibited criminals and prostitutes from legally entering the United States and extended the ban upon contract labor from China.[38] In 1882, Congress passed a general Immigration Act that banned all "lunatics, idiots, convicts, those liable to become public charges, and those suffering from contagious diseases" and expanded the 1862 and 1875 bans on the coolie trade by prohibiting all Chinese laborers from entering the United States.[39] To fund the growing bureaucracy of migration control, the 1882 Act also introduced a 50-cent tax on each person entering the United States. In 1885, Congress expanded the prohibition upon Chinese contract labor by making it unlawful to import any contract laborer into the United States.[40] In 1891, Congress added polygamists to the list of banned persons and authorized the deportation of any person who unlawfully entered the United States.[41] In 1903, epileptics, anarchists, and beggars joined the growing group of excluded persons, and Congress transferred the Bureau of Immigration to the newly created Department of

Commerce and Labor.[42] The 1903 Immigration Act also provided for the deportation of immigrants who became public charges within two years of their arrival in the United States and extended to three years the period during which an immigrant could be deported if found to have been inadmissible at the time of entry. The Immigration Act of 1907 increased the head tax to four dollars per person and added each of the following to the list of excluded persons: "imbeciles, feeble-minded persons, persons with physical or mental defects which may affect their ability to earn a living, persons afflicted with tuberculosis, children unaccompanied by their parents, persons who admitted the commission of a crime involving moral turpitude, and women coming to the United States for immoral purposes."[43] The 1907 Immigration Act also extended the period during which immigrants could be deported if they became public charges from causes existing prior to entry and defined entering the United States without official inspection to be a violation of U.S. immigration restrictions. The Bureau of Immigration was transferred to the newly independent Department of Labor in 1913.[44] The Immigration Act of 1917 created the Asiatic-Barred Zone, which prohibited entry by any immigrant of Asian descent while raising the head tax to eight dollars, imposing an additional ten-dollar visa fee, requiring all eligible immigrants to pass a literacy test, broadening the scope of deportation to a period of five years, and prohibiting entry into the United States at any point other than an official port of entry.[45]

By 1917, the list of persons prohibited from entering the United States included all Asians, illiterates, prostitutes, criminals, contract laborers, unaccompanied children, idiots, epileptics, the insane, paupers, the diseased and defective, alcoholics, beggars, polygamists, anarchists, and more. The penalties for violating U.S. immigration laws varied. For example, importing an immigrant "for the purpose of prostitution or for any other immoral purpose" was a felony punishable by a prison term of up to ten years and a fine not to exceed five thousand dollars. Both unauthorized entry and immigrant smuggling were defined as misdemeanors punishable by up to five years in prison and a fine of two thousand dollars. An assortment of Anglo-American nativists, labor unions, progressives, and others had pushed these many exclusions and penalties into U.S. immigration law. Still the most ardent Anglo-American nativists were not satisfied, and their collective influence was growing in American society, politics, and culture during the 1920s.

THE NATIVISTS' CRUSADE

Comprised of eugenicists, xenophobes, scholars, Klan members, labor organizers, and others, nativists united in opposition to what they viewed as the menacing growth in immigration from eastern and southern Europe.[46] Beginning in the early 1900s, Italians, Poles, Slovaks, and others had rushed into U.S. industrial centers such as New York and Chicago. Their arrival fueled the rise of American manufacturing, but nativists regarded these groups as "undesirable immigrants" who were socially inferior, culturally alien, and politically suspect. Fearing the "contamination" of Anglo-American society and culture by these "new stock" immigrants, nativists demanded an end to immigration from anywhere other than northwestern Europe.[47]

In 1924, Anglo-American nativists played a crucial role in crafting and passing the National Origins Act of that year. The act was a dense bill that outlined, in detail, the limitations placed upon legal immigration. Most important, it ratified all previous immigration restrictions and introduced a nationality-based quota system that strictly limited the number of immigrants allowed to enter the United States each year. According to the intricate quota system, Germany, Britain, and Northern Ireland were afforded 60 percent of the total number of slots made available to all immigrants subject to the national origins system. Europeans of any background grabbed 96 percent of the total available slots. Beyond the quota system, the National Origins Act reconfirmed total Asian exclusion from the United States. Historian John Higham described the National Origins Act as a "Nordic Victory," a triumph of the narrow racial nationalism of Anglo-American nativists during a decade he has characterized as the "tribal twenties."[48] Ironically, however, as Mae Ngai has deftly argued, the long-term impact of that triumph was the reconstitution of a "white American race, in which persons of European descent shared a common whiteness distinct from those deemed to not be white. In the construction of whiteness, the legal boundaries of both white and nonwhite acquired sharper distinction."[49] The National Origins Act, in other words, remapped and broadened the category of white to include previously "hyphenated" Europeans against the total exclusion of those defined as nonwhite, namely, Asians.

The powerful lobby of southwestern agribusinessmen tempered the nativists' quest for a "whites-only" immigration policy by supporting an exemption from the national quota system for all immigrants from countries in the Western Hemisphere such as Canada, Cuba, and Mexico. Mexico's immigrant workers, therefore, were allowed to continue entering the United States without any preset numerical limit. In agreeing to the Western Hemisphere exemption, the nativists capitulated to the growers' lobby in 1924, but after the passage of the National Origins Act, a committed core of nativists continued to oppose Mexican immigration to the United States. As one congressmen complained during the 1924 hearings, "What is the use of closing the front door to keep out undesirables from Europe when you permit Mexicans to come in here by the back door by the thousands and thousands?"[50] After the passage of the 1924 National Origins Act, the nativists campaigned to add Mexico's migrant workers to the quota system. Mexico was a nation of mongrels, they argued. As such, Mexicans were inassimilable racial inferiors, and unrestricted Mexican immigration jeopardized the core objective of the National Origins Act. "The continuance of a desirable character of citizenship is the fundamental purpose of our immigration laws. Incidental to this are the avoidance of social and racial problems, the upholding of American standards of·wages and living, and the maintenance of order. All of these purposes will be violated by increasing the Mexican population of the country," explained Congressman John C. Box (Texas), who co-sponsored a 1926 bill to limit Mexican immigration to the United States.[51] The growers defeated the 1926 Box Bill, but the nativists tried again in 1928, arguing that the exemption for Mexican workers needed to be terminated because, as they forebodingly warned, "Our great Southwest is rapidly creating for itself a new racial problem, as our old South did when it imported slave labor from Africa."[52]

Throughout their debates with the nativists, southwestern growers fully agreed with the notion that Mexico's immigrant workers presented a "racial problem" and thereby conceded the nativists' point that Mexican immigration posed a threat to American society. As S. Parker Frisselle of the California Farm Bureau Federation explained during the 1926 hearings, "With the Mexican comes a social problem. . . . It is a serious one. It comes into our schools, it comes into our cities, and it comes into our whole civilization in California."[53] But after assuring the nativists that "we, gentlemen, are just as anxious as you are not to build the civilization of California or any other western district upon a Mexican foundation," the growers countered the nativists' call to place a numerical limit upon Mexican immigration to the United States by arguing that without unrestricted access to Mexican workers, the rising empire of agribusinesses in the American southwest would turn to ruin.[54] Instead of ending Mexican immigration, they offered the nativists a promise. "We, in California," vowed Frisselle, "think we can handle that social problem."[55] For, as another agribusinessman from Texas explained, "If we could not control the Mexicans and they would take this country it would be better to keep them out, but we can and do control them."[56]

The pledge that "we can and do control them" referred to the social world of agribusiness in the U.S.-Mexico borderlands. Agribusinessmen and the demands of their enterprises dominated the political, social, and cultural life of borderland communities as the racialized organization of work refracted throughout community life. Whites held land or managed workers, while Mexicanos harvested, plowed, picked, tended, reaped, and migrated. As Devra Weber, Paul Schuster Taylor, and others have detailed, the racialized divisions in California were so crude that "the owners and top managers were white: foremen, contractors and workers were Mexican."[57] In Texas, one young white farmer explained that white landholders and tenants lived a life of leisure because "we have the Mexicans here and don't work."[58] The hierarchy between Anglo-American landowners, white managers, and Mexicano workers reverberated throughout the region where highly racialized practices of social segregation, political repression, and community violence accompanied the patterns of economic exploitation that locked the region's large Mexicano population into low-wage work. From Texas to California, white and Mexicano youth graduated from separate and unequal schools. Poll taxes and political bosses effectively disenfranchised Mexicano voters. Mexicans had limited employment options outside of agriculture. Police violence against Mexicanos was common. Labor organizing among Mexican workers prompted swift and violent community-wide responses. And, where such prejudice was most extensive, "No Negroes, Mexicans, or Dogs" signs were posted on restaurant doors.[59]

Agribusinessmen of the borderlands lobbied on behalf of their industry and held up the social world that they had built as evidence that unrestricted Mexican immigration would profit American businesses without infiltrating American society, culture, and politics. The hierarchy of race in the U.S.-Mexico borderlands, they promised, provided barriers against Mexican incorporation. But in a nation most intimately versed in the black/white divide as the basic unit of racial control and social inequity, nervous onlookers worried about the place of Mexican immigrants— neither black nor white—in America. As Professor William Leonard explained, Mexicans "are not Negroes . . . they are not accepted as white men, and between the two, the white and the black, there seems to be no midway position."[60]

The nativists' concerns were not assuaged by the class-based flexibility of the borderlanders' system of racialized social organization. For example, the assistant superintendent of schools in San Diego, California, described middle-class Mexican Americans as "Spanish" and argued that middle-class Mexican American children were "the equal of our white children."[61] According to Mexican scholar Manuel Gamio, a similar class- and complexion-based flexibility was accorded to Mexicanos by private proprietors. Although some Mexicans were denied entry to certain facilities, Gamio found that Mexican immigrants who were "white and even blue-eyed" were considered to be American and given "first place in everything."[62]

The nativists hounded the borderlanders for a clear answer as to where Mexicans fit within the presumably crisp racial orders of eugenics, national origins, and the one-drop rule of the black/white divide. Texans typically referenced the logic of the black/white racial hierarchy to explain the place that they had assigned Mexican immigrants. For example, when asked about Anglo-Mexican relations by economist Paul Schuster Taylor in the late 1920s, one Texan stated that Mexicans were "not so bad as the Negroes," while another elaborated that "The mexicans will eat in the restaurants and at the tables in the drug stores, but the niggers would not," because even a "nigger with money couldn't associate with white persons."[63]

Californians often deployed a multirelational approach that positioned Mexicans against the Chinese, Japanese, Hindus, Filipinos, and others that had worked in the fields before Mexican immigrants began to dominate the agricultural workforce during the 1920s. In defense of Mexican immigration, Fred Bixby of Long Beach, California, explained during the 1928 hearings to restrict Mexican immigration that "we have no Chinamen; we have not the Japs. The Hindu is worthless; the Filipino is nothing, and the white man will not do the work."[64] But engaged in a debate with outsiders—namely, when battling the nativists who discussed the social threat of Mexican immigration by constantly evoking the "negro problem"—Bixby and the Californians proved capable of mapping Mexicans against the prevailing black/white divide. "I want to tell you that you people have no understanding at all of the Mexicans. They are loyal," charged Bixby. "I have a family—three of them are girls," he explained. "Ever since they were that high," he indicated, "I have had them out on the range, riding the range with Mexicans. . . . Do you suppose we would send them out with a bunch of negroes? We would never think of such a thing."[65] In these very strategic discourses that negotiated the differences between regional particularity and national trends, the Californians drew upon the black/white divide to explain the social position of Mexicans north of the border. African Americans, they argued, represented the unmitigated bottom of the racial hierarchy, and Mexico's migrant laborers, they suggested, presented a superior alternative of racial inferiors to labor in the fields of the American southwest.

Struggling to fit Mexicans into the prevailing discourse of racial difference, inequity, and control, the borderlanders constructed Mexicans as more or less black or more or less white: they were an in-between people without a clear place in a racial order grounded in the black/white divide.[66] The overwhelmingly marginalized but generally unfixed position of Mexicanos in the separate and unequal borderlands contrasted sharply with the America that the nativists were trying to formulate through U.S. immigration restrictions. In metaphor, comparison, and everyday social practices the borderlanders had created an unequal but ambiguous place for Mexicans north of the border.

To calm the ardent nativists who did not believe that the southwestern growers could control the racial meanderings of Mexican immigrants in American social and cultural life, the growers made one final pitch. "The Mexican is a homer. Like a pigeon he goes back to roost" explained Frisselle.[67] Mexican immigrants, in other words, were at least temporary if not contained, and their transitory presence in the fields of the southwest would benefit agribusiness without having any major or long-term impact upon American society. From the standpoint of the early twenty-first century, Frisselle's promise appears foolish. During the 1920s, hundreds of thousands of Mexican immigrants entered the United States. The notion that they would have no impact upon American life was a massive miscalculation drenched in the fundamentally flawed philosophy that Mexicans were both temporary and innately marginal. Mexicans, according to Frisselle, were nothing more than a source of cheap and disposable labor whose impact upon America would only be measured in dollars and sweat. "He is not a man that comes into this country for anything except our dollars and our work," testified Frisselle, who promised that Mexicans would always go home and leave nothing but profit behind.[68] With such promises of control, containment, and, at the very least, impermanent Mexican settlement in the United States, the agribusinessmen triumphed in their clash with the nativists, and the numerical limits of the quota era were never placed upon Mexican immigration to the United States.[69]

With the exemption provided for immigrants from the Western Hemisphere, the National Origins Act of 1924 capped Congress's sixty-two year drive for increasingly restrictive immigration legislation. Yet legislators understood that the passage of the National Origins Act did not automatically translate into a new social reality. Many years of experience had taught them that without aggressive U.S. immigration law enforcement, persons excluded from legal entry would simply disregard and violate U.S. immigration law by entering the United States without authorization. "So long as the border is not adequately guarded," explained F. W. Berkshire, supervising inspector of the U.S.-Mexico Border District for the Immigration Service, "the restrictive measures employed at ports of entry, simply tend to divert the illegal traffic to unguarded points."[70] For example, since the passage of the Chinese Exclusion Act of 1882, an enterprise of smuggling Chinese immigrants into the United States had thrived along the U.S.-Mexico and U.S.-Canada borders and between Florida and Cuba.[71] In addition to the categorically excluded Chinese workers, other classes of immigrants—persons infected with contagious diseases, illiterates, and those unable to pay the head taxes and visa fees—also chose the poorly guarded land borders as a "back door" entry into the United States.[72] The vibrant world of unsanctioned migration along the U.S.-Mexico border registered in the United States District Courts that heard immigration cases. Between April of 1908 and the spring of 1924, for example, more than one-third of the persons tried for immigration offenses in the Laredo Division of the U.S. District Court carried non-Spanish surnames.[73] And between July of 1907 and September of 1917, only 15 percent of the persons tried for immigration violations in the Southern California Division of the U.S. District Court carried Spanish surnames, most of whom were tried for immigrant smuggling.[74] The majority of persons standing trial in U.S. District Courts were Chinese, Japanese, Eastern European, and East Indian immigrants who had evaded U.S. immigration restrictions by entering the United States without sanction. Therefore, to prevent unlawful entry into the United States, three days after passing the National Origins Act of 1924, Congress set aside one million dollars to establish a "land-border patrol" in the Immigration Bureau of the U.S. Department of Labor.[75]

THE ESTABLISHMENT OF THE U.S. BORDER PATROL

The Border Patrol's beginnings were inauspicious. The million-dollar kick-off appropriation comprised less than 25 percent of the Immigration Bureau's total budget of $4,084,865 for that year. Funded as a small corner of the Immigration Bureau, the Border Patrol's position within the broader apparatus of U.S. immigration control did not improve significantly over time. Edging up to just $1,150,000 in 1926, the Border Patrol's budget climaxed at $2,198,000 in 1932 before dropping to $1,735,000 in 1939; all the while holding an ever-smaller share of the Immigration Bureau's total budget, which hovered around $10,000,000 throughout the 1930s. The Border Patrol's limited funds were used for basic operational and equipment costs such as buildings, horses, cars, guns, and uniforms, but, most of all, they paid for the salaries of U.S. Border Patrol officers as the patrol's authorized force increased from 472 in 1925 to 916 in 1939.[76]

The Border Patrol's small beginnings however can best be understood when examined within the context of federal law enforcement during the 1920s, namely, in the realm of liquor and drug control. Most efforts to expand federal law enforcement were stymied during the early twentieth century by anxious southerners who opposed federal intervention in southern race relations. In particular, the powerful southern bloc opposed federal response to African American activists who demanded an end to the rising number of lynchings occurring in the south. The development of federal immigration law enforcement at the nation's borders therefore was tempered by efforts to protect white supremacy in the southern states. However, federal efforts at drug control and liquor control grew during these years.[77] In 1914, the U.S. Congress had passed the Harrison Act, which required all persons involved in the manufacture, distribution, and sale of narcotics (morphine, cocaine, opium, and heroin) to be registered and to pay a tax on all narcotics sales. Enforcement of the Harrison Act was given to the Bureau of Revenue within the Treasury Department. The passage of the Eighteenth Amendment to the United States Constitution (1919–1933) and the Volstead Act of 1919 prohibited the manufacture, sale, transport, import, or export of intoxicating beverages. The Prohibition Unit within the Internal Revenue Board was established to enforce federal liquor prohibition, and the enforcement of the Harrison Act was transferred to the Narcotics Enforcement Division within the Prohibition Unit. In comparison to the Border Patrol's original appropriation for $1,000,000 in fiscal year 1925, the 1925 appropriation for the Narcotics Division of the Prohibition Unit was $11,341,770, a figure more than ten times greater than the Border Patrol's annual budget but only an estimated 10 percent of the total combined funds provided for the enforcement of federal liquor and narcotics control.[78] Similarly the month before Congress established the U.S. Border Patrol, it had provided the U.S. Coast Guard with a $12,000,000 boost to enhance its interdiction efforts along United States coasts.[79] In the world of federal law enforcement, the U.S. Border Patrol and immigration control had very low priority, and significant growth was unlikely until the south's black/white divide was challenged.

Congress seconded its paltry funding of U.S. immigration law enforcement by failing to define clearly the new land-border patrol's mandate and authority. According to its foundational act, the Border Patrol was instructed to enforce the provisions of the Immigration Act of 1917 and subsequent acts and, more specifically, to prevent the unlawful entry of aliens into the United States. But by 1924 there were so many methods of unlawful entry (unsanctioned border crossings, fraudulent documents, breaking the conditions of legal residence) and so many classes of persons explicitly prohibited from legally entering the United States that U.S. immigration restrictions provided a broad field of possible subjects for U.S. immigration law enforcement. Prostitutes and anarchists were categorically excluded from the United States, so Border Patrol officers could have spent their time searching brothels and investigating radical immigrants, particularly the labor organizers. Or they could have raided hospitals and clinics in search of immigrants who unlawfully entered the United States with a communicable disease. Or the patrol could have reviewed cases of fraudulent documentation or, as its official title seemed to suggest, the new "land-border patrol" could have patrolled the border line to prevent all unauthorized border crossings. The original mandate was so broad that it was entirely unclear what the new "land-border patrol" was supposed to do. Further, Congress provided the Border Patrol with no authority as a law enforcement entity. The Department of Labor Appropriations Act of May 28, 1924, therefore, officially established the U.S. Border Patrol but provided only limited funds and a vague mandate with no authority to act. Still, with money in hand and a broad mandate on the table, the Bureau of Immigration quickly organized the U.S. Border Patrol. Officers were on duty along the Canadian and Mexican borders by July 1, 1924.

The early months were defined by disorganization and an overarching lack of clarity. From Spokane, Washington, the regional district director admitted that "not being familiar with the provisions of the Congressional Act establishing the Border Patrol and having received no definite information from the Bureau, considerable doubt and uncertainty exists as to the authority vested in the Border Patrol officers and the scope of their duties."[80] He followed with a request for guidance from the Bureau of Immigration regarding what the districts were supposed to do with this new patrol force. "It would therefore seem that the work would be greatly facilitated, and more in conformity in the different Districts, if the Bureau would issue some specific instructions," he wrote.[81] The commissioner-general of the Bureau of Immigration responded with little substantive guidance when he explained, in August of 1924, that he, too, was unsure of the new patrol force's authority and function. "If the Bureau is right in its understanding of the matter," he wrote, "the border patrols are now without the slightest authority to stop a vehicle crossing the border for the purpose of search, or otherwise, nor can they legally prevent the entry of an alien in violation of law. In other words, they possess no more powers than does the ordinary citizen, who can exercise police powers only at the request of a duly constituted officer of the law, or to prevent the commission of a felony."[82] Without any clear authority to enforce U.S. immigration restrictions, the commissioner-general of Immigration advised the district director in Spokane that Border Patrol officers "would be guilty of assault" if they used any amount of physical coercion while attempting to "prevent a violation of the immigration laws."[83] With no authority to act in the enforcement of U.S. immigration restrictions, the new patrolmen were little more than ordinary citizens. The confusion among top administrators regarding what to do with these new ordinary citizens on the Immigration Bureau's payroll naturally spread to the new recruits in the summer of 1924. Wesley Stiles, for example, entered on duty as a U.S. Border Patrol officer on July 28, 1924, in Del Rio, Texas. "No one knew what we were supposed to do or how we were supposed to do it. . . . So we just walked around and looked wise," recalled Stiles of his early days on patrol in the U.S.-Mexico borderlands.[84]

With neither direction nor authority, the Border Patrol officers stammered through the summer and fall of 1924. In December of 1924, the Immigration Bureau took the first step toward distinguishing Border Patrol officers from the "ordinary citizen" by providing uniforms for the officers.[85] The uniforms flagged the U.S. Border Patrol as an emergent police force, but two more months passed before Border Patrol officers were invested with police powers to enforce U.S. immigration laws. Congress established the Border Patrol's law-enforcement authority with the passage of the Act of February 27, 1925 (43 Stat. 1049–1050; 8 U.S.C. 110). According to this act, a Border Patrol officer was authorized to "arrest any alien who in his presence or view is entering or attempting to enter the United States in violation of any law or regulation made in pursuance of law regulating the admission of aliens, and to take such alien immediately for examination before an immigrant inspector or other official having authority to examine aliens as to their rights to admission to the United states." In the case of *Lew Moy vs. the United States* (1916), the U.S. Supreme Court had determined that an "alien is in the act of entering the United States until he reaches his interior destination."[86] The 1925 Act and the *Lew Moy* decision gave Border Patrol officers broad authority to interrogate, detain, and arrest any person they believed to be engaged in the act of illegal entry, a violation of U.S. immigration law that extended from the moment unauthorized immigrants crossed the border until they reached their interior destination. The 1925 Act also authorized a Border Patrol officer to "board and search for aliens any vessel within the territorial waters of the United States, railway car, conveyance, or vehicle, in which he believes aliens are being brought into the United States, and such employee shall have power to execute any warrant or other process issued by any officer under any law regulating admission, exclusion, or expulsion of aliens."[87] As such, the 1925 Act invested Border Patrol officers with broad powers of arrest without warrant in the pursuit of U.S. immigration law enforcement and defined a massive jurisdiction for Border Patrol work.

Over the years, there would be many shifts in the policies guiding the interpretation of the Border Patrol's jurisdiction and authority, but the 1925 Act defined the substance and limits of the Border Patrol's law-enforcement capacities until

1946. According to the 1925 Act, Border Patrol officers could chase unsanctioned immigrants and search vessels within the broader borderlands and, without a warrant, arrest those they suspected of being engaged in the act of unlawful entry. Border Patrol officers also held the power to serve warrants in the enforcement of all U.S. immigration laws. These powers defined the U.S. Border Patrol as the uniformed, law-enforcement wing of the U.S. Immigration Service. Still the patrol's job remained mired in questions and complexities.

Given the various classes of exclusion, the many methods of unlawful entry, and the extended periods during which immigrants were subject to deportation, the United States Border Patrol was confronted with forging a manageable program for U.S. immigration law enforcement. In particular, from the long list of U.S. immigration restrictions, Border Patrol officers needed to prioritize the many possibilities of migration control and develop everyday practices of U.S. immigration law enforcement. The rapid localization of U.S. Border Patrol personnel and supervision allowed the officers of the U.S. Border Patrol to direct this project.

THE MEN OF THE U.S. BORDER PATROL

Clifford Alan Perkins first arrived in El Paso, Texas, in 1908. He needed a job, but—as he recalled—"nobody seemed to be interested in hiring an inexperienced, nineteen-year-old semi-invalid."[88] A suspected case of tuberculosis had forced Perkins to move away from his family in Wisconsin and seek out relatives in Texas. The dry El Paso climate improved his health, but finding work in the border town was difficult. Fortunately, low pay and bad hours caused the Post Office to have "trouble filling an opening in the registered mail division."[89] Within days of applying for the position, Perkins was behind the desk at the El Paso Post Office.

The monotony of the work quickly frustrated Perkins, who "finally popped off one day about being sick and tired of [his] job to May Brick, the middle-aged spinster who relieved [him] at the registry window."[90] She suggested that Perkins apply for a job with the Immigration Service. He did not know what the Immigration Service was, but when his co-worker explained that officers for the Immigration Service dealt with "immigration, exclusion, deportation and expulsion of aliens" and that the starting salary was twice what he was earning at the Post Office, Perkins recalled, "that was enough for me."[91] He signed up for and passed the Immigration Service's next civil service exam. On January 4, 1911, the Immigration Service appointed Perkins as a Mounted Chinese Inspector within its Chinese Division.

In 1904, the U.S. Immigration Service had established a small force of officers assigned to enforce the Chinese Exclusion Acts along the nation's borders. Never numbering more than seventy-five men for the Mexican and Canadian borders, the Mounted Guard monitored border towns and patrolled the borderlands to apprehend undocumented Chinese immigrants. As a Mounted Chinese Inspector,

Clifford Perkins worked from Nogales, Arizona, to Brownsville, Texas, looking for, questioning, and deporting undocumented Chinese immigrants. He quickly moved up within the Immigration Service and in 1920 became inspector-in-charge for the Chinese Division. When Congress provided funds for a land-border patrol in May of 1924, the U.S. Immigration Service drew upon its resources in the Mounted Guard and promoted the head of the Chinese Division, Clifford Perkins, to build the small police force that could broadly enforce U.S. immigration restrictions along the massive U.S.-Mexico border.

The U.S.-Mexico border stretches more than two thousand miles, crosses five ecological zones, spans four states, includes twenty-eight counties, and binds two nations. As a political boundary, it is a physical space that twists in the Rio Grande and turns in the sands along specific points of longitude and latitude. This is the line that the U.S. Congress had defined as unlawful to cross without authorization. But the Border Patrol's jurisdiction also extended far north of the U.S.-Mexico border, and Perkins' job entailed developing a police force capable not only of enforcing a line in the sand but also of patrolling a massive territory composed of multiple small localities. The path he pursued effectively regionalized and localized the enforcement of U.S. immigration restriction.

Perkins's first act was to divide the U.S.-Mexico border jurisdiction into three Border Patrol districts.[92] The Los Angeles Border Patrol District stretched from the Pacific Ocean to about fifty miles east of Yuma, Arizona, and extended northward in California to San Luis Obispo. The El Paso Border Patrol District picked up where the Los Angeles District left off and extended to Devils River, Texas. The San Antonio Border Patrol District reached from Devil's River to the Gulf of Mexico at Brownsville, Texas. Each District was then divided into subdistricts.[93] Each subdistrict was further divided into several stations to which a chief patrol officer and several senior patrol officers and patrol officers were assigned.[94]

Perkins anticipated that the various district directors for the Department of Immigration would closely manage the Border Patrol, but their many administrative responsibilities and the isolation of Border Patrol stations prevented them from keeping a close eye on the new patrol force. The lack of formal training or clear directives were an indication of the distance between Immigration Service supervisors and the officers of the U.S. Border Patrol. For example, when Edwin Reeves joined the Border Patrol, he laughed at the early training. All he received was a ".45 single-action revolver with a web belt—and that was it."[95] Therefore, outside of the broad directive provided by Congress, the new patrol force was left without any substantial direction. In the breaches of command, the distances between stations and headquarters, and the absence of regional coordination, patrol officers exerted significant control over local Border Patrol strategies.

The first men hired as Border Patrol officers were transfers from the Mounted Guard of Chinese Inspectors. Twenty-four percent of the original 104 Border Patrolmen hired by July 1, 1924, were transfers from the Mounted Guard.[96] These officers carried their experiences with enforcing the Chinese Exclusion Acts into the formation of the U.S. Border Patrol. Among them was Jefferson Davis Milton, a legendary officer who is still remembered as the father of the U.S. Border Patrol.

Born at the dawn of the Civil War to a large slave-owning family, Jefferson Davis Milton grew up in the defeated South. His father died soon after his birth, but had been the governor of Florida and named his son after his close friend and the president of the Southern Confederacy, Jefferson Davis. After the war, the Milton family struggled to live life as they always had; the end of slavery had broken the foundations of their world. In the past, they had lived lives of leisure and plenty, but after the war, many of their black field hands fled the plantation, forcing the Milton family to take to the fields. At the age of sixteen, Jeff decided he wanted more adventure than plantation life could offer, so he headed west to Texas.[97]

There, Jeff began a law-enforcement career that spanned more than fifty years, crossed four states, straddled two nations, and made him a legend among officers of the U.S. Border Patrol. In 1879, at the age of eighteen, he joined the Texas Rangers. Three years later, Jeff moved to the New Mexico territory, where he served as a deputy sheriff and a peace officer. As the Indian Wars raged around him, Jeff joined the "hunt for Victorio and Geronimo."[98] After helping to settle the nomadic nations of what was becoming the American West, Jeff roamed the region. He was chief of police in El Paso, Texas; a fireman on the Southern Pacific Railroad; a U.S. marshal in Texas, Arizona, and Mexico; a prospector in California; and deputy sheriff for Santa Cruz County, Arizona. Whether working as a Texas Ranger, an Indian fighter, or the chief of police, Jeff developed a reputation as a fearless officer who dared to venture alone into the desert lands, a vigilant enforcer of the law at the outskirts of society. He chased down bank robbers and cattle thieves, bandits and Indians. After countless battles in the backcountry, Jeff always returned alive, while many of his adversaries did not.[99]

During his tenure in the U.S.-Mexico borderlands, Jeff earned many admirers, but made few friends. He was a nomad who moved often, spent long periods of time working alone in remote places, and spoke little when he came to town. Still, his name was a "byword and his exploits legendary."[100] The favored memory of Jeff is the time he disappeared after pursuing three bandits. Confident in his skills as a law-enforcement officer, but worried for the man who alone dared to challenge three train robbers, anxious borderlanders began to wonder if Jeff had fought his last fight. Their worries subsided when Jeff sent a characteristically simple telegraph message, "Send two coffins and a doctor. Jeff."[101]

In 1904, Jeff joined the Immigration Service of the Labor Department as a Mounted Chinese Inspector. When Congress established the Border Patrol in 1924, Jeff was sixty-three years old and had already spent twenty years enforcing immigration restrictions. Still, he was not a wealthy man and joined the new organization out of a love for law enforcement and, most likely, because he needed to work. To this day, Jefferson Davis Milton—a man born in the shadow of slavery, hardened by the battles to settle the American West, and a pioneer in the enforcement of Chinese Exclusion laws—is remembered as the father of the U.S. Border Patrol. He is often referred to as the "one-man Border Patrol," and generations of U.S Border Patrol officers focus less on Jeff's long career and prefer to remember him as a legendary loner and social nomad who represents their origins in a "hardy band of border law enforcement officers."[102] Yet the representation of Jeff as a man without deeply consequential historical entanglements is, most likely, as much a myth as it is a misleading representation of the men who served as Border Patrol officers in the 1920s and 1930s. The officers who worked along the U.S.-Mexico border were not legends, nomads, or loners. They did not aggressively enforce the law or secure the border without compromise. Like Jeff, most early officers joined the Border Patrol because they needed a job, and the new organization offered steady work.

The position of U.S. Border Patrol officer was subject to civil service regulations, but the quick organization of the Border Patrol between May 28 and July 1, 1924, did not allow time for the Border Patrol to draft and administer an exam for new recruits. Perkins, therefore, began to hire men who had passed the railway mail clerk civil service exam instead. Recruits from the railway civil service exam filled the majority of Border Patrol positions in 1924, but they did not remain in the organization for long. Turnover of Border Patrol officers in the first three months hovered around 25 percent and did not settle until 1927. "So fast did resignations occur that the register soon became exhausted," recalled the commissioner of immigration, who admitted that the Border Patrol was quickly forced to hire patrol inspectors "without regard to civil-service regulations."[103] The main benefactors of the Border Patrol's dire need to fill positions quickly were men already in the borderlands looking for work—men such as Dogie Wright.[104]

Despite Dogie's rich family history in the Texas borderlands, in September of 1924 he was out of work and roaming about in El Paso, Texas. There he ran into Grover Webb, an old family friend with whom he had served in the Texas Rangers and who had become the head of the U.S. Customs Mounted Patrol in El Paso. Webb suggested that Dogie go see the new Border Patrol chief, Clifford Perkins, saying "Tell him I sent you."[105] Two months after the U.S. Border Patrol began policing the border, Perkins was still scrambling to hire officers with law-enforcement or military experience. Dogie walked straight to the Border Patrol office, and upon the recommendation of Webb and another friend, Sheriff Jeff Vaughn of Marfa, Texas, Perkins immediately hired him.

The influence of local men such as Dogie Wright within the U.S. Border Patrol outweighed their numbers because early commendations and promotions focused upon officers with "a wide knowledge of people and customs of this vicinity," who knew "everyone in that part of the country," or had been "employed practically all of their lives in ranch work in this immediate vicinity."[106] In 1929, for example, of the men who held the leadership positions of senior patrol inspector or chief patrol inspector, at least 87.5 percent were borderlanders before joining the Border Patrol.[107] Their concentration was heaviest in the Texas-Mexico borderlands, where 90 percent of the chief patrol inspectors were borderlanders, compared to 42.9 percent in the California subdistricts. In Texas subdistricts, 84.6 percent of senior patrol inspectors were borderlanders, compared to 50 percent in the California subdistricts.

E. A. "Dogie" Wright was one of the benefactors of Perkins's scramble to hire officers for the U.S. Border Patrol during the 1920s. His presence in El Paso, Texas, and his unemployed status made him quickly available to Perkins. Dogie's experience as a law-enforcement officer was an additional benefit, given that Perkins preferred to hire men who had served as law-enforcement officers or in the military. Yet such preferences did not always materialize into realities. Extensive research with a 1929 roster of Border Patrol personnel shows that only 28.6 percent of early officers had served in civilian law enforcement or the military before joining the patrol. Border Patrol officers and their early chroniclers spun tales of officers as frontiersmen, military men, and career officers, but historical inquiry suggests that many of the early Border Patrol officers entered with eclectic working-class résumés. Most important, few owned land in the agriculture-dominated borderlands.

Only 24 percent of the officers working along the U.S.-Mexico border in 1929 worked in agriculture before joining the Border Patrol, and only 10 percent owned or operated their own farms.[108] Overall, most of the early officers, a total of 47.4 percent, worked outside of agriculture before joining the patrol. For example, Horace B. Carter was a senior patrol inspector in Laredo, Texas, in 1929, but he had worked as a tram operator in Hood County, Texas, in 1920.[109] Don G. Gilliland was a patrol inspector in San Antonio in 1929 but a salesman at a grocery store in Floresville, Texas, in 1920.[110] Orville H. Knight was a patrol inspector in Chula Vista, California, in 1929 but a chauffeur in Illinois in 1920.[111] Even the famous Dogie Wright, who was a senior patrol inspector in El Paso, Texas, in 1929, was selling tickets at the movie theater in Marfa, Texas, in 1920.[112] Although Dogie had had several short stints as a Texas Ranger, he had also worked as a clerk, as a chauffeur, in construction, and in a café.[113] And, while the commissioner of the Immigration Service often suggested that the Border Patrol was an organization of independent young men, more than 40 percent of the Border Patrol officers identified by all sources on the 1929 roster were married, and nearly half were between the ages of thirty and forty. Therefore, while some young, single men with law-enforcement and military experience joined the patrol, overall the early officers were less a "hardy band of law enforcement officers" than average working-class men, namely, white men, who used law enforcement as one strategy to earn a living in the agriculture-dominated U.S.-Mexico borderlands.[114]

In a region where power was rooted in land ownership, early Border Patrol officers were neither elite members of borderland communities nor active participants in their core economies. These were precisely the working-class white men in the Texas-Mexico borderlands whom Paul Schuster Taylor found to be vigorously opposed to unrestricted Mexican immigration to the United States when he conducted interviews in the region during the 1920s. In contrast to the borderland farmers whose vocal and persuasive protest halted congressional efforts to limit Mexican immigration—"without the Mexicans we would be done," feared the powerful agribusinessmen—average white workers in the region often interpreted Mexican immigration as a source of competition in the labor market. "I hope they never let another Mexican come to the United States," said one south Texas labor union official.[115] "The country would be a whole let better off for the white laboring man," explained another, "if there weren't so many niggers and Mexicans."[116] Hired from the ranks of the borderlands' white working class, the officers of the Border Patrol operated within a political economy that privileged the interests of large landholders, but they did not necessarily wholly share nor strive to protect those interests. The agribusinessmen were powerful, but there were class-based cleavages among whites on the issue of Mexican immigration to the United States. White workers had lost the congressional battle over U.S. immigration law, but when they were hired as U.S. immigration law-enforcement officers, they gained considerable influence over the everyday management of Mexican labor entering the United States. This, in the borderlands, was a new source of power, and the Border Patrol's working-class officers leveraged their federal authority to police unsanctioned migration in complicated and often contradictory ways that were only consistent in their mindfulness of opportunities to extract bits of dignity, respect, status, and power from the region's social elite by policing their workforce. The Border Patrol's turn toward policing Mexicans, in other words, was much more than a matter of simply servicing the interests of agribusiness in capitalist economic development. It was a matter of community, manhood, whiteness, authority, class, respect, belonging, brotherhood, and violence in the greater Texas-Mexico borderlands.

On the back roads and in the small towns where U.S. immigration law enforcement unfolded during the 1920s and 1930s, the men that became Border Patrol officers pursued something more elusive than the singular class interests of the region's elite. Their working-class and landless backgrounds had long located their labor at the edges of borderland societies, where the profits of southwestern agriculture were unevenly distributed along a racial hierarchy of productive labor. Early officers may have lived in white neighborhoods, worshipped at white churches, and sent their children to white schools, but as salesmen, chauffeurs, machinists, and cowpunchers they had labored at the edges of whiteness in the borderlands. The steady pay and everyday social authority of U.S. immigration law-enforcement work dangled before them the possibility of lifting themselves from a marginalized existence as what Neil Foley has examined as the "white scourge" of borderland communities.[117] Policing Mexicans, in other words, presented officers with the opportunity to enter the region's primary economy and, in the process, shore up their tentative claims upon whiteness. As immigration control was emerging as a critical site of simultaneously expanding the boundaries of whiteness while hardening the distinctions between whites and nonwhites. The project of enforcing immigration restrictions therefore placed Border Patrol officers at what police scholar David Bayley describes as "the cutting edge of the state's knife" in terms of enforcing new boundaries between whites and nonwhites.[118]

The project of policing the boundaries between white and nonwhite was also important for the small number of Mexican American men who joined the U.S. Border Patrol during the 1920s and 1930s. According to the 1929 roster of Border Patrol personnel, six officers had Spanish surnames. Among them was Manuel Saldaña, the Texas-born son of Mexican immigrant parents.[119] His father had been a stock dealer in Brownsville, Texas, but by the time he registered for the U.S. Army in 1917, Saldaña had taken over the care of both his mother and an adopted son.[120] In 1920, he was listed on the United States census as a bridge watchman for the U.S. Immigration Service in Brownsville. Manuel Uribe was another of the six Mexican American officers listed on the 1929 roster. Uribe was born and raised in Zapata, Texas, and was praised as "know[ing] practically everyone from Laredo to Roma."[121] He had gotten to know many people as he grew up working on his father's farm in the area.[122] By 1920, his father had allowed both Manuel and his brother, Enrique, to operate their own sections of the family farm. Manuel took on this work to provide for his wife and four young children.[123] But by 1923 he was working for the U.S. Immigration Service, and in 1924 he became a U.S. Border Patrol officer. Jesse Perez, a legend within the Border Patrol, was the son of a Texas Ranger and married to one of the founding families of Rio Grande City, where his father-in-law was a Texas Ranger, a sheriff, and a U.S. marshal. Jesse was stationed in Rio Grande City for his entire tenure with the Border Patrol and, for several years, worked alongside his father, who also served as a patrolman.[124] Pete Torres was a member of an established and influential "Spanish-American" family in New Mexico.[125] One more officer identified by Border Patrol correspondence as "partly of the Spanish race" is listed on the 1929 roster. Before joining the Border Patrol, he had served as a Texas Ranger for the influential King Ranch family in south Texas, a family that he married into several years after joining the Patrol.[126] This is not an exhaustive list of the Mexican American Border Patrol officers during the 1920s and 1930s. Border Patrol correspondence records tell of other Mexicano officers who cycled in and out of the patrol, and not all of the Mexicano officers can be identified by searching for Spanish-surnamed individuals, but these few biographies suggest that while Anglo Border Patrol officers tended to come from working-class backgrounds, Mexican American officers joined the patrol from the middle and upper echelons of the borderlands' Mexican American communities.

As suggested by the League of United Latin American Citizens (LULAC), a leading Mexican American political and cultural organization of the era, middle-class Mexican American officers brought a unique ensemble of social investments to the development of U.S. immigration control. The Mexican American middle class enjoyed uncertain access to whiteness in the borderlands. Although many were often able to participate in centers of social, cultural, political, and economic power, the class-based flexibility in the application of racial segregation could be unpredictable. Organizations such as LULAC, established in Texas in 1929, emerged to promote Mexican American integration into mainstream American society. LULAC members cherished American institutions, political philosophy, and capitalism, but they protested the discrimination that prevented their full participation. Rather than challenging the racial hierarchies that organized American society, namely, the black/white divide that operated as the foundation of racial inequity, Mexican American political leaders worked to construct themselves as white ethnics.[127] So although they sponsored festivals and activities to instill pride in their Mexican heritage, many middle-class Mexicanos simultaneously demanded that their European origins be acknowledged by defining themselves as "Spanish Americans." Therefore, as U.S. immigration control was remapping the boundaries of whiteness, Spanish Americans of Mexican descent fought to be included within the margins of white ethnicity. According to much of the LULAC leadership, it was their association with the "colored races" that prevented them from gaining full inclusion in white American society. Therefore, they put distance between Mexican Americans and the colored races, particularly African Americans. However, the particular conditions of the U.S.-Mexico border region also forced Mexican American political leaders to construct their ethnic white identity in contrast to Mexican immigrants. Mexican immigrant laborers were poor, dark-skinned, and did not speak English.[128] These new arrivals, many believed, undermined the quest of acculturated Mexican Americans for civil rights through the highly racialized politics of citizenship and whiteness in the U.S.-Mexico borderlands. In other words, as middle-class Mexicanos stepped up on the ledges of the black/white divide, many feared that the continuous arrival of Mexican laborers would pull them toward nonwhite status according to the sharpening distinctions of the emerging regime of immigration control. Therefore, the small, Mexican American middle class represented by LULAC tended to advocate limiting Mexican immigration and supported increased border enforcement.[129] What evidence remains of the work of the Border Patrol's first Mexicano officers firmly points toward their grounding in the racialized politics of whiteness and citizenship in the U.S.-Mexico borderlands. No one made this clearer than Patrol Inspector Pete Torres when, one day, an acquaintance began to tease him by calling him a Mexican. In response, Torres "pulled out his revolver

and shot right at his feet. He says, 'I am not a Mexican. I am a Spanish-American,'"
recalled an onlooker.[130] In the Border Patrol and through Mexican exclusion, he
and the others literally shot their way into whiteness.

From Pete Torres to Dogie Wright, these were the men to whom the development of U.S. immigration law enforcement was assigned in the early years of the
U.S. Border Patrol. Though it was established to function as a national police force
dedicated to broad enforcement of federal immigration restrictions, the disorganization of Border Patrol supervision and coordination effectively granted control
over that enforcement to the officers of the patrol. The intense localization of U.S.
immigration control empowered local men to determine the direction of U.S. immigration law enforcement. For these sons of the borderlands, immigration law
provided the basic framework for their work, but local interests and customs defined
by the social world of agribusiness provided the immediate means of interpreting
the priorities of immigration law enforcement. As chapter 2 details, not only did
the introduction of the Border Patrol to the Texas-Mexico borderlands allow its
officers to rise from the working class—often from work as unskilled laborers to
positions with significant authority—but, by joining the patrol, these landless laborers found a unique way to participate in the agricultural economy: they policed
the region's primary workforce. In the process, they created a new axis of racial division in borderland communities by linking Mexican immigrants to the crimes,
conditions, and consequences of being illegal in the United States.

2

A Sanctuary of Violence

When they were kids, Jean Pyeatt and Fred D'Alibini would "gather up rocks and pile them up on the school grounds so that they'd fight the Mexicans during recess."[1] They were children of the U.S.-Mexico borderlands who defended the inequities between whites and Mexicanos when the borderlands' sometimes ambivalent system of racialization failed to clearly mark the difference. Years later, as officers of the United States Border Patrol, they traded their rocks for shotguns and converted their child's play into police practice. As Border Patrol officers, their violence introduced a new way of marking the meaning of race in the U.S.-Mexico borderlands. In particular, by substituting policing Mexicanos for patrolling the border, Border Patrol officers linked being Mexican in the U.S.-Mexico borderlands with being illegal in the United States.

This chapter tells the story of how, why, and with what consequences officers of the United States Border Patrol policed Mexicanos as proxy for policing illegal immigration in the U.S. Immigration Service's Texas-based districts. It is the story of ordinary men—neither powerful nor dispossessed members of their communities—who had grown from boys of the borderlands to officers of the state. They were few in number—several hundred, at most—and few people outside of the borderlands region took note of how they did their jobs. But it was these men and the intersection of their lives and their work that defined the formative years of U.S. immigration law enforcement in the greater Texas-Mexico borderlands.

TRACKING MEXICANS

With little supervision and no formal training, U.S. Border Patrol officers tested a variety of techniques for enforcing U.S. immigration laws. The simplest method was "line watches," which consisted of patrolling the political boundary between official U.S. immigration stations to apprehend unauthorized immigrants as they surreptitiously crossed into the United States. In their first year of duty, Border Patrol officers in Texas-based stations reported turning back a total of 3,578 immigrants as they attempted to cross the U.S.-Mexico border.[2] But with many desolate miles to patrol between the official ports of entry and with fewer than two hundred officers spread across multiple shifts, Border Patrol officers could not provide effective line watches against illegal entry. In December of 1926, Chief Patrol Inspector Chester C. Courtney of the Border Patrol's subdistrict office in Marfa, Texas, conducted a study of the efficiency of line patrols. Courtney was an Arkansas native who was a drugstore clerk in his home state before serving in the United States Army between 1912 and 1915.[3] By 1920, Courtney had taken up residence in Dimmit County, Texas, where he owned and operated his own farm to provide for his wife and infant son.[4] By 1926, Courtney had left farming and was the chief patrol inspector for the United States Border Patrol several miles up the Rio Grande in Marfa, Texas. In this position, Courtney estimated that 40 percent of unsanctioned border crossers evaded the Border Patrol's line watches in his subdistrict.[5] He computed the percentage of missed apprehensions by comparing the number of persons apprehended since 1924 to the growth in the region's Mexicano population. Any growth in the Mexicano community, Courtney assumed, was attributed to unsanctioned migration, and no group other than Mexican nationals engaged in unauthorized border crossings in the region. His calculation reflects the Border Patrol's very early focus upon policing Mexicanos in the Texas-Mexico borderlands. Officers assumed that only Mexicans crossed the border illegally and that the broader Mexicano community in the region was under suspicion for illegitimately entering into the United States.

To capture the floating mass of Mexico's unsanctioned border crossers, Border Patrol officers utilized their broad jurisdiction to apprehend undocumented immigrants as long as they were en route to their final destination. Beginning in 1927, most of the activity in the Border Patrol's Texas-based districts developed in the greater borderlands region rather than along the border line. That year, Border Patrol officers in the El Paso and San Antonio Districts reported turning back only nine immigrants.[6] Instead of enforcing the boundary between the United States and Mexico, Border Patrol officers patrolled backcountry trails and conducted traffic stops on borderland roadways to capture unsanctioned Mexican immigrants as they traveled from the border to their final destination.[7] Along major and minor transportation routes, the officers reported questioning hundreds of thousands of people. Border Patrol officers in the Texas-Mexico borderlands thus broadly policed Mexicano mobility instead of enforcing the political boundary between the United States and Mexico.

As the officers pulled back from the border, they could not witness violations of U.S. immigration law; instead, they used what the United Supreme Court would later describe as "Mexican appearance" as a measure for identifying unauthorized border crossers. For example, on March 23, 1927, Border Patrol Inspectors Pete A. Torres, a member of the Spanish-American middle-class from New Mexico, and George W. Parker Jr., an Arizona native from a ranching family, were "driving slowly up the El Paso-Las Cruces Highway when this Ford Car and the two Mexicans in question passed us going north."[8] Torres turned to Parker and said, "I believe the two in that car are Mexicans, let us go and see if they are wet aliens."[9] In a clear example of policing Mexicans as proxy for policing unsanctioned border crossers, they used "Mexican appearance" as an indicator that the two men, Mariano Martínez and Jesus Jaso, had violated U.S. immigration restrictions. The inspectors ordered Martínez and Jaso to "drive over to one side off the road and stop, or words to that effect, which they did."[10] Torres then approached the car to "investigate them as aliens." As he walked closer to the car, "Torres saw something in the car that appeared to be sacks, with the impression of cans on the inside" and rather than inquiring into the men's immigration status, Torres asked, "What you boys got?"[11] When Martínez admitted to carrying liquor, the Border Patrol officers quickly arrested the two men for violating federal prohibition laws.

Martínez and Jaso protested their arrest and sparked a rare investigation into the racial logic of Border Patrol practice in the Texas-Mexico borderlands. They protested their arrest on the grounds that Border Patrol officers had neither the authority nor reasonable evidence to investigate them for violating prohibition laws. Since February of 1925, Border Patrol officers had been authorized to enforce U.S. immigration restrictions, but the constant intersections of undocumented immigration and liquor smuggling created many questions regarding the limits of the Border Patrol's authority to enforce federal law. As one chronicler of the Border Patrol explained, "Professional contrabandistas (smugglers) enter incidentally because they smuggle. Others smuggle incidentally because they enter," but the U.S. Border Patrol was only specifically authorized to enforce U.S. immigration laws.[12]

The Bureau of Immigration declined to navigate the complex intersections of prohibition and customs laws with immigration control at the nation's borders by blithely responding to pleas for clarification from district directors and Border Patrol officers. "What is the status of an Immigrant Patrol Inspector in regard to Prohibition and Narcotic Enforcement. . . . I have never been in a position to get a satisfactory opinion from any one in authority," wrote Patrol Inspector William A. Blundell on February 3, 1926. "I am not sure of my ground and do not know how far I can go . . . several times [I have] been placed in a rather difficult position by not knowing just what the policy of the Immigration Service is in regard to the above matter."[13] Blundell's district director sought clarification from the Bureau of Immigration's headquarters in Washington, D.C., but all he was told was that there was no uniform policy on Border Patrol officers participating in the enforcement of prohibition laws. "This is a matter which the Bureau has left to the discretion of the District heads," explained a memo from the Bureau of Immigration.[14]

Understanding the Border Patrol's unclear jurisdiction in terms of enforcing federal prohibition laws, the lawyer for Martínez and Jaso argued that the evidence against his clients should be excluded "on account of illegal arrest; the officers did not have reasonable belief that the car contained liquor."[15] The U.S. commissioner reviewing the case concurred with the defendants' position that Border Patrol authority was limited to immigration law enforcement but upheld the arrest of Martínez and Jaso because "if the Immigration Patrol Inspectors stopped these Mexicans to inquire into whether or not they were aliens . . . and . . . during the course of the investigation of the persons' alienage, the officer saw sacks in the car and asked, 'Boy what have you in the car,' and one of the defendants answered, 'We have liquor,' then it was the officer's duty under Section 26 National Prohibition Act to arrest the persons and seize the car and liquor."[16] The commissioner upheld the actions of Inspectors Torres and Parker, including their use of race as an indicator of illegal entry, and sent the case to the Federal Grand Jury.

Reviewing the decision for the U.S. Border Patrol in El Paso, Texas, Chester C. Courtney, by then the acting chief patrol inspector of the Border Patrol's El Paso station, interpreted the case's significance for the use of race as a measure of immigration status. Courtney advised his officers that "as long as Patrol Inspectors [officers] use their heads when stopping Mexicans to inquire into their alienage, and later find liquor, the arrest will be upheld."[17] But, he warned, "Had the two persons been white Americans the case would have been thrown out on account of illegal search, as it would have been absurd to say they believed the Americans to be aliens."[18] In this explicit discussion of the logic of U.S. immigration law enforcement, Chief Patrol Inspector Chester C. Courtney reveals that Border Patrol practice pivoted upon racialized notions of citizenship and social belonging in the U.S.-Mexico borderlands. In particular, by describing the defendants as "Mexican" regardless of their formal citizenship status while seamlessly interchanging the terms of white and American, Courtney revealed that Border Patrol tactics were profoundly shaped by the deeper histories and broader social systems that marked Mexicanos as marginalized and temporary outsiders within the region's dominant social, cultural, political, and economic systems. Immigration law, therefore, provided the basic framework for Border Patrol operations, but the histories of conquest, displacement, and the rise of Jim Crow in the era of agribusiness penetrated the Border Patrol's everyday translations of immigration law into immigration law-enforcement practices. Although Torres and Parker had not witnessed Martínez and Jaso illegitimately cross the border, the evidence of their infractions was plainly inscribed in the social world of the borderlands.

Racialized notions of citizenship and social belonging penetrated the Border Patrol's development of the pseudo-science of tracking. Tracking is a method by which

Border Patrol officers read the markings left by people traveling across the land. Broken twigs, human litter, and footprints are all indicators of human passage that Border Patrol officers used to locate unsanctioned border crossers. The officers would pick up a footprint at the border and then track the human's movement inland. Tracking is a simple and low-technology technique, but it requires training and experience to learn how to follow a human trail across miles of thick brush, mountain terrain, and open desert.

In the Texas-Mexico borderlands, some men entered the U.S. Border Patrol with extensive experience in tracking, especially if they had worked in agriculture or ranching prior to joining the patrol. Among the experts was Fred "Yaqui" D'Alibini, who taught tracking to many of the new recruits who passed through his station. D'Alibini liked to joke around, recalled retired officer Bill Jordan, and he would dazzle new recruits with his tracking abilities by "squat[ting] over a clear track—horse or man—study it a bit, and, apparently communing with himself, pontificate. 'Hmmm. A Mexican male; about 5'5" to 5'8"; dark brown hair; brown eyes; dark complexion; wearing huaraches . . . and so on.' "[19] As D'Alibini explained to writer Peter Odens in the early 1970s, human tracks reveal racial characteristics: "A Mexican always walks heavy on the outside of his feet. When he walks, he puts his foot down on the heel first and then rolls it off—Indians will do that, too. Whites and blacks ordinarily put their feet down flat."[20] So, after reading a track for the gender, complexion, and national origins of its maker, D'Alibini would follow the tracks, and "when the last tracks were found with the maker standing in them, sure enough!" exclaimed Jordan, "That's what he looked like!"[21] According to Border Patrol tracking lore, therefore, undocumented immigrants fit a specific profile that could be tracked north from the border by following the particular imprints that Mexicans made upon the land. Illegals were Mexicans—poor, rural, brown, and male Mexicans—and evidence of such an equation was pressed into the landscape by the peculiar gait of Mexican workers as they walked north from Mexico. In a region crisscrossed by Mexicano workers, Border Patrol officers often found what they were looking for when following tracks heading north from Mexico.

On June 28, 1936, two Border Patrol officers tracked nineteen-year-old José Hernández to a store in Esperanza, Texas (just outside of Fort Hancock). That morning, Hernández left his home, a shack near the U.S.-Mexico border, and began walking north toward the store.[22] When he was about halfway there, a man who worked in the store was driving by and stopped to give him a ride. After arriving at the store, Hernández stood outside talking with two other men for awhile. This is when two Border Patrol officers pulled into the driveway. One of the officers walked past Hernández and headed into the store. Hernández followed him in to buy a soda. Nothing transpired between Hernández and the patrolmen until the officers were preparing to leave. Before leaving the premises, one of the officers decided that he should interrogate Hernández about his citizenship status. This officer instructed one of the other men who was standing outside the store, an "American" as described by the officers, to go inside and tell Hernández to come out.[23] "If they want to talk to me they could come in the store," responded Hernández. The officers entered the store, jerked Hernández by the arm, forced him into their patrol car, and drove off.

Apprehended, detained, and accused of illegal entry, Hernández carried the burden of proof. The officers took him to his shack, where he showed them his baptismal certificate as evidence of citizenship. "Shut up you son of a bitch!" yelled one of the officers, who did not believe that the certificate was valid, and he pushed Hernández back in the patrol car. This time they took him down to the river where there were the fresh tracks that they had been following before arriving at the store. The officers forced Hernández to "put one of his tracks down opposite the tracks on the river," and then declared, "They are just the same . . . yes, you crossed tonight, you son of a bitch."[24]

The Hernández incident exemplifies the significance of the borderlands' social world of racialized difference and inequity in the Border Patrol's enforcement of U.S. immigration laws. The officers had been tracking an unsanctioned border crosser when they arrived at the store. At the end of the tracks stood three men: two were "American" men as described by the officers, and the other man, they explained, was Hernández, "the Mexican standing outside of the store."[25] The officers' decision to question Hernández was unrelated to the tracks; instead, it was rooted in racialized notions of belonging in the borderlands, which Border Patrol officers imported into their tracking techniques. The Hernández incident thus demonstrates that the social world of the borderlands informed how the U.S. Border Patrol narrowed its mandate for migration control into a project of policing Mexicanos.

The Hernández incident also demonstrates how Border Patrol work introduced a new zone of violence and marginalization to the region. Despite its disorganization and lack of funding, the arrival of the U.S. Border Patrol in the Texas-Mexico borderlands introduced the legal/illegal divide to the region's established systems of inequity while creating a new apparatus of violence and social control. The Border Patrol's narrow enforcement of U.S. immigration laws was an intrinsically violent process, sanctioned by the state, that linked Mexicans to illegality and illegality to Mexicanos. The Border Patrol's racialized sphere of violence and social formation, therefore, reinvented and reinvested what it had drawn from the borderlands by creating a new mechanism and logic for the marginalization of Mexicanos in the borderlands.

As a fundamentally social process, the Border Patrol's policing of Mexicanos was a contested project. The Hernández incident, for example, was recorded and investigated because the store's proprietor, Mr. G. E. Spinnler, argued that his rights as a landholder and property owner had been violated by U.S. Border Patrol officers who entered his store to enforce U.S. immigration restrictions against a "Mexican laborer."[26] Eighteen months later Spinnler's complaint was included in a broader protest by members of the Hudspeth County Conservation and Reclamation District no. 1, who provided the Hernández incident as evidence of "high-handed" behavior by Border Patrol officers, whose actions produced a "shortage of farm laborers in Hudspeth County."[27] Such concerns were unfounded because the Border Patrol's impact upon the flow of Mexican workers into the Texas-Mexico borderlands was nominal. In 1926, the 175 Border Patrol officers in the two Texas-based districts registered apprehending 1,550 persons for immigration violations. The next year, they apprehended a total of 10,875 persons for immigration violations.[28] In 1928, they apprehended 16,661 persons.[29] And after reaching a high of 25,164 such apprehensions in 1929, the number apprehended for immigration violations in the Texas-based Districts of the U.S. Border Patrol plunged to just 14,115 in 1930 and continued to drop during the 1930s.[30] Therefore, while the Texas "army" of migrant workers reached an estimated three hundred thousand at the height of the season in the late 1920s, Border Patrol officers reported apprehending only a small fraction of the number of workers needed for the region's seasonal harvests. Still, the long life of Spinnler's complaint indicates that the Border Patrol's policing of Mexican immigrants had created a powerful yet contested institution in the borderlands by introducing a new regime of authority over the region's labor supply.

Mexicanos also contested the authority and attentions of Border Patrol officers. Although Border Patrolmen carried enormous authority in their jobs as armed immigration law-enforcement officers, Mexicanos did not always quietly submit to the officers' demands. Retired Patrol Inspector E. J. Stovall told the story of a time when he quickly assessed the limits of his authority according to the immediate context of his work. One day in 1928, explained Stovall, he was patrolling alone near San Elizario, Texas, when he decided to drive through town. "San Elizario was this little Mexican town on the Rio Grande," said Stovall, who remembered that when he got into town that day he saw a Mexicano "come out from behind the bank of the drainage ditch and then duck back."[31] Stovall admitted to knowing the man but stopped the car and asked him, "What do you have there in your bosom?"[32] The man reached into his shirt pocket and "pulled out two bottles of beer and put them down on the bridge and broke them, so we wouldn't have any evidence."[33] Reflecting upon the incident, Stovall wondered, "Why I didn't pull out my gun and fire at that Mexican. I don't know. I don't know why."[34] Instead of reaching for his gun and firing, Stovall fled. "I got in my car and got away from there," remembered Stovall, because "it was in daylight about one o'clock. If I had pulled my gun and fired there would have been fifty Mexicans around me that quick."[35] According to Stovall, God spared his life that day by "taking charge" of his hands and preventing him from shooting at the Mexicano. Perhaps Stovall instinctively knew that his only immediate supervisor was "this little Mexican town" whose residents may have immediately challenged his actions. All alone in San Elizario, Stovall fled before

TABLE 1 Principal activities and accomplishments of the U.S. Border Patrol for the years ended June 30, 1925–1934

	1925	1926	1927	1928	1929	1930	1931	1932	1933	1934
Total number of persons apprehended	N/A	35,274	19,382	25,534	34,591	22,448	23,593	23,750	21,809	11,016
Number of persons apprehended for immigration violations	14,078	33,159	17,225	23,896	33,002	21,149	22,504	22,884	21,066	10,459
Number of persons apprehended, Mexican border region	N/A	N/A	13,759	19,850	28,805	17,027	18,072	18,648	16,950	7,637
Number of persons apprehended for immigration violations, Mexican border region	N/A	22,326	12,232	18,686	27,731	16,261	17,522	18,222	16,462	7,265
Number of persons questioned, Mexican border region	N/A	1,580,754	723,123	844,706	785,420	614,991	594,066	511,968	457,497	345,530
Total number of persons questioned	1,252,379	2,220,952	1,265,690	1,385,103	1,356,543	1,100,152	989,005	906,721	877,278	722,120
Value of all seizures	$475,663	$461,000	$809,938	$773,864	$695,778	$766,042	$342,591	$304,955	$283,744	$123,187

SOURCE: Data compiled from principal activities and accomplishments of the U.S. Border Patrol, *Annual Reports of the Immigration and Naturalization Service, Fiscal Years Ending June 30, 1925–1934* (Washington, DC: GPO).

beginning a battle he could not win. And borderland resident Julio Santos Coy recalled a time when Border Patrol officers were "[yelling] at one person like in the movies when sergeants yell loudly at new recruits three millimeters from their faces."[36] Coy challenged the officers and was warned, "Shut up or you'll be where he is," but his opposition to the officers' aggression is evidence of Mexicano resistance to Border Patrol work.[37] Resistance in the moment of interrogation was critical because street-level investigations, examinations, and confrontations were at the heart of Border Patrol work.

Quite often, the impact of Border Patrol work is measured according to the number of people apprehended or deported each year. While this is a critical indicator of Border Patrol activity, apprehension statistics provide only a partial snapshot of what was occurring in the development of U.S. immigration law enforcement. Each year Border Patrol officers apprehended less than 3 percent of the number of persons they reported having questioned, examined, or investigated during the year. Border Patrol activity, therefore, constructed a broad net of surveillance that far exceeded the product of their police work as captured by the annual apprehension statistics.

In 1925, the eight officers working out of the Del Rio, Texas, station referred 102 people to a U.S. Immigration inspector for suspicion of immigration violations. To refer these 102 people, the Del Rio officers questioned or investigated 32,516 persons. These officers did not conduct 32,516 extensive individual interrogations; rather, they included a variety of interactions in their tally of interrogations. For example, when officers boarded a train and walked through the cabins, they recorded the total occupancy of the train in their tally for persons questioned. In Del Rio in 1925, this amounted to 12,109 people riding on 2,092 trains. Similarly, they included all occupants of the cars that they stopped and questioned. In Del Rio in 1925, this included 20,055 persons riding in 5,599 automobiles. Statistics for the total number of people questioned or investigated by the Border Patrol reflect a broad net of surveillance rather than a specific set of individual interrogations. In the sparsely populated border counties of the Del Rio station, Border Patrol racial profiling practices concentrated the officers' wide net of surveillance upon the region's Mexicano workers.[38]

The Del Rio station's territory stretched 137 miles along the U.S.-Mexico border across Kinney, Val Verde, and halfway through Brewster Counties. In 1930, the total population of these three counties combined was 25,528, of whom 14,559 (57 percent) were Mexicano.[39] In addition to resident populations, there was the seasonal arrival and departure of migrant laborers, linked most closely to the amount of cotton that had to be harvested.

In the 1920s, Kinney, Val Verde, and southern Brewster County farmers were only beginning to raise cotton. Although statistics for the amount of cotton harvested in the three counties in 1925 are not available, in 1924 only 27,970 acres of cotton were planted in Kinney, Val Verde, and Brewster Counties combined.[40] Using Paul Taylor's calculation that a good cotton crop would yield 170 lb./acre, and a good picker can pick 200 lb. of cotton per day, it would only require 792 workers to pick all three counties' cotton in five weeks. The three counties were already home to 2,166 male farm workers who would have performed much of the labor during the cotton harvest, leaving little work for migrant laborers.[41] Compared to the rapid expansion of cotton in areas such as the Lower Rio Grande Valley, Texas, or the Imperial Valley, California, the three counties in the Del Rio station's territory had few labor needs, and the Del Rio area was not a major beltway for migrant laborers heading north. Therefore, the bodies present and marked for interrogations in the Del Rio station's territory would rise and fall over the year but hovered around 15,000 Mexicanos. Still, setting the Del Rio station's 32,516 interrogations beside the estimated 15,000 possible subjects of their work only begins to reveal the impact of Border Patrol police practices upon Mexicano communities in the borderlands.

Gendered racial profiling dropped the number of "suspicious" Mexicans in the Del Rio area to 7,500, if approximately half of the resident Mexican population was male. And, assuming that only half of the Mexican population was over the age of fifteen, the number of suspicious Mexicans would be further reduced to 3,750. Understanding that Del Rio's officers reported questioning and investigating 32,516 persons within a region that was home to an estimated 3,750 racialized and gendered adult subjects of Border Patrol work reveals that the patrol's work amounted to police harassment of Mexicano laboring men in the Texas-Mexico borderlands. Despite occasional complaints from regional elites such as storeowner E. G. Spinnler and the members of the Hudspeth County Conservation and Reclamation District no. 1, farmers typically appreciated the Border Patrol's policing of Mexicano workers as a new tool of labor control in the region.

IMMIGRATION ENFORCEMENT AS LABOR CONTROL

Farmers and ranchers wanted migrants to come and go with the seasons, but they did not want workers to deploy their mobility as a strategy to improve their labor conditions and wages by seeking work elsewhere in the middle of the harvest. In response to the agribusinessmen's concerns regarding migrant mobility, municipalities placed restrictions upon out-of-state labor contractors and passed vagrancy laws that threatened migrant workers with arrest while en route to new jobs. The power vested within the United States Border Patrol was just another weapon in the arsenal of agribusinessmen who understood the advantages that Border Patrol work presented. As one farmer admitted, "The mexicans are afraid to run off they are afraid of what will be done to them and they don't know the law. They are afraid to come to town now because of the immigration officers."[42] Some regional elites protested Border Patrol intrusions upon their property and, at times, objected to the policing of Mexican laborers. In 1929, for example, a resident of Cameron County, Texas, protested that "our immigration officials are like dog catchers the way they go after the Mexicans."[43] A farmer in Carrizo Springs complained that Border Patrol officers "think their job is to pack a gun and to shoot even if a man is running."[44] But others recognized that without Border Patrol surveillance on the county roads and even of their own fields, migrant workers would "leave to go where wages were higher."[45] As one farmer explained, "We tell the immigration officers if our mexicans try to get away into the interior, and they stop them and send them back to Mexico. Then in a few days they are back here and we have good workers for another year."[46]

The Border Patrol's contributions to the agribusinessmen's interests in limiting and regulating the mobility of the industry's primary workforce cannot simply be explained by describing Border Patrol officers as the lackeys of agribusinessmen or as the tools of the capitalist state. Agribusinessmen often had the opportunity and ability to exercise direct influence over the development of Border Patrol practices, but the officers were local men, community members, and workers who maximized and manipulated the project of policing Mexican workers. Dogie Wright, for example, understood the interests of local agribusinessmen and utilized his position as a Border Patrol officer to demand respect from local elites. Indicating his authority to police Mexican workers, Dogie explained that "an officer's job is he's got to enforce the law."[47] The price for flexible enforcement against Mexico's unsanctioned border crossers was respect for his authority. So long as ranchers "treat me alright. And they always did," Dogie explained, he was happy to remain flexible in the enforcement of federal immigration restrictions against Mexican workers.[48] "We used our head. We wasn't rabid," recalled Dogie. "It makes a lot of difference right here on the border," he explained, "'cause we can't be too observant . . . they need labor right here on the border."[49] Structured by the political economy of Mexican labor migration to the Texas-Mexico borderlands, Dogie's strategic approach to U.S. immigration law enforcement reveals the more nuanced dynamics at work when Patrol officers—former tram conductors, auto mechanics, salesmen— extracted dignity, respect, and authority from the region's social, political, and economic elite by selectively policing the region's primary low-wage labor force.

The Border Patrol's contributions to the interests of agribusinessmen and ranchers were also a matter of self-protection because upsetting relations with local farmers and ranchers would have estranged officers from a critical source of assistance in the backcountry regions where Border Patrol officers worked alone, in pairs, or, at most, in groups of three. In particular, officers depended upon the support of local ranchers and farmers when policing the dangerous intersections of unsanctioned migration and liquor smuggling because, unlike migrant workers, liquor smugglers were typically armed and willing to engage Border Patrol officers to protect and move their loads. Prohibition, therefore, created a context in which protecting the interests of ranchers and farmers afforded the small and scattered force of Border Patrol officers with a crucial network of support.

Patrol Officer Frank Edgell understood the value of maintaining close relations with local ranchers and farmers. A Texan by birth, Edgell was a farmer in Pima County, Arizona, before joining the Border Patrol in 1924. Edgell was assigned to a series of Arizona stations and knew many of the local farmers because of his personal history in the region. Two of his acquaintances were Mary Kidder Rak and her husband, who owned a cattle ranch in the southeastern corner of Arizona. Rak broke the tedium of ranch life by writing about her life and experiences. In 1938, she published *Border Patrol*. Although *Border Patrol* is often cited as a text that chronicles the history of the U.S. Border Patrol, it is better understood as an artifact of the close relations between borderland ranchers and farmers and the officers of the U.S. Border Patrol's greater El Paso District during the 1930s.

Edgell told Rak of the dangers of Border Patrol work and celebrated the critical support provided by local ranchers such as Rak and her husband. For example, in December 1924, Edgell recalled, he had spotted the tracks of a horse in a desolate region near Sasabe, Arizona. Suspicious of off-road traffic in this isolated area, Edgell drove to the nearby Palo Alto Ranch and borrowed a horse.[50] He followed the tracks and found liquor concealed in a thicket. Crossing the thin line between enforcing U.S. immigration restrictions and policing liquor smugglers, Edgell continued to follow the tracks. Soon he came upon six armed men. Rather than confront the six men, Edgell opted for a distraction. " 'I am a Federal Officer,' he began frankly, taking his tobacco sack from his shirt pocket and rolling a cigarette as he sat at ease on his horse," wrote Rak, who admired her friend's bravery and ingenuity. " 'I hear that two Chinamen have come across from Mexico and are headed for Tucson, on foot. Have any of you men seen their tracks when you were riding around?' " The smugglers answered that they had not seen any Chinese passing through the area, and Edgell's successful ruse allowed him to avoid a conflict and continue on without incident. Edgell circled back and took a concealed position near the liquor hidden in the thicket. The smugglers were sure to return for their stash. Soon, two of them did. Edgell took them by surprise and placed them under arrest, but he was alone, and the two liquor smugglers had four friends in the area. One of smugglers' friends approached from a far-off hilltop and quietly prepared to shoot Edgell. Fortunately, explained Rak, Edgell's borrowed horse alerted him to the man in the distance. Edgell took cover, shot first, and downed the accomplice. Still, there were three other smugglers wandering about the area, and it was only the fortuitous arrival of "a trusted Mexican cowboy" that allowed Edgell to escape.

Together, Dogie Wright's reflections and Frank Edgell's anecdote provide unique insight into why the officers of the United States Border Patrol actively policed Mexicans while only meekly attempting to cut off the flow of Mexican workers into the greater Texas-Mexico borderlands. The corridors of migration between Mexico and the southwestern United States were certainly too broad, deep, and embedded for several hundred officers in scattered stations to patrol effectively, but, in addition to the systems of mass labor migration that the farmers and ranchers had lobbied to protect, Border Patrol officers empowered themselves by demanding respect in exchange for selective immigration law enforcement and protected themselves in an era of prohibition by fostering collaborative relationships that allowed them to call upon farmers and ranchers for support in times of need. The Border Patrol's simultaneously flexible and focused policing of Mexican workers was thus a complicated matter, a deeply social and political tactic of law enforcement that developed within the very specific socio-historical context of race, labor, power, and policing in the greater Texas-Mexico borderlands.

The violence that emerged from the Border Patrol's narrow enforcement of U.S. immigration restrictions also evolved in the dense social world of policing Mexicans in the Texas-Mexico borderlands. As of February 1925, Border Patrol practice was rooted in each officer's authority to use physical coercion. When their efforts at U.S. immigration law enforcement intersected with prohibition, Border Patrol coercion escalated into spectacular gunfights that became the backbone of border lore that painted the men of the Border Patrol as a "band of hard-bitten patrol officers."[51] While these legends of Border Patrol violence appropriately capture the extreme possibilities of Border Patrol work, they overlook the more everyday manifestations of Border Patrol authority, such as the net of surveillance, and elide the ways in which Border Patrol violence was often grounded in community life and folded into the fabric of family relations.

JACK'S REVENGE: THE SOCIAL WORLD OF BORDER PATROL VIOLENCE

John H. (Jack) and James P. (Jim) Cottingham were brothers. Jack was born in El Paso, Texas, in January 1881, and Jim was born five years later, in Brownsville, Texas, in March 1886. Although Jack was the older brother, he was born with limited mental facilities, and his younger brother watched over him as they grew from childhood to adulthood in the Texas-Mexico borderlands.[52] In 1900, their father was a farmer in Cameron County, Texas, their mother was a homemaker, and Jack, Jim, and their sisters, Susie and Mary, were in school.[53] By 1910, their father had left farming to become a real estate agent in Uvalde, Texas, and Jack and Jim had moved with the family to Uvalde, where they worked as merchants.[54] By 1920, the family had moved back to Cameron County. Jack and Jim were in their thirties and working as peace officers, and their father had returned to farming. Living with the family in Cameron County was their sister Susie's new husband, John Peavey. Peavey was a military man who had been born in Missouri but came to the Lower

Rio Grande Valley as a child with his family. Between 1920 and 1924, Peavey and the Cottingham brothers joined the U.S. Customs Mounted Guard and then switched over to the U.S. Immigration Service Mounted Guard.[55] In July 1924, they were transferred into the new U.S. Border Patrol. In the patrol, they all worked closely together, but Jack and Jim were inseparable partners, as Jim spent his days enforcing U.S. immigration restrictions and looking after his brother.[56]

The stories of Jack and Jim tell of two brothers deeply dedicated to one another. They worked together and lived together almost all their lives. Jack, the older and slower brother, never married, but rumor has it that when Jim got married, Jack joined him and his new bride on their honeymoon. Out on patrol, they shared the responsibilities of driving the patrol car. Regardless of where they were, every hundred miles they would trade. Every now and then, one officer recalled, "the time to change drivers would come right in the middle of downtown Mission or McAllen, or where ever . . . so they stopped their car, got out, changed sides, and then went on about their business."[57]

While on patrol one evening, their partnership almost came to an end when Jim was shot by a Mexican liquor smuggler. Jim shot back and killed the smuggler, but he was critically wounded. The bullet had gone through his arm and chest and punctured his lung. Jack picked up his brother and took him to the hospital. Jim's wounds were serious, and it was "touch and go for him in the hospital for some time."[58] He did recover, but on the day that Jim had been shot and it seemed as if Jack was to be left behind, Jack headed to the border to take vengeance for his wounded brother. As Jim lay in the hospital, "someone came to the bridge from across the river to complain because some one was down there doing a lot of shooting. When they went to investigate, they found Jack. He had gone on down to the river below where Jim had been when he was shot, and just stayed there. He killed every person who came in sight on the Mexican side of the river during that time."[59]

The story of Patrol Inspectors Jack and Jim Cottingham exemplifies the social entanglements of Border Patrol violence. In the course of enforcing U.S. immigration law, the transitions from investigation to aggression and lethal violence were often embedded in a world of family relations among the local officers of the Texas-Mexico borderlands. What had begun as a matter of immigration law enforcement ended as a matter of brotherhood. Border Patrol violence moved outward and onward through a socially integrated network of officers who sought vengeance against those who had harmed their own. Chief Patrol Inspector Herbert C. Horsley acknowledged this when he wrote to the parents of Patrol Inspector Benjamin T. Hill. Hill had joined the Patrol on May 14, 1929, and sixteen days later he was killed in a shootout with liquor smugglers. As Horsely wrote to Hill's parents, "We are leaving no stone unturned in our search for the murderer whose hand caused the death of your son, our beloved comrade."[60] Adding Hill's name to the Honor Roll, the list of officers killed in the line of duty, Horsley pledged that "your son's name will go down in Border Patrol history as a martyr to the cause of justice and as an example of fearlessness in the enforcement of the Laws of our Country."[61]

Hill was the twelfth Border Patrol officer to be killed in the line of duty. By 1933, nine other officers had died.[62] Each death and injury brought a search for vengeance. For example, on January 20, 1939, Presidio County Sheriff Joe Bunton delivered the body of Gregorio Alanis to his relatives living near Presidio, Texas. The delivery finished a battle that had begun eight years earlier between Alanis, a Mexican American, and officers of the U.S. Border Patrol. During a daybreak raid upon his father's property, Gregorio shot Patrol Inspector James McCraw just below the left clavicle and then fled to Mexico. Immediately after the shooting, Senior Patrol Inspector Earl Fallis secured a felony warrant against Alanis from the county sheriff "in the event it should become necessary to shoot Gregorio Alaniz, for in all probability he will resist arrest."[63] Time did not distract the officers, and on the evening of January 20, 1939, Patrol Inspector Dorn assigned all his men to a remote trail outside of Presidio, Texas. At 9:30 P.M., in an abandoned house along the trail, Dorn shot and killed Gregorio Alanis.

At the inquest, Justice of the Peace W. G. Young of Presidio County found that "Gregorio Alaniz came to death at the hands of Patrol Inspector Edwin Dorn, who while in the line of duty, commanded Gregorio Alaniz to halt and hold up his hands, Gregorio having refused and put up fight with a razor, the said Edwin Dorn shot him with a shotgun, in self-defence."[64] The other man who had crossed with Alanis that night and who had witnessed the shooting "offered no resistance, but while being conveyed to the patrol car which was some distance from the scene of the encounter by Inspectors Dorn and Temple, succeeded in escaping from them."[65] Eight years after the shooting of Patrol Inspector McCraw, Gregorio Alanis was dead, the witness was missing, and a brotherhood of law enforcement exonerated Dorn without any further investigation.

The composition of the Border Patrol (an ensemble of white men, including the Spanish or Mexican Americans who fought for whiteness by enforcing U.S. immigration laws against Mexican Browns) and the composition of its subjects (poor, male, brown-skinned Mexicans) structured the vengeance campaigns as struggles between white men and brown men of the borderlands. In the case of Jack Cottingham, Jack headed to the border to exact revenge for the shooting of his brother. With the gunman already dead, Jack's vengeance followed the Texas Rangers' tradition of "revenge by proxy." Jack shot Mexicans, any Mexicans, for the offense of one, and his outburst was implicitly gendered as he randomly subjected Mexicans to a highly masculine and public form of violence, pistol shooting. In the case of Gregorio Alanis, the officers of the patrol pursued a more slow, patient, and temperate approach: they waited eight years to avenge the shooting of Patrol Inspector James McCraw and took their vengeance at the often violent intersection of migration control and liquor interdiction.

In the case of Lon Parker, the murder of a fellow officer sparked years of violence as men who were both kin and colleague to Parker sought vengeance for their losses. Lon Parker was born in Arizona in 1892 and grew up in southern Arizona. In 1924, both Lon and his brother, George W. Parker Jr., joined the United States Border Patrol. By any measure, Lon was popular and epitomized the early Border Patrol officer as a man who was familiar with local customs and highly integrated into local communities. "It was said that if one met a strange man anywhere within a wide radius of the Huachucas, one could say "Good morning, Mr. Parker,' and be right four fifths of the time," explained Mary Kidder Rak.[66]

On a Sunday afternoon in the summer of 1926, Lon left a family picnic to follow the tracks of two liquor smugglers into the mountains. The smugglers, however, found Lon before he found them, and they shot him when he came into range. Seriously wounded, according to the stories told to Mary Kidder Rak, Lon drew his gun and killed one of the smugglers and his horse. The other smuggler fled, and Lon slowly rode to the nearest ranch for help. Lon barely made it to the ranch, where he fell off of his horse and collapsed against a fence; but nobody was home to help him, and within hours Lon was dead.[67]

A few days later, when Washington, D.C., transplant Alvin Edward Moore reported for duty in Patagonia, Arizona, he was handed the badge of the recently slain Lon Parker and told the story of the smuggler who got away. After Lon's body was discovered, brother Border Patrol officers followed his trail back into the mountains and found the dead smuggler. It was Narciso Ochoa, a noted liquor smuggler in the area. The officers presumed that it was his brother Domitilio Ochoa who had left the tracks fleeing the area.[68] Soon after Moore arrived in Arizona, Senior Patrol Inspector Albert Gatlin got a tip that Ochoa was going to try to return to Mexico that night. Gatlin told Moore to find Patrol Inspector Lawrence Sipe (Gatlin's brother-in-law), Deputy Sheriff Jim Kane (raised with Lon on the same ranch and "ate out of the same beanpot") and "anybody else he can get" and meet at Campaña Pass along the border. When Moore, Sipe, and Kane arrived, they were met by Gatlin and a "posse of officers from Douglas County." According to Moore, ranchers were "turning out of bed to patrol the line that night . . . stalking off in the moonlight, rifles ready, prepared to shoot and be shot at."[69] During such vengeance campaigns, the line between officers and community members disappeared. Together, they took to the night to avenge the murder of Lon Parker.

It was Lon's partner, Albert Gatlin, who led the posse. "Lon had been as near to Gatlin as his own brother, and his murder had all but turned him from an impartial officer into an avenging nemesis," remarked Moore.[70] Before he stationed the posse at posts along the border, Gatlin gave the officers, ranchers, and farmers who had been deputized for the evening some advice: "All I've got to say, men, is if you see anybody comin' toward the line tonight, yell at 'em in English. And if he don't answer you in English, shoot!"[71] With that advice, the men took to their posts for the night.

Several hours later, Moore saw a figure move in the dark. When a bullet blasted through his car window, Moore took aim and shot back. After the figure dropped, Moore ran over. It was Ochoa, and he had been shot in the chest. As daylight broke, Moore proudly displayed the wounded Ochoa to Gatlin, who moaned, "It's too bad you didn't kill the son-of-a-bitch," but "you qualify for the Border Patrol."[72] Moore was not a local, but in the blood of Domitilio Ochoa, he was baptized as a Border Patrol officer. Ochoa survived the shooting but was sentenced to death by hanging soon after—at least, this was Moore's tale of Lon Parker.

Ralph Williams joined the Border Patrol long after Lon had died, but he was related to Lon by marriage and had heard the legends from family and from brother officers. Williams knew that Lon was an uncle to Sheriff Jim Hathaway of Cochise County. Jim grew up with Officers Jean Pyeatt and D'Alibini and had been with them when they fought the Mexicans during recess. When Lon lost his final fight on that mountain trail, Jim vowed, "That smuggler will never die a natural death."[73] Two years later, Jim found the man he believed had killed Lon, and "in the middle of the night with that boy, he eliminated him. Him and that guy who was riding shot-gun for him."[74] According to Williams, two men were dead for the murder of Lon Parker, when only one was accused of fleeing the scene. Still, according to the legend of Lon Parker, the pursuit of justice in the name of their brother officer did not stop.

Patrol Inspector Robert Moss had his own version of the story to tell. According to Martin, three men were involved in the murder of Lon Parker. Two of the men were later found "hanging from a tree, right where they had killed him. I don't know how they got back there, but they were found dead, hanging from a tree."[75] Moss believed that he later caught a third accomplice in downtown El Paso. When the man saw Moss and his partner coming, he began to run and "started screaming in English 'Don't let them kill me.'" The man must have known that Patrol Inspector Gatlin had long ago set English as the code for not getting shot by the Border Patrol for the murder of Lon Parker. He too was sent to jail.

All together, the legends of Lon Parker tell of seven men dead and one in jail after a Sunday afternoon in 1926. Lon and Narciso were the first to die. Then, after one man fled the scene, a posse shooting and jury hanging, a dual nighttime elimination, two mountain lynchings, and a final El Paso apprehension followed. The legend tells of violence that was dispersed but not random. Patrolmen serving as officers of the state, brothers of the deceased, and men of the community exacted compensation from Mexicano men for the murder of Lon Parker. The legends suggest that in many ways and on many nights, Border Patrol violence was used to exact personal vengeance and defend community interests. In the battles that ensued between Border Patrol officers and Mexicanos, schoolyard clashes were replayed between grown men, but the white boys who had become Border Patrol officers had gained the authority of the state. As immigration law-enforcement officers, their violence carried new meaning by unfolding in the field in which illegality was being defined. When Border Patrol officers shot, killed, arrested, hung, eliminated, or otherwise brutalized Mexicanos, the violence that had so long defined the differences between whites and Mexicans in the borderlands—those of conquest, land ownership, employment, and so on—became inscribed within the violence that marked the differences between being legal and illegal.

But the legend of Lon Parker must be read as a matter of both fact and fiction. As historian Alexandra Minna Stern has observed, Border Patrolmen of the 1920s and 1930s actively embraced, among other things, a "primitive masculinity" whereby they forged their institutional identity in the image of frontier cowboys and other pioneering conquerors of the American West, namely, the Texas Rangers.[76] Such notions elided the complex personal and employment histories of the early officers—the tram drivers, the mechanics, and the Texas Rangers included—but it was a powerful narrative that officers carefully projected to one another and to the world around them. Whether or not their predecessors had actually engaged in the exploits that comprised the legends of Lon Parker, they spent years swapping stories of having brought a more primitive and manly form of justice to some smuggler, some night, at the hands of some Patrol inspector. The legends of Lon Parker were a form of cultural production in which Border Patrol officers defined themselves as inheritors of a masculine and highly racialized renegade tradition of violence in the U.S.-Mexico borderlands.

The life, career, and celebrated lethality of Patrol Inspector Charles Askins Jr. was another source of bravado for the early officers. Askins is heralded as one of the twentieth century's greatest gunfighters. At the time of his death in 1999, a hesitant but admiring obituary in the gun-enthusiast magazine *American Handgunner* described Askins as a "stone cold killer. For those of us who knew him, there was just no gentler way to put it."[77] Askins himself listed his official body count at "Twenty seven, not counting [blacks] and Mexicans."[78]

Askins was not from the borderlands. He was born in Nebraska and grew up in Oklahoma before moving to Montana, where he took a temporary job fighting fires in Flathead Forest.[79] He then moved down to New Mexico, where he again worked fighting fires, this time on the Jicarilla Indian reservation. When fire season ended, he worked in logging camps. By 1929, he was working full-time as a forest ranger in the Kit Carson National Forest. In 1930, Askins's friend, George W. Parker Jr. recruited him to the U.S. Border Patrol. Parker had boasted of "a gunfight every week and sometimes two."[80] Always in search of a gunfight, Askins "succumbed to the glowing reports from my amigo Parker who was having a hell of a good time in the Border Patrol."[81] Stationed in El Paso, Texas, Askins had plenty of opportunities to do battle with *contrabandistas* attempting to bring liquor into the United States.

Askins disagreed with Prohibition—"an ill-fated attempt to force the thirsty American public to give up John Barleycorn," as he described it—but liquor control presented him with the opportunity to engage in the "sport" of human hunting.[82]

Askins recounted his life of guns, violence, and immigration law enforcement in his autobiography, *Unrepentant Sinner*. Recalling his first day on the job as a Border Patrol officer, Askins explained that there was "no training school for recruits. . . . I was handed a badge and since I had my own shooting irons I did not draw the old .45 Colt Model 1917 nor one of the next to worthless Enfield rifles."[83] With his own weapon and a U.S.-issued Border Patrol badge, Askins headed out for his first "tour of duty." That evening, at about 9:30 P.M., Patrol Inspectors Jack Thomas and Tom Isbell "ran into an ambush and killed a smuggler." Askins had not been at the fight, but he arrived soon after and helped to collect the body of the dead *contrabandista*. "I was enthralled, I'll tell you!" exclaimed Askins, "I hadn't fired a shot but I'd been close to the smell of gunpowder and I thought, 'Boy, this is for me!' "[84]

Askins eagerly pursued gunfights with the smugglers and reveled in the Border Patrol's besting of the *contrabandistas*. He estimated that while Border Patrol officers killed five hundred smugglers between 1924 and 1934, the Border Patrol's Honor Roll listed only twenty-three officers lost in the process.[85] Askins so enjoyed the sport of battling the liquor smugglers that he seemed to forget the primary function and authority of the United States Border Patrol. "Actually the primary job of the Border Patrol was not alcohol at all but illegal aliens," he said.[86] "The BP was part of the Immigration Service and, believe it or not, was part of the Department of Labor."[87]

When Askins did engage in immigration law enforcement, his methods were rough. "I was really in favor of banging a suspect over the ears with a sixshooter and then asking him when he crossed out of Mexico," explained Askins, "This I found reduced the small talk to a few syllables and got a confession in short order."[88] Although he was transferred from the El Paso station after the district director read one too many gunfight reports that included his name, Askins believed that his chief patrol inspector sanctioned his excess and aggression because "only those jazbos who had not been raised along the border, were not happy with this system."[89]

Over the years, Askins was promoted for his enthusiasm, expertise, and knowledge in firearms. First, he was tapped to organize a pistol team. Under his tutelage, the Border Patrol Pistol Team won multiple regional and national competitions. While Askins routinely complained about the average patrolman's inexperience with guns, the success of the Border Patrol Pistol Team helped brand the organization as an outfit of straight shooters. In 1937, Askins was appointed as the firearms trainer at the Border Patrol Training School in El Paso, Texas, boasting that this position made him the highest paid officer in the U.S. Border Patrol. That Askins not only survived but prospered in the patrol during the 1930s is particularly significant because it was an era of reform in federal law enforcement.

In 1929, widespread concerns regarding crime and crime control, focused on issues emerging from Prohibition, prompted President Herbert Hoover to establish the National Committee on Law Observation and Enforcement, popularly known as the Wickersham Commission. The Wickersham Commission assessed the causes of crime, concentrating on the rise of organized crime and efforts to stem liquor consumption and trafficking, and examined the many problems of enforcing Prohibition. As the Wickersham Commission examined the enforcement of Prohibition, it uncovered patterns of police corruption and brutality that exposed all arms of federal law enforcement to increased scrutiny.

In 1930, the Department of Labor began to investigate corruption and excessive violence within the Border Patrol by compiling a list of all criminal charges that had been filed against Border Patrol officers since July 1, 1924.[90] The officers had been convicted of everything from murder to speeding. Then, in 1933, the Department of Labor reorganized the Immigration Service and Naturalization Service by forming the joint Immigration and Naturalization Service (INS) and attempted to clean out the Border Patrol by firing all officers and rehiring them on a temporary basis. To secure a permanent position with the Border Patrol, the officers had to appear before a board of officials from the Department of Labor and the Immigration Service, popularly remembered as the Benzene Board. Dogie Wright explained that the board's function was "to cut out the men who were doing a lot of gun fighting, too prone to use their guns."[91] Some were removed, but many of the officers, including Charles Askins, made it through.

As suggested by Askins' retention, the impact of the Benzene Board was limited. The country was in the depths of the Great Depression, and jobs were hard to come by. The board made a quick pass over Border Patrol personnel, but even someone as unrepentant as Charles Askins must have spoken wisely and judiciously before the Benzene Board. Further the board depended upon local law-enforcement systems to expose and document cases of corruption and brutality. However, as in the case of Gregorio Alanis, local law enforcement typically buried incidents of Border Patrol violence.

Just a few months before the Benzene Board began, the death of Miguel Navarro exemplified how local law enforcement concealed Border Patrol violence. On August 18, 1932, two patrol inspectors and a special state ranger heard that some liquor smugglers were going to try to cross the border illegally that evening at the Las Flores crossing near La Feria, Texas. At around 9 P.M., they hid behind a tree and waited for the smugglers to cross. The inspectors had been waiting about forty-five minutes when they "saw three men carrying something on their shoulders . . . from the direction of the river."[92] When the smugglers got within fifty feet of the officers, Patrol Inspector John V. Saul stepped out from behind the tree and told the men to halt. Two of the men—Anselmo Torres, a U.S. citizen, and José Sandoval, a Mexican national—stopped and raised their hands. The third smuggler, a U.S. citizen and resident of Mercedes, Texas, named Miguel Navarro "half turned and threw his right hand to his body reaching under the sack he had across his left shoulder," according to Saul, who was "sure he [Navarro] was drawing a gun and fired."[93] Navarro fell to the ground, shot in the leg. With the help of the "other two Mexicans," the officers loaded Navarro into the back of their car and drove him to the nearest hospital in Mercedes before they took the other two men to the jail in Weslaco, Texas. The officers then returned to the scene of the shooting with their chief patrol inspector, a U.S. Customs officer, at least two deputy sheriffs of Hidalgo County, and the assistant supervisor of the Customs Border Patrol.[94]

At daylight, the officers "began searching for a gun which we believed must be there for we were certain the Mexican wounded had attempted to draw one."[95] Saul depended upon his brother officers to exonerate him of excessive force by locating Navarro's gun. After a short search around the "pool of blood there on the road where the Mexican fell," one of the deputy sheriffs called out, "Here it is," and "picked up a 32 double-action revolver . . . about five or six feet from where the Mexican fell."[96] The officers passed the gun around for inspection and agreed that it was the one carried by Navarro. With no further investigation, the deputy sheriff's discovery of the gun allowed the Border Patrol to find Saul's shooting of Navarro justifiable and close the case.

Within a few days, Navarro died from the gunshot wound. During the external investigation by local law-enforcement authorities, the sheriff assured the Border Patrol that he was "entirely satisfied the matter was a justifiable homicide and that they [saw] no reason . . . to investigate or proceed with the matter any further."[97] The local justice of the peace followed suit and declared that "the deceased came to his death from shock and hemorrhage caused by a bullet wound inflicted on him while resisting lawful arrest with a deadly weapon."[98] In the end, Miguel Navarro— the "Mexican" born in Mercedes, Texas—was dead, and Patrol Inspector Saul was exonerated without further inquiry.

Quick exonerations by a brotherhood of local and state officers shielded the men of the Border Patrol from the potentially less sympathetic scrutiny of a federal grand jury or even the Benzene Board. Such impunity fortified the localized structure of Border Patrol operations. Still the broader effort to professionalize federal police practice during the 1930s did prompt the establishment of the Border Patrol Training School (BPTS) in 1937, which brought a new level of uniform training into the Border Patrol project.

THE BORDER PATROL TRAINING SCHOOL

The BPTS was actually the expansion of a training program first developed in 1935 by the chief patrol inspector of the El Paso District, Herbert C. Horsley, and his supervisor, district director of the Immigration Service in El Paso, Texas, Grover C.

Wilmoth. Wilmoth had spent years struggling with a rag-tag group of officers in his district. He repeatedly issued circulars requiring officers to wear their uniforms, to stop drinking, gossiping, and sleeping on the job, to cease their cavorting in Mexican border towns, and to stop over-reaching their authority by conducting random traffic checks. But nobody seemed to listen. The culture of immigration law enforcement in the far-flung offices seemed resistant to his interventions by memo. In February of 1928, for example, Wilmoth found it necessary to recirculate a memo dated September 2, 1924, which asserted that "employees must not while on duty indulge in the use of intoxicating liquors in Nogales, Sonora, Mexico, or elsewhere."[99] In October 1929, incidents of officers "accept[ing] gifts of small value" prompted Wilmoth to instruct officers as to the "impropriety of any officer or employee of the Immigration Service accepting gratuities of any sort from any alien or from any person in any way interested in the immigration status of an alien."[100] The next month Wilmoth wrote that "despite frequent warnings . . . certain officers and employees have continued to indulge in useless and harmful talk to outsiders . . . concerning official matters," and he advised his staff that "upon proof of receipt of a copy of this formal warning, no leniency will be shown one who offends in the respect indicated."[101]

In 1930, Wilmoth attempted to forge a measure of uniformity and a culture of professionalism within his district by providing a detailed welcome letter for all new recruits. "You are congratulated on having been selected as a member of the U.S. Immigration Service Border Patrol, which we . . . believe to be the finest law-enforcing agency of the Federal Government," the letter began.[102] After listing a series of "don'ts"—don't fail to tell the truth, don't drink, don't gamble, don't grumble, and so forth—the letter explained the Border Patrol's on-the-ground training process by urging the new recruits to submit themselves to the more experienced officers. "For the next few months your attitude should be that of a student," advised the letter.[103] "You should show a desire and willingness to learn this business from officers who have served long and faithfully and who KNOW IT. You may have had excellent training in other lines of police work but bear in mind that you are expected to learn to do things the Border Patrol way."[104] Wilmoth spoke of a "Border Patrol way" but, as he well knew, the El Paso District was fraught with disorder. From his office in El Paso, Wilmoth had little direct control over Border Patrol officers working in stations spread from Nogales, Arizona, across New Mexico and over to the western edges of the Lower Rio Grande Valley of Texas. There was no consistency or uniformity that amounted to a "Border Patrol way"; rather, there was an assortment of localities that received and trained new recruits, each in their own way. If Wilmoth doubted the disorder in his district, he was reminded in March 1931, when he toured stations along the border and found that officers did not regularly wear their uniforms. "It is a matter of regret for the writer," explained Wilmoth "that it is again necessary for him thus formally to call attention to the wide-spread disregard of the uniform regulations. He recently noted that some of the officers were on duty without any pretense of wearing the uniform; that some of the uniforms were unbelievably shabby; and that some of the officers, both on and off duty, violated instructions by wearing merely a portion of the uniform."[105]

One decade after the establishment of the U.S. Border Patrol, G. C. Wilmoth attempted to impose order and uniformity on his region by establishing the El Paso District Training School.[106] The first session of the three-month training course was held at the El Paso headquarters on December 3, 1934. During the morning, the trainees received instruction in the Spanish language, immigration law, conduct, rights of search, seizure, evidence and court procedure, firearms, fingerprinting and identification, line patrolling, and equitation. After listening to lectures by instructors such as Charles Askins, who served as the firearms instructor, the trainees spent their afternoons working alongside experienced patrolmen for a ground-level education in the application of U.S. immigration law. On patrol and in the classroom, the new recruits learned from the old-timers how U.S. immigration law was interpreted on a daily basis in the U.S.-Mexico borderlands. Wilmoth's efforts to impose uniformity and discipline therefore simply formalized the localization of immigration law enforcement in the El Paso District. Without improving lines of ongoing supervision and training, Wilmoth allowed the old-timers to continue to exert significant control over the development of U.S. Border Patrol practices.

In 1937, the Immigration Service renamed the El Paso District Training School the Border Patrol Training School (BPTS) and began requiring all new recruits, nationwide, to attend. The establishment of the BPTS in El Paso, Texas, represents an important moment in the history of the U.S. Border Patrol. The informalism, disorder, and regionalism that characterized the patrol's first ten years were certainly reduced by the adoption of a national training program. But the establishment of the BPTS is most remarkable in the ways that it centralized the Texas-Mexico borderlands in the making of U.S. immigration law enforcement.

The year that the BPTS opened, the U.S.-Mexico border was not the epicenter of Border Patrol activity. That year, 325 officers worked along the U.S.-Canada border, while 234 worked along the U.S.-Mexico border; another 34 worked in Jacksonville, Florida, and there was 1 officer in New Orleans, Louisiana.[107] However, requiring all officers to attend the BPTS and to conduct their first patrol activities in the El Paso district forged uniformity and commonality around the particularities of the Texas-Mexico borderlands. Further the establishment of the BPTS in El Paso, Texas, greatly empowered the officers of the turbulent El Paso District to shape the definition of the "Border Patrol way."[108] The establishment of the BPTS, therefore, was significant for the Border Patrol's focus on the U.S.-Mexico border, with an area of concentration in the Texas-Mexico borderlands.

Among the first officers to be trained at the BPTS was Harlon B. Carter. Harlon grew up in Laredo, Texas, where the disjointed structure of U.S. immigration law enforcement had once allowed the city's Mexicano majority and elite to dominate the development of local Border Patrol operations. In 1927, however, Clifford Perkins made an inspection trip to the area and was alarmed by the development of U.S. immigration control in the city. "Laredo was strictly a Mexican town. . . . probably ninety-percent of the people were either Mexican or of Mexican descent," wrote Perkins, who distrusted the Laredo sector's ability to enforce U.S. immigration restrictions independently. "The only Anglo on the police force was the chief himself," which distressed Perkins. During his two-week investigation, Perkins waged a "full-scale housecleaning." He charged local officials, the chief patrol inspector, and Border Patrol officers in the Laredo station with immigrant smuggling and forced just under half of Laredo's twenty-eight Border Patrol inspectors and the chief patrol inspector to quit or be fired. Perkins then transferred select Border Patrolmen who had all been Texas Rangers into the Laredo sector because "all were experienced, well-disciplined fighters who knew the country well."[109]

Detailing former Texas Rangers to Laredo was a strategy used to divorce the Border Patrol station from the local Mexican-American political elite. Tension quickly mounted between the ex-Rangers and the Laredo community, particularly the Laredo Police Department. While the Border Patrol enjoyed close relations with the local police in most borderland communities, in 1927 several officers of the Laredo Border Patrol "got in their Model T automobiles and spent about a half hour circling and shooting up the police station."[110] The 1927 cleanup of the Laredo station reflected the limits of Border Patrol disorganization that allowed for local management of immigration law enforcement. Although most local stations developed their own strategies, policies, and procedures, the Laredo station was exempt until the men and the infamously brutal racial violence of the Texas Rangers slashed away at the bonds between the Laredo Border Patrol and local Mexican-American leadership. The cleanup transformed the Laredo Border Patrol into a refuge for white violence within Mexican-dominated Laredo. One of the men who found sanctuary in the U.S. Border Patrol was Harlon B. Carter.

Harlon had a history of violence before joining the Border Patrol. On March 3, 1931, in Laredo, Texas, a teenaged Harlon returned home to find his mother upset. Several young Mexican American boys had been loitering in front of the house, she complained. Harlon's father, Horace B. Carter, was not home. He was an officer with the U.S. Border Patrol and was most likely on duty and not expected to return home soon. So young Harlon picked up his shotgun and headed out to find the boys who had upset his mother.[111]

He found them not too far away. Ramón Casiano, fifteen years old, Salvador Peña, twelve years old, and two others were just leaving a local swimming hole when young Harlon approached them. With shotgun in hand, Harlon demanded that the four boys return to his home with him. Ramón, the oldest of the boys, spoke for the group and refused. "We won't go to your house and you can't make us," he said. The defiance sparked some bitter words between the two until Harlon raised his shotgun to Ramón's chest and shot him dead. A Laredo policeman arrested Harlon, and a Laredo jury found him guilty of murder. Harlon served two years in prison—and joined the National Rifle Association—before being released upon appeal when a higher court ruled that the "trial judge's jury instructions had been incomplete."[112] After wandering for awhile, Harlon followed in his father's footsteps by joining the Border Patrol.

Harlon joined many other local men who became immigration law-enforcement officers in the greater Texas-Mexico borderlands. Among them were the Cottingham brothers from south Texas, Fred D'Alibini from southern Arizona, and Pete Torres from southern New Mexico. They too had come of age in this region claimed by conquest and dominated by agribusiness. As men, they took up the mandate of immigration control. Holding more than 87.5 percent of all supervisory positions in the stations along the Texas-Mexico border, these local men made a significant imprint upon the development of U.S. immigration law enforcement. Most important, although they were federal officers enforcing national laws along an international boundary, Border Patrol officers in the 1920s and 1930s were entrenched in the local realities of race, labor, migration, masculinity, and violence that structured their lives as working-class men in the Texas-Mexico borderlands. They used the monopoly on violence granted them as immigration law-enforcement officers to both maintain and manipulate the world in which they lived by policing Mexicans as a proxy for policing illegals. In the process, they filled the caste of illegality with Mexican Browns and introduced a unique site of racialization to the U.S.-Mexico borderlands.

These were the formative days of the U.S. Border Patrol in the Texas-Mexico borderlands, but the Border Patrol's turn toward policing Mexican immigrants and its rise in the U.S.-Mexico borderlands was far from an undifferentiated process. Along the California and western Arizona border, which was policed by the U.S. Immigration Service's Los Angeles District, Border Patrol practices developed according to very different dynamics. Chapter 3 draws upon the fragmentary record of Border Patrol work in the Immigration Service's westernmost region to examine the unique conditions that shaped the enforcement of U.S. immigration restrictions in that region.

3

The California-Arizona Borderlands

When the U.S. Border Patrol archived its discontinued correspondence records with the National Archives in 1957, very few records were forwarded from the Los Angeles District, which stretched from the Pacific Ocean to east of Yuma, Arizona, and extended north in California to San Luis Obispo. The bulk of the records addressed Border Patrol activity in the Texas-based districts and the Canadian border region. But in records ranging from oral histories and press accounts to U.S. District Court records and annual statistical reports for Border Patrol activities, the story of the U.S. Border Patrol in the western U.S.-Mexico borderlands emerges and reveals that this was a regionally distinctive zone for the development of U.S. immigration law enforcement. Here, Border Patrol officers began their work by policing a wide range of unsanctioned border crossers. Asians, Europeans, and Mexicans were all subject to migration control efforts. Yet the shifting political and fiscal limitations of comprehensive immigration law enforcement soon narrowed the Border Patrol project in the region, and, here, the swing toward policing Mexicans accompanied a shift away from policing Asians and Europeans.

POLICING THE PACIFIC CORRIDORS OF MIGRATION

Legal Asian immigration into the western U.S.-Mexico borderlands slowed after the Chinese Exclusion Act of 1882 prohibited Chinese workers from entering the United States and came to a near halt after the "Asiatic Barred Zone" of the Immigration Act of 1917 had effectively prohibited all Asians from legally entering the United States. By the time the U.S. Border Patrol was established, illegal immigration was the only route available for most Asian immigrants seeking entry into the United States. Many tried to enter with forged documents through U.S. ports of entry, while others tried their luck with unsanctioned border crossings along the Mexican and Canadian borders.[1] Others simply avoided U.S. immigration restrictions by heading to destinations that did not restrict Asian immigration, such as Mexico.

As immigration restrictions against Asians tightened in the United States, Mexican President Porfirio Díaz encouraged Asian immigration to Mexico by signing the Treaty of Amity, Commerce, and Navigation with Japan in 1888 and the Treaty of Amity and Commerce with China in 1893. Díaz hoped that Asian immigrant workers would help fuel projects of industrialization in Mexican agriculture.[2] Between 1900 and 1920, an estimated 10,000 Japanese immigrants arrived in Mexico and, by 1930, an estimated 15,960 Chinese lived in Mexico. Both Japanese and Chinese immigrants tended to settle in northwestern Mexico, primarily in Baja California.[3]

In addition to immigration from China and Japan and a smaller number of arrivals from Korea and India, the Asian population in northern Mexico also expanded as Chinese workers and Japanese farmers crossed into Mexico to flee anti-Asian hysteria in California. They headed south, encouraged by U.S.-based agribusiness companies operating in Mexico's Mexicali Valley that were building enormous cotton farms with Asian workers. Most important was the Colorado River Land Company (CRLC), which actively recruited Chinese laborers to plant and pick cotton on their land in the Mexicali Valley, the cross-border extension of the Imperial Valley in Southern California. The CRLC preferred to use Chinese immigrant labor in the Mexicali Valley so as not to interrupt the flow of Mexican migrants to the United States. By 1919, the CRLC had recruited 7,000–8,000 Chinese laborers to the Mexicali Valley. About 500 Japanese and 200 East Indians also worked for the CRLC, but an estimated 80 percent of the CRLC fields were tended by Chinese immigrants.[4] In 1920, the U.S. Consul in Mexicali wrote that the arrival of Chinese workers in Baja California and departure of Mexican workers to Norte California was "creating on the California-Lower California border a community more distinctly Chinese than Mexican."[5] To the east of the Mexicali Valley, 3,571 Chinese had also taken up residence in the state of Sonora, Mexico, by 1930.[6]

Asian immigrants in the northern Mexico borderlands fostered anxieties north of the border that Mexico would serve as a staging ground for unsanctioned Asian entry into the United States. As Congress debated the National Origins Act during the spring of 1924, Southern California newspapers reported that Japanese immigrants were planning "an invasion" of California.[7] Reporting on the impending Japanese invasion was matched by regular coverage of the smuggling of East Indians across the U.S.-Mexico border and, most important, the threatening presence of a Chinese-Mexican community in the Mexicali, Baja California region.[8] For many, therefore, the establishment of the U.S. Border Patrol promised to place a barricade between the United States and the Asian population of the northern Mexico borderlands.[9] For U.S. agribusinessmen north of the border, however, the establishment of the U.S. Border Patrol also threatened unrestricted access to the Mexican workers who cycled in and out of the borderlands during the great boom in California agriculture of the 1920s. But as the National Origins Act of 1924 made its way through Congress and into effect, farmers in the Imperial Valley seemed to have little reason to worry that immigration restrictions would significantly restrict their labor supply. Local coverage of U.S. immigration law-enforcement activities told stories of Europeans rather than Mexicans being apprehended for unsanctioned entry into the United States. In April and May of 1924, for example, the *Calexico Chronicle* followed the story of Conrad Meiers, a Swiss rancher who had been found guilty of smuggling three Swiss workers across the U.S.-Mexico border.[10] On May 8, 1924, the *Calexico Chronicle* covered the story of Hans Martens, a German immigrant, who had illegally crossed the U.S.-Mexico border with the assistance of Martens Kraeger. Hans was arrested and deported, and Kraeger stood trial for immigrant smuggling.[11] On June 2, 1924, the *Calexico Chronicle* reported a story of U.S. Immigration Inspectors capturing five Italian immigrants and their smuggler.[12] Nothing was written of Mexican workers encountering increased immigration restrictions. Further, local officials promised that the new changes in U.S. immigration law would have a limited impact upon Mexican workers. On June 13, 1924, for example, an article in the *Calexico Chronicle* explained that "the new immigration law, which goes into effect on July 1, will probably be responsible for some confusion on the border for a matter of two or three days . . . during which Mexicans crossing the line unaccompanied by properly visaed passports will be required to give evidence of their nativity."[13] But the article then affirmed that "while it does not mean that Mexicans will be prevented from crossing the line as freely as in the past, the requirements which will go into effect need a certain amount of time to complete."[14] A few days later the inspector-in-charge of the local U.S. Immigration Service station promised that "Mexicans will not be molested excepting in extreme cases and in accordance with regulations which have been enforced through the past several years, [because] the rigid rules now in effect [apply] chiefly to European aliens."[15] By July 3, 1924, the new immigration regime seemed only to affect southern Europeans, who were said to be "assembled in Mexicali and desiring to make entry to the United States [but] are encountering a great deal of grief."[16]

Yet just six days later, the U.S. Immigration Service clarified its position on Mexican workers. The estimated 400–600 "Mexicans who have been in the habit of crossing the line daily for the purpose of working in the fields of lettuce, cantaloupes and cotton or other crops on this side of the line" would be exempt from the eight-dollar head tax and ten-dollar visa fee, explained Chief Nielsen of the Immigration Service, but all other Mexican border crossers would be required to comply with all U.S. immigration restrictions and fees. The thousands of Mexican workers seasonally employed in the upper valley region would be required to pay eighteen dollars each time that they crossed into the United States. Employers feared that the cost of legal immigration would discourage Mexicans from seeking work north of the border, and the evasion of U.S. immigration requirements would become more difficult after the impending arrival of "20 additional inspectors" (i.e., U.S. Border Patrol officers), who, Nielsen explained, would be "stationed along the border to stop illegal crossings at points other than at the port proper."[17] Despite all of their lobbying efforts to keep Mexican immigrants out of the quota system, the application of the administrative requirements for legal entry and the establishment of a police force to prevent unsanctioned border crossings threatened to stem Mexican labor migration into California. "If rigidly enforced," explained the *Calexico Chronicle*, "the new immigration law, as it applies to Mexicans, is likely to work considerable of a hardship in the valley." Protesting impediments to Mexican labor migration, the *Calexico Chronicle* reported that "local people as well as employers from the north end of the valley are preparing to make an attempt to have the law modified, or at least its enforcement modified to the extent where it will not work a hardship, and for this purpose organized effort is to be made within the next few days, with the likelihood that committees will be appointed from civic organizations to make an active fight to have its application less harmful to valley interests."[18] Before the U.S. Border Patrol ever began work in the Imperial Valley, the local press was encouraging farmers and community members to challenge any interruption to Mexican labor migration.

As local agribusinessmen gathered their forces, the newly hired U.S. Border Patrol officers in El Centro, California, began work on August 2, 1924, from their makeshift office in the local County jail.[19] The officers were an eclectic group. Alfred E. Thur was a fifty-four-year-old German immigrant who had tried his hand at poultry farming in northern California before joining the U.S. Immigration Service in Los Angeles.[20] Ralph V. Armstrong was a North Dakota native who relocated with his family to San Diego, California, where his father worked as a railroad conductor.[21] Ralph lived at home and found a job as a fireman in San Diego before he joined the U.S. Border Patrol in the summer of 1921.[22] Four years later, he joined the U.S. Border Patrol. Thirty-two-year-old Frank P. McCaslin was a Pennsylvania native who worked as a production clerk at a machine factory before settling with his young family in Southern California in the early 1920s.[23] The lead officer for the El Centro station was Frank G. Ellis, a forty-four-year-old California native. His mother was described as "Mexican/Spanish" by the 1910 census taker, and his father was a Norwegian immigrant who owned and operated his own farm in San Diego County, California. Frank's older brother worked on the family farm, but Frank pursued an education until at least the age of nineteen and worked at a dairy before he was recruited to the U.S. Mounted Guard by Harry Weddle, a family friend and the inspector in charge of the U.S. Immigration Service office in San Diego, California.[24] Ellis's initial stint with the Mounted Guard was in 1909. He policed the California-Mexico borderlands looking for Asian immigrants attempting to illicitly cross into the United States but left the Mounted Guard after three months and went to work as a chain man for a local surveying company. He returned in 1913 and served the next thirty-five years with the U.S. Immigration Service. In the days and months leading up to the formation of the U.S. Border Patrol, Ellis was credited with capturing a wide range of unauthorized European immigrants in the Imperial Valley.[25] But with a much broader mandate than the one he had as a Mounted Guardsman, Ellis led the El Centro Border Patrol in an expanded effort; he promised that his officers would immediately deport all illegal immigrants from his jurisdiction, including unsanctioned Mexican workers.[26] Just eleven days after the U.S. Border Patrol began operations in El Centro, California, the *Calexico Chronicle* reported the first major catch by Ellis's officers: four Hindus and six Mexicans.[27]

By the end of the Border Patrol's first fiscal year on June 30, 1925, Ellis and the officers in the El Centro station had emerged as among the most aggressive of the new patrol force. The El Centro station reported questioning 535,252 persons, representing 42.7 percent of all persons questioned by the U.S. Border Patrol along both the Canadian and Mexican borders. They also referred 934 persons to immigration inspectors for administrative hearings regarding their immigration status in the United States. And they reported having directly prevented 985 persons from crossing into the United States.[28] Further, the officers of the El Centro, California, office arrested seven Chinese immigrant smugglers, more than any other station, excluding the Montreal station, which also arrested seven Chinese immigrant smugglers.[29] The local press heralded the new patrol for its efforts and, in particular, praised the officers of the U.S. Border Patrol for stemming the threat of unsanctioned Asian immigration along the California-Mexico border. But Ellis and the other officers in the California-Mexico borderlands also policed unsanctioned Mexican border crossings, which brought quick and fierce protest from local farmers.

Tension between new Border Patrol officers and farmers in the Imperial Valley exploded in early 1926. C. B. Moore of the Imperial Valley Chamber of Commerce complained that "we had considerable trouble with the Immigration Department— it was trouble to us—possibly due to the fact that the inspector in charge of our district wished to show a large number of deportations to his credit, and they started the border patrol that worked throughout the valley deporting Mexicans that had entered the country illegally. As a result of it, the Mexicans were like a lot of jack rabbits that were being hunted."[30] The limited Border Patrol personnel could not have significantly threatened the supply of Mexican workers in the valley region. In 1926, the Imperial Valley depended upon the labor of an estimated 3,000–7,000

Mexican workers, but the entire Los Angeles District of the U.S. Border Patrol employed only sixty-three officers. That same year, the officers reported questioning 1,034,212 persons but directly interrupted only 806 unsanctioned border crossings and apprehended only 375 persons for immigration violations. Further, as C. B. Moore admitted, the Border Patrol failed to close the border effectively because after the officers apprehended Mexicans and "put them across the line, one day and the next day they would be back across the line at some other place."[31] Regardless, the farmers of the Imperial Valley grew anxious that the arrival of the Border Patrol would deny them free and unrestricted access to Mexican workers.

For help, the farmers of the Imperial Valley turned to higher authorities within the U.S. Department of Labor. Imperial Valley farmers had long depended upon the federal government to support agricultural production in their desert homeland. They turned to the federal government when a botched diversion of the Colorado River had flooded the region between 1904 and 1907. And, in 1909, the U.S. Department of Agriculture had helped to launch cotton farming in the region by testing for the most profitable and productive strains in the Imperial Valley. So when the new Border Patrol officers began arresting their workers and interrupting the flow of labor migration, the farmers quickly "went to the Department of Labor and asked them to come to our rescue and help us out in the matter."[32] The Department of Labor could not offer the farmers a blanket exemption from the new regime of U.S. immigration law enforcement, but a compromise was reached by which "the people of the valley, upon their own initiative, entered into a system of registration of these Mexicans that were working there," explained Moore.[33] The Department of Labor thereby intervened on behalf of the farmers by creating a system of immigration registration that protected Mexican workers from the U.S. Border Patrol. Yet fiscal troubles and the Great Depression soon changed the political economy of policing Mexicans. By the end of the 1930s, Border Patrol officers in the California-Arizona region focused almost entirely on policing unsanctioned Mexican immigrants.

THE FISCAL SQUEEZE

The U.S. Immigration Service was never generously funded, and after Congress passed the National Origins Act of 1924, the organization struggled to keep up with the multiplying demands of immigration control. By 1927, the Immigration Service's expenses for immigration hearings, detention, and deportation far outstripped its appropriations. Officials searched for ways to cut costs. Records from the U.S. Border Patrol office in El Paso indicate the organization's financial troubles. Grover C. Wilmoth, the district director in El Paso, Texas, explained in March of 1927 that fiscal limitations required that all Border Patrol officers judiciously and economically pursue immigration law enforcement. "It is desired to impress upon all concerned that a real emergency in the matter of finances now confronts the entire Service as well as this district and it is desired and expected that each and every officer and employee will cooperate to the limit in effecting the necessary economies."[34] According to Wilmoth, "European [and Chinese] aliens now on hand will more than exhaust the funds available for maintenance, including a considerable amount taken from the Border Patrol allotment. In order to handle additional aliens who may be apprehended during the fiscal year, it will be necessary to make still further inroads upon the Border Patrol allotment for funds with which to pay maintenance and detention expenses, leaving the Border Patrol practically afoot."[35] The Immigration Service's limited funds required that "we must husband our resources, and the money gathered at the sacrifices which must be made will not be spent inadvisedly."[36]

The Immigration Service created resources for expensive deportations to Asia and Europe by streamlining the process of Voluntary Return (VR) for unsanctioned immigrants from Canada and Mexico. VR was the process by which unsanctioned immigrants opted out of an official deportation hearing and, instead, voluntarily returned to their home country. In 1927, the U.S. Immigration Service began to offer VR to Mexican nationals to save time and money by reducing the number of deportation hearings. Mexican immigrants tended to accept the offer because the VR process allowed them to depart the United States without submitting themselves to possible detention or incurring a deportation record that would prohibit them from legally entering the United States at another time. But in March of 1927, the U.S. Immigration Service made a critical change in VR procedures that broadened the U.S. Border Patrol's authority. Advising that "no money should be spent for the maintenance or detention of any Mexican alien, or of any Canadian alien, or any able-bodied alien seamen of whatever nationality, if such can possibly be avoided," Wilmoth explained that whereas Border Patrol officers had previously delivered Mexican and Canadian immigrants to the nearest U.S. Immigration station to be processed for deportation or voluntary return, the financial crisis of 1927 prompted the Immigration Service to authorize the officers to issue their own Voluntary Return orders.[37] The 1927 fiscal squeeze on the Immigration Service and the U.S. Border Patrol, therefore, prompted a dramatic change in Border Patrol authority and practice by allowing Border Patrol officers to quickly, cheaply, and independently expel Mexican nationals without an administrative hearing. The dire straits of U.S. immigration law enforcement institutionally discouraged the policing of Asian immigrants, while the streamlining of VR procedures for Mexican nationals economized the policing of unsanctioned Mexican immigration.

The Border Patrol's endemic lack of resources combined with the enormous influence of agribusinessmen and anti-Asian politics to create a peculiar predicament for immigration law enforcement in the California-Mexico borderlands. Mexicans were the most affordable immigrants to police, but the local power structure vigorously opposed the U.S. Border Patrol's efforts to regulate Mexican labor migration. The political climate supported and heralded the Border Patrol's efforts to deport unsanctioned Asian and European immigration, but aggressively enforcing restrictions against Asians and Europeans was costly. Local power structures and fiscal shortages rendered the U.S. Border Patrol anemic in the California-Arizona borderlands. In 1928, the 59 officers of the Los Angeles District of the U.S. Border Patrol apprehended only 2,025 persons for immigration violations in comparison to the 7,102 apprehended by the 82 officers of the El Paso, Texas, District and the 9,559 apprehended by the 84 officers of the San Antonio, Texas, District.[38] In 1929, the 65 officers of the Los Angeles District reported apprehending 2,567 persons for immigration violations in comparison to the 9,980 apprehended by the 87 officers of the El Paso District and the 15,184 apprehended by the 85 officers of the San Antonio District.[39]

AN EXPENSIVE SURGE

Not until 1932 did a surge in unsanctioned Chinese immigration from Mexico prompt a flurry of Border Patrol activity in the western U.S.-Mexico borderlands. The surge was the result of a wave of anti-Chinese activity along Mexico's northern border that forced thousands of Chinese into the United States. For many years, an anti-Chinese campaign had been mounting in Mexico's northern borderlands. In addition to *mestizaje*, the prevailing theory of racial nationalism in postwar Mexico, which defined Asians as racial foreigners within a Mexico, Mexican workers complained that Chinese immigrants lowered wages for and stole jobs from native Mexicans. In 1924, for example, the Governor of Baja California responded to specific anti-Chinese complaints by funding the deportation of fifty Chinese nationals from Baja, and Mexican labor leader Manuel Talavera advocated the deportation of all Asian workers from Mexico.[40] The onset of the Great Depression intensified the ongoing anti-Chinese movement in Baja California and resulted in the creation of a Chinese barrio to restrict and control Chinese activities.[41] The anti-Chinese movement in Mexico, however, was most extreme in the state of Sonora, Mexico.

The Chinese presence in Sonora was small and dispersed, but by 1916, sixteen anti-Chinese committees had been formed in the state, and at least one newspaper was dedicated to the anti-Chinese movement.[42] The committees constructed Chinese immigrants as a racial threat that undermined efforts to build Mexico into a modern nation of mestizos and operated under the slogan "For Nation and Race." Many Sonoran citizens harassed Chinese immigrants whom they believed stole jobs, lowered wages, and underbid businessmen; all of which, they argued, committed the ultimate sin of forcing Mexican citizens to emigrate to the United States. In 1919, Sonoran Governor Victoriano de la Huerta (Mexico's president from 1913 to 1914) signed a labor law that required all foreign-owned businesses to give 80 percent of their jobs to Mexican citizens—a law targeting Chinese business owners. The Great Depression further strained Mexican-Chinese relations in Sonora and provided the context for an aggressive campaign to purge the state of its Chinese residents.

The purge began in 1930 and ramped up in 1932, literally pushing thousands of Chinese into the United States. For example, on August 1, 1932, the municipal president in Esperanza, Sonora, told all Chinese immigrants to pack up and leave within four days. They could leave quickly and voluntarily or neglect the order and be forcibly deported without their belongings after August 5, 1932.[43] Yee Chu Chim, a fifty-five-year-old Chinese immigrant, did not heed the warning. He had lived in Guaymas, Sonora, for twenty years, but soon after the decree, "Four policemen, all armed with pistols, came to my place where I was living and told me that I had to leave Mexico."[44] The officers took him to the railroad station and placed him in the custody of the conductor, who "told me to get off the train" when it arrived in Nogales, Arizona.[45] "I was alone," recounted Chim, who "did not have any money or anything to eat."[46] Alone and hungry, he followed the orders he was given upon being kicked out of Guaymas, and, despite U.S. Chinese Exclusion laws, he crossed the border into the United States. Others, however, were taken directly to the border and pushed across.

After dark on March 15, 1932, a car carrying luggage on its fenders headed west along the border in Nogales, Mexico. In its headlights marched three Chinese men. The driver turned the car and the men around, shut off the headlights, and marched the men for two hundred yards in the other direction along the same road before coming to a stop. Then, the driver got out of the car and led the men to a patched hole in the border fence. The driver kicked the patching and directed the Chinese men to crawl through the hole. Suddenly Ivan Williams of the U.S. Border Patrol "jumped from behind the bushes and shoved the Chinese back through the hole."[47] The driver—a Mexican police officer—protested, but Senior Patrol Inspector Williams still refused his efforts to deport the three Chinese men into the United States. At that moment, fourteen more Chinese men "came out of the darkness" to be marched with the other three away from the border.[48]

Later that night, Williams apprehended three of the Chinese men he had earlier turned away. In the same area, Patrol Inspector Albert Gatlin also saw someone escort four Chinese across the line, but "was too far away to prevent it."[49] At 4:00 A.M., Patrol Officers Corley and Nichols turned back seven Chinese who were attempting to enter. And at 8:00 A.M., Patrol Officers Sevy and Todd apprehended ten Chinese who had been forced across the border just two miles west of Nogales.

His persistence enabled the Mexican officer to forcibly deport all of his Chinese charges during the early morning hours.

Because the anti-Chinese movement was strongest in Sonora, Mexico, and because the railroad linked Sonora to the United States through Nogales, most illegal deportations of Chinese from Mexico took place in the Nogales region. Still Mexican officers forced Chinese into the United States all along the border. For example, Border Patrol officers reported that on March 14, 1932, in Naco, Arizona, a Mexican officer fired several shots "to scare the Chinese across the line or to keep them from going back to Mexico once they were in the U.S."[50] And, in April of the same year the U.S. Attorney's office in Los Angeles submitted the following report: "GREAT INFLUX OF CHINESE COMING ACROSS MEXICAN BORDER. . . . WE HAD FORTY SEVEN CASES LAST FRIDAY AT SAN DIEGO AND . . . ONE HUNDRED AND SIXTEEN ADDITIONAL CHINESE HAVE SINCE BEEN CAUGHT NEAR THE LINE. . . . MEXICAN AUTHORITIES ASSIST IN RUSHING THESE ALIENS ACROSS THE LINE" (capitals in original).[51]

Deported from Mexico but unwelcome in the United States, Chinese immigrants in Northern Mexico endured a double deportation from Mexico to the United States and from the United States to China. In interviews with U.S. immigration officials, Chinese deportees from Mexico reported being forced to leave their homes in places such as Navojoa, Esperanza, Guaymas, and Cajeme, Sonora. With only a few of their belongings, sometimes only the clothes on their back and the money in their pockets, Chinese immigrants were detained by Mexican officers and placed on trains heading for the border. At the border, Mexican officers detained them once again and pushed them through holes in the border fence. When pushed back into Mexico by officers of the U.S. Border Patrol, their bodies became the focus of a battle between U.S. and Mexican officers over controlling migration across a shared border.

The two nations shared anti-Chinese immigration policy and popular sentiment.[52] Along the border between 1930 and 1933, this mutual xenophobia and racism resulted in a clash. Neither nation wanted the Chinese. Mexico tried to solve its problem by deporting Chinese to the United States, but the Chinese Exclusion Acts in the United States prohibited the entry of most Chinese nationals. Estimates of the number of Chinese immigrants forced north of the U.S.-Mexico border reach into the thousands.[53] Only a fraction of the deportees were apprehended by U.S. authorities, but 468 cases, or 53.2 percent of the total number of cases heard in the U.S. District Court of Southern California between January 4, 1932, and December 31, 1933, involved persons with Chinese surnames.[54]

Still, the Border Patrol's efforts at controlling unsanctioned Chinese immigration were greatly hampered and shaped by fiscal limitations. To finance the surge in deportations to China, the U.S. Immigration Service required its employees to take thirty days leave without pay in fiscal year 1932. "Federal appropriations were not enough to cover their journeys home, so employee's wages were docked at a rate of two and one half days per month for one year," explained Gary Charles, who processed the Border Patrol's payroll between 1929 and 1935.[55] By the close of fiscal year 1933, the Immigration Service's budget remained overstretched, and G. C. Wilmoth once again urged "the exercise of every possible economy for the remaining portion of this fiscal year and during the ensuing fiscal year. Every contemplated expenditure," he explained "must be carefully considered, and the necessity therefore must clearly appear before the obligation is incurred." The crisis, he explained, would continue into the following year, and to leave no doubt as to how the U.S. Immigration Service was going to economize immigration law enforcement, Wilmoth instructed his officers that "*commencing immediately* [emphasis in original] there must be a sharp reduction in maintenance expenses, our principal item of expenditure. This will be accomplished by extending the voluntary departure privilege to a larger number of Mexican aliens, and by paroling a larger number of such aliens made the subject of formal warrant proceedings. In general, Mexican aliens apprehended in the act of crossing the International Line illegally, or thereafter while in travel status, will be accorded the voluntary departure privilege unless criminal proceedings are to be instituted."[56] Once again, streamlining the deportation of Mexican nationals financed the expensive return of Chinese to China. This time, however, financing deportations to China directly affected the lives and pockets of all employees of the U.S. Immigration Service, and reducing the number of Chinese deportees became a matter of institutional and individual fiscal interest, while offering VR to Mexican nationals emerged as the most judicious and economical option for U.S. immigration law enforcement.

THE POLITICAL ECONOMY
OF POLICING MEXICAN IMMIGRATION

The fiscal strains on comprehensive immigration law enforcement unfolded alongside dramatic changes in the political economy of policing Mexicans. In particular, whereas agribusinessmen had once demanded unrestricted Mexican migration, the Great Depression created a surplus of domestic labor and a sparked a rise in anti-immigrant activity that opened new possibilities for Border Patrol work in the California-Arizona region. The implosion of the global economy in 1929 generated new streams of displaced workers—an estimated three hundred and fifty thousand people entered California during the 1930s—while agribusinessmen benefited from the federal government's incentives to reduce acreage in production under the provisions of the Agricultural Adjustment Act of 1933. The Great Depression therefore reduced the dependence of California's agribusinessmen upon the flow of Mexican workers across the U.S.-Mexico border, while the lack of work north of the border discouraged Mexican workers from trekking north. Further, during the early years of the Great Depression, Mexican nationals and Mexican Americans throughout the United States fell prey to those looking for quick and local answers to the economic crisis. "Deport the Mexicans" became a battle cry of those attempting to create jobs and squeeze pennies from public services. Most powerful in California but extending to Illinois and parts of Texas, local governments and charities sponsored train fares to force Mexican nationals and their U.S.-born children to return to Mexico.[57]

Efforts to push Mexicanos out of the United States coincided with efforts by the Mexican government to coordinate the repatriation of Mexican nationals and their children to Mexico. The hope was that repatriated Mexicans would return to Mexico with stockpiles of social and financial capital to invest in Mexican development. An estimated 1.6 million Mexicans and Mexican Americans crossed south into Mexico between 1929 and 1939. Ironically, it was at this moment when more Mexicans were leaving the United States than entering that the U.S. Border Patrol in the California-Arizona region began to focus on policing Mexicans. The U.S. Border Patrol in the California-Mexico borderlands, in other words, targeted Mexicans during a downswing in both migration and migration control, so that, although the total number of persons expelled from the United States (deported, ordered to depart, or voluntarily removed) fell from 29,861 in 1931 to 17,792 in 1939, Mexican nationals apprehended and removed from the United States as a percentage of the total number of persons expelled increased from 28.2 percent in 1931 to 52.7 percent in 1939. By the end of the Great Depression, therefore, the officers of the U.S. Border Patrol in the U.S.-Mexico borderlands had developed a distinctively narrow interpretation of U.S. immigration law enforcement by focusing their attention, resources, and authority upon policing unsanctioned Mexican immigration.

For Mexico's emigrant workers, the establishment of the U.S. Border Patrol ended the era of casual labor migration to the United States. As George Sánchez has most eloquently described, the 1924 consolidation in U.S. immigration control transformed the once "fluid" U.S.-Mexico border into a "rigid line of demarcation, [which] made it clear that the passage across this barrier in the desert was a momentous occasion, a break from the past."[58] Confronted by a new regime of U.S. immigration control, a regime increasingly dedicated to policing Mexicans, Mexican labor migrants had to make new choices when they reached the northern edge of Mexico: they could either deliver themselves for inspection and be confronted with unaffordable fees, humiliating exams, and the possibility of exclusion, or they could try their luck at illicitly crossing the border and cautiously avoiding the Border Patrol. Many tried their luck and surreptitiously entered the United States. In doing so, they not only made their way across an increasingly policed border but also entered the United States as illegal immigrants targeted and chased by the officers of the U.S. Border Patrol. The new conditions of their fugitive lives north of the border dramatically altered the meaning of Mexican labor emigration to the United States. Chapter 4 explores how the 1924 changes in U.S. immigration control broadly rescripted the meaning of Mexican labor emigration and thereby encouraged Mexican authorities to prevent Mexican nationals from violating U.S. immigration restrictions by extending the project of policing unsanctioned Mexican migration south of the U.S.-Mexico border.

4

Mexico's Labor Emigrants, America's Illegal Immigrants

In 1910, a widespread uprising brought an end to Porfirio Díaz's thirty-five year reign as the president of Mexico. Campesinos, exiles, anarchists, and middle-class malcontents all rebelled against the processes of land dispossession, capital accumulation, and political centralization that were embedded within Díaz's vision of "order and progress." Díaz's ouster came quickly: it took just several months to send him into exile. But the fighting lasted seven years as the various factions and leaders of the revolution battled for dominance. By 1917, the fighting finally eased, and the promise of a new day glimmered at the edges of a society frayed by nearly a decade of civil war. In these years, the new leaders of Revolutionary Mexico stood upon the rubble of *el Porfiriato* and began the business of reconstructing the nation.[1]

As Mexican officials worked toward rebuilding Mexico—its economy and society—Mexican citizens made an unprecedented one million border crossings into the United States during the 1920s. The flight of Mexican workers to the United States worried many Mexican nationalists, who wondered how revolutionary Mexico could develop socially and economically if emigration drained the country of its citizens and laborers.[2] One Mexican official despaired, "If I could, I would build a Chinese wall clear across our northern border and keep our laborers at home."[3] The Mexican public, too, ardently opposed Mexican labor emigration to the United States. Emigrating workers, they argued, betrayed the nation by dedicating their energies to the expansion of American wealth rather than to the building of revolutionary Mexico.

Despite these concerns, Mexican authorities could not and would not stop the exodus of workers across the border. The Mexican Constitution of 1917 [Section 26 of Article 123] required Mexican nationals seeking work abroad to secure a labor contract signed by municipal authorities and the consulate of the country where they intended to work.[4] The contract needed to provide a minimum wage, maximum hours, and medical care, and the employer had to pay the cost of repatriation for the worker. But the Mexican Constitution also protected the right of Mexican nationals to freely enter and exit the national territory, and Mexican authorities therefore refused to prevent Mexican nationals from crossing the border, regardless of the administrative requirements for legal emigration. More important, perhaps, political elites in postwar Mexico were reluctant to interfere with struggling families who sent their most able members north to work. The Mexican Revolution had been built upon promises of economic equity and social justice, but unrelenting poverty continued to define the everyday life of the average Mexican worker in postwar Mexico. Given the harsh differences between the rhetoric of the Mexican Revolution and the realities of Mexican life, political elites calculated that allowing laborers to emigrate and send back remittances diminished the threat of rebellion in the countryside. Mass labor emigration to the United States, in other words, enhanced political stability within Mexico. Therefore, despite a popular culture that smeared emigrants as traitors to the nation, both constitutional and political considerations combined to prevent Mexican authorities from taking action to stop Mexican nationals from crossing the U.S.-Mexico border.

However, in the middle of the Mexican emigration boom of the 1920s, the U.S. Congress passed the National Origins Act of 1924 and, three days later, established the U.S. Border Patrol. The 1924 innovations in U.S. immigration control dramatically altered the dynamics of Mexican labor migration to the United States. Most important, the 1924 changes hardened the U.S.-Mexico border against informal border crossings and transformed Mexico's labor emigrants into America's illegal immigrants. The deep social impact of the new U.S. regime of immigration control forced Mexican authorities to reconsider how they managed Mexican border crossings into the United States.

This chapter tells the little-known story of how the tightening of U.S. immigration control forced Mexican authorities to take a new look at how they managed Mexican labor emigration to the United States. The chapter draws upon the records of the Archivo Histórico del Instituto Nacional de Migración (AHINM) to detail how Mexican authorities attempted to prevent Mexican nationals from violating U.S. immigration laws in the years after the 1924 consolidation in U.S. immigration control. Mexican efforts at emigration control were weak, poorly funded, and scattered, but dusty government records gathered from a nearly forgotten warehouse in Mexico City tell of Mexican officers policing Mexico's northern boundary, interrupting unsanctioned border crossings, and arresting migrant smugglers. Records detailing rising concerns over the problem of illegal immigration to the United States and textual snapshots of Mexican migrants ducking and dodging Mexican authorities long before they ever reached the U.S.-Mexico border directly challenge the popular notion that efforts to control Mexican migration at the U.S.-Mexico border was a wholly unilateral effort.[5] Mexican authorities responded to the consolidation of U.S. immigration control by policing Mexican emigration to the United States. While the U.S.-Mexico border would remain the most difficult barrier for unsanctioned migrants to cross, the rise of Mexican emigration control created a crescendo of migration control in the greater U.S.-Mexico borderlands rather than a sudden deployment at the U.S.-Mexico border.

The crescendo in migration control is a story that does not fit comfortably on either side of the border. Mexican emigration control developed within Mexico and evolved according to Mexican national interests in preventing the many costs associated with unsanctioned Mexican immigration to the United States. But it is important to note that the officers of the Mexican Department of Migration attempted to prevent Mexican nationals from breaking U.S. immigration laws and always operated under pressure from U.S. authorities to reduce the number of unsanctioned border crossings made by Mexican nationals. Mexican enforcement of U.S. immigration restrictions makes clear that Mexican emigration control did not arise as a discrete Mexican regime of migration control; rather, it was the product of the broad and cross-border social impact of the changes in U.S. immigration law and law enforcement.

THE POLITICS AND PROMISES OF MEXICAN LABOR EMIGRATION

The politics of migration and national development shaped the rise of emigration control in postwar Mexico. Mexican authorities launched ambitious projects of reconstructing the nation that attempted to touch, if not transform, all aspects of what many political elites regarded as the wretched lives and backward culture of Mexican peasants. As Alan Knight has argued, governance in postwar Mexico was dominated by "ideas that stressed the need to develop Mexican society and economy, above all by disciplining, educating, and moralizing the degenerate Mexican masses."[6] Everything from agrarian reform to industrial relations, artistic expression, and child development theory were all explicit "exercise[s] in state building and social engineering" explains Knight.[7] Mexican labor emigration did not escape the social engineering projects of the revolutionary state in postwar Mexico.[8]

The work of Dr. Manuel Gamio clearly articulates the ways in which Mexican authorities hoped to harness mass labor emigration in the rebuilding and remaking of Mexico. Throughout the 1920s and 1930s, Gamio, an anthropologist, was Mexico's foremost scholar on Mexican migration to the United States. He formally and informally influenced Mexican migration policy by providing the research that shaped the positions taken by Mexican officials, and he advised the state-sponsored repatriation projects during the 1930s.[9]

Gamio identified three critical benefits that Mexico and Mexicans derived from mass labor emigration to the United States. First, he argued, the economic reality of postwar Mexico was that Mexican families suffered from low wages and underemployment. In his seminal 1927 publication, *Mexican Immigration to the United States; A Study of Human Migration and Adjustment,* Gamio estimated that while the average Mexican household needed $123.74 monthly to live above the "misery" line, the average Mexican head of household earned only $17.67 per month.[10] Mindful of the painful differences between what was earned and what was needed for a decent life in Mexico, U.S. labor contractors aggressively recruited Mexican workers with promises of an average monthly wage of $105.[11] Although mass labor emigration upset many nationalist sensibilities in postwar Mexico, Gamio encouraged his readers to interpret the exodus as "fundamentally, an economic phenomenon."[12] For many Mexican *campesinos,* he explained, the social calculus of emigration was simple: they could pledge their hearts to Mexico, but their basic economic survival demanded that they cross the border to work in the United States. The benefit of migration for Mexican families, Gamio insisted, was shown clearly by the five million dollars in remittances that migrants sent home each year during the 1920s.[13] There may have been many concerns regarding the flight of Mexico's workers and citizens in an era of national reconstruction, but labor migration was a lifeline for many Mexican families, a means of economic survival.

The economics of migration bolstered by national dignity drove Mexican officials to oppose the 1924, 1926, and 1928 efforts by Anglo-American nativists to limit the number of Mexican immigrants legally allowed to enter the United States each year. For example, in response to the 1928 Harris Bill, Manuel Tellez, Mexican Ambassador to the United States, stated that "the Mexican Government cannot sit idly by in this event," and he requested that the heads of key federal departments examine the potential impact of the proposed immigration legislation.[14] Writing for the Secretaría de Gobernación and drawing upon the work of Dr. Manuel Gamio, Andrés Landa y Piña, director of the Statistics Office, argued that any limit upon legal Mexican immigration would "intensify" Mexico's unemployment problem by locking Mexicans in Mexico at a time when "neither the local nor federal government is in the position to transform the economy in the affected regions in a manner that would provide the emigrant workers the opportunity of work that was lost if the neighboring country (U.S.) shut its doors to them."[15] Furthermore, Landa y Piña argued, a reduction in Mexican emigration to the United States would mean disaster for Mexican railroads. Just as families depended upon the remittances that Mexican workers sent home each year, railroads relied upon the fares paid by emigrants heading to and from the border. Mexican immigration, therefore, was critical for both Mexican families and industries; without it, the tentative hold that the revolutionary governments had upon social order and economic development would deteriorate. "It is absolutely necessary," Landa y Piña implored, "that Mexico's campesinos and workers can continue their activities in the United States."[16] The directors of the departments of Agriculture and Industry and Commerce and Labor and the Secretaría de Gobernación all concurred with Landa y Piña's position.

In addition to recognizing the economic benefits of emigration, Gamio encouraged Mexican authorities to consider the departure of Mexican workers as a political strategy. Discontent among the dispossessed, Gamio explained, was "one of the principal causes, and perhaps the most important, of the revolutions that have agitated Mexico for more than a century."[17] Mexico's annual exodus, he argued, operated as a critical "escape valve" that averted potential rebellions by draining the countryside of "hundreds of thousands of men who had no lands of their own and whose small wages were not enough for them to live on."[18] By linking mass labor emigration to the maintenance of political stability within Mexico, Gamio inverted the logic of emigration as a loss of citizens and laborers into emigration as a mechanism of political stability.

Gamio presented the Cristero Rebellion of 1926 to 1929 as evidence of the political value of mass emigration.[19] Since the Spanish conquest, the Catholic Church had been a core institution in Mexico. The secularism of the Mexican Revolution weakened the Church's influence within Mexican society. Rather than accept diminution of the Catholic Church, priests and piety rebelled. In 1926, their political dissent exploded into armed conflict with the Mexican military. For three years, the forces of God and government battled each other in the Mexican countryside. Most of the battles were fought in the Mexican states of Guanajuato, Michoacán, Jalisco, and Zacatecas, each of which Gamio had identified as core sending states for labor migrants to the United States. Emigration, Gamio argued, mitigated the bloodshed and strengthened the state's hand in the conflict by draining these battle zones of the displaced campesinos whose underemployment represented a constant political threat in a region already destabilized by religious strife. Therefore, although labeling emigrants as traitors was a popular trope in revolutionary Mexico, Gamio cited the outbreak of the Cristero Rebellion as irrefutable evidence that mass emigration actually served the basic political needs of the Mexican state in its ongoing struggle to assert, consolidate, and legitimate its authority in contested regions.[20]

Finally, in addition to economic practicalism and the political dividends of unrestricted labor emigration, Manuel Gamio encouraged Mexican politicians to harness emigration to the United States as a social and cultural development technique in the remaking of Mexican society. Emigrants left Mexico as provincial and backward peasants, argued Gamio, but in the United States they received "injections of modern culture."[21] Working on the industrial farms of the American southwest, absorbing Anglo-American cultural sensibilities, and acquiring modern material goods, Gamio explained, was an intensive program in social transformation that penetrated the souls, homes, aspirations, work habits, and sensibilities of Mexico's poor and backward labor emigrants. Mass emigration therefore was a mechanism of modernization within Mexico by providing Mexican peasants with the opportunity to transform themselves into modern Mexican citizens. As Gamio described it, so long as the emigrants returned home with all of their goods and resources, the United States functioned as a "marvelous incubator" for making Mexicans modern.[22]

To demonstrate the broad social and cultural dividends of mass labor emigration to the United States, Gamio assessed the belongings of Mexico's returning emigrants. Thirty-eight percent of returning Mexicans brought bathtubs, 21.82 percent brought phonographs, almost 78 percent brought metal kitchen utensils, another 82.88 percent brought beds, and just about everybody brought chairs and multiple trunks and bundles stuffed with clothing. "Taking into consideration the generally miserable conditions of the great mass of immigrants," Gamio argued that the goods carried home by labor migrants symbolized both a cultural and material enrichment.[23] Further, more than one-third of the returning migrants drove home in cars, which Gamio argued would indirectly modernize the Mexican countryside by "stimulat[ing] the owners to build roads."[24] Migrants who returned to Mexico at the end of each season brought with them wages, cultural capital, and material goods that could drive a micro-economic revolution in the Mexican countryside and serve projects of social and cultural modernization in Mexico.[25]

There were, then, many reasons why Mexican authorities refused to interrupt the flow of Mexican workers across the U.S.-Mexico border. But the tightening of U.S. immigration control reconfigured the meaning of Mexican emigration by splitting Mexican labor migration into two parts, one legal and the other illegal. The rise of illegal immigration undermined the prevailing hope among Mexican political elites that mass labor emigration to the United States could operate as an engine of political stability, social uplift, and economic progress within Mexico. Most important, the deportation of unsanctioned border crossers transformed the challenge before them from one of maximizing the potential benefits of emigration into one of managing the problems of deportation. The hardening of the U.S.-Mexico border and the rise of illegal immigration forced Mexican authorities to reexamine how they managed Mexican emigration to the United States.

THE PROBLEMS OF ILLEGAL IMMIGRATION

Since the beginning of mass labor emigration from Mexico to the United States, many of Mexico's emigrants had informally crossed the U.S.-Mexico border. As immigration restrictions tightened against other groups, Mexican workers still casually crossed the border with little interference from U.S. authorities. The U.S.

Immigration Service even declined to regularly record the number of Mexican nationals entering the country until 1908.

The regulation of Mexican labor migration began to change with the passage of the Immigration Act of 1917, which required all prospective immigrants to submit themselves to official inspection prior to entry, pay eighteen dollars for head taxes and a visa fee, and pass a literacy test and health examination before they could legally enter the United States. Mexico's labor migrants were often unable to comply with the new requirements. They found reprieve from the 1917 restrictions at the outbreak of World War I because many U.S. agribusinessmen and industrialists complained that the new immigration law would limit their access to Mexican migrant workers. During the war, the U.S. Immigration Service exempted Mexican immigrants from having to pay fees and pass literacy exams.[26] The Immigration Service lifted the exemption in 1921. Facing new fees and exams at U.S. ports of entry, tens of thousands of Mexican laborers entered the United States by crossing elsewhere along the border and evading inspection. By doing so, they continued a tradition among both Mexicans and Americans of crossing the border at will and at their convenience, but they also violated U.S. immigration restrictions. After 1921, therefore, many Mexicans crossed into the United States as unsanctioned immigrants. Three years later, the United States Congressed established the U.S. Border Patrol to forcibly prevent unauthorized migration.

The total number of Mexican nationals apprehended for violating U.S. immigration laws was actually quite small during the 1920s. The U.S. Immigration Service recorded returning only 25,570 Mexican nationals to Mexico between 1925 and 1929. This represents a small fraction of the number of Mexican nationals that illicitly crossed the U.S.-Mexico border in these years because, while we cannot precisely quantify the number of unsanctioned border crossings by Mexican laborers during the 1920s, estimates suggest that a substantial proportion of the one million border crossings during the decade were made in violation of U.S. immigration restrictions. Examining discrepancies between Mexican immigration records, which registered the number of Mexican nationals leaving Mexico, and U.S. immigration statistics, which registered the number of Mexicans entering the United States, Manuel Gamio estimated that 228,449 Mexican nationals crossed into the United States without officially registering with U.S. officials between 1920 and 1925.[27] According to Gamio's estimate, nearly 50 percent of the total number of Mexican border crossings between 1920 and 1925 were made in violation of U.S. immigration law. Similarly, U.S. census data suggests that more than five hundred thousand Mexicans entered the U.S. without passing through a U.S. port of entry between 1920 and 1930.[28] These different methods of assessing unsanctioned migration into the United States each suggest that a significant portion of Mexican labor migration during the 1920s was unsanctioned.

For Mexican officials, the transformation of mass labor migration into mass illegal immigration converted the profits of labor emigration into the problems of illegal immigration. In particular, when crossing the border without official authorization, Mexican immigrants entered the United States not as laborers with a set of enforceable protections but as fugitives targeted and chased by the U.S. Border Patrol. If arrested, they risked being deported with neither goods nor resources, losing investments they had made in the trip north. For example, as recorded in reports submitted by officers of the Mexican Department of Migration, "they [United States Immigration authorities] are deporting people from the United States and they arrive in disastrous health and material conditions."[29] When taken straight to the border for voluntary departure, Mexico's labor emigrants reported that they had to leave behind basic goods that they had either brought with them from Mexico or purchased while in the United States.[30] "A large number of deportees," reported Inspector José Bravo Betancourt of the Mexican Department of Migration, "are persons with resources," but U.S. officials did not provide them with "time to communicate with family [or] gather their things and money."[31] Animals, clothing, furniture, and even cars were all forfeited by Mexico's labor emigrants when they were forcibly removed from the United States. Instead of returning to Mexico with goods and wages that would support their families and fuel the project of modernization in Mexico, deportees, explained Betancourt, returned to Mexico "without enough resources even to eat."[32] Thus, the varied hopes for Mexican labor emigration to the United States unraveled when Mexican workers returned to Mexico as deportees.

Working along the U.S.-Mexico border, the officers of the Mexican Department of Migration were among the first to register the ways in which U.S. immigration control was fundamentally rescripting the meaning of Mexican labor emigration to the United States. Lobbying for an expansion of Mexican emigration control efforts, they argued that what had once been a system of labor migration to the United States had become a network of crime that spanned the U.S.-Mexico border.

Mexican immigration authorities compiled the harrowing stories of unsanctioned border crossings into cautionary tales that dramatized how the consolidation of U.S. immigration control affected the lives of Mexico's emigrant workers. The problem of illegal immigration to the United States, they warned, began south of the border, where migrants hired the services of "coyotes," that is, human smugglers, to guide their illegal entry. In passionate and dramatic memos, Mexican immigration officials described coyotes who stalked the train stations and enticed their "victims" with offers of reduced cost for entry into the United States.[33] To comply with the administrative restrictions placed upon leaving Mexico, migrants needed to acquire a Mexican passport that would both facilitate their entry into the United States and their return to Mexico. It would cost an additional eighteen dollars to cover the visa fee and head tax required for legal entry into the United States. Legal immigration was expensive, explained the coyotes, who would "grab them [migrants] in the street and advise them to not get their passports."[34] Instead, coyotes promised that they could help migrants to surreptitiously exit Mexico and enter the United States for the bargain fee of two to three dollars.[35]

For migrants, the possibility of entering the United Status at a fraction of the cost of legal entry must have been appealing. Train fare from central Mexico to the northern border averaged $40–$50 during the 1920s.[36] Along the way, migrants purchased food and, if they had to wait at the border before crossing over, they had to secure shelter.[37] Regardless of how they crossed into the United States, if they found work through a labor contractor, they could expect to surrender a portion of their wages to the contractor. Once they found jobs, they would have to purchase food, shelter, and possibly rent work supplies, such as cotton sacks, from their employer. Migration north, therefore, was a major investment that campesinos funded by squeezing savings from their already taxed earnings, selling property, or taking on debt. If they could get in and out of the United States without sacrificing the fees required for a Mexican passport and the eighteen dollars required for legal entry, they could return home with that much more in their pockets or, at least, enter the United States with a little something to carry themselves over if work was not easy to find.

As U.S. immigration restrictions had begun to tighten around Mexican immigrants, authorities within the Secretaría de Gobernación clearly understood that illicit border crossings were cheap in comparison to complying with the requirements for legally entering the United States. But, as explained in a 1924 circular just prior to the passage of the U.S. National Origins Act of that year, migrants paid dearly for the discount because "the exploitation began" once they accepted the coyote's offer.[38] Coyotes took migrants from the train station to a safe house to wait until night. The safe house was usually managed by an accomplice of the coyote who locked the workers in their rooms. For their rooms, which were often little more than an "enormous cage," the owner charged the migrants about twenty pesos.[39] At night, the coyote would return and take the migrants to the river. After a long walk through the "intense cold and brutal rain," Inspector Ricardo Zavala told of coyotes who raped female migrants or abandoned the migrants altogether after relieving them of their cash. Others, however, made good on their promise to smuggle migrants into the United States. To cross the river, smugglers and migrants slipped into boats made of metal and wood and began to cross the rapids of the Río Bravo (Rio Grande). U.S. officers often sat concealed in the bushes and shot across the river to prevent smugglers from successfully landing their cargo on the other side. Vividly describing scenes of chaos, the circular warned that husbands and wives, parents and children would become lost from one another as boats tipped and the river's rapids pulled the unlucky under and washed the fortunate ashore. Although Mexican labor emigration was a recognized if despised means of financial survival for many Mexican campesinos, this early circular from the Secretaría de Gobernación contended that illegal immigration ensnared Mexico's migrants in a world of crime, exploitation, and danger that threatened to literally drown the Mexican family. And, if migrants successfully crossed into the United States, they lived as fugitives "at the mercy of their employers."[40]

The consolidation of U.S. immigration control allowed immigrant smuggling to become a big business in the border region. As one officer in the Piedras Negras station explained, some border communities were "plagued by smugglers whose immoral occupation has become their 'modus vivendi.' "[41] By 1931 José Bravo Betancourt reported that immigrant smuggling had emerged as a core enterprise in small pueblos in Mexico's northern borderlands as an increasing number of peasants became coyotes and "made this reproachable industry into a lucrative, but criminal business."[42] "El Soliceño, El Capote, La Palangana, San Luisito, La Baquetería, La Barranca, La Palma, [and] La Palmita," he reported, were towns dominated by "natives who dedicate themselves to emigrant smuggling."[43]

The U.S. Congress deepened the problem of crime that was embedded within the rise of illegal immigration by passing the Immigration Act of March 4, 1929, which defined unsanctioned border crossings as a misdemeanor for first-time offenses and a felony punishable by 2–5 years in prison and a fine of ten thousand dollars for second offenses. The criminalization of illegal entry into the United States subjected those apprehended to lengthy jail terms and costly fines prior to deportation. Jails in the border region were quickly beginning to fill with unsanctioned Mexican border crossers. In Southern California between April 19, 1929, and April 18, 1930, 236 Spanish-surnamed immigrants were convicted of felony illegal entry. On average, these immigrants spent 80.97 days in jail prior to being deported for violating the 1929 Immigration Act. During the same period, U.S. District Court judges in southern Texas convicted 513 Spanish-surnamed immigrants for illegal entry. Of the 210 convicted immigrants for whom sentences are listed in the U.S. District Court Docket books, they spent an average of 36.72 days in jail prior to deportation. For these emigrant inmates and the thousands to follow, each workday spent in jail represented, if nothing else, a payday lost, while fines reduced whatever savings they had accumulated prior to arrest.[44]

Enrique Santibáñez, the Mexican consul in San Antonio, Texas, organized a political response to the imprisonment of Mexico's emigrant laborers. "I do not deny that the Border Patrol has the right to apprehend" undocumented immigrants, admitted Santibáñez, but he believed that "the new immigration laws that have been put into effect are too severe and even cruel." Jail terms for illegal immigration were "inhumane" he argued, since Mexican nationals had illegally entered the United States to "work and build their [U.S.] agricultural riches."[45] Hoping to expose the imprisonment of the borderlands' labor force, Santibáñez asked Mexican consuls throughout south Texas to conduct regular visits to local and county jails and to interview Mexican nationals convicted of immigration offenses. On July 23, 1929, for example, the Mexican consul in Brownsville, Texas, visited the county jail, where he found sixty-three Mexican nationals serving sentences ranging from twenty-four days in the county jail to one year and one day to be served in the Atlanta, Georgia, federal penitentiary before formal deportation.[46] Throughout 1929, Santibáñez and the south Texas consuls continued to collect reports about the number of Mexican nationals serving time for undocumented entry, but by the next year conditions had grown worse. Jails in Edinburg, Hidalgo, and Brownsville were packed beyond capacity.

Seeking relief for Mexico's emigrant workers, Santibáñez encouraged the Mexican ambassador to the United States to discuss the deepening impact of U.S. immigration law enforcement with higher authorities in the U.S. Department of State. He hoped that higher authorities could command the local Border Patrol officers to suspend apprehensions until the jails could be emptied.[47] However, national influence upon local Border Patrol activity was limited in the Texas-Mexico borderlands. As the consul in Brownsville understood, Border Patrol officers might be instructed to stop apprehensions for illegal entry, but they could not be expected to comply.[48] Therefore, while Manuel Gamio depicted the United States as a school where Mexico's backward peasants could learn how to become modern citizens and, if nothing else, earn what they needed to survive, the criminalization of unsanctioned entry in 1929 routed Mexico's emigrant workers away from American worksites and communities and delivered them instead to U.S. jails and prisons prior to deportation.[49] Fines and incarceration further diminished the basic pecuniary function of labor emigration, while time in jail placed Mexico's emigrants next to American criminals rather than American citizens. The 1929 criminalization of unsanctioned migration therefore deepened the social, cultural, and economic threats created by the transformation of Mexico's labor emigrants into America's illegal emigrants.

MEXICO'S SYSTEM OF EMIGRATION CONTROL

By 1930, the many problems created by illegal immigration forced Dr. Andrés Landa y Piña, then director of the Mexican Department of Migration, to modify his once strong support for unlimited immigration to the United States. The changes in U.S. immigration control had split Mexican labor migration into legal and illegal streams, and Landa y Piña identified unsanctioned border crossings into the United States as "the most important problem" to be addressed by the Mexican Department of Migration.[50] As Consul Enrique Santibáñez had concluded at the end of his review of jails in south Texas in 1929, America's emergent problem of illegal immigration was profoundly reshaping the meaning of Mexican emigration; whereas Mexico's emigrant workers had once been "admitted like workers," the changes in U.S. immigration control meant that Mexicans were increasingly "persecuted like criminals."[51] Mexico, he suggested, had an interest in stopping Mexican nationals from making unsanctioned border crossings into the United States.

But the Mexican Department of Migration could do little more. Since its establishment in 1926, the poorly funded agency had maintained a three-tiered system of emigration control. As the first line of defense, the Mexican Department of Migration contributed to widely dispersed efforts among Mexican nationalists and industrial leaders to discourage Mexican workers from leaving Mexico. Radio notices, newspaper articles, and flyers warned potential emigrants to stay home unless they were able to comply with the requirements for legal entry into the United States, including entrance fees, a literacy exam, and a health inspection.[52] If migrants attempted to evade U.S. immigration restrictions and enter the United States illegally, the notices warned that smugglers and labor contractors would take advantage of them. The propaganda also warned of racial discrimination and violence in the United States.[53] In 1930, the Mexican Secretaría de Gobernación sponsored a competition that would award five hundred pesos to the person with the best plan to prevent Mexican emigration to the United States.[54] Mexican citizens living in both Mexico and the United States suggested everything from developing the mining industry in Mexico to prohibiting Chinese immigration to Mexico.[55] It is unclear what the Secretaría de Gobernación did with the proposals, but the announcement functioned as a piece of propaganda that underscored the national government's opposition to unsanctioned emigration.

Despite the warnings, many Mexican nationals headed north in search of work in the United States. In Mexico's northern borderlands, the officers of the Mexican Department of Migration implemented second and third tiers of defense against unsanctioned Mexican border crossings. The second tier of emigration control was comprised of checkpoints at train stations along routes leading from central Mexico to the U.S.-Mexico border. In Matamoros, Nuevo Laredo, Irapuato, Empalme de González, Torreón, Saltillo, and Monterrey, the officers boarded incoming trains to "check that the braceros have enough money, that they know how to read and write."[56] As a 1926 report from the office of the Mexican Department of Migration in Nuevo Laredo, Tamaulipas, explained, officers checked the trains heading into the city each day. In general, the passengers riding in second-class "are braceros who want to emigrate."[57] The officers of the Mexican Department of Migration took these migrants off the trains and verified that the emigrants could fulfill the conditions required by "U.S. Immigration law for entering their territory."[58] If migrants could not meet the requirements for legal entry into the United States, officers of the Mexican Department of Migration prohibited the migrants from traveling north.[59] The second tier of Mexican emigration control, therefore, was a system of Mexican officers enforcing the provisions of U.S. immigration law.[60]

All along the border, the officers of the Mexican Department of Migration found that many of the migrants passing through the region could not satisfy the requirements of legal entry into the United States. "A considerable number of emigrants do not know how to write and are not legally married to the women that accompany them," wrote Fernando Félix in May of 1926 after conducting an inspection of the operations at the Mexican Department of Migration office in Nuevo Laredo.[61] To prevent the migrants from illicitly crossing into the United States, the officers of the Mexican Department of Migration confiscated their passports.[62] Passport confiscation was an indirect form of emigration control that discouraged unsanctioned entry into the United States by making the migrants' return to Mexico more difficult: without a Mexican passport, Mexican nationals could not prove their right to freely return to Mexico. Although the Mexican Constitution of 1917 prohibited Mexican authorities from coercing Mexican nationals to remain in the national territory, passport confiscation functioned as a bureaucratic disincentive to unsanctioned migration.

Checkpoints at train stations and passport confiscation extended the regime of U.S. immigration control well south of the U.S.-Mexico border. For many of Mexico's labor migrants, therefore, the attempt to enter the United States illegally began by evading the officers of the Mexican Department of Migration. To stop Mexico's emigrants from illicitly entering the United States, the officers of the Mexican Department of Migration first had to catch them, and, as Félix reported, the emigrants quickly learned how to dodge the train station checkpoints. For example, to elude the checkpoints in Saltillo and Monterrey, migrants took a circuitous route from San Luis Potosí to Tampico and then to Monterrey. From there, they hired cars to take them to small, outlying train stations that were unmonitored by the limited personnel of the Department of Migration, or the hired cars dropped them somewhere along a recently built road that would deliver them within kilometers of the Río Bravo (Rio Grande).[63] The Mexican Department of Migration established a horse patrol along the route between Monterrey and Matamoros, but with limited personnel the patrol could not cover the long road effectively, and, according to Félix, coyotes routinely helped migrants to evade the Mexican immigration officers.[64]

Although Mexico's second tier of emigration control was underfunded and permeable, it was only with preparation, defiance, and assistance that Mexico's unsanctioned border crossers headed north toward work in the United States. By the time they arrived at the U.S.-Mexico border, they had already dismissed warnings of various Mexican authorities and industrialists and had either evaded or ignored Mexican officers. The U.S.-Mexico border certainly remained the most difficult and dangerous barrier. Neither the Río Bravo, with its rushing currents, nor the U.S. Border Patrol, with its guns, held much sympathy for Mexico's unsanctioned border crossers. The migrants' journey of unsanctioned entry into the United States reached its climax rather than its beginning along the U.S.-Mexico border.

At the U.S.-Mexico border, the officers of the Mexican Department of Migration made their third and final effort to prevent Mexican nationals from illicitly crossing into the United States. Although the Mexican Constitution of 1917 prohibited Mexican authorities from forcibly stopping Mexican nationals from exiting Mexico, the 1926 Ley de Migración levied a fine of one hundred to one thousand pesos upon persons found guilty of attempting to take migrants from the country without official inspection and sanction. Furthermore, the 1926 law outlined stiff penalties of one to two years in prison or fines of one hundred to two thousand pesos for smugglers who assisted laborers, in particular, to leave the country without official review and authorization. After at least two years of lobbying for greater authority to prevent Mexican workers from crossing the border illegally, officers of the Mexican Department of Migration dedicated whatever resources they could spare to enforcing the anti-smuggling provisions of the 1926 Ley de Migración.

Mexican efforts at patrolling the U.S.-Mexico border were sporadic and dictated by the availability of personnel. In September 1926, for example, the office of the Mexican Department of Migration in Villa Acuña, Coahuila, had insufficient personnel to guard the Río Bravo against coyotes and still conduct regular immigration business at the office. Placing the minimum number of personnel at the official immigration station to manage the legal movement of people in and out of Mexico meant that no officers could be assigned to work along the line and prevent unsanctioned exits and entries.[65] Similarly, the office in Matamoros, Tamaulipas, was severely understaffed. The Matamoros office covered the region from the Gulf of Mexico to Camargo, Tamaulipas, and filed the greatest number of reports regarding human smuggling along the U.S.-Mexico border. In 1930, however, only ten officers worked in the Matamoros office.[66] After assigning officers to guard the bridge and to establish checkpoints at the train station, no officers were available to patrol the Río Bravo. A 1930 report from the office in Ciudad Juárez describes the personnel situation as so dire that the officers enforced only Mexico's immigration restrictions against the Chinese and left all others to enter and exit Mexico at will.[67]

The limited personnel working along the border struggled to enforce Mexican emigration restrictions against coyotes. At times, however, they could shake loose enough personnel to send officers out on patrol to prevent *coyotaje* (smuggling). By focusing on coyotes, "those that facilitate clandestine emigration," officers of the Mexican Department of Migration were able to interrupt unsanctioned emigration without directly policing Mexican citizens who held the constitutional right to freely enter and exit Mexico.[68] For example, on the afternoon of September 11, 1933, seventy-year-old Agustín Bautista paid José Martínez 20 pesos to ferry Bautista and his five children across the Rio Grande.[69] Martínez agreed, but just before they left the riverbank, two officers arrived. The officers took Martínez,

Bautista, and the five children to the Mexican Department of Migration for questioning. After providing information about his negotiations with Martínez, Bautista and the children were allowed to leave the office and, most likely, try their luck with another coyote on another day. Martínez spent five days in jail for his crime.

Too few officers and too little support rendered Mexico's program of emigration control almost entirely ineffective against the tens of thousands of migrants heading north each year, many of whom would successfully enter the United States by also evading the United States' poorly funded and disorganized effort at immigration control. North and south of the border, migration control was far from a priority of governance, and it was only the deep economic decline of the 1930s in the United States that effectively turned back Mexico's unsanctioned border crossers.[70] Still, Mexico's broken system of emigration control reveals that U.S. immigration control rippled south to rescript the meaning of Mexican labor emigration and challenges popular notions that attempts to police Mexico's illegal emigrants began north of the U.S.-Mexico border. However weak, Mexico's efforts at emigration control place the U.S. Border Patrol's early formation within a broad cross-border context of migration control. In the years ahead, World War II would reopen the corridors of Mexican migration to the United States and, together, the officers of the U.S. Border Patrol and the Mexican Department of Migration would intensify their activities in the U.S.-Mexico borderlands. They did so according to a new era of immigration control during which the U.S. and Mexican governments collaborated in the close management of Mexican labor migration to the United States.

PART TWO

Transformation

A Border Patrol boat circles the S.S. *Veracruz* on leaving Port Isabel, Texas, January 18, 1956. U.S. Border Patrol Photograph, SW40/McA. Courtesy of the National Border Patrol Museum—El Paso, Texas.

BY THE END OF THE GREAT DEPRESSION, Border Patrol work in the U.S.-Mexico borderlands was almost entirely dedicated to the project of policing unsanctioned Mexican immigration. The project had a massive social impact, rescripting the story of race in America by binding Mexicanos to the caste of illegals. Still, in relationship to the broader matrix of federal law enforcement, the Border Patrol remained a tiny outfit, and its presence in the U.S.-Mexico borderlands was smaller than the distribution of Border Patrol personnel along the U.S.-Canadian border. Part two examines the shifts in U.S. immigration law enforcement during the early 1940s, which simultaneously amplified Border Patrol resources and swerved its personnel toward an accumulation in the U.S.-Mexico borderlands. In these years, Dogie Wright and the Cottingham brothers became relics, "old-timers," in a rapidly changing organization as an onslaught of new recruits, new technologies, new interests, and new partners introduced a new era of immigration law enforcement in the U.S.-Mexico borderlands. At the center of the Border Patrol's World War II transformation was the Bracero Program, which intimately linked the U.S. Border Patrol to national and bi-national efforts to manage the cross-border migrations of Mexican laborers.

On August 4, 1942, the United States and Mexico signed a bilateral agreement called the Bracero Program, under which the U.S. government contracted Mexican laborers to work in the United States, particularly on southwestern and northwestern farms. Although first introduced as a wartime effort, the Bracero Program lasted from 1942 to 1964. In that time, more than two million Mexican laborers fulfilling nearly five million bracero contracts worked in the United States. The Bracero Program had a significant impact on U.S. Border Patrol work by altering the political context and expanding the possibilities of migration control along the U.S-Mexico border. In particular, the establishment of a bi-national program to manage the importation of legal Mexican laborers into the United States provided new possibilities for the cross-border management of deporting illegal Mexican laborers. Within the context of the Bracero Program, the Border Patrol responded to cross-border concerns regarding the unsanctioned migration of Mexican laborers and tested cross-border techniques of migration control. This new era of migration control extended the penalties that migrants paid for their crimes of illegal immigration and drove the violence they faced deep into the border landscape. Farmers and ranchers in southern Texas would rebel against the delocalization of U.S. immigration law enforcement, but they could not stop the rise of a new era of migration control.

5

A New Beginning

When the United States entered World War II, the scope of Border Patrol responsibilities expanded. For example, during the war, Officer Bob Salinger was moved from his station along the Texas-Mexico border and assigned to guard against enemy submarines by patrolling along the Gulf of Mexico.[1] In California, Border Patrol officers transported Japanese Americans and Japanese immigrants to internment camps operated by the Immigration and Naturalization Service. Officers also served as guards at INS internment camps throughout the war.[2] In New York, Border Patrolmen interrogated German and Italian nationals regarding their sympathies for Hitler and fascism. The assignment of U.S. Border Patrol officers to submarine watches, internment camps, and immigrant investigations indicates the world of change that World War II introduced to the practices and priorities of U.S. immigration control.[3] The anxieties of a nation at war rushed through the U.S. Border Patrol, transforming its national organization, swelling the number of personnel, and introducing new concerns regarding border enforcement and immigration control. Substantive structural reorganization of Border Patrol administration meant that, for the first time, U.S. immigration law enforcement was designed to respond to national concerns and centrally defined imperatives. Despite these shifting and expanding demands, these were the years when the U.S. Border Patrol took a sharp turn toward policing unsanctioned Mexican immigration in the U.S.-Mexico borderlands. This chapter addresses the dramatic transformation in the men, the mandate, and the organization of the U.S. Border Patrol during World War II and examines how, both in spite of and because of these dramatic changes, the U.S. Border Patrol's focus upon policing unsanctioned Mexican immigration intensified during the early 1940s.

IMMIGRATION CONTROL AND BORDER
ENFORCEMENT IN A WORLD AT WAR

World War II did not touch U.S. territory until the bombing of Pearl Harbor on December 7, 1941, but fears of invasion and subterfuge produced new anxieties regarding border enforcement and immigration control. In particular, the poorly guarded U.S. land borders came into focus, and concerns of sabotage by enemy aliens heightened during the late 1930s. In 1939, the commissioner of the Immigration and Naturalization Service argued that "the international situation which is developing in Europe furnishes strong reason for strengthening the Border Patrol without undue delay."[4] In 1940, Congress transferred the INS from the Department of Labor to the Department of Justice and supplemented the U.S. Border Patrol's budget with a $2,000,000 appropriation for 712 additional officers.[5] Overall, the Border Patrol's appropriation doubled from $1,735,000 in 1939 to $3,883,400 in 1941.

The transfer to the Department of Justice signaled a new era for the INS and the U.S. Border Patrol. Now located within the Department of Justice alongside the Federal Bureau of Investigation (FBI) and U.S. attorneys and marshals, the Bureau of Prisons, and the Bureau of Prohibition (later renamed the Drug Enforcement Agency), the Border Patrol entered into the growing bureaucracy of federal law enforcement. There, the U.S. Attorney General's office launched a project of centralization and consolidation in U.S. immigration control and border enforcement. In 1941, the Department of Justice created the position of chief supervisor of the Border Patrol to remove past breaks in command and provide direct supervision for the U.S. Border Patrol by closely monitoring, directing, and coordinating station activities. No longer were local officers in control of Border Patrol strategies and priorities, and the hundreds of new recruits entering the Border Patrol after the 1940 appropriation never experienced the system of decentralized and local leadership that the old-timers had developed.

Complementing the incorporation of the Border Patrol within the Department of Justice's matrix of federal police forces and the new lines of authority within the Border Patrol, improvements in mobile communications during the 1940s contributed to the consolidation of its activities. In particular, the procurement of increasingly effective car radios improved Border Patrol mobility and capabilities. The Border Patrol first experimented with radio technology during the 1930s, but the equipment was far from ideal. To use it, officers first had to learn Morse code, and the radios were of limited use when in pursuit because an officer had to "stop the car, assemble a long antenna and mount it on the back of the car, and then get the engine running good so it would generate its maximum electrical output."[6] "Even then," explained an INS electronics engineer, "the station desired could seldom be reached, but with luck, another station might be contacted which could relay the message."[7] But rapid improvements in FM radio technology during World War II allowed officers to transmit messages from a moving car. By the mid-1950s, the U.S. Border Patrol had linked its radio operations throughout the southwest region. With improved mobile communications, officers could coordinate their activities across wide areas. As one officer explained, "Prior to the FM radio, plans could be made; you could go out to work, but even trying to time coordinated efforts with your watches, it never was really smooth and didn't work right. Once we got the radios, we could coordinate various kinds of equipment, any number of people. . . . We could coordinate the movement of the vehicles so that we could do just about what we wanted; . . . it was a major element in the improvement and efficiency of the Border Patrol."[8] Further, if officers needed assistance while patrolling isolated areas, they could contact each other instead of depending upon ranchers and farmers.

New additions to the Border Patrol's transportation fleet accompanied the improvements in mobile communications. In particular, in late 1945, the military provided the Border Patrol with three surplus Stinson L-5 airplanes. "The L-5 was a distinguished little all-purpose workhorse used by the army in World War II for observation, reconnaissance, artillery spotting and direction, ambulance [work], photography, short field air supply craft, and 'you name it,'" explained one of the first officers to deploy the L-5s in Border Patrol operations.[9] Distributed to Border Patrol stations along the U.S.-Mexico border, the Stinson L-5 became a "workhorse" for the Border Patrol. When cars and radios were coupled with the use of a plane, officers could coordinate their movements to increase apprehensions. Border Patrol pilots circled above and directed officers via radio to locations where laborers were illegally crossing the border or hiding. By 1953, at least one plane and pilot was assigned to each sector along the U.S.-Mexico border.[10]

In many ways, World War II was a rebirth for the national police force that had long ago yielded to local control. The wartime appropriations and reorganization transformed the U.S. Border Patrol from a series of small and locally oriented outposts into a national police force with the resources to pursue immigration control on a much larger scale. World War II, in other words, ripped the U.S. Border Patrol from its local roots and marked a new era in its development.

It was a time of uncharted possibilities for U.S. immigration law enforcement. Internment camps, enemy aliens, and submarines all demanded the U.S. Border Patrol's attention. Further, as high-level INS officials warned, saboteurs lurked at America's borders, waiting to slip into the United States. At the outset of the war, INS officials advised Border Patrol inspectors, "It is entirely possible that such Axis agents may endeavor to look the part of a local farmer or at night may even black their hands and faces, particularly in isolated areas, to look like negroes."[11] Such worries about European saboteurs illegally entering the United States threatened to break the Border Patrol's focus upon policing persons of Mexican origin, because, as the INS instructed, "officers should not be too prone to accept outward appearance as being indicative of nativity of the locality."[12] In a time of war, everyone was suspect. Precautions pressed the U.S. Border Patrol to break with the practice of narrowly focusing upon unsanctioned Mexican immigration. Mexican nationals would continue to cross illegally into the United States, but many questioned whether Mexican laborers should be the priority of U.S. immigration law enforcement at a time when saboteurs seemed to be conspiring everywhere.

The old-timers were typically resistant to changing "the Border Patrol way" that they had developed over the years. But World War II also sparked a massive shift in Border Patrol personnel. While the old-timers held onto their old ways, the onslaught of new recruits played pivotal roles in incorporating, interpreting, and implementing the new demands upon Border Patrol work.

THE NEW RECRUITS

The 1940 appropriation doubled the authorized force of U.S. Border Patrol officers from 773 in 1939 to 1,531 in 1941. But the organization struggled to recruit and retain new officers. War mobilization had brought a wave of new jobs to American cities and towns. Wages were high, and American workers had many options. The Border Patrol expanded its efforts to recruit officers by probing into new regions. They recruited farm boys from Indiana, lawyers from Tennessee, and, as in the case of officer Bob Salinger, teachers from the south. "I had been coaching and teaching mathematics in a little high school in Mississippi called Calcun Academy, right out of Vicksburg, making $135 a month. . . . I was taking every civil service exam or anything that was making more money than I was making," explained Salinger about his choice to become a U.S. Border Patrol officer.[13] At the time, new Border Patrol officers earned two thousand dollars annually, which was "quite an improvement salary wise" according to Salinger.[14] Salinger entered on duty as a Border Patrol officer on March 11, 1941, and stayed with the Patrol until his retirement on December 31, 1977. Many of the new recruits from distant places, however, knew nothing about the job before signing up and, once on patrol, quickly learned that they simply did not like the day-to-day work of being a patrolman. "Some would come in and not even stay until they got a pay day. That's how they disliked it. They come from all over you know. They didn't like to go lay in on the river," explained retired Patrolman J. R. Breechen.[15] In the competitive wartime labor market, struggles to recruit and retain new Border Patrol officers quickly reshaped Border Patrol leadership in the 1940s and 1950s.

To increase the number of eligible recruits, the Border Patrol eased recruitment standards and simplified the civil service entrance exam but was still unable to fill its appropriation. G. C. Wilmoth of the El Paso district complained to the new chief of the U.S. Border Patrol that the shortages forced him to "accept many recruits who by no means would have been acceptable before the present emergency," but he was glad that "approximately half of the candidates selected at this time [were] veterans of the current war."[16] From planes to personnel, the Border Patrol received the human and manufactured surplus from the war. But what the war delivered, it also recalled. Officers constantly cycled through the military and the Border Patrol. Those who had not served in the military before joining the Border Patrol were typically called to duty sometime after joining the organization.

The expanded recruitment efforts failed. As early as September of 1941, the Border Patrol returned to its old recruitment strategies to supplement the civil service recruits. Border Patrol officers were asked to recommend friends for the job. Although these local recruits were described as "better prospects than the average new appointee received at the training school during the past year," they still did not fill the appropriation.[17] After administering more exams, easing recruitment standards, sponsoring publicity campaigns, and turning to local friends of Border Patrol officers, the Border Patrol was still unable to fill its appropriation. Vacancies and shortages plagued the Border Patrol throughout the war.

In 1942, old-timer Carson Morrow, chief patrol inspector of the Tucson station, informed the Central Office, "the shortage of personnel in this subdistrict has become so acute that it is impossible to properly man all of our substations."[18] To counter the lack of personnel and quickly get men on duty, the Border Patrol shortened the sessions of the Border Patrol Training School (BPTS) to one month and assigned probationary officers to duty before they had attended the BPTS. Faced with untrained recruits, local stations depended on experienced officers to train and supervise new recruits. All along the U.S.-Mexico border, however, the number of new recruits outnumbered old-timers. El Paso's chief patrol inspector, old-timer Griffith McBee, observed that "the number of the probationary patrol inspectors assigned to this sub-district is considerably greater than the number of older officers who are available for their training."[19]

The chief patrol inspector of El Centro, California, Richard H. Wells, warned upper officials, "A distinct problem of no mean proportions presents itself in the efficient training of new officers."[20] Without enough old-timers, Wells had recently "found it necessary in this sub-district to place five officers in charge of important stations who each had less than two years experience." Although "not one of these officers had ever apprehended a smuggler of aliens . . . they [were], among their other duties, expected to lecture and counsel the new officers under their supervision [about] the methods employed by smugglers, the detection and handling of such cases, etc."[21] And, within the El Centro subdistrict stations led by inexperienced officers, several patrol inspectors "of less than one year's experience" were assigned to be crew leaders.[22] Wells argued that "during this resultant recruiting and training period, which must from necessity be carried on by officers many of whom only have partial training themselves, the Patrol from necessity operates on a greatly retarded effectiveness."[23]

By 1942 the new recruits significantly outnumbered the old-timers, and they brought new social backgrounds into the Border Patrol. For example, according to a 1944 listing of new recruits being sent to the BPTS, only 40 percent had lived in the border region prior to joining the patrol. Men from distant places, in other words, began to comprise a larger share of Border Patrol officers. Among them was William Blaise, who had recently graduated from Oklahoma Teachers College and was working for a tire company in central Oklahoma when a friend told him about the U.S. Border Patrol. "I had never seen a Border Patrolman and I had no idea what their job was, but I thought it sounded real good," explained Blaise.[24]

The old-timers tried to school the fresh recruits in "the Border Patrol way." For example, they regaled the new recruits who did attend the BPTS at El Paso with parables from the old days. "There's a story about a smuggler who was supposed to have pitched his gun into the canal," recalled one of the new recruits of a story told to him while at the BPTS. In this story, the Border Patrol officer needed a defense because, although the smuggler never fired a gun, the officer shot and killed him. "When asked why he shot him since there was no shooting the other way that he could prove—the man didn't have a pistol—he said, 'He must have thrown it in the canal because I saw something flash in his hand. It was night and I didn't want to take a chance and I went ahead and shot him.'" From this story, the new recruit learned that aggressive caution was to be taken in unsure moments. In what followed, he learned that the old-timers' way was defined by a brotherhood of officers: to escape prosecution "all of his [the Patrol officer's] friends knew that he had to have an alibi gun—he had to have a gun in the canal if that's where this man threw one. When they drug the canal the next day, they got five or six guns out of there, because all of his buddies had pitched guns out in there the night before to make sure that this smuggler had actually thrown a gun out there."[25] Without specifics—such as the morning in 1932 when officers stood around a pool of Miguel Navarro's blood passing the gun that exonerated Patrol Inspector John V. Saul— this story instructed the new recruits in the old-timers' definition of brotherhood in the Patrol.

Yet the old-timers were dramatically outnumbered by the new recruits, and, with so little local control, the seasoned officers rarely had the opportunity to dictate Border Patrol strategies; at best, they were limited to offering guidance from afar. For example, when a Mexican national resisted apprehension, probationary Patrol Inspector Burnett refrained from using excessive force to control the situation. Back at the station, old-timer Jim Cottingham heard of the incident. About ten years earlier, when Jim had been shot by a smuggler, he was saved and avenged by his brother, Jack. Jim's stern advice to the new recruit was that he had "done the wrong thing" and "should have killed the alien," but his teachings fell upon deaf ears among the new generation of Border Patrol officers, many of whom objected to the raw violence of the early Border Patrol in the Texas-Mexico borderlands.[26] Burnett believed that lethal violence in response to nominal resistance would have been un-justified and left his conversation with Cottingham wondering how he "had all of this reconciled in his mind, about right and wrong."[27]

Burnett represented the new patrol that was emerging. Aware that coercive force was required to enforce U.S. immigration restrictions but uncomfortable with the physical brutality that was common in Border Patrol practice and folklore during the 1920s and 1930s, the new recruits built a new professional culture of violence. The new chief of the Border Patrol, W. F. Kelly, supported their rejection of raw violence, and soon after assuming his new post, Kelly pushed the Border Patrol's unrepentant sinner and firearms instructor, Charles Askins, out of the service. There was no longer a place for Askins and his methods in the Border Patrol. With nothing to do but move forward, the new recruits struck out on their own "without experienced key officers to instruct and direct."[28] Soon, the severe personnel shortages placed the new recruits in leadership positions, and they led the Border Patrol in a fundamentally new direction of U.S. immigration law enforcement shaped by the rapidly changing dynamics and politics of migration control along the U.S.-Mexico border.

MANAGING MEXICAN LABOR MIGRATION

Mexican labor migration to the United States had declined during the Great Depression, and the repatriation movement returned more Mexicans to Mexico than the number that crossed north throughout the 1930s, but World War II reopened and formalized the corridors of mass migration between Mexico and the United States. Beginning in 1940, the U.S. Congress had called upon all American farmers to increase production for the war effort. Growers in the southwestern United States expanded their acreage and anxiously recruited Mexican workers. Complaining of labor shortages and seeking increased control over the arrival and departure of Mexican workers, southwestern farmers—namely, the Californians—lobbied Congress for a labor recruitment program to increase and guarantee the number of Mexican laborers available to U.S. farms. In 1941, U.S. officials approached the Mexican government with the idea of establishing a bilateral labor program that would facilitate the short-term labor migration of Mexican workers into and out of the United States.

Mexican officials had reservations about facilitating Mexican immigration into the United States, but experience had shown that as U.S. agribusinessmen called south to Mexican campesinos, many of whom remained unemployed or under-employed during the 1940s, the Mexican Department of Migration would be unable to prevent unsanctioned exits across Mexico's northern border. A controlled and managed system of legal migration—and all of the associated benefits for Mexico—seemed better than a rise in unregulated and illegal border crossings.

Therefore, after negotiating a basic labor contract that satisfied the requirements established by the Mexican Constitution of 1917, Mexican officials agreed to participate in a bilateral system of state-managed labor migration.[29] This system became known as the Bracero Program.[30]

The Bracero Program offered Mexicans wanting to work in the United States the opportunity to do so legally. Bracero contracts quickly became valued commodities in the Mexican countryside, where underemployed Mexican campesinos once again hoped that work in the United States would provide sustenance in Mexico. This time, however, officials of the U.S. and Mexican governments hoped to exercise greater control over the flow of Mexican labor migration.

Scholars have offered many ways of understanding the U.S. and Mexican effort to manage Mexican labor migration through the Bracero Program. Working as a labor activist with California farm workers during the 1940s and 1950s, Dr. Ernesto Galarza wondered aloud, "Is this indentured alien—an almost perfect model of the economic man, an 'input factor' stripped of political and social attributes that liberal democracy likes to ascribe to all human beings ideally—is this *bracero* the prototype of the production man of the future?"[31] Galarza's critique of the Bracero Program as a system of "administered migration" by which U.S. agribusinesses extracted labor and profit from a reserve labor supply contained south of the border was an indictment conceived at the intersection of theory and empiricism in the fields where California farmers had strategically used braceros to lower wages, break strikes, and demean working conditions. Gilbert González and Raúl Fernández have built upon the work of Galarza by placing the Bracero Program within the context of U.S. empire and examining the program as a system of "colonial labor exploitation."[32] Against this backdrop of the Bracero Program as a system of cross-border labor exploitation, Kitty Calavita, Deborah Cohen, and Ana Rosas have pushed for textured perspectives on the making and meaning of the Bracero Program. Calavita, for example, has examined the program as a bureaucratic response to the conflicting demands of U.S. immigration law and capitalist economic development.[33] Deborah Cohen and Ana Rosas, on the other hand, have broadened our understanding of the Bracero Program by considering the gendered dynamics and various Mexican interests in managing Mexican labor migration to the United States. Their work takes the eligibility requirements for the Bracero Program as a point of departure and examines the meaning of the program's development within Mexican politics, culture, and society. As their work reminds us, not all Mexican campesinos were eligible for bracero contracts. Only healthy, landless, and surplus male agricultural workers from regions not experiencing a labor shortage within Mexico were qualified to apply. Many Mexicans—those who were too young, too old, or too sick, along with rural landholders, urban dwellers, or women—were all categorically ineligible for the Bracero Program. Examining the interests of Mexican elites and considering the gendered dimensions of Mexico's effort to manage the international labor migration of rural Mexican men provides a richly nuanced understanding of the Bracero Program. According to Cohen, the Mexican officials of the 1940s continued to invest in the social, political, and cultural possibilities of mass labor migration to the United States and cast the Bracero Program as a modernization project that would transform Mexicans and Mexico by sending rural campesinos to learn, save, and absorb all that they could from their experience in the United States.[34] In particular, argues Cohen, the Bracero Program was a highly gendered project of modernization that lifted up Mexican men as the "ideal actors and agents of modernity."[35] Ana Rosas examines the Bracero Program as "a transnational and gendered immigrant family experience."[36] By sponsoring the exodus of millions of rural Mexican men, the program, argues Rosas, interrupted family life and reshaped gender norms and relations. In turn, however, bracero workers and their families significantly affected the development of the Bracero Program by refusing its limits, exploiting its opportunities, and defying the ideals pinned to managing their labor migration between the United States and Mexico.

The Bracero Program was all of these things—a system of labor exploitation, a matter of empire, a project of masculinity and modernization, a family experience, and a site of gendered resistance—and the enormous complexity of the making, meaning, and evolution of the program strongly influenced how the U.S. Border Patrol policed unsanctioned Mexican migration during the 1940s.

Although the Bracero Program delivered legal, temporary, male Mexican workers to U.S. farms and ranches, a large number of Mexican nationals illegally crossed into the United States at the same time. In particular, those disappointed by the limits of the Bracero Program or otherwise unable to secure a bracero contract often decided to contract themselves by heading north, illegally crossing the border, and finding work on border area farms. The rise in illegal immigration from Mexico would have seemed familiar to U.S. Border Patrol officers who had worked along the U.S.-Mexico border prior to the Great Depression, but the broader political context within which unauthorized Mexican immigration now had to be controlled was dramatically new. Not only had concerns of national security increased Border Patrol funding, streamlined Border Patrol authority, and enhanced Border Patrol capacities, but the geopolitics of World War II opened U.S. Border Patrol practice to Mexican influence.

World War II turned U.S.-Mexican relations upside down. Emboldened by a history of conquest and economic imperialism, the United States had long accorded Mexico little power in U.S-Mexico relations prior to World War II; during the war, however, sharing a two-thousand-mile border with the United States gave Mexico new leverage in her relations with the United States. If Mexico turned or fell to the Axis powers, the threat to the United States would be magnified by proximity. Bombs could rain down on U.S. communities from Mexican bases, and saboteurs could easily access the United States through Mexico. Accordingly, the Americas in general, but Mexico in particular, gained new significance for the United States during the war.

As battles erupted across Europe in the late 1930s, Mexican President Lázaro Cárdenas (1934–1940) declared neutrality. Both the United States and Mexico were holding onto formal neutrality when the Japanese bombed Pearl Harbor on December 7, 1941. The United States immediately entered the war, and Mexico was forced to consider how it was going to protect itself against a conflict that seemed to be creeping up on its Pacific shores. But when a German ship torpedoed a Mexican ship, Mexico officially joined the Allied Forces in May of 1942.

World War II directly linked Mexico's national security and economic development to those of the United States. Mexico's new president, Manuel Avila Camacho (1940–46), hoped to strengthen Mexico's economy through industrialization. Two decades had passed since the Mexican Revolution ended, but inequality still gripped the Mexican economy. The agrarian vision for Mexican social equality that revolutionary governments had proposed had vanished, and many invested in the belief that industrialization would produce social justice by wrenching Mexico from its persistent land-based inequalities.[37] Mexican labor activists, intellectuals, elites, artists, and politicians all championed industrialization as the cure for Mexican economic struggles. Many, however, including some of the country's most influential labor activists, believed that the ideals of social justice needed to be suspended while Mexico produced the necessary capital to redistribute wealth. Capital accumulation, therefore, was placed ahead of the redistribution of wealth. World War II provided an opportunity to court U.S. investments in Mexican economic development.

United States elites were eager to regain access to Mexican land and natural resources. Many had had their land seized and their companies crippled when Lázaro Cárdenas nationalized oil production in 1938.[38] President Camacho settled their claims against the Mexican government, which gave U.S. businessmen renewed confidence in investing in Mexico.[39] Mexican and U.S. businessmen took advantage of the systems of economic cooperation that were established when Mexico joined the United States in its battle against the Axis forces.

Improving transportation systems was a crucial first step in Mexican industrialization. Through the U.S.-Mexican Commission for Wartime Cooperation, the United States provided Mexico with both technical assistance and goods to improve Mexican railroads, while the Export-Import bank spent $10 million dollars on Mexican road bonds in 1941. The next year, the United States spent $9.1 million on the Pan American Highway in Mexico and spent another $13.5 million dollars on Mexican railroad bonds.[40]

With work on improved transportation systems underway, U.S. and Mexican elites focused upon increasing the number of products being produced for export from Mexico. The Mexican-American Commission for Economic Cooperation (MACEC) was formed in 1942 and boasted members from among the top business leaders in each country. That year alone, the MACEC launched sixteen projects that mixed war mobilization with Mexican industrialization. They targeted "agricultural development, transportation, industry, public works, tourism, and fisheries," but nowhere was their effect felt more swiftly and deeply than in the industrialization of agriculture.[41]

In 1943, the U.S. and Mexican Commission on Agriculture advocated shifting Mexican agricultural production away from domestic products and toward oil and seeds deemed necessary for the war effort. Between 1942 and 1943, seven hundred thousand hectares were reassigned from the production of corn, a staple in the Mexican diet, to the production of war-related products.[42] Crisis quickly set in. In 1943 there was a bad harvest. The combination of fewer hectares being planted and bad conditions created a dangerously low yield of corn. On September 21, 1943, the Mexican Ministry of Agriculture prohibited farmers in Nayarit, Sinaloa, Nuevo León, San Luis Potosí, Tamaulipas, Veracruz, Colima, and the coast of Jalisco from growing anything other than corn, but the conditions for a near famine were already in motion. Mexico had to import almost seventy tons of corn to prevent massive starvation. The governor of Durango seized a railroad car of corn that was heading to Mexico City in order to feed people in his state.

The poor, for whom corn was a staple, were hardest hit by the crisis of 1943. A recovery in corn production did not begin until 1945. The decisions made by U.S. and Mexican officials to shift production away from domestic products reflects the primacy of war production in their decisions and the collusion of the Mexican and U.S. elite in the pursuit of a system of Mexican economic development that did not benefit the Mexican poor. Despite the lessons of 1943, Mexico continued its program to industrialize agriculture and produce crops for export. Domestic food shortages continued to plague the Mexican poor through the 1940s as the elites of each country grew closer.

The rapid industrialization of Mexican agriculture and the domestic food shortages, compounded by a dramatic rise in the Mexican population, once again forced many Mexican campesinos to seek economic survival through migration. They took the new roads and railroads funded by the United States to Mexico's urban centers, northern states, and the U.S.-Mexico border. Many learned of the opportunity to work in the United States through the Bracero Program and headed to bracero recruitment centers in Mexico. When they arrived, many learned that they were not eligible for the program. Disappointed by the limits of the program, Mexican workers illegally crossed the border in search of work.

Just as it was in the past, the unsanctioned immigration of Mexican nationals into the United States was of concern to the Mexican government. Unsanctioned immigration gutted the profits of labor emigration and drained the country of one of its greatest natural resources, a cheap and flexible labor supply.[43] The loss of laborers and the inability to regulate labor mobility once again worried many social, political, and economic leaders at a moment when national leaders had committed the country to a project of rapid industrialization driven by U.S. capital and Mexican labor. Mexican political leaders imagined the Bracero Program as a way to manage migration that offered the Mexican government the opportunity to control the international mobility of poor Mexican campesinos.[44] Control, however, was elusive, as undocumented migration increased alongside the Bracero Program.

Various Mexican interest groups pressured their government representatives to end unsanctioned Mexican migration across the U.S.-Mexico border. President Camacho received requests from a business leader in the state of Jalisco complaining about the loss of 350–400 men who had abandoned their land to seek work in the United States.[45] Agribusinessmen along Mexico's northern border were particularly vocal in their protests that cotton was rotting in the fields because Mexican laborers chose to cross the border for higher wages rather than work in Mexico. Some of the earliest and most pressing demands came from landholders in Mexico's most productive and profitable zones of cotton farming, the Mexicali Valley of Baja California and the Matamoros region in Tamaulipas. Businessmen in these regions demanded placement of the Mexican military along the border to prevent Mexican cotton pickers from illegally crossing into the United States.[46] They and other businessmen had objected to establishing the Bracero Program. As they saw it, the program was a bilateral system that facilitated the loss of agricultural laborers to the United States. They had argued that the Mexican government should not encourage Mexican migration while pursuing an internal project of economic development and industrialization that needed Mexican laborers. Their protests were joined by the voices of braceros working within the United States who resented undocumented emigration because they believed that undocumented workers lowered wages and worsened working conditions.[47] Mexicans in general resented the loss of citizens and workers to the north. The Mexican government, with its mind fixed upon industrialization, responded to these demands by pressuring U.S. officials to intensify border vigilance and guarantee the apprehension and deportation of all Mexican nationals working illegally within the United States.[48]

The pressure placed upon U.S. Border Patrol officers from south of the border first exploded in El Paso, Texas. Just one month after the first braceros arrived in California, old-timer and chief patrol inspector Griffith McBee recommended that a "state of emergency" be declared in the El Paso district.[49] Despite the Bracero agreement that facilitated the legal importation of Mexican laborers to the United States, McBee wrote that Mexican nationals were pushing across the Texas-Mexico border in unprecedented numbers. Defiantly opposed to the minimum wage and other provisions of the bracero contracts, Texas farmers declined to participate in the Bracero Program.[50] By the spring of 1943, McBee explained that "this situation is taxing to the utmost the limited patrol force available for line duty in and near El Paso, Texas," and he ordered a suspension of holidays for patrol inspectors in the El Paso district and required all officers to work fifty-six hours per week.[51] Yet, while McBee wrote that Mexican nationals were illegally crossing the border in "unprecedented numbers," and officers were required to work more hours, the apprehensions in the El Paso district actually decreased in 1943. During that year of crisis, the El Paso subdistrict reported only 2,299 apprehensions— the lowest number ever in the El Paso subdistrict.[52] What was the "state of emergency" that McBee declared?

When the 1940 appropriation increased the number of personnel along the southern border, the El Paso station was slated to receive a large number of new recruits. Although the appropriation for officers in the El Paso area was increased to one hundred, shortages plagued the station. In 1943, McBee complained to his supervisors that only fifty-nine officers were actually assigned to work in his district, and the assignment of officers to non-patrol duties further reduced potential Border Patrol effectiveness. Of the fifty-nine officers in El Paso, McBee wrote that "5 are doing office work in the Mexican Border Identification Unit, 2 are assigned to the office of the local Inspector in Charge as Acting Immigrant Inspectors, 2 are working in the multilith and photographic department on the Central Office Lecture Course, and 18 are scheduled to enter the next term of the Border Patrol Training School."[53] Soon, the understaffed force of fifty-nine officers would drop to thirty-one, and, after assigning the men to shifts, as few as fifteen officers would be available for line patrol at any given time. In the context of poor recruitment, drafts into the armed services, and war-related details that kept all stations undermanned, McBee had reason to be concerned that his force might be further "skeletonized." He requested a "state of emergency" to shield his officers from additional details and to place El Paso first in line for new recruits.

McBee's discussion of El Paso's "state of emergency" also hinted at an emerging concern for the officers and officials of the U.S. Border Patrol. McBee wrote that "there is reason to believe that there is a feeling among local Mexican authorities that we are not cooperating with them in their efforts to prevent the entry of agricultural laborers."[54] McBee registered Mexican concerns regarding migration control as a top priority for the U.S. Border Patrol in El Paso and warned officials working out of Washington, D.C., that "should our present line force be decreased for any reason within the next several weeks, the number of illegal entries would increase in proportion thus giving cause for just criticism of this Service for failure to effectively patrol the El Paso Line Sector."[55] Unlike the situation in the 1920s and 1930s, the new political matrix of World War II and the Bracero Program forced local Border Patrol officials to respond to Mexican demands for more effective immigration law enforcement. McBee's emergency represented a crisis of faith between U.S. and Mexican officers in the shared project of controlling Mexican labor migration.

The Department of State did not oversee U.S. immigration law enforcement, but its officials did pressure the Department of Justice, the INS, and the U.S. Border Patrol to close the border to undocumented Mexican immigrants and to apprehend more Mexican nationals. Soon after the Bracero Program began, Mexican officials hosted a meeting in Mexico City with representatives of the Department of State, the Department of Justice, the INS, and the U.S. Border Patrol. At this meeting "the Mexican Government complained that great numbers of laborers were succeeding in effecting unlawful entry . . . [and] . . . urged definite steps be taken by this [U.S.] Government effectively to deal with the problem."[56] In response to Mexican demands, INS officials agreed to "strengthen the Patrol force along the Mexican Border by means of filling all existing vacancies and detailing approximately 150 Patrol Inspectors from other areas to the Mexican border."[57]

The majority of new officers hired after 1943 were assigned to stations along the U.S.-Mexico border.[58] The growth of the Border Patrol budget in 1940 and the shift of personnel in late 1943 almost doubled the number of Border Patrol inspectors working in the U.S.-Mexico borderlands.[59] Shifting more officers to the southern border transformed the national organization of the U.S. Border Patrol. Prior to 1943, more officers worked along the northern border than along the southern. After 1943, however, the Mexican border became the center of operations for the U.S. Border Patrol. Mexican officials also demanded that Border Patrol officers enumerate the number of Mexican nationals apprehended separately from all others. In effect, they called for special attention to undocumented Mexican nationals. The Mexican demands of 1943 contributed to the concentration of U.S. immigration law enforcement personnel along the U.S.-Mexico border and emphasized policing unsanctioned Mexican immigration. Therefore, at a time when an expanding politics of migration control opened the U.S. Border Patrol to new concerns regarding the illicit entry of European saboteurs and the management of domestic enemy aliens, the establishment of a cross-border system of managing labor migration refocused the officers of the U.S. Border Patrol upon unsanctioned Mexican immigration.

The several hundred new officers assigned along the U.S.-Mexico border—many of whom cycled in and out of wartime duties—were no match for the steady rush of unsanctioned migrants who pushed across the U.S.-Mexico border in the 1940s. In 1942, Mexican officials had successfully prevented enough migrants from crossing the California border to create a labor shortage in the Imperial Valley. Their isolated successes, however, were eclipsed by the steady rush of migrants that crossed the border during the Mexican famine of 1943, and Mexico continued to use the bureaucracy and politics of the Bracero Program to press the United States for results. On December 11, 1943, the Mexican Embassy in Washington, D.C., warned the U.S. Department of State that if control was not established over the flow of illegal immigration into the U.S., Mexico would "effect a complete revision of the [Bracero] agreements."[60] The threat was passed from the Department of State to the Department of Justice, the INS, and the chief supervisor of the U.S. Border Patrol, who, by 1943, was prepared to take centralized action to increase border enforcement along the U.S.-Mexico border.

SPECIAL MEXICAN DEPORTATION PARTIES

Within six months of the Mexican Embassy's threat to revise the Bracero Program, the chief supervisor of the Border Patrol, W. F. Kelly, launched a new program of aggressive immigration law enforcement. The documentation of the new methods employed by the Border Patrol in the 1940s is voluminous, but disorganized and unspecific. Randomly placed throughout dozens of files are memos discussing "drives on Mexican aliens," "special Mexican details," "Mexican deportation parties," and the "Mexican expulsion program." The purpose of the parties, details, drives, and programs was to increase apprehensions of undocumented Mexican nationals by transferring Border Patrol officers from relatively quiet stations to "hot spot" locations for a limited amount of time. These temporary details of officers allowed Kelly to increase the number of apprehensions despite personnel shortages.

By June 1944, Kelly had initiated an "intensive drive on Mexican aliens" by deploying Special Mexican Deportation Parties throughout the country. For example, on June 14, 1944, Kelly ordered the Border Patrol stations in Minnesota and North Dakota to detail officers to Chicago and to perform special raids against Mexican nationals.[61] The next day, Border Patrol officers in McAllen, Texas, completed a drive upon Mexican nationals that resulted in more than 6,900 apprehensions.[62] By November of 1944, 42,928 Mexican nationals had been deported by Mexican Deportation Parties out of California.[63]

Despite concentrated efforts in California during the summer of 1944, in October of that year, Chief Kelly was still receiving reports from the Los Angeles Border Patrol District that "aliens are literally pouring over the border in the El Centro sector." The authorized number of officers in El Centro, California, was sixty-eight, but the station was functioning eighteen officers short, which meant "only four officers are available for 'line patrol.'"[64] Given that the El Centro sector was responsible for patrolling the U.S.-Mexico divide between El Centro, California, and Yuma, Arizona, four officers could not begin to prevent illegal immigration across the region.

In November of 1944, Kelly began plans to answer the requests of the El Centro sector for increased personnel. He announced a plan to detail thirty officers from the El Paso district to the El Centro station. Just one year earlier, Chief Patrol Inspector McBee had declared a "state of emergency" and complained about the se-

Mexican deportees wait in a holding area for apprehended aliens. U.S. Border Patrol
Official Photograph, File No. 96–12. U.S. Immigration Border Patrol, McAllen, Texas.
Courtesy of the National Border Patrol Museum—El Paso, Texas.

vere personnel shortage in El Paso. He and others protested that the detail of thirty
officers out of El Paso would jeopardize Border Patrol work in the area. Kelly disagreed and reasoned that the relatively stable conditions in El Paso did not "jus-
tify us in leaving your patrol force alone when a number of your officers would ob-
viously be of such great assistance, at least for the time being, in another district."[65]

The detail of El Paso officers began work in El Centro on November 7. Three
weeks later, the detail reported apprehending "1994 Mexican aliens," an average
of 110 apprehensions per day. By December 6, only 600 more "Mexican aliens had
been apprehended." Given that the El Centro station had estimated that 6,000 Mexican aliens had illegally entered the U.S. through Mexicali between October 10 and
16, the apprehension of slightly more than 2,500 Mexicans attempting to cross the
border was unimpressive. Regardless, the Central Office kept the detail of forty men
in El Centro until at least January 2, 1945.[66]

The extension of the nominally productive detail prompted Earl Fallis, now chief
patrol inspector in the El Paso station, to complain that "a considerable number of
the officers from this Sector have written letters expressing their utter dissatisfac-

tion with being kept on detail in the El Centro Sector."[67] Fallis argued that the men were frustrated because "long details away from their homes are always hard on our officers,"[68] and he encouraged Kelly to return the officers to their home communities. In the new order of centralized authority and under pressure to increase apprehensions, Kelly dismissed Fallis's protest, because it was "sound border patrol practice to put the men at the points of greatest activity."[69]

The constant detailing of officers was a strategy developed in 1944 that would remain with the Border Patrol well into the 1950s. The new strategy forced officers to move or to quit the Border Patrol. One unintended result of detailing and re-stationing officers was to undermine the ability of new recruits to become integrated within the local communities. Regularly assigned to details away from their base states, Border Patrol officers depended upon their wives to build their local social networks.

BORDER PATROL WIVES

The new recruits and their families came from all over the country and were stationed in small towns, such as La Feria, Texas, Nogales, Arizona, and Blythe, California. Upon arriving in a new town, Border Patrol wives depended upon each other to soften the blow of frequent moves. Norma Hill recalled that, on her husband's first day of official duty in 1940, they "drove to Lordsburg and got a motel room about 2 P.M. At 3 O'Clock, the senior came by, picked Bill up and they disappeared for the next 24 hours! That was a proper intro into a Border Patrol wife's life!" Such scenes were replayed many times in their tenure with the Border Patrol. Alone and in a new community, Hill depended on other Border Patrol wives for support in her new community.[70]

At about the same time that Norma Hill was leaning on Border Patrol wives in Lordsburg, Mary Clint moved "1,000 miles away from my family in Kansas" to Laredo, Texas, with her husband, who was a new Border Patrol recruit in 1941. "We were informed the rental housing was scarce," recalled Clint, but "another patrolmen had just moved out of a two room apartment that we could rent." When her husband left for El Paso to begin training at the BPTS, Mary "visited other Border Patrol wives and learned of other better apartments to be had on the East side of town." Upon the recommendations of resident Border Patrol wives, the Clints soon moved "to an apartment building next to another Border Patrol couple." Whenever possible, Border Patrol families chose to live near each other for instant friendships and support.[71]

In October of 1941, New Yorker and new recruit John Rosier entered onto duty in Fabens, Texas. "Of course, there was no housing at the time," so Rose and his wife boarded with a local family until "we found a little place to live which was then called the Bungalow Apartments."[72] Rosier and his wife eagerly moved to the Bungalow Apartments, because "several of the fellows in the Patrol and their wives were living there."[73] For the wives, who were often left alone while their husbands were on detail, the quick and close Border Patrol friendships cushioned their families against the disruptions of constant moves because "you would always count on other BP friends becoming closer than family."[74] Although there were "frequent tearful partings," numerous transfers meant "always knowing you'd see them again somewhere 'along the line.' "[75]

Border Patrol families formed communities within communities along the line. Transferring from town to town was eased by always remaining within the Border Patrol community. But the social survival strategy of depending upon the Border Patrol community further distanced new arrivals from established borderland communities. Border Patrol officers did not integrate themselves into the local community life, interests, or customs. When the Central Office demanded increased enforcement and higher apprehension rates, the Border Patrol's new personal and social distance from local communities made officers less hesitant to upset local interests in flexible immigration law enforcement.

The new officers, armed with planes, radios, and trucks, and operating under a system of national coordination, brought rapid results. By the end of 1944, total apprehensions doubled from 16,330 in 1943 to 33,681 in 1944 (see table 2). Scholars have often interpreted the rise in Border Patrol apprehensions in 1944 as a reflection of a dramatic increase in undocumented crossings, but close observation of patrol operations during these years suggests a combination of factors at work. In addition to the economic struggles of workers in the Mexican countryside and the expansion of employment opportunities in the United States, there were new recruits with improved resources operating under a more centralized system of administration within a binational politics of deporting Mexican workers.[76] Although a rise in undocumented Mexican immigration certainly did occur during the 1940s, the transformation in U.S. Border Patrol authority, resources, personnel, and priorities also contributed to the dramatic rise in the number of Mexican nationals apprehended in the Mexican border region. According to these many dimensions of U.S. immigration law enforcement in the U.S.-Mexico borderlands during the early 1940s, the Border Patrol's project of policing unsanctioned Mexican immigration clearly intensified.

The consequences were high for persons of Mexican origin in the U.S.-Mexico borderlands as the Border Patrol's net of surveillance expanded in the region. For example, the number of interrogations reported by the U.S. Border Patrol skyrocketed from 473,720 in 1940 to 9,389,551 in 1943—an almost twentyfold increase. The number of apprehensions did not keep up with the number of interrogations; the ratio of apprehensions to interrogations declined from 1.5 percent in 1940 to 0.009 percent in 1943. Under intense pressure to deport unsanctioned

TABLE 2 Principal activities and accomplishments of the U.S. Border Patrol for the years ended June 30, 1935–1944

	1935	1936	1937	1938	1939	1940	1941	1942	1943	1944
Total number of persons apprehended	11,674	12,406	13,825	13,655	12,685	11,092	12,649	15,237	16,330	33,681
Number of deportable aliens located	N/A	N/A	N/A	N/A	N/A	N/A	N/A	N/A	N/A	N/A
Number of persons apprehended for immigration violations	11,144	11,881	13,217	12,963	12,174	10,618	11,390	11,872	11,238	31,653
Number of persons apprehended, Mexican border region	8,430	9,010	9,544	9,263	8,879	7,438	N/A	8,708	11,775	28,173
Number of persons apprehended for immigration violations, Mexican border region	8,076	8,768	9,266	8,982	8,606	7,161	N/A	6,705	8,246	26,810
Number of persons questioned, Mexican border region	388,377	362,884	435,262	474,489	486,400	473,720	N/A	N/A	9,389,551	3,954,353
Total number of persons questioned	812,007	812,110	858,256	942,985	1,012,242	987,274	N/A	13,240,125	24,598,186	5,925,036
Value of all seizures	$96,517	$65,476	$71,639	$57,789	$39,062	$36,452	N/A	$75,373	$144,488	$128,243

SOURCE: Data compiled from principal activities and accomplishments of the U.S. Border Patrol, *Annual Reports of the Immigration and Naturalization Service, Fiscal Years Ending June 30, 1935–1944* (Washington, DC: GPO).

TABLE 3 Immigrants deported (total), immigrants departing voluntarily (total), and Mexican immigrants returned to Mexico for the years ended June 30, 1925–1975

Year	Immigrants Deported (Total)	Immigrants Departing Voluntarily (Total)	Mexican Immigrants Returned to Mexico
1925	9,495	—	2,961
1926	10,904	—	4,047
1927	11,662	15,012	4,495
1928	11,625	19,946	5,529
1929	12,908	25,888	8,538
1930	16,631	11,387	18,319
1931	18,142	11,719	8,409
1932	19,426	10,775	7,116
1933	19,865	10,347	15,865
1934	8,879	8,010	8,910
1935	8,319	7,978	9,139
1936	9,195	8,251	9,534
1937	8,829	8,788	9,535
1938	9,275	9,278	8,684
1939	8,202	9,590	9,376
1940	6,954	8,594	8,051
1941	4,407	6,531	6,082
1942	3,709	6,904	N/A
1943	4,207	11,947	8,189
1944	7,179	32,270	26,689
1945	11,270	69,490	63,602
1946	14,375	101,945	91,456
1947	18,663	195,880	182,986
1948	20,371	197,184	179,385
1949	20,040	276,297	278,538
1950	6,628	572,477	458,215
1951	13,544	673,169	500,000
1952	20,181	703,778	543,538
1953	19,845	885,391	865,318
1954	26,951	1,074,277	1,075,168
1955	15,028	232,769	242,608

Mexican immigrants, officers and the Special Mexican Deportation Parties directed the millions of additional questions, suspicions, and interrogations against U.S. citizens and legal immigrants of Mexican origin. The Border Patrol's search for unsanctioned migrants of Mexican origin was motivated in part by the demands of the Mexican government through the bilateral bureaucracy of the Bracero Program. The project of policing unsanctioned Mexican immigration therefore evolved and intensified according to circumstances very distant from the regional and local politics of migration control that had once led U.S. Border

TABLE 3 *(continued)*

Year	Immigrants Deported (Total)	Immigrants Departing Voluntarily (Total)	Mexican Immigrants Returned to Mexico
1956	7,297	80,891	72,442
1957	5,082	63,379	44,451
1958	7,142	60,600	37,242
1959	7,988	56,610	30,196
1960	6,892	52,610	29,651
1961	7,438	52,383	29,817
1962	7,637	54,164	30,272
1963	7,454	69,392	39,124
1964	8,746	73,042	43,844
1965	10,143	95,263	55,349
1966	9,168	123,683	89,751
1967	9,260	142,343	108,327
1968	9,130	179,952	151,000
1969	10,505	240,958	201,000
1970	16,893	303,348	277,377
1971	17,639	370,074	348,178
1972	16,266	450,927	430,213
1973	16,842	568,005	577,000
1974	18,824	718,740	709,959
1975	23,438	655,814	680,392

SOURCE: Data for total immigrants deported and total immigrants departing voluntarily compiled from *Annual Reports of the Immigration and Naturalization Service, Fiscal Years Ending June 30, 1960–1975.* Data for Mexican immigrants returned to Mexico compiled from the following sources: For 1925–73, Julian Samora, "Mexican Immigration," in *Mexican-Americans Tomorrow: Educational and Economic Perspectives,* ed. Gus Tyler (Albuquerque: University of New Mexico Press, 1975), 70. For 1974–75, *Annual Reports of the Immigration and Naturalization Service, Fiscal Years Ending June 30, 1974 and 1975.* For years 1925–73, data includes the various categories used to define force removal, deportation, and voluntary departure. For years 1974 and 1975, data refers to the number of deportable Mexican immigrants located.

NOTE: U.S. immigration statistics are inconsistently recorded across the annual reports of the commissioner general of immigration, the annual reports of the secretary of labor, the annual reports of the Immigration and Naturalization Service, and the INS statistical yearbooks. However, the overall trends in the various categories of immigration, exclusion, apprehension, and forced removal are constant.

Patrol officers to focus their energies upon targeting and apprehending unsanctioned Mexican immigrants. Beneath the surface of continuity, ruptures in the world of U.S. immigration law enforcement dramatically shaped the Border Patrol's rise in the U.S.-Mexico borderlands.

Chapter 6 digs deeper into the changes in the mechanics of migration control in the U.S.-Mexico borderlands by examining how the U.S. Border Patrol built upon the opportunities provided by the Bracero Program to gain greater control over the unsanctioned border crossings of Mexican nationals. In particular, chapter 6 tells the story of how the officers of the United States Border Patrol worked closely with Mexican officers south of the border. Together, U.S. and Mexican officers launched new enforcement practices and established new systems of deportation that stitched together U.S. and Mexican systems of migration control. Chapter 6, in other words, examines how new dynamics of migration control chased unsanctioned border crossers along the familiar corridors of migration between the United States and Mexico.

6

The Corridors of Migration Control

On January 17, 1948, funeral home owner M. K. Fritz sat down to read his morning paper in Chicago, Illinois. In it he read about a case of racial discrimination against a Mexican national. He was so enraged by the incident that he mailed the clipping to Miguel Alemán, the president of Mexico, to let him "get a look at the way people of color are treated here in this country of ours."[1] Fritz did not understand racial discrimination as an aberration of life in America. "We the Negro people," he wrote "have been subject to it for a many year without any seeming let up."[2] According to Fritz, what the Mexican national had experienced was a fact of life in the United States, and he "sympathize[d] with any fellow man of color that receives such unjust treatment."[3] With this, he advised President Alemán that "it might not hurt to let your people know what treatment one of your nationals got here so that when Americans of white descent are in your country they might be given a dose of their own medicine."[4]

As many civil rights activists and organizations were doing throughout the 1940s, Fritz sought international alliances against racial discrimination and violence within the United States. Often, international pressure and cross-border alliances were enormously influential in encouraging, shaming, and compelling American presidents, members of Congress, and U.S. Supreme Court justices to press for an end to racial segregation within the United States.[5] From his kitchen table in Chicago, Illinois, Fritz hoped that Mexico too would help dismantle American systems of racialized inequity.

President Alemán never answered his letter, but Fritz's hope was not totally unfounded. Episodes of organizing and resistance among African Americans and Mexicanos had before threatened the racial order of American life. For example,

125

during the economic struggles of the 1930s, African American and Mexicano workers in Chicago and elsewhere had participated together in that decade's great up-
surge in interracial labor organizing.[6] But Mexican officials of the 1940s were not
interested in broadly tackling the problem of racial inequity in the United States.
Rather, they pursued a more cautious approach of opposing discrimination toward
people of Mexican origin.[7] During the early 1940s, for example, Mexican officials
had refused to send braceros to the state of Texas, where anti-Mexican discrimination was most public and unapologetic. Mexican officials also worked with Mexican American civil rights organizations to pressure Texas to officially recognize
Mexicanos as Caucasian.[8] By fighting for inclusion within the realm of whiteness,
Mexican officials simultaneously drew upon and reinforced the black/white divide
as the most basic and fundamental racial/ethnic division in American life. As a
struggle for immigrant incorporation, this was a strategy that had worked for many
other immigrant groups in other places at other times: the Irish had donned black-
face, and Italians had defended residential segregation.[9] But along with their battle for whiteness, Mexican officials participated in the buildup of U.S. immigration
law enforcement in the U.S.-Mexico borderlands. By contributing to the U.S. Border Patrol's turn toward the U.S.-Mexico border and to its deepening project of
policing unsanctioned Mexican immigration, Mexican officials participated in the
Mexicanization of the caste of illegals in the United States.

　　This chapter continues the story of Mexican influences on U.S. Border Patrol
practice by chronicling the rise of cross-border migration control strategies in the
mid-1940s. Building upon the Bracero Program's bilateralism in managing the importation of legal labor migrants into the United States, U.S. and Mexican immigration officers imagined and implemented cross-border methods of deporting illegal Mexican migrants out of the United States. Further they worked collaboratively
to transform the permeable U.S.-Mexico border into a clear boundary that held
unsanctioned migrants south of the border or that swallowed them in the process
of their unsanctioned border crossings. In this era of cross-border cooperation, U.S.
and Mexican officers drove the violence of immigration law enforcement deep into
the landscape of the border and far into the interior of Mexico. The bodies of unsanctioned Mexican migrants were still maimed and mangled but—unlike what
happened in the past—U.S. Border Patrol officers rarely delivered the blows. M. K.
Fritz, the professional coroner and perceptive social critic, was most likely unaware
of the ways in which cross-border innovations in migration control strengthened,
deepened, and extended the violence that damaged and dislocated the bodies of
Mexico's illegal immigrants. This chapter demonstrates that the violence of immigration law enforcement took place in a context of cooperation between U.S. and
Mexican systems of migration control. In exploring the rise of new corridors of
cross-border migration control, this chapter examines the bi-national dimensions

of the problem of race according to the Border Patrol's narrow policing of the legal/illegal divide.

THE UNITED STATES, MEXICO, AND THE
TRANSFORMATION OF DEPORTATION

The Special Mexican Deportation Parties delivered an increasingly large number of unsanctioned Mexican immigrants across the U.S.-Mexico border. Yet mass deportation failed to solve the problems of unsanctioned migration. Arriving with few resources, deportees stretched the resources of Mexican municipal authorities who grappled with the realities of mass deportation, and deportees often crossed back into the United States. Although mass deportations looked good on paper, they aggravated Mexican border communities and were ineffective in terms of preventing unsanctioned border crossings. With this in mind, U.S. and Mexican officials sat down to discuss migration control along the U.S.-Mexico border.

On January 11, 1945, U.S. and Mexican authorities reached an agreement designed to control the return of undocumented Mexican migrants to Mexico through close U.S. and Mexican cooperation. According to this agreement, the U.S. Border Patrol would deport Mexican nationals who were residents of Sonora, Sinaloa, and Jalisco through Nogales, Arizona; residents of eastern and southern Mexican states would return through El Paso, Texas. At the border, Mexico would "accept delivery of the aliens" and "divert them to localities in the Interior."[10] Whereas in the past, U.S. Border Patrol officers had released deportees at the U.S.-Mexico border, according to the January 1945 agreement, they would begin to release deportees into the custody of Mexican officers who forcibly relocated them to places south of the U.S.-Mexico border.

Collaborative deportations began in April of 1945. The preferred method of transporting deportees to the interior of Mexico was by train. On and off throughout the 1940s, 1950s, and 1960s, trainlifts removed between 600 and 1,000 migrants weekly to Monterrey in the state of Nuevo León, Torreón in the state of Coahuila, or Jiménez in the state of Chihuahua. In addition to the more cost-effective trainlifts, in June of 1951, U.S. and Mexican officials introduced daily plane flights, or airlifts, from Holtville, California, and Brownsville, Texas, to Central Mexican states, such as San Luis Potosí, Guadalajara, and Guanajuato (see map). That year, 34,057 migrants were airlifted to the interior of Mexico. The following year, 51,504 Mexicans were airlifted to central Mexico, but Congress made no appropriations for planelifts in 1953, and the practice was stalled until funding resumed in 1954.[11]

Whether using trains or planes, the procedure for coordinating deportation into the interior of Mexico was similar. Typically, U.S. Border Patrol officers apprehended undocumented Mexican nationals somewhere within the United States and bused them to an INS detention center along the California or Texas border. At the detention center, officers determined the method of removal that would be offered to each immigrant. Residents of an adjacent border area were allowed to cross back into Mexico and remain in the border area without further penalty or surveillance. If they were from the interior, however, Border Patrol officers tagged them for a trainlift or airlift. Residents of northern Mexican states were generally designated for deportation by train to Monterrey, Torreón, or Chihuahua, while residents of "the balance of Mexico" were designated to return by plane to Central Mexico.

As described in a 1956 memo, the procedure for the trainlift to Chihuahua was for U.S. Border Patrol officers to drive a busload of migrants to the "middle of the bridge" that connected Presidio, Texas, to Ojinaga, Mexico.[12] At the middle of the bridge, all Border Patrol and INS personnel would "leave the bus and return to the inspection station."[13] As the U.S. officers left the bus, Mexican officers entered to "conduct the party from the middle of the bridge to the railroad station."[14] At this point, the deportees and the financial responsibility for their detention, supervision, transportation, and care were officially transferred from the United States to Mexico.

On the Mexican side of the Presidio-Ojinaga bridge, the Mexican officers directed the bus to the train station in Ojinaga. There, they placed the migrants under armed guard. To make the transfer complete, a few of the Mexican officers returned the empty bus to the center of the bridge where they would disembark, and U.S. officers would reenter and drive the bus back to the U.S. Immigration station in Presidio. Meanwhile, back at the train station in Ojinaga, the migrants waited until a train was ready to take them south. As they waited, they might be lectured by a Mexican official that "it was useless for them [returnees] to return to the United States, as no demand existed for labor."[15] If they complained about being forcibly relocated to the interior of Mexico, an officer of the Mexican Department of Migration may have explained that they had broken Mexican law by emigrating without the proper authorization and were in no position to dispute their removal to the interior.[16] When the trains were ready, the guards placed the migrants on board and escorted them to their final destination somewhere farther south of the U.S.-Mexico border.

Cross-border cooperation introduced a system of immigration law enforcement far removed from the one developed by local boys who enforced federal law during the early decades of Border Patrol work along the U.S.-Mexico border. Local sheriffs, police, farmers, and Texas Rangers had once been the primary partners of U.S. Border Patrol officers. Now, the officers spent a considerable amount of time working with Mexican officials to coordinate the movement of deportees into the custody of Mexican officers south of the border. In the direct and coercive transfer of Mexican deportees from U.S. to Mexican custody, a new era of immigration law enforcement rooted in bilateral strategies was born.

Mexican guards supervise deportees awaiting the trainlift in Mexico, circa 1952–53. U.S. Border Patrol Official Photograph, File No. 46–21. U.S. Immigration Border Patrol, McAllen, Texas. Courtesy of the National Border Patrol Museum—El Paso, Texas.

For officers, cross-border collaboration expanded the possibilities of migration control. Police practice is defined as a site of state violence that is limited by the boundaries of the nation-state, but by coordinating deportation across the border, U.S. and Mexican officers linked the distinct territories of U.S. and Mexican police authority. At all times, U.S. and Mexican officers respected the limits represented by the border. They disembarked from the buses and exchanged custody of deportees at the line between the two countries. With cross-border collaboration, U.S. and Mexican officers were able to transform the border that marked the limits of their jurisdictions into a bridge that linked rather than divided the two distinct systems of migration control. Upon that bridge, the consequences for unsanctioned border crossing were merged. For migrants, cross-border collaboration extended the price they paid for illegal entry into the United States. No longer were the detentions and dislocations that accompanied migration control isolated north or south of the border. In the United States, those identified as illegal immigrants were subject to surveillance, detention, and deportation. In Mexico, they faced the disruptions and anxieties of forced dislocation to unfamiliar places. In each location, however, the consequences of having committed the symbiotic trespasses of unauthorized exit from Mexico and illegal entry into the United States were bound together through the collaborative practices of U.S.-Mexican migration control.

"NO MARKS OF VIOLENCE": BILATERALISM, GENDER, AND THE EVOLUTION OF STATE VIOLENCE

The trainlifts and airlifts were a strategy of migration control that targeted the bodies of unsanctioned migrants. The objective was to reduce the number of unsanctioned border crossings by removing unsanctioned migrants from the border region. Transforming the U.S.-Mexico border into an impenetrable barrier, however, presented another option for migration control.

In 1945, U.S. Border Patrol authorities began to recognize a shift in illegal border crossings away from the El Paso, Texas, area to the California border. To confront the rise in illegal crossings across the California border, the Immigration and Naturalization Service delivered "4,500 lineal feet of chain link fencing (10 feet high, woven of No. 6 wire) to the International Boundary and Water Commission at Calexico, California." INS and Border Patrol officials believed that a fence would turn away unsanctioned border crossers and decided to recycle its resources by sending to the Mexican border the chain-link fence that had been used at the Crystal City, California, internment camp.[17] The wires and posts that had imprisoned Japanese Americans during World War II were dug up from the deserts of Crystal City and driven into the sands of the U.S.-Mexico border to keep Mexicans out, at least for 5.8 miles on either side of the All-American canal in Calexico, California.

Although the INS could not erect a continuous line of fence along the border, they hoped that strategic placement of the fence would "compel persons seeking to enter the United States illegally to attempt to go around the ends of the fence."[18] What lay at the end of the fences and canals were desert lands and mountains extremely dangerous to cross without guidance or sufficient water. The fences, therefore, discouraged illegal immigration by exposing undocumented border crossers to the dangers of daytime dehydration and nighttime hypothermia.

The construction of the fence sparked immediate resistance in Mexican border communities. "Through our sources of information in Mexicali, several rumors have been picked up from the cantinas that the lawless element of Mexicali is going to start cutting holes in the fence as soon as it is up."[19] While the Border Patrol lobbied for funds, arguing "a lighting system with observation towers should be provided" to protect the fence, the governor of Baja California detailed Mexican soldiers to patrol and protect the fence "during its erection."[20] Without Mexican cooperation, U.S. efforts to solidify the border line with fences and barbed wire would probably have succumbed to wire cutters. While the Mexican government demanded protection for Mexican braceros from discrimination and abuse by U.S. employers, Mexican border officials helped the U.S. Border Patrol to erect fences

· designed to reduce illegal immigration by making undocumented border crossings more dangerous.

Border crossers constantly cut holes in the new border fences. For example, on July 3, 1951, all of the holes in the Calexico fence had been repaired. By the July 7, "there [were] to be found 14 holes cut in the mesh of this fence on the east side of Calexico, as well as 11 panels torn out from the bottom which, when pulled out, will permit a person to slide out underneath; in addition, 7 strands of barbed wire had been cut. On the West side of Calexico, 13 panels were torn loose from the bottom, and one strand of barbed wire had been cut."[21] The migrants cut through, dug under, and even jumped over the barbed-wire fences. "You'd go along there in the daytime and see the results of the night before's crossing. They'd throw mattresses and coats and everything else to keep from getting scratched," noted one officer, describing the ineffectiveness of the fences in keeping people south of the border. He and other Border Patrol officers routinely described the fences as "just a constant hassle" rather than an effective barrier.[22] Still, many migrants were frustrated by the fences and the presence of Border Patrol personnel in popular crossing areas, and increasingly risked the march around its edges.

After the fence was complete, officers in the Imperial Valley of California turned their attention to making apprehensions by sweeping through the desert at night and picking up migrants who sat still in the freezing cold. Although the Border Patrol kept no written record of the number and conditions of the migrants they found, Patrol Inspector Ben A. Parker did recall many years later that it was during the 1940s and 1950s when officers began picking up migrants from the deserts and mountains. "I know it was one of the worst snow storms that I've ever seen in this country," explained Parker of one night in the Texas-Mexico borderlands when he picked up a migrant whose "feet were frozen. Blood was seeping from under his toenails. They were black and swollen."[23]

Migrants themselves also recognized the new dangers presented by border fences that pushed them into the deserts and mountains. For example, after being apprehended by the U.S. Border Patrol while trying to get across the border fence, a Mexican deportee reported to the *Los Angeles Times* that "next time I will cross over in the desert country. When, with companions, I will take a road through the desert sand where there are no people." He recognized that beyond the fences "it is hard, and many die on such a road," but he hoped that "maybe my water bottle will last, and I will come to some place like San Bernardino, or to Los Angeles, and become lost there, from *la migra*."[24] Many who shared his dream, however, perished along the way.

On February 4, 1952, an irrigation district employee discovered five dead Mexican males near Superstition Mountain in the Imperial Valley of California. The bodies were found "near small shrubs with a flax straw water bag, two cans of sardines and two loaves of bread." Apparently the men had readied themselves for a long trek through the desert, but they had underestimated the ravages of the back-lands along the U.S.-Mexico border. Local law enforcement deduced from the significant decomposition of the bodies that the men had died "while they attempted to pass by immigration officials" during the "terrific summer heat" of 1951.[25]

Although U.S. officials were unable to identify many of the bodies they discovered, migrants quickly registered the deaths and disappearances of the companions who traveled through the deserts. Many continued to use the deserts, particularly with the hired help of coyotes, but others tested new methods, such as crossing the All-American canal. As with the Rio Grande, when the canal's waters rushed high and fast, the Border Patrol left it relatively unguarded because of the inherent threat it presented to undocumented crossers. On May 26, 1952, twenty-five-year-old Mario Ramírez stepped into the canal six miles west of Calexico and drowned.[26] Several days later, canal authorities discovered the battered corpse of an unidentified Mexican male that had been entangled in the head gate of the All-American canal for at least one month.[27]

Border Patrol officers had given up their brutality, but the body count of migrants paying the penalty of death while trying to evade apprehension for illegal immigration continued. In a bitter twist from the past, however, immigration law-enforcement techniques shifted responsibility for the number of deaths associated with undocumented immigration to migrants themselves. No longer were apprehensions the primary site of danger. Rather, the Border Patrol had relocated the danger of immigration law enforcement to the natural landscape of the borderlands. Migrants battled deserts and rivers rather than men with guns.

The new strategies of the U.S. Border Patrol pushed the violence of immigration law enforcement away from visible interactions with individual officers and toward unobserved encounters with the environment. These were tactics that muddied the authorship of state violence. When bodies shriveled in the desert or washed up on the banks of the Rio Grande, no one could be named in the death of the migrants. Fingerprints could not be dusted from the sand, and the rapids left no tracks to be followed. The new strategies created the circumstances for violent deaths with no human assailants. Danger, damage, and death continued, but fortifying the border structured a system of violence without perpetrators. As a county coroner declared over the dead bodies of five migrants who had attempted to cross through the Imperial Valley desert, "No marks of violence were found [on] any of the five bodies."[28] This was a system in which the Border Patrol retreated from its authority to strike and, instead, embraced what Michel Foucault has described as "the power to let die."[29]

Migrants quickly realized that danger lay outside of their interactions with officers. In time, they learned how to exploit the new opportunities for resistance provided by the changes in Border Patrol violence. By the early 1950s, Border Patrol officers were complaining that Mexicans demonstrated an "increasing tendency to resist arrest."[30] Not only did they run, but many used their large numbers to intimidate officers. For example, in March 1953, in Andrade, California, a "near riot" erupted when "three to four hundred" Mexicans effected illegal entry on a Southern Pacific freight train and "milled around the railroad gate shouting threats of violence and curses against the Immigration Officers and Americans in general, for . . . well over an hour."[31] In a separate incident, a large group of Mexicans "pointed out their numerical superiority and indicated they would have disarmed the officers and effected their escape had they been arrested under different circumstances."[32] After migrants were apprehended, their active resistance did not end. On Sunday March 1, 1953, thirty-two "aliens in detention in the Indio [California] Border Patrol Unit building effected their escapes by climbing through a ventilating hole in the ceiling."[33]

Migrants constantly ran, scattered, and escaped Border Patrol apprehension, causing officers to complain in the early 1950s that "the problem is already serious and grows steadily worse."[34] Frustration mounted within the Border Patrol. Officers worked long hours in hot deserts, isolated regions, and freezing mountains. They were sent on details, and their families were regularly transferred along the line. They made significant family sacrifices to serve the Border Patrol, but "the odds are too uneven with a few dozens of officers pitted against tens and hundreds of thousands of aliens."[35] It seemed impossible to "combat these hordes of aliens."[36] Some officers began to request transfers away from the southern border "to get away from what they regard[ed] as a hopeless and back-breaking task."[37] It was an unenviable job, particularly since undocumented workers had increasingly taken to "running to escape apprehension, and the task of chasing them across the cotton fields, plowed ground, canals and *resacas,* and brush and sand in the blazing 100 degree plus temperature and choking dust [had] become a most grueling and exhausting task, and the men complete[ed] each tour of duty so exhausted they [could] hardly walk."[38] The constant chases made the young officers "tired and weary," and the "older men in their late thirties and early forties [were] exhausted and worn out."[39] However, for most, morale was "unbelievably high, and the greater the odds against them the harder they worked, but they [were] wearing out."[40] Exhausted, defied, and often defeated, Border Patrol officers still rarely resorted to physical brutality. They responded to the daily frustrations of Border Patrol work by upsetting the cycles, pathways, and rhythms of migration that allowed migrants to constantly return.

To minimize the risks of undocumented immigration, migrants depended heavily upon social networks that assisted them with successful passage, housing, jobs, and community life while far from home. Social networks provided necessary shelter and protection against the dangers of undocumented immigration. The Border Patrol and Mexican officials could erect fences, pull bodies out of the desert, and deport hundreds of thousands of individual migrants each year, but unsanctioned Mexican immigration continued. U.S. and Mexican officers realized that any successful attempt to reduce undocumented immigration would have to disrupt the social networks that facilitated it.[41] Mexico's program of removing deportees from the border was, in part, intended to disrupt those social networks. Mexican officials, however, exempted deportees claiming residency in a border region for at least six months before apprehension from forced removal to the interior. As border towns grew in size, and migrants learned about the exemption, more and more deportees claimed exemption from trainlifts, thus forcing the U.S. Border Patrol to return to deporting migrants directly across the border, from where they quickly returned to the United States.

In response to migrant resistance, the Border Patrol designed a system of buslifts to reduce constant crossing and recrossing by migrants deported within the borderlands. Officers might apprehend a migrant in McAllen, Texas, and buslift him to Laredo, Texas, for deportation, or they might apprehend migrants in Los Angeles and buslift them to Nogales, Arizona, before escorting them south. The buslifts grew out of the recognition that Mexican migrants did not come from an abstract national space but journeyed north through particular routes, places, and networks. Returning deportees through ports far from where they entered or in areas that were "real isolated, on both sides of the river" interrupted social networks by removing migrants from the regions that hosted the migration routes and social networks with which they were familiar.[42] Describing the buslift to Zapata, Texas, one officer noted that "the little village on the Mexican side was a good many miles, seems like it was about 15, or maybe 20, miles north of the highway, . . . [and] there was no transportation there, so the aliens had to walk at least to that road, and maybe farther, to get away from that village. There was no incentive for them to return en masse at Zapata because there were no jobs on the American side in that area. It was tough traveling, too, to get back to the Valley from Zapata."[43] Deporting migrants thru Zapata, Texas, functioned as a system of spatial and social dislocation: removing migrants from familiar regions and networks increased the likelihood that they would become wanderers, itinerants in an unfamiliar region. A Mexican officer of the Department of Population reported that deportees returning via the buslift could be found wandering the border region asking locals for the "times and places that are best to enter the United States illegally."[44] Buslifts also made deportees increasingly vulnerable to the muggers who made a business of relieving returning migrants of their cash and goods. Without the protections of an established social network, which often included housing and food, the wandering deportees were particularly vulnerable to the criminals waiting along the border. In June of 1946, for example, Mexican authorities reported a wave of robberies and pulled nineteen bodies from the Rio Grande, each with bullet wounds and empty pockets.[45]

The changing, gendered composition of unsanctioned Mexican migration during the 1940s and 1950s limited the Border Patrol's application of buslifts. In part, U.S. and Mexican officials imagined the Bracero Program as a program that would reduce illegal immigration by expanding the pathway to legal labor migration for Mexican laborers. However, only men were eligible for bracero contracts. U.S. and Mexican officials, therefore, formed their approach to controlling unsanctioned Mexican border crossings in terms of limiting the unsanctioned border crossings of husbands, fathers, sons, and brothers.[46] This narrow construction of the Bracero Program ignored the possibility that Mexican women, children, and family groups would also participate in labor migration to the United States. The establishment of the Bracero Program in 1942, therefore, introduced an implicitly gendered, two-tiered system of labor migration to the United States: legal bracero migration, which was limited to Mexican men, and illegal non-bracero migration, which included the women and families excluded from the Bracero Program. The bracero era was a crucial period during which millions of husbands, sons, brothers, and fathers were lifted into legal streams of migration, while women, children, and families were left to cross the border without sanction.

The waters of the Rio Grande provided much of the evidence of the rising numbers of women and children crossing illegally into the United States during the 1940s and 1950s.[47] In 1949, Ignacio Garza Jr. of the Lower Rio Grande Valley in Texas estimated that one person died every day while trying to cross the Rio Grande.[48] On June 27, 1946, that person was 11-year-old Francisca Cantu Hernández.[49] On Monday, April 12, 1948, it was Eugenia Rodríquez and her sixteen-month-old daughter, Hortencia.[50] And, in February of 1950, it was young Héctor Martínez, who drowned while trying to cross with his father.[51] When scooping Héctor from the river, Mexican authorities found the body of an unidentified Mexican woman.[52] Border Patrol officers also noted an increase in unsanctioned border crossings by women and children, and, by 1953, the El Paso Border Patrol station reported that more than 60 percent of all apprehensions in the region were of women and children.[53]

The shifting gender dynamics of unsanctioned Mexican migration complicated the Border Patrol's use of violence. The new recruits had retired the old-timers' preference for brutality and typically favored more indirect methods of applying coercive force. Trainlifts, airlifts, buslifts, and fences were all methods that concealed the coercions of migration control by displacing migrants and shifting responsibility for the danger, injury, and death that migrants suffered as they crossed out of Mexico and were deported from the United States. The arrival of women and children, however, exposed the continued physical violence of Border Patrol work. Women and children abandoned in unfamiliar places violated the gendered norms of police violence, which typically targeted men and male juveniles. Border Patrol officials recognized the dangers that buslifts created for migrants and devised a gendered policy that exempted women, children, and family groups from the program. Many believed that the general public would not support the abandonment of women and children in unfamiliar spaces. Only single men at least fifteen years old were subject to the buslifts. To meet daily quotas for the number of Mexican males needed to fill the buses waiting to take them elsewhere along the line, U.S. Border Patrol officers often released from their custody women, children, and family groups.[54]

Migrants studied the Border Patrol's gendered policies of deportation and exploited its weaknesses. Chief patrol inspectors requested that the ban on buslifting women and children be lifted because the migrants understood "every angle and soft spot in our Immigration Laws and use every method of escaping prosecution."[55] Wherever the Border Patrol raided, migrants first ran; if they were apprehended, male and female migrants joined hands and claimed to be married. Instant nuptials of friends and strangers protected single male migrants from buslifts to distant places. One officer later complained that "when the wetback grapevine buzzed the news that we were not hauling [buslifting] married couples, every male and female that could do so grabbed an opposite. . . . Men and women who had never before set eyes on each other were suddenly man and wife with quickie facts to back up the claim. . . . When it became known that small children were not buslifted, families loaned, and lend, their children to single wets."[56] Officers had to work extra hard to apprehend a quota of migrants eligible for buslifts as "instant families" allowed some migrants to escape the struggles of being abandoned far from anything familiar.

Mexican migrant workers crafted methods of resistance according to the challenges they met and the assets they held. As they sought entrance into the United States, they confronted an expanding web of surveillance and force that threatened them not only with deportation, but with forced relocation to places far from both home and work. Still, they had rocks to throw, feet to run with, and minds to manipulate the gendered forced-removal policies of the Border Patrol. In the process, the men, and especially the women and children, strengthened the resolve of Border Patrol officers to build the new era of migration control upon practices that concealed and displaced the physical coercions required to stop unsanctioned border crossings.

The new breed of U.S. Border Patrolman was far less likely to use physically brutal tactics, but officer David Snow reported that rebellious women and children exposed the implicit violence of immigration law enforcement. Upon apprehension, he explained, children would "immediately begin to cringe and cry."[57] In the public places where apprehension quite often occurred, the "shrieking" and "struggling" of children who had been grabbed by Border Patrol officers often forced the "embarrassed officers" to set the children free.[58] Women, Snow elaborated, were just as likely to employ this "professional method" of shrieking and struggling to evade apprehension, detention, and deportation. If their initial attempts failed to "draw the attention and sympathy of the people in the near vicinity," women would persist. "I personally have apprehended several alien women crossing the river into Brownsville," he recounted "that kicked and barked up my shins in good style."[59] The public resistance of rebellious women and children turned U.S. Border Patrol officers enforcing federal law into men embarrassed by their mandate and created what Snow described as a "spectacle" that was becoming an "untenable situation" for the U.S. Border Patrol.[60] It was an increasingly unbearable source of embarrassment, as the border emerged as a local tourist attraction for onlookers sitting on the river bank, explained Snow. The solution, he argued, was to erect a "well designed fence along the U.S. side of the river."[61] If successful, the fence would "eliminate entire classes of the present illegal crossers, such as the small shoe shine boys and other juvenile urchins, women, family groups with women and small children."[62] If not, the fence would at least redirect the spectacle of shrieking children and struggling women to the remote regions at the fence's end. Snow's plea for a border fence indicates that while U.S. and Mexican officers had not initially erected border fences to address gendered problems of state violence, the increasingly common and troublesome confrontations between unsanctioned women, undocumented children, and embarrassed officers affirmed the Border Patrol's turn toward displacing the violence of immigration law enforcement onto the landscape of the borderlands.

MEXICO AND THE PROBLEM OF EMIGRATION

The emergence of unsanctioned Mexican immigration alongside the Bracero Program ignited familiar problems in Mexico. Mexican border towns still lacked sufficient resources to feed or house the increasing number of laborers and families that headed north each year in search of work. The trainlifts and airlifts helped to alleviate their concentration along the border, but for each migrant sent to the interior, another dozen seemed to arrive. Officers of the Mexican Department of Migration reported that an "avalanche" of workers was pushing north against their understaffed and underfunded offices along Mexico's northern border.[63] Echoing requests from twenty years past, officers from along the line requested additional personnel because emigrants were crossing out of Mexico without any significant opposition. "Unfortunately," explained one Mexican immigration officer along the California border, Mexican workers were leaving Mexico "without our even knowing it."[64] Mexico's system of emigration control had never been strong, and the resurgence of unsanctioned migration in the 1940s exposed the persistent weaknesses in the Mexican Department of Migration's system of migration control.

In Mexicali and Matamoros, agribusinessmen requested that the Mexican government place the military along the border to prevent unsanctioned emigration. For agribusinessmen in the northern Mexico borderlands, unsanctioned emigration was emerging as a labor problem at a moment when Mexico's program of rapid industrialization and intensive irrigation development fostered a reorientation of Mexican agriculture toward centralization, mass production, and export. Whereas their competitors to the north seemed to have a constant supply of undocumented Mexican labor, agribusinessmen in northern Mexico needed workers and complained of constant labor shortages.[65] The cotton growers in the lucrative Matamoros-Reynosa region and the Mexicali Valley pressed particularly hard for an end to unsanctioned emigration.[66] In February of 1944, the military commander in Baja California requested permission to assign troops along the border to stop workers from making unsanctioned border crossings into the United States.[67] But, until a crisis along the Texas-Mexico border region in October 1948, Mexican officials generally preferred to rely upon the U.S. Border Patrol to stop the unsanctioned exit of Mexican nationals.

During the weekend of October 16–17, 1948, thousands of Mexican migrants stormed the El Paso, Texas, border. For some time, U.S. and Mexican officials had been bickering over the minimum wage that would be paid to bracero cotton pickers. U.S. authorities insisted that $2.00 to $2.50 per pound was fair, while Mexican officials demanded that braceros be paid no less than $3.00 per pound of cotton. They had reached an impasse, while Mexican bracero hopefuls crowded into Ciudad Juárez, just south of El Paso, Texas. Many of the migrants worried that the program would collapse in the disagreements between U.S. and Mexican representatives. They had waited patiently while their resources dwindled, and resolution of the wage dispute seemed to grow more distant each day. On October 16, their frustration and anxiety broke. An estimated four thousand migrants rushed across the border.

The memories that U.S. Border Patrol officers have of those few days in October of 1948 vary.[68] Some remember obeying orders to allow the migrants into the United States and to transport undocumented migrant workers to local farmers. Others recall working hard to stem the unstoppable tide. The confusion taught Mexican officials that they could not trust the United States (via the Border Patrol) to effectively prohibit illegal emigration when disputes over the Bracero Program emerged. Therefore, when Mexico terminated the Bracero Program until a workable wage agreement could be reached, Mexican officials placed the Mexican military along the border to stop illegal border crossings and instructed Mexican immigration officials to turn back migrants who intended to cross into the United States. The activities of Mexican military and law-enforcement officers climaxed in July 1949, when the Mexican government declared a national emergency because cotton farmers in the Reynosa-Matamoros region did not have enough laborers.[69] That month five thousand Mexican troops patrolled the U.S.-Mexico border in San Pedro, Tamaulipas, and worked within the cities and countryside to detain migrants until they accepted labor contracts with Mexican cotton growers.[70] The Mexican

Agricultural Bank supported the military's efforts to turn Mexican migrants into Mexican workers and encouraged the use of "forced labor" if migrants did not willingly submit to working within Mexico. Government officials denied coercing migrants to work in the fields, but local journalists published interviews with migrants who claimed that they were "sold like slaves."[71] Soldiers were also accused of threatening migrants with imprisonment unless they worked for Mexican agribusinessmen.[72] Migrant compliance was further secured by rumors of soldiers shooting at migrants along the border. Most of all, however, officers and soldiers actively enforced a 1947 law that established a punishment of 2–5 years imprisonment and a fine of up to ten thousand pesos for persons who attempted to take Mexican citizens out of Mexico without the proper authorization from the Mexican Secretaría de Gobernación.[73] North of the border, the penalties for migrant smuggling were widely published in U.S. newspapers.[74] With the assistance of officers of the Mexican Department of Migration and municipal police, the military claimed to have stopped all illegal emigration in the area.[75]

The Mexican military, Mexican Migration officers, and municipal officials remained vigilant in the Reynosa-Matamoros area until a new bracero agreement was signed in August of 1949. Once again, Mexican authorities reported good relations with officers of the U.S. Border Patrol who deported Mexican workers into areas experiencing labor shortages in the Reynosa-Matamoros region.[76] The Mexican military pulled back from the border until the summer of 1952, when the U.S. Border Patrol announced plans to abandon the Lower Rio Grande Valley. The intensification of Border Patrol operations had enraged growers and agribusinessmen in South Texas, who were long accustomed to influencing the rhythm of apprehensions and deportation. The Border Patrol's threat to leave the Lower Rio Grande region was designed to discipline growers who routinely interrupted its operations in South Texas. South of the U.S.-Mexico border, Mexican growers feared that the Border Patrol's withdrawal would deepen labor shortages on their farms by allowing Mexican laborers to cross into the United States without fear of apprehension and deportation. Again, in response to the demands of Mexican agribusinessmen between Reynosa and Matamoros, Mexico launched a "wetback campaign," in which military and municipal officers targeted *pateros* (smugglers) for apprehension and federal prosecution. The Mexican president also authorized officers of the Department of Migration to stop illegal emigration and to work closely with the U.S. Border Patrol, whose threat never materialized.[77]

Mexican immigration law enforcement simmered until negotiations with the United States over the bracero contract returned to boiling point in 1953. In April of that year, Mexico returned five thousand troops to the border to stop undocumented emigration. By August, reinforcements arrived, and patrols were placed well south of the border.[78] Rather than risk another mass exodus of Mexican laborers that would threaten the cotton crop of the lucrative Reynosa-Matamoros

Mexican smugglers being questioned by the Mexican Border Patrol. U.S. Border Patrol
Official Photograph, File No. 84–2. U.S. Immigration Border Patrol, McAllen, Texas.
Courtesy of the National Border Patrol Museum—El Paso, Texas.

region, the Mexican Department of Migration established a full-time Mexican Border Patrol comprised of twenty-five officers assigned to police the border just below South Texas. The captain of the Mexican Border Patrol, Alberto Moreno,
worked with a "hand of steel" to arrest migrant smugglers and apprehend undocumented immigrants when they illegally crossed back into Mexico.[79] The establishment of a direct Mexican counterpart to the U.S. Border Patrol along the South
Texas border provided new opportunities for cross-border cooperation.

THE POSSIBILITIES OF BILATERALISM

The U.S. and Mexican Border Patrols worked independently and collaboratively
to police unsanctioned migration along the border. South of the border, the Mexican Border Patrol focused upon stopping unauthorized migration by policing coyotes. Chief Patrol Inspector Fletcher Rawls of the U.S. Border Patrol in El Paso,
Texas, valued Captain Moreno's work on the southern side of the border. He "is
tearing up boats by the bunches (I think shooting up a few) and is cooperating
with us very good," explained Rawls to his district director. "If we can keep this

man over there and he continues to receive the backing from Mexico City, he is going to be a big help to us," argued Rawls, who recognized the value of complementary police forces working on each side of the border. Both U.S. and Mexican immigration officers worked at the edges of their authority. The U.S.-Mexico border was permeable to unsanctioned border crossers but marked the limits of police authority to deploy state violence for the purposes of domestic law enforcement. Unsanctioned migration was intrinsically transnational, while the authority of Border Patrol officers to police the crime of illegal immigration was limited by the boundaries of the nation-state. At the border, therefore, U.S. and Mexican Border Patrol officers were both committed to combating the transnational crime of unsanctioned migration. But, as Ethan Nadelmann has described, U.S. and Mexican Border Patrol officers confronted the question of how to police criminals that "either ignore or take advantage of national borders when the powers of the state remain powerfully circumscribed by the political, geographical, and legal limitations that attend notions of national sovereignty."[80] Cross-border deportations and fences were examples of collaboratively policing transnational crime, but these methods required significant coordination between the top officials of each country. The establishment of the Mexican Border Patrol in 1953 allowed officers to explore innovations in the art of exploiting the limits of the border for the purposes of law enforcement.

By the late 1940s, on average, one-third of all apprehensions were of "repeat offenders," persons who had previously been deported.[81] Some repeat offenders had been apprehended and deported several times in a year, and others were apprehended and deported several times a day. One day in the early 1950s, Bob Salinger, patrol inspector in Charge of the Mission, Texas, station "got fed up" with the "chronic offenders" who "you'd see . . . day after day. You'd take them across the river and sometimes they beat you back across."[82] Salinger "promoted a pair of clippers" that were to be carried in each Border Patrol car and instructed the officers to shave the heads of "chronic offenders."[83] After they had put migrants through the Border Patrol "barber shop," Salinger instructed his officers not to process the "clipped" deportees through the official detention center: "You're going to have to take them straight over the river and kick them across after you clip their heads. We can't run them through the camp."[84] Salinger was aware that the practice of shaving heads was unsanctioned and unofficial, and consciously pushed the practice underground.

Head-shaving was an act of subordination and a strategy of power designed to punish the chronic offenders and discipline any migrant who heard the stories and rumors of the Border Patrol barber shop. Developed by Salinger, a southerner and teacher before he joined the U.S. Border Patrol, head-shaving emerged in the new patrol of the postwar era when more indirect methods of physical coercion replaced explicit brutality as a primary method of U.S. immigration control.

Knowing that higher authorities would most likely shut down the Border Patrol barber shop, Salinger had tried to keep the practice underground, but the officers became lax in their efforts. When eight "aliens" broke free of an officer one day and began "thumbing their nose" at him, he caught them and "decided they needed their heads clipped, so he peeled all of them. He did a good job of it," remembered Salinger.[85] "He had made an Apache out of some of them, cut crosses on their heads, just the long-haired ones. One ole boy had a big bushy mustache, he'd shaved off half of it."[86] But when some of them were processed through the local INS detention center, Chief Patrol Inspector Fletcher Rawls ordered the Mission, Texas, station to stop "peeling" Mexican heads while he determined whether or not head-shaving violated the civil rights of detainees. When Mexican newspapers began to expose and condemn the practice, which had also independently emerged in California, Rawls was forced to put distance between the Border Patrol and head-shaving.[87] The political distance needed was available just a few feet away. Rawls contacted the captain of the Mexican Border Patrol, who agreed to pick up the practice of head-shaving until the civil rights issues it presented in the United States could be worked out.[88] This agreement exemplifies the ways in which cross-border collaboration made the boundary between the U.S. and Mexico permeable to distinct systems of state violence. Forbidden practices in postwar America were pushed southward along a cross-border corridor of migration control.

In Mexico, the practices of migration control unfolded far removed from the public eye. There had long been significant public pressure within Mexico to end undocumented emigration, but the violence, dislocation, and disorder that migration control required was typically unwanted and unwelcome. Officials involved in the forced removal of deportees to the interior removed reporters from the trains and steered the lifts away from Mexico City, the hub of Mexico's media, and toward locations that either needed the labor or appreciated the dollars that deportees returned with in their pockets.[89] With less public scrutiny focused upon its practices, Mexico agreed to practice head-shaving while officials of the U.S. Border Patrol investigated the civil rights issues involved in using humiliation as a tactic of immigration law enforcement. Members of the Mexican Border Patrol used it until several years later, when head-shaving was officially reincorporated by the INS as a public health initiative at INS detention centers, creating what Michael Ignatieff has examined as a "hygienic ritual" that buried a mechanism of social subordination within a public health program.[90]

Still, the chronic offenders laughed at the officers of the U.S. Border Patrol. "They take their apprehension as a joke, and laugh and kid one another about it," complained the chief patrol inspector of El Centro, California.[91] Against the acts of dehumanization and the hidden violence of U.S. immigration law enforcement, migrants exposed the limits of Border Patrol authority by taunting officers. Migrants deployed what James C. Scott has called "the weapons of the weak" by demeaning

Border Patrol officers and their work as, ultimately, an ineffective joke.[92] Border Patrol officers could deport rising numbers of unsanctioned border crossers—apprehensions increased from 70,639 in 1945 to 289,400 in 1949—and, in the process, try to strip the deportees of their dignity, but migrants continued to cross the U.S.-Mexico border without sanction and refused to accept the authority of the Border Patrol officers.

By most measures, U.S. immigration control was failing along the U.S.-Mexico border. Mexican and U.S. officials had expected that deportation to homes or farms far from the border would reduce illegal immigration, but they were wrong. Then they tried fences to discourage illegal immigration. But, again, they had miscalculated, and immigrants continued to cross through, around, over, and under the fences. Trainlifts, airlifts, buslifts, and fences may have slowed the illegal reentry of those deported to the interior, but determined laborers often returned to the United States. As one officer commented, "They are like the leaves in the forest and the sands on the beach. They keep coming from a seemingly inexhaustible reservoir across the river."[93]

By the early 1950s, Border Patrol officers were apprehending so many Mexicans that there was no place to keep them as they awaited deportation. INS detention centers were filled beyond capacity. While officials lobbied for additional funds to build two new detention centers in Brownsville, Texas, and El Centro, California, officers erected temporary detention centers in barns and fields. Municipal governments recognized an opportunity in the Border Patrol's lack of space and allowed the INS to rent beds for migrants in local jails for $1.50 per day. Renting jail beds to the INS was so financially successful for border counties that they invested in expanding their jail facilities to accommodate the thousands of migrants being apprehended.[94] As of July 1949, the INS maintained contract agreements with 211 jails and institutions for the detention of aliens.[95] That year, the INS held 102,523 aliens in detention for an average of 7.5 days.[96] More than one-half of these detainees were held in non-INS facilities.[97]

Many officers hoped that stays in overcrowded detention centers and county jails would discourage migrants from coming north, but apprehensions increased from 468,581 in 1950 to 509,040 in 1951. As far as the officers of the U.S. Border Patrol could tell, nothing seemed to be working. In 1953, the U.S. Border Patrol added boatlifts as a new deterrent. The boatlifts returned deportees from Port Isabel, Texas, to Tampico and Veracruz on the S.S. *Emancipación,* the S.S. *Mercurio,* and the S.S. *Veracruz.* Between 1953 and 1956 the S.S. *Emancipación* and the S.S. *Mercurio* transported two thousand deportees monthly (eight hundred per trip). For the migrants, the trip was long and trying on these ships that transported Mexican bananas to south Texas before taking Mexican deportees to the ports of Veracruz and Tampico. In May of 1956, INS Commissioner Joseph Swing described the boatlifts as a deterrent because "these interior Mexicans don't like the sea water.

A boatlift convoy arrives in Port Isabel, Texas, September 3, 1954. U.S. Border Patrol Official Photograph, File No. 112–11. Courtesy of the National Border Patrol Museum— El Paso, Texas.

I understand they get a little sea sick and they are a long way from home."[98] Three months later, just a few days after U.S. Representative Joseph Kilgore condemned the boatlift as a "penal hellship," deportees aboard the S.S. *Mercurio* rioted. Thirty-six deportees jumped from the ship as it pulled into Tampico for an emergency docking, and five drowned.[99]

The bloated bodies pulled from the Tampico harbor map the violence of migration control far south of the U.S.-Mexico border. Along the border, men, women, and children drowned in the Rio Grande. An increasing number of those who pushed into the desert suffered from dehydration. And U.S. and Mexican officers dislocated deportees far from their homes in Mexico and away from their jobs in the United States. Deportee Juan Silos spoke with a journalist from *El Heraldo de Chihuahua* as he awaited a trainlift in Reynosa, Mexico. Silos complained that Mexican officers had beaten him over the head with an iron rod. The irony of the beating was not lost upon Silos. For years the Mexican press and politicians had warned migrants against going to the United States, where they would be subject to racial discrimination and violence. But, according to Silos, the violence experienced by him and the other deportees within Mexico made him wonder "why they talk about discrimination toward workers abroad, when here brothers of our own race almost kill us."[100]

The geographical dispersal of the bodies moved and mangled in the pursuit of migration control represented a fundamentally new era of policing and punishing Mexico's unsanctioned border crossers. In the past, migrants had to cross many hurdles to secure unauthorized exit from Mexico and illicit entry into the United States. U.S. and Mexican systems of migration control, however, were distinct and divided. Their lack of cooperation allowed migrants to forge partial refuges on either side of the border. Beginning in 1945, however, U.S. and Mexican officers passed migrants back and forth between their jurisdictions. Linking the violence of U.S. and Mexican migration control across the border brought a fundamentally new era of immigration law enforcement.

There is a well-known photo of U.S. and Mexican immigration officials standing on their respective sides of the U.S.-Mexico border and pulling in opposite directions with all their might on the arms of a Mexican man. Taken in January of 1954 during one of the many breakdowns in the Bracero Program, this photo vividly discloses the persistent struggle between U.S. and Mexican officials to control the mobility of Mexican workers, particularly young Mexican men. At this moment, U.S. officials and employers wanted Mexican workers north of the border and Mexican officials wanted them to remain south of the border until a new bracero agreement was established. Yet, this snapshot conceals the many ways in which U.S. and Mexican officials also collaboratively policed Mexico's unauthorized border crossers according to the shifting politics of migration control within Mexico, within the United States, and between the two. When U.S. and Mexican officials disagreed—usually because of one of the many ruptures in the bracero agreements—the U.S. Border Patrol clashed with Mexican officers along the line. When they were in agreement, Border Patrol officers worked closely with the various Mexican officers assigned to police migration from south of the border. During these times, in contrast to the image of U.S. officers pulling Mexican workers north and Mexican officers pulling them south, U.S. and Mexican officers collaboratively pushed and squeezed Mexican unsanctioned border crossers between their two jurisdictions.

Another example of U.S.-Mexican collaboration emerges from a handwritten note from Chief Patrol Inspector Fletcher Rawls regarding Border Patrol efforts to clear out Tampico, a large encampment of undocumented families along the border near Donna, Texas. Home to "more than five hundred men, women and children" and spreading over a half-acre just off of a major freeway, the Tampico encampment was "passed daily by hundreds of U.S. citizens and tourists who are unaware of its existence."[101] But for officers of the U.S. and Mexican Border Patrols, Tampico was an enforcement obsession and obstacle because migrants adeptly exploited the border to evade apprehension, especially when the river ran low through this region due to drought, diversions, and damming during the 1940s

"Border foot-tag": A Mexican farmworker, center, tries to jump onto Mexican soil while evading the Mexican border guards at Mexicali, in order to reenter the United States legally. *Los Angeles Times,* January 26, 1954. Los Angeles Times Photographic Archive, Department of Special Collections, Charles E. Young Research Library, UCLA.

and 1950s. Setting up shanty homes just north of the border line, migrants lived outside the grasp of Mexican authorities, and fled the jurisdiction of U.S. officers when the U.S. Border Patrol raided the camp. The scene of Border Patrol failure along the border was described by two members of the Mexican American veterans' association, the American G.I. Forum, whom the Border Patrol allowed to witness a 1951 raid upon Tampico. "The Task Force," they reported, was a mobile and modern detachment of "eight patrolmen, a truck, a passenger bus and two cars, with all vehicles controlled and directed by a two-way radio system." Yet the residents of Tampico easily evaded the well-trained and well-outfitted officers of the U.S. Border Patrol. According to the G.I. Forum representatives, the officers raided the camp "from the north, the east, and west." To the south, however, was Mexico. The officers launched their three-sided raid and "approached simultaneously." "As the first clouds of dust rose from the roads . . . the camp of inhabitants scattered like quail into the brush and across the dry river bottom to the Mexican side." By the time the Border Patrol task force reached the camp, they explained, "the able-bodied and speedy of both sexes had already 'flown the coop' "; the only people left north of the border were "the children, the sick, the old and the feeble." South of the border, the escapees "sat there in full view of the patrolmen, laughing, joking, and gesticulating at the discomfiture of the practically empty-handed officers. Some climbed trees on the high Mexican bank, scouting the situation and preparing to give a signal on the departure of the patrolmen.[102] The Tampico raid demonstrated the struggles of Border Patrol officers who worked at the limits of their authority, while migrants used the border as a barrier against the state authorities who policed them.

Cross-border cooperation allowed U.S. and Mexican officers to deny migrants the partial refuges provided by the border. Without the American G.I. Forum, the U.S. Border Patrol returned to Tampico on another day. "This morning we made a run at 'Tampico,'" scribbled Chief Patrol Inspector Fletcher Rawls, who was eager to notify his supervisor of his office's new successes along the south Texas border.[103] When the task force descended upon the camp from the north, east, and west, "as usual all the aliens ran for the river," he admitted. But this time, to the immigrants' "amazement, . . . the Mexican officials were on the *Mexican* side and several shots were fired from the Mexican side (pretty close) directing the aliens to remain on the American side, which they did, and all were picked up by the patrol."[104] The collaborative raid of the U.S. Border Patrol from the north, east, and west, and the gunfire of the Mexican Border Patrol from the south created what Rawls described as "a very surprised and frightened group of people."[105]

The Tampico residents, along with tens of thousands of Mexico's labor emigrants, were caught in the new era of immigration law enforcement in which U.S. and Mexican officers collaborated on the shared problem of illicit border crossings. By prohibiting migrants from utilizing the border as a barrier against police authority, such collaborative efforts denied migrants even the partial refuges that the separate systems of immigration law enforcement had once allowed. Between the U.S. Border Patrol on the north and the Mexican Border Patrol to the south, Mexico's unsanctioned border crossers and America's caste of illegals were caught by the interlocking systems of state violence that policed the crime of unsanctioned migration.

The cross-border methods of migration control demonstrated the dramatic changes that had occurred within and around the U.S. Border Patrol during the 1940s and early 1950s. The new men with new technology did not just conduct business as usual within the borderlands. They had retired the casual use of brute force as the Border Patrol's primary method of negotiating its conflicts with Mexico's unsanctioned border crossers. In its place, they implemented indirect means of applying physical pressure to the bodies of Mexican nationals who pushed north without first complying with U.S. immigration law. Fences pushed migrants to risky and remote regions. Buslifts abandoned them in places far from their familiar social networks. And at the core of the U.S. Border Patrol's dramatic changes were the cross-border alliances that allowed U.S. and Mexican immigration officers to negotiate and exploit the limits of the border. Trainlifts, airlifts, and boatlifts removed deportees from the United States and forcibly relocated them into the interior of Mexico. At the border, cross-border collaboration allowed the boundary to function as a bridge between U.S. and Mexican systems of migration control and, at times, squeezed migrants between the guns, clippers, and batons of the officers waiting for them on either side of the border.

For the U.S. Border Patrol, the cross-border alliances strengthened the officers' focus upon policing persons of Mexican origin. Not only had the majority of personnel been shifted to the southern border, but officers began and ended their days trying to fill the trains, planes, boats, and buses waiting to take Mexican deportees into Mexico. In turn, the number of Mexicans returned to Mexico as a percentage of the total number of forced removals from the United States increased from 51 percent in 1943 to 68 percent in 1944 and to 78 percent in 1945. By the mid-1940s, removing Mexicans from the United States had emerged as the central project of the U.S. Border Patrol.

The deepened correlation between Mexican immigration and illegal immigration carried a strange irony for the evolution of the racialized marginalization of Mexicans in the borderlands. Much had changed in the borderlands. World War II ushered in a new era of inclusion for the Mexican American middle-class. The military-industrial complex boomed in the southwest. Economic diversification provided Mexican Americans with employment options outside of agriculture and broke the hegemony of agribusiness in the borderlands. For decades, the growers' unfettered access to cheap Mexican labor was the foundation of the borderlands social, racial, and economic order. Farmers had unabashedly admitted that "we have the Mexicans here and don't work."[106] A society of deep segregation developed out of, around, and in support of this racial division of agricultural labor. But economic expansion displaced growers as the economic core of borderland societies and broke their political stronghold on local communities.[107] As David Montejano argues, when economic transition toppled the political and economic hegemony of the farmers and ranchers, the corresponding social order was also displaced.[108]

By the late 1940s, "No Mexicans allowed" signs had disappeared, and high schools were often integrated.[109] In general, the customs of racial segregation eased toward persons of Mexican origin. Even Texas officially recognized Mexicans as members of the white race with the passage of a resolution entitled "Caucasian Race—Equal Rights," which prohibited racial discrimination against Mexicans in public facilities. INS employee Stanley Childs recalled that even Mexican deportees were allowed access to a wide range of public places that had once steadfastly excluded the poor, Mexican workers that Border Patrol officers targeted for immigration law enforcement. Childs had joined the INS as a general laborer in El Paso, Texas, in August of 1940. In 1947, he was promoted to deportation officer, and several years later he was given the job of supervising the INS detention officers in El Paso. For extra cash, Childs drove the busses that carried migrants assigned to be deported from distant places such as Presidio or San Antonio, Texas. "We usually left El Paso around 7 or 8 o'clock and we drove all night," recalled Childs. On the way, the officers and migrants often stopped to eat prepacked lunches.[110] When food was not prepacked, the drivers and migrants stopped at restaurants to eat. As Childs explained, "the aliens could go in and sit down at the restaurant and eat." Childs, however, was an African American, and for him the rules of segregation in south Texas had yet to bend. Childs felt pained and ashamed that Mexican deportees being buslifted to distant places for deportation from the United States ate inside, while he "had to go into the kitchen or bring it out."[111]

The black citizen/Mexican illegal paradox represented by this story from south Texas during the late 1940s reminds us that the racialization of Mexicanos in twentieth-century America was always a complicated matter. The deportees, in the past, almost certainly would have been denied access to the same restaurants as African-Americans. They were the Mexican Browns whom the black/white divide had once swerved to envelop. By the late 1940s, the aggressive pursuit of statutory whiteness by Mexican American activists and Mexican authorities allowed the deportees to walk in the front door and sit in the places once exclusively reserved for Anglo-Americans and upper-class Mexicanos. Outside, however, they were illegals on locked busses en route to deportation from the United States. In short, the deportees' migration to the zones of whiteness was temporary, as the practices of migration control had forged powerfully constitutive equations between the caste of illegals and Mexican Browns.

Writing to President Alemán from his kitchen table in Chicago, Illinois, it is unlikely that M. K. Fritz knew much of Mexico's contributions to the story of race in America through the Mexicanization of the caste of illegals. In the late 1940s, the Border Patrol made relatively few incursions into Chicago, and press coverage of Border Patrol activities was overwhelmingly limited to the U.S.-Mexico border region. But records dug up from forgotten and overlooked archives north and south of the border make it clear that the Border Patrol's Mexicanization of the caste of illegals evolved upon a cross-border foundation that allowed Mexican authorities to function as partners in migration control along the U.S.-Mexico border. This story challenges the tendency to interpret the international influences upon U.S. race relations after World War II as singularly progressive. In the postwar era, many nations, diplomats, and international social critics confronted the United States on the issue of racial inequity in the self-professed land of liberty, freedom, and human rights. Their protests quite often contributed to significant changes in the American racial landscape. The case of cross-border migration control, however, provides an example of how Mexican authorities contributed to the racialization of the caste of illegals, a deeply consequential political category in American life and law, by participating in the consolidation and intensification of the U.S. Border Patrol's targeted enforcement of U.S. immigration restrictions. Built upon a binational foundation of policing Mexico's unsanctioned border crossers, the Border Patrol pushed Mexico's emigrants to gain illicit entry into the United States across some of the borderland's most dangerous pathways. Along the way, an increasing number of men, women, and children were swallowed by the evolving nature of Border Patrol violence. If they were caught, the Border Patrol subjected unsanctioned Mexican migrants to bus lifts, plane lifts, train lifts, boat lifts, jail stays, and the humiliations of head shavings. Mexican authorities helped shape this new era of migration control and thus helped shape the evolution of racial subordination within the United States.

Just as the Border Patrol's project of policing Mexico's unsanctioned border crossers pivoted upon unexpected partners and penetrated into new spaces, opposition to the many changes in U.S. Border Patrol practice during the 1940s emerged from the most unpredictable of players. Chapter seven examines the rebellion among growers in south Texas against the delocalization of Border Patrol authority. In their uprising, the growers offered some of the earliest critiques of the broad social consequences of the racialization of the caste of illegals.

7

Uprising

A Farmers' Rebellion

In May of 1947, the remaining old-timers sat vigil. The U.S. Border Patrol they had built was gone, and the man they had idealized was dying. Jefferson Davis Milton had been with the Border Patrol since its first day on patrol on July 1, 1924, but after a long career as a patrolman, Milton had entered the last days of his life. For Milton, it had been a "long period of excruciating illness."[1] The once powerful man was weakened by old age and debilitated by illness. His old-timer friends tried to visit as much as possible, but they were busier than ever. Multiple details kept them on the move, and every year they felt more pressure to catch Mexican nationals who crossed illegally into the United States. Nothing was as it had been; still, for years, these old-timers had found time to chauffeur Milton when he needed to go to town, and in the last week of his life, they organized shifts to sit with his wife twenty-four hours a day. They were there to help the man they had known, loved, and respected pass on.[2]

After his death, the old-timers eulogized Jefferson Davis Milton. They exalted him as an "institution rather than an individual," because "no other immigration officer [had his] value in cultivating for the Service the good will and friendship we must have for effective enforcement of the law."[3] In the past, farmers, ranchers, and patrolmen had worked together to enforce federal immigration restrictions. The "goodwill and friendship" of locals, they remembered, had been the cornerstone of Border Patrol work in the Texas borderlands. But the new era of immigration law enforcement that ripped the Border Patrol from its local origins sparked a borderland rebellion against the U.S. Border Patrol in South Texas.

By 1947, goodwill and friendship between the patrol and borderland ranchers and farmers was gone. World War II had unleashed global and national forces that shook the basic foundation of U.S. immigration law enforcement. The Border Patrol's primary target remained unsanctioned Mexican migrants, but local ranchers and farmers exerted less control over how, when, and why its officers policed Mexican Browns in the borderlands. Farmers and ranchers fought back with guns, lobbies, and propaganda against the patrol's use of Special Mexican Deportation Parties, airlifts, trainlifts, and raids. Battles erupted in the cotton fields, courtrooms, and newspapers as farmers and ranchers protested the delocalization of U.S. immigration law enforcement and challenged the legitimacy of the new era of migration control. At the funeral for Jefferson Davis Milton, old-timers eulogized both the man and the era he represented.

This chapter tells the story of the farmers' rebellion against the U.S. Border Patrol in south Texas during the late 1940s and early 1950s. Since the dramatic transformations of the World War II era, the arrival of new officers and new tactics shook the small borderland communities familiar with local boys enforcing federal laws. The new recruits routinely violated established systems of flexible immigration law enforcement and, when farmers objected, officers offered no apologies. Beginning during World War II, the officers of the Border Patrol directly answered to supervisors outside of the borderlands and operated according to a complicated politics of migration control that extended as far north as Washington, D.C. and as far south as Mexico City. Farmers and ranchers in south Texas rebelled against their loss of influence over migration control and fought to return the Border Patrol to its local roots. In the process, they emerged as unexpected critics of the patrol's racialized focus upon policing persons of Mexican origin.

RESISTANCE IN SOUTH TEXAS

Egbert Crossett knew well the changes that had transformed the U.S. Border Patrol during World War II. Crossett grew up in southern Arizona's Parker Mountains. As a young man he joined the U.S. Border Patrol with childhood friends, such as expert tracker Fred D'Alibini and Lon Parker. Throughout the 1920s and 1930s, Crossett served as a patrolman, but by the early 1940s, he had left the Border Patrol and begun farming in Doña Ana County, New Mexico.[4] Crossett remained committed to the old philosophies and tactics of the U.S. Border Patrol and was enraged when a detail of new recruits raided his farm in September of 1947. He confidently challenged the "authority" of the Border Patrol officers "to come upon his place and search," but the new officers recognized neither Crossett nor his philosophy of casual enforcement. They were of a new generation, and Crossett was "badly beaten" for his defiance by a new recruit.[5]

The farmers' annoyance with the new era of aggressive migration control simmered throughout borderland communities. Patrol Inspector Bob Salinger recalled that in Del Rio, Texas, "people they kinda looked up to you if you were a Border

Patrol man," but that in Mission, Texas, "they looked down on you."[6] Contempt for the new recruits manifested itself in many ways. Thinking back upon these difficult years, Salinger remembered "a sign in a restaurant saying 'coffee a dime, 25 cents for Border Patrol.' "[7] One officer's wife instructed her children to say that their father worked for the Immigration and Naturalization Service, because "some natives didn't like Border Patrolmen taking their wetbacks."[8] But in small towns most children knew whose fathers worked for the Border Patrol. When inviting friends to a birthday party, children would announce "I am having a birthday party and everyone is invited but the Border Patrol kids."[9]

Tension filled the growing social distance between local communities and the new Border Patrol officers. Before the introduction of new tactics in 1944, old-timer officers could often ease the tension between new recruits and community members by encouraging new officers to obey local customs. When the chief patrol inspectors in Eagle Pass and Del Rio, Texas, heard gossip "about the Patrolmen living at a Mexican's house," they promptly instructed the new recruits to move to the home of "some *respectable American* family" (emphasis in original),[10] protested Mrs. Concepción Nuncio, who was providing room and board for the officers. The removal of new recruits from the home of Mrs. Nuncio represents one of many cases of old-timers softening the changes sweeping over the Border Patrol. In these early days, new recruits had few options but to obey the orders of the still-dominant old-timers, who envisioned U.S. immigration law enforcement according to local customs and interests. But increasing numbers of new recruits quickly assumed positions of authority and refused to bow to the pressure of locals. When Special Mexican Deportation Parties arrived at the gates of belligerent farmers and ranchers, officers, ranchers, and farmers who had once been neighbors, friends, and kin became strangers and foes. Old-timer Fletcher Rawls, for example, recalled that in times past ranchers and farmers would give a "sly, knowing wink to let me know that [they] had plenty of wets and that I was fully aware that [they] had them but would do nothing as our policy was to do nothing."[11] But after the new era of immigration law enforcement swept through the Border Patrol, Rawls began to receive "a lot of cussing remarks . . . and instead of the wink I now [got] a glare." Rawls later admitted, "I kinda like this way the best as before I always felt just a little guilty."[12] But, as the raids and mass deportations continued, the tension soon exploded in the greater Texas-Mexico border region.

"I will kill the first man that goes any further into that field," threatened L. S. Fletcher from the gate of his farm in Las Cruces, New Mexico.[13] For years, Fletcher had hired undocumented Mexican workers. He had cooperated with Border Patrol officers to insure that all undocumented workers returned to Mexico rather than staying in the United States. But, World War II and the Bracero Program revised all previous agreements he had had with officers of the U.S. Border Patrol. It was November 4, 1947, and the Border Patrol detail standing at his gate had in-

structions to raid the Fletcher farm and deport all undocumented Mexican nationals. The officers drove around the irate farmer and into the field; Fletcher rushed
back to his house for his rifle.

The lead patrol inspector warned his officers, "It is liable to be pretty tough here
in a minute," so they checked and readied their weapons before they "called all of
the Mexicans out of the field."[14] Within a few minutes, the officers apprehended
eighteen undocumented Mexican workers and "herded them down the ditch road
and into the cars."[15] As the officers turned their cars to leave, Fletcher's son
charged them with his jeep. Just before crashing into the Border Patrol cars, the
Fletcher boy came to a quick stop. He tried to jump out of the jeep and turn his
gun upon the closest officer, but was stopped when a new recruit aimed his pistol
at him and told him to "drop that gun," while old-timer Patrol Inspector Griffith
McBee cocked his pistol "and took aim at the spot between young Fletcher's eyes."[16]

It was a standoff between a defiant farm family and the U.S. Border Patrol. Between them sat eighteen unarmed and unpaid Mexican laborers. Young Fletcher
had a .45 automatic pistol, a 12-gauge automatic shotgun, and a .300 rifle loaded
in the front seat of his car, but he was outnumbered, and his father had yet to return from the house. Young Fletcher was not up to the battle and dropped his gun.
Fletcher senior soon arrived with more weapons, but he too conceded defeat when
surrounded by the well-armed officers. For that day, the Border Patrol had won,
but the Fletchers did not surrender.

When the Border Patrol filed obstruction of justice charges against them, the
Fletchers defended themselves by challenging the authority of the Border Patrol to
enter their farm without specific warrants of arrest, providing the first legal test to
a 1946 expansion in Border Patrol authority to "arrest any alien in the United States
in violation of any law or regulation made in pursuance of law regulating admission, exclusion or expulsion of aliens, and likely to escape before a warrant could
be obtained for his arrest."[17] Ranchers and farmers rallied around the Fletchers and
their cause. During the trial, the "court room was filled with spectators," particularly farmers, who had journeyed from as far as the Lower Rio Grande Valley to
support the Fletchers. The Lower Rio Grande Valley of Texas was the epicenter of
resistance. There, farmers and ranchers had recently organized the Ten-Dollar Club
to fund a letter-writing campaign to U.S. Congressmen against the Border Patrol.[18]
But others, including ex-Patrolman Egbert Crossett, came as well.

The crowd of farmers and ranchers was matched by Border Patrol officers from
along the line who also attended the trial. They supported the actions of their brother
officers and knew that if the Fletchers won the case, the Border Patrol would be
forced to retreat and submit to the will of employers in the region. All knew that
the Fletcher case was about the distribution of power over the development of immigration law enforcement in the U.S.-Mexico borderlands. Farmers, ranchers, and
Border Patrol officers packed the courtroom to hear the outcome. The Fletchers

lost. Not only were they charged $150 each for "interfering and impeding Border Patrol officers in the performance of their official duties," but the judge also affirmed the Border Patrol's authority to conduct raids upon farms and ranches near the border without first securing individual warrants for arrest.[19] The Border Patrol left the trial victorious. The farmers and ranchers had failed in their attempt to use the courts to trim back what some farmers had begun to describe as "a nasty, sprawling weed."[20]

Farmers and ranchers used a variety of methods to resist the changes in U.S. immigration law enforcement. The most belligerent threatened to use physical retaliation or hired armed guards to challenge, undermine, and intimidate Border Patrol officers. Many others stationed lookouts along the perimeter of their property to signal alarms or to yell "Patrol!" when Border Patrol vehicles entered the gates for a raid. The warnings allowed undocumented workers time to scatter and hide before officers could reach the fields.[21] When officers could not be turned back with force or evaded with lookouts, many chose "cursing, shouting, and threatening to hire armed guards, have us all transferred, put locks on gates, etc." as counterstrategies.[22] But, most of all, the region's elite flooded Border Patrol and congressional offices with complaints. In 1950, a storm of farmer and rancher complaints against the U.S. Border Patrol erupted in the borderlands. Anger that had been simmering since the mid-1940s exploded after Inspector Albert Quillin experimented with a new strategy that increased the ability of the Border Patrol to apprehend large numbers of Mexican nationals.

Albert Quillin was a new recruit in 1940. He was first stationed for two months in Laredo, Texas, before the Border Patrol sent him on a three-week detail to Alice, Texas, to work with "an old timer character, Charlie Rhyne."[23] Without much supervision and ignored by Rhyne, Quillin began testing new techniques for apprehending undocumented immigrants. "Quillin was young, imaginative, eager beaver, all kind of ways of doing undercover work and having informers. Charlie thought that that was a bunch of foolishness," explained retired officer Brad Thomas.[24] Charlie was accustomed to the old system of targeting migrants in transit, rather than at work—a method that rarely resulted in large apprehensions. According to Charlie, "If you just sat in the bus station in Alice . . . everybody in south Texas comes through this bus station at sometime or another."[25] Quillin, however, was of the rising generation of officers who, upon receiving instructions from the chief supervisor of the Border Patrol to increase apprehensions of Mexican nationals, devised new strategies.

"At 5 A.M., Tuesday, February 11" 1950, a detail of twelve patrolmen led by Albert Quillin took "two buses, one plane, one truck, a carryall, and . . . nine automobiles" and convened at a "point four miles east of Rio Hondo, Texas," where a miniature immigration station was established with typewriters and tables. The men split into two teams, and each team was given maps of the area and the instructions to "clean as well as possible a certain section" of "illegal aliens." The plane looked for aliens attempting to escape, while the buses were used to "haul . . . wets" to the border. About one hundred were apprehended and processed for deportation from the Rio Hondo area to Brownsville, Texas, where they would be deported into Mexico. The next day, this same detail moved on to Crossroads Gin near Los Fresnos, Texas, and raided farms until 561 "wets" were apprehended and deported. On the third day, this detail moved into San Benito, Texas, where they apprehended 264 and on the fourth and final day in San Benito, another 134.[26] In all, Quillin's detail apprehended more than one thousand undocumented laborers in four days of work.[27] Quillin's enhancements of the details model impressed Border Patrol officials, who introduced the strategy to Border Patrol stations throughout the southwest. Within two weeks of Quillin's raids, constant details of Border Patrol inspectors were "pounding away on these 'wets.'"[28] Quillin's model details were renamed "task forces" and then coordinated into multiple operations that struck throughout California and Texas. Officials named the new model of migration control Operation Wetback.[29]

By 1952, the Operation Wetback model was a well-funded strategy utilized by most Border Patrol stations throughout the southwest.[30] For example, at dawn on July 30, 1952, "Some 100 Border Patrolmen in trucks, cars equipped with radios, and airplanes, touched off a mass raid in the Russelltown area between Harlingen and Brownsville." By 8 A.M., the officers had apprehended more than three thousand Mexican nationals. By noon, total apprehensions for the day reached five thousand. "All through the morning, trucks and buses shuttled between huge tomato warehouses at Russelltown, used as a temporary detention camp, and the bridge at Hidalgo." At the bridge, the patrolmen handed the deportees the following note:

> You have entered the United States illegally and in violation of the laws of your land and also those of the United States. For this reason you are being returned to your homeland. If you return again illegally you will be arrested and punished as provided by law. . . . We understand that the life of a wetback is difficult. Wetbacks are unable to work for more than a few hours before they are apprehended and deported. Remember these words and transmit the news to your families and countrymen if you want to do them a favor.[31]

The deportees were then "escorted across the river" and "turned over to Mexican authorities and placed under military guard."[32] Mexican authorities had built a "wire-enclosed detention camp" to hold the deportees until they could be placed on trains with armed guards and transported to the interior of Mexico.[33]

The Operation Wetback model blended the aggressive targeting of persons of Mexican origin in the United States with mass deportations into the interior of Mexico. Supported by an increase in personnel in the U.S.-Mexico border region and by improved equipment, such as radios and planes, the model boosted the number of annual apprehensions. Between 1950 and 1953, U.S. Border Patrol apprehensions almost doubled from 469,581 to 839,149. The number of Mexican immigrants returned to Mexico as a percentage of the total number of forced removals from the United States increased from 79 percent to 96 percent in 1953. Again, although these statistics are often read as an indication that more Mexicans were illegally crossing into the United States, such innovations in Border Patrol practice along with the steady rate of repeat offenders make it difficult to decipher the actual volume of unsanctioned Mexican immigration. What is clear is that the Border Patrol was apprehending more Mexicans or the same Mexicans more times. The patrol's increased activity and efficiency enraged borderland employers, who felt they had lost control over the apprehension and forced removal of Mexico's unsanctioned workers. In response to the Border Patrol's 1950 innovations, complaints poured into the Border Patrol Central Office, across the desk of the INS commissioner, and into the district offices of state representatives. In their protests, farmers and ranchers rarely challenged the U.S. Border Patrol's basic mandate of migration control. Rather, they demanded that control over immigration law enforcement be returned to borderland communities.

One such example involved thirty-six residents of El Indio, Texas, who had held their complaints about local Chief Patrol Inspector Tom Karnes until they could do so no longer. In 1950, they sent a formal petition and protest to the Border Patrol Central Office in Washington, D.C. The El Indio residents complained, "Mr. Karnes has always been an extremely difficult man to deal with."[34] Karnes was not a local. He was transferred into El Indio in 1946 "or thereabouts," they explained, and immediately aggravated the community residents because "his attitude [was] one of sarcasm and truculence with all the local people, and [he seemed] to care nothing about the good will of the local people or their problems."[35] Most important, explained one local resident, Karnes "has been so efficient" in his apprehension of undocumented laborers "that our community has been hurt by that."[36] The El Indio residents wanted Karnes out of Maverick County, requesting that he be "transferred from the Indio Section of Maverick County, Texas, and some other official of the United States Immigration Service be put in his place."[37] The U.S. Border Patrol declined the request.

In contrast to the relatively polite request of the El Indio residents, some ranchers and farmers raged against the realignment of power created and symbolized by the delocalization of migration control. They had built empires based upon controlling land, water, and the mobility of Mexican migrant workers, but the region's agribusiness elite was losing its grip. Economic diversification and the expansion of federal government into the southwest in the postwar era each challenged the reign of agribusinessmen in the borderlands. The inability to dominate the flow of labor migration and, more broadly, the loss of influence over the various mechanisms of authority in the region represented and fostered the decline of the agribusinessmen's world. Grasping for the past, prominent farmers such as Bill Allison, from Marfa, Texas, challenged the authority of the U.S. Border Patrol.[38] In the summer of 1951, Allison had taken three of his workers to the bus depot to buy a ticket for one of the workers to go home to Mexico for a short visit. While he went inside to purchase the ticket, the three men remained in the car. Border Patrol inspector Bassham saw three men of Mexican appearance in the car and began to question them about their immigration status. Allison soon returned and demanded to know what authority Bassham had to question his workers, given that he had no evidence that the men had entered the country illegally. Despite Allison's protests, Bassham completed his investigation, found the three men to be in the United States legally, and then replied, according to Allison, "In case you are not completely satisfied about this, I want you to know there's not a goddam thing you can do about it."[39]

Allison was enraged and "resented such treatment on the part of a Border Patrolman."[40] Relations had always been complicated between farmers, ranchers, and the patrolmen who policed their workforce, but Bassham seemed to have no regard for the farmer's position, and others in the area had also grown increasingly frustrated with Bassham's disregard. So Allison "hunted up a rancher named Bennett and told him what had just happened."[41] In his conversation with Bennett, Allison said that he wanted the sheriff to "take the gun off Bassham and that then, 'a rancher and a Border Patrolman would have it out.'"[42] Perhaps, in days gone by, a fistfight or a shootout might have resolved this dispute, but Bennett wisely advised Allison that the local sheriff could not disarm a federal law-enforcement officer. Undeterred, Allison devised a new plan; he went to District Judge Alan Fraser and told him of "his trouble with Bassham." Judge Fraser heard Bassham's complaint and called the Border Patrol station in Marfa. Judge Fraser insisted that other local ranchers had similar complaints about Bassham and suggested that Bassham "be moved by transfer from Marfa."[43]

The INS district adjudication officer, Taylor C. Carpenter, investigated the complaint from the rancher and a district judge. During an interview, Allison warned Carpenter, "If Bassham continues in his attitude and his Gestapo ways, . . . the next time he jumps on [me] there will be trouble."[44] He directly threatened Bassham with physical retaliation, but he never clearly explained what Bassham and the Border Patrol could do to avoid violent confrontation with ranchers and farmers in Marfa. Another local rancher, Cherry Bryant, elaborated upon the situation. Bryant explained that Bassham "probably makes more apprehensions than anyone else."[45] Like Karnes, Bassham was too effective, too inflexible, and too unconcerned with the farmers' position. Cherry explained that Bassham "should be willing to 'live and let live,' meaning that when officers find 'wet' aliens on various ranches that are badly needed at that time, they should be willing to parole them to the rancher," as older officers had done, who "at times in the past paroled aliens to them."[46] But times in the past were gone, and the Border Patrol left Bassham in Marfa against the wishes of local ranchers and farmers.

Such incidents are examples of farmers seeking to regain local control over immigration law enforcement by filing complaints against the least flexible officers. But these ranchers and farmers had misidentified the source of the Border Patrol's new effectiveness. Details and the Operation Wetback model lay at the heart of the Border Patrol's increased effectiveness. The removal of individual officers from local stations would have offered only partial relief from the new era of immigration law enforcement. World War II had wiped the past away. Growers and the U.S. Border Patrol would have to find a resolution to their conflicts within the present mandates of immigration law enforcement. Until then, south Texas growers and the Border Patrol would continue to clash as officers relentlessly raided border farms, and growers protected their property with ingenuity, political influence, and force.

THE LOGIC OF RESISTANCE

South Texans believed their defiance was justified because the U.S. Border Patrol was attempting to unravel their lives. In places such as Brownsville and Hidalgo, growers maintained deep social, cultural, and economic commitments to utilizing undocumented Mexican labor, and they expected cooperation instead of interference from U.S. immigration law-enforcement officers. When the new recruits began raiding and refusing to parole workers to the custody of growers, they not only threatened the supply of undocumented workers but also significantly challenged the farmers' position of authority in the borderlands by intervening in the rhythms of migration and the lives of migrants. Therefore, although mass deportation created an atmosphere of fear among undocumented workers upon which growers capitalized, many Texans tended to regard the new era of aggressive immigration law enforcement as an unwanted shift in the world that they were struggling to maintain. So they cursed and shouted, booby-trapped their farm gates, placed lookouts along their property perimeters, hired armed guards, and even threatened to arm undocumented immigrants. But the officers kept on coming, threatening to undo their world by deporting their workers.[47] The farmers' struggle, some believed, was so monumental and fundamental that it reminded them of the battle between North and South during the U.S. Civil War.

"We had a large old 17-room farmhouse," and "we had quarters for the Mexicans in the back . . . three good houses, and then they made some *portales* for themselves," remembered D. C. Newton, whose family posted guards to warn of Border Patrol raids.[48] But one night in 1952, after everyone had gone to bed, he reported, "We heard motor noises, . . . and suddenly the whole farmhouse compound is lit up, and there's jeeps at the closure of every driveway to our house."[49] The Border

Patrol had entered slowly and quietly before flashing on their headlights, surprising everyone who was settling to sleep in the farmhouse, back quarters, and *portales*. "I was petrified," recalled Newton, who was a small child at the time. He saw "men running everywhere" and believed that the Border Patrol was "gonna come and take us all, everybody, take everybody, 'cause this is what I understood happened."[50] As he watched the Border Patrol officers search in the dark for undocumented Mexicans, his mother or older brother held him tight.

The officers did not find many undocumented migrants that night because Newton's eldest brother had already "run out" to "tell the Mexicans that the Border Patrol was here and to haul it, run south, or get into a tree."[51] By the time the officers reached the back houses that night, the migrants had scattered. Almost empty-handed, the "ranking officer" of the Border Patrol and other officers came into the Newton home. They entered Newton's parents' bedroom and began "shining the flashlights in my mother's eyes and my father's eyes telling them to 'Get up. We're gonna go out and find where your Mexicans are.'"[52] With his father in pajamas, his mother in a nightgown, and no one wearing any shoes, the officers forced the family out of the house while "pushing, physically pushing my mother in the back, pushing my father in the back and demanding [to know] where the wetbacks [were]."[53] Most of the workers had fled, including Newton's nanny, Lupe, for whom the officers claimed to be searching in particular. She had heard the arrival of the patrolmen and climbed out of the window on the second floor of the farmhouse, "rolled down onto the roof of the garage and [run] off to the southeast and was gone."[54] Although the Newtons believed they had outsmarted the Border Patrol by alerting the migrants to the raid, the head patrol inspector still led fifty-three apprehended workers away, saying, "See how you handle your groves now."[55]

Newton's father likened his family's struggle against the U.S. Border Patrol to the southern slaveholders' war with northern aggressors. With all the romantic paternalism of a southern slave owner, Newton's father believed that by taking away their workers, the "damn yankee Border Patrol" were "splitting up a household."[56] As he explained it to his son, the south Texans protected their homes, their families, their property, and their very way of life from the Border Patrol raids. He was the master, the Mexican illegals were equivalent to the black slaves, and together they formed a household, a system of labor relations, in a world of tightly bound intimacy and inequity. The Border Patrol threatened their household by reducing the farmer's control over Mexico's unsanctioned migrant workers. So, as the southerners had rebelled against intrusions upon their labor relations and plantation lives, the Newton family had to defend itself against the U.S. Border Patrol. Newton's brother took the lesson to heart. When the Border Patrol raided on another night, he stood in the family driveway with a shotgun aimed at the officers. Startled by the hostile twelve-year-old boy, the officers left the property and returned on another day.[57]

Newton's family story provides a glimpse into the world that his father and others fought to maintain by opposing the new era of U.S. immigration law enforcement. It was a world of unquestioned inequity between Anglo-American landholders and Mexican migrant workers: a world that agribusinessmen had paraded before Congress during the 1920s as evidence that unlimited Mexican immigration would profit American employers without influencing American culture, politics, and society. But the genocidal campaigns of racial purity during World War II had sufficiently discredited the language of racial hierarchies so that what Newton's father shared with his sons remained a private history of resistance. In contrast, the farmers' public pleas and protests against the changes in U.S. immigration law enforcement tended to call upon postwar commitments to human rights, American justice, and racial equality.

World War II and the Cold War fundamentally altered the politics of race within the United States, which had emerged from World War II as the self-proclaimed leader of the free world. Racial segregation, inequity, and violence within the United States, however, consistently and powerfully undermined the legitimacy of U.S. global leadership. Leaders of African, Asian, and South American nations were quite familiar with the problems of race in the United States and aggressively questioned the nation's ability to lead a world inhabited primarily by the so-called colored people that Anglo-Americans degraded and segregated within the United States. As countless journalists and politicians around the world observed, American justice fractured along lines of race.[58]

Under massive international pressure and facing an increasingly powerful social movement among African Americans, national leaders began to dismantle the systems of racial segregation that had long defined social, political, and economic relations in the United States. For example, in 1941, under pressure from African American labor activist A. Phillip Randolph, President Franklin Roosevelt issued Executive Order 8802, banning racialized employment discrimination in defense industries. Still, communities proved more resistant. Throughout the American south, local elites resisted change until African American activists, congressional legislation, and federal marshals left them with no other option. In the U.S.-Mexico borderlands, however, change came a bit sooner. Economic diversification forced the world that the agribusinessmen had built into retreat, and U.S. dependence upon the allegiance of neighbors reinvigorated the spirit of the Good Neighbor Policy during World War II, allowing the Mexican American middle-class and Anglo-American reformers to demand an end to anti-Mexican discrimination in the U.S.-Mexico borderlands.[59]

The rebellious farmers and ranchers deployed the Cold War discourse of human rights, good neighborliness, and racial equality to turn back the Border Patrol. In particular, farmers and ranchers began to argue that Mexicans were unfairly targeted for deportations. "Why the Mexicans?" asked a 1953 editorial in the

El Paso Times. "Without a doubt, hundreds of thousands of Europeans are in this country illegally," charged the newspaper's editor, who criticized the Border Patrol for "singling out . . . Mexican aliens and turning all the resources of the federal government into stopping them or rounding them up."[60] The ranchers and farmers who had built agricultural empires upon unequal social relations between Mexicano laborers and Anglo-American landholders, therefore, took the politically perceptive position that the U.S. Border Patrol was guilty of racial discrimination by targeting unsanctioned Mexican immigrants. Further, they argued, the systems of displacement—the buslifts, airlifts, and trainlifts—were "cruel," "inhuman," and "outrageous" practices that were nothing more than "trading in human misery."[61] Wages were lower in Mexico, and work was scarce; deportation to the interior, therefore, sentenced deportees to starvation or to forced labor for "cruel" Mexican employers.[62] When Border Patrol officers arrived at her door to deport her maid, Mrs. Esther Potts of Harlingen, Texas, followed the south Texas script by opposing the deportation of her "faithful femme sole, who came to this valley to get away from starvation" and an abusive husband in Mexico.[63] According to another south Texan, "these poor devils need the work, and they and their families are starving."[64] The jobs they offered Mexican workers, in other words, were acts of international kindness and hemispheric neighborliness toward a "safe, high-class people," who were not only "family men" but loyal and worthy refugees from poverty and tyranny. Mexican laborers, they argued, deserved sanctuary as laborers in the United States.[65] The Border Patrol, in their view, was guilty of damaging U.S. global legitimacy by committing acts of racial discrimination and fostering communism in Mexico. Further, they argued, the U.S. Border Patrol posed a threat to American citizens—Anglo and Mexican—who deserved equal protection under the law and the right to live free of unwarranted police attention.

C. B. Ray, executive manager of the Valley Farm Bureau [Texas], for example, recounted the following incident to the INS commissioner. "On Saturday of last week a resident of the Valley and his wife started into town to do their week's shopping. He is a citizen, approximately fifty years of age, and of Latin extraction," explained Ray.[66] The couple picked up a hitchhiker on the way into town and was then pulled over by a Border Patrol officer. According to Ray, the officer demanded that they provide proof of citizenship. When the hitchhiker admitted to being an undocumented immigrant, the Border Patrol officer threatened the couple with a fine or jail time for "transporting an alien."[67]

Ray was enraged by the incident. "Has it come to the point in this land of ours that one dares not let a brown-eyed man ride in his car?" he asked.[68] Mexican Americans were routinely pulled over for roadside interrogations in the Border Patrol's quest to identify and deport all undocumented Mexican nationals. However, Ray's complaint was not made only on behalf of Mexicanos. "How are we to judge at all times our actions so as to be on the safe side from Border Patrol questioning?" he asked.[69] Ray recognized that when he was alone, he was white and safe, but if he associated with those suspected of unsanctioned migration, he would be subject to Border Patrol interrogations when officers pulled him over to check the status of his associates. The traditional targeting of Mexicanos, he argued, trespassed upon the civil and constitutional rights of all Americans caught within the Border Patrol's net of surveillance. "Must we segregate ourselves from the society of these people," he challenged the INS commissioner, "or shall we continue to associate with the Garcias' and Gonzales'?"[70] Ray warned the commissioner, "Most of the people here are well aware of their legal responsibilities. They are also aware of their constitutional rights as citizens of the United States and resent deeply any encroachment upon these rights and are prepared to demand that an armed guard respect these rights."[71]

Opposing the U.S. Border Patrol's racial profiling tactics was an unexpected protest from south Texas farmers and ranchers, who had long since accepted Border Patrol practice as an additional mechanism for marginalizing the region's agricultural labor force. The farmers, however, drew upon powerful discourses, concerns, and anxieties of postwar America to legitimate their rebellion against the new era of U.S. immigration law enforcement.

Despite resistance, the Border Patrol continued to "pound away" in the borderlands. Apprehensions rose and outpaced the patrol's capacity to detain the number of people being arrested each year. The officers erected temporary detention centers in barns and flew three planeloads a day of Mexican nationals to places like San Luis Potosí, Guadalajara, and Durango, Mexico. But they needed more detention centers, more planes, and more officers to remove apprehended Mexican nationals from the United States. In 1953, in anticipation of a needed supplemental appropriation, Willard Kelly hired 240 additional officers for the south Texas area, made plans for two new detention centers, and arranged to purchase another plane. These preparations infuriated the farmers and ranchers of the Lower Rio Grande Valley.

The frequency of armed encounters between resistant farmers and the Border Patrol increased, and the tenor of rebellion escalated. One farmer "threatened to arm his wetback laborers against the border patrol, threatening 'there is liable to be a couple of dead border patrolmen.'"[72] Another threatened that "during my earlier years on the border, such governmental tactics would have strewn dead border patrolmen from Brownsville to Laredo," and added that "the old American spirit is 'not dead, but sleepeth.'" He predicted that "if the present situation is permitted to continue, some high-handed patrolman will sooner or later invade the premises of a hot-tempered farmer and be carried out."[73] Death-threats against patrolmen became common. Farmers and ranchers lobbied their Congressmen to "turn back" the Border Patrol and turn down the supplemental appropriation request before anyone got hurt. They did not lobby on their behalf, they explained, but for the thousands of Mexican immigrants who were victims of the Border Patrol's "cheap vindictiveness—a great hunger to rule or ruin; to control, to govern—anything to carry a point, reckless of the consequences to the poor workmen which they herd around as cattle."[74]

Farmers and ranchers condemned the proposed detention center as a "concentration camp" and a "Korean-type wire stockade" that was a "contradiction to our good neighbor policy."[75] The detention center was more evidence of the Border Patrol's "gestapo" tactics, they argued. But the airlifts were even worse. It was "inhumane" to deport Mexican nationals to the interior of Mexico, decried ranchers and farmers, and the local press routinely ridiculed Border Patrolmen and their airlift as "Operation Squander."[76]

The ranchers and farmers pressured their elected representatives, and the Senate vetoed the Border Patrol's supplemental appropriation. The valley's successful campaign against the appropriation meant that "some 240 eligible border patrolmen who had reported for duty will be sent home at their own expense," according to Willard Kelly, who added that "they came from all parts of the U.S., some with their families."[77] The loss of the additional funding was a significant blow to the Border Patrol in their mounting battle against valley farmers and ranchers. The Border Patrol had won the right to use aggressive tactics, but lacked sufficient funding to implement its new tactics. Similarly, in 1952, valley farmers had participated in a successful lobby against a measure to criminalize the employment of unauthorized immigrants.[78] Underfunded for its massive mandate, the Border Patrol needed a new strategy against the ranchers and farmers who protested that "the whole trouble is that we have far too many officers assigned to this immediate locality."[79]

One month after losing the supplemental appropriation, Chief Kelly announced the Border Patrol's "withdrawal from the Rio Grande Valley to a 'new defense' line 10 miles to the north of Kingsville, Falfurrias, and Hebbronville."[80] Rather than fight a losing battle in the Lower Rio Grande Valley, the Border Patrol decided to pull out of the area, because "with limited forces we can best control the wetback invasion at the line farther north."[81] But if the Border Patrol intended the withdrawal to persuade valley farmers to desist, they miscalculated. Farmers declared that the Border Patrol was trying to "bring us to our knees," but vowed to "fight until hell freezes over."[82] Supportive of valley growers, Congressman Lloyd Bensten dismissed the Border Patrol's plan as a "scare campaign."[83] Many growers, however, welcomed the proposed pullout, hoping that with the withdrawal, life and labor in the Valley could "be like old times."[84] But there would be no simple return to the old days when "the immigration officials [had] not bothered the 'wetbacks' a great deal when they were in the field harvesting crops."[85] INS supervisors called off Chief Kelly's withdrawal from the south Texas region: the farmers and the Border Patrol would have to resolve their conflicts; each side, in the end, would have to compromise.

Support by the local press guaranteed that the ranchers' and farmers' rebellion remained front-page news, but cracks in agribusiness hegemony did not allow their voices to dominate. Before World War II, the federal government had maintained a minimal presence in the Texas-Mexico borderlands, and the federal officers of the Border Patrol operated under local control. But with economic expansion and a creeping federal authority in local politics, the borderlands' established leaders lost significant control over their communities. New political interests had emerged, not only in border enforcement, but in the borderlands. Businesses that had developed in connection with the economic diversification of World War II and the Cold War did not depend upon undocumented labor. Mexican Americans who demanded increased border enforcement were gaining a new political voice. The battles erupting between borderland growers and the Border Patrol represented broader changes sweeping across the borderlands' power structures.[86]

Farmers and ranchers wanted a return to "old times." Access to undocumented Mexican immigrants was the foundation of those times, and they used everything in their arsenal. They met officers at their gates with shotguns. They ostracized officers in the community. They charged the Border Patrol with violating American freedoms at home, and they accused officers of fostering communism abroad. But the farmers and ranchers could not trim back the "nasty weed" that the Border Patrol had become. The politics and practices of migration control now extended far beyond the U.S.-Mexico borderlands. Despite all of the farmers' protests, the work of the U.S. Border Patrol could not be rolled back to an earlier day when local officers enforced federal law according to local customs and interests.

The south Texas rebellion made the work of Border Patrol officers extremely difficult along the migration corridor that their supervisors identified as the priority hot zone for U.S. immigration law enforcement. The daily assaults damaged morale among officers who never knew what to expect when they raided a local farm, entered a community restaurant, or attended a community event. What was at stake, however, was the viability and legitimacy of the Border Patrol's basic organizing principle: the focus upon policing unsanctioned Mexican immigration. The agribusinessmen's motives may have been entirely suspect, but the basic organizing principle of U.S. immigration law enforcement was under attack. Chapter 8 tells the story of how the U.S. Border Patrol fought back against the farmers' rebellion to restore the goodwill, friendship, and legitimacy that had passed away with the death of the old-timers' patrol. They turned the farmers' slaveholder stories into an abolitionist narrative that defended the project of aggressively policing Mexicans and, with both coercion and compromise, the Border Patrol won the support of the south Texas rebels and stabilized its position in the U.S.-Mexico borderlands.

PART THREE

Operation Wetback and Beyond

Mexican families await deportation, circa 1954. U.S. Border Patrol Official Photograph, File No. 108–6. U.S. Immigration Border Patrol, McAllen, Texas. Courtesy of the National Border Patrol Museum—El Paso, Texas.

BY THE EARLY 1950S, U.S. Border Patrol officials readily confessed to a crisis of control along the U.S.-Mexico border. A little more than two million Mexican men entered the United States as legal braceros, but many others, quite often the men, women, and family groups categorically excluded from the Bracero Program, entered the U.S. illegally. Amid the Border Patrol's crisis of control, the south Texas rebellion represented a crisis of consent among influential growers who refused to concede to the new era of migration control. The recalcitrant farmers were few, but they leveled damaging indictments against the Border Patrol and its focus upon policing persons of Mexican origin. The U.S. Border Patrol stabilized its position in the U.S.-Mexico borderlands by confronting the interrelated crises of control and consent with a campaign now known as Operation Wetback of 1954. Typically, Operation Wetback is interpreted as a mass deportation campaign targeting Mexican nationals, but Border Patrol officials entered the summer of 1954 with intentions reaching far beyond mass deportation. In particular, officers sought an end to the crises of consent and control along the U.S.-Mexico border. Mass deportation, or at least the threat of mass deportation, was a means to reaching these ends.

After the close of Operation Wetback of 1954, U.S. Border Patrol apprehension rates dropped dramatically. Whereas the chaotic decade between 1944 and 1954 had been known as the "wetback era," the years after 1954 were quiet. In these years, Border Patrol practice could have headed in many directions, but resources remained clustered in the U.S.-Mexico border region, and Border Patrol officials reinvented immigration control as a site of crime control. The explicit turn toward crime control marked a momentous shift in the development of the U.S. Border Patrol. While Border Patrol officers had once pursued U.S. immigration law enforcement at the intersection of policing unwanted foreigners and undocumented workers, the linguistic turns, strategy innovations, and policy priorities of the post-wetback era reconfigured daily practices and powerfully redefined the meaning of migration control in the United States. Taking shape at the dawn of the carceral era—a time when crime and punishment were emerging as primary ways of understanding and managing social problems—the Border Patrol's explicit recoding of migration control as a site of policing crime and punishing criminals made the work of the immigration law-enforcement officers at the nation's borders resonate with the discourses and panics regarding social order and control in late twentieth-century America. In other words, by linking migration control to the problem of crime, Border Patrol officers and INS officials bound their efforts in the borderlands to an increasingly central dynamic of American culture, politics, and governance. Part 3 tells the story of how U.S. Border Patrol officials transformed the making and meaning of migration control in the borderlands by deporting the "wetbacks" in 1954 and, in the days and decades that followed, battling the criminals who dared to return.

8

The Triumphs of '54

In June of 1954, the U.S. Border Patrol announced that it would soon launch its most aggressive and innovative Operation Wetback campaign to date. The U.S. attorney general and the recently hired commissioner of the INS, retired general Joseph Swing, chronicled the campaign as it unfolded. Beginning at dawn on June 10, 1954, hundreds of U.S. Border Patrol officers on detail from throughout the country set up roadblocks in California and western Arizona, where they nabbed almost eleven thousand unsanctioned Mexican immigrants in the next seven days. In the following three months, Border Patrol task forces swept through south Texas, Chicago, Illinois, and the Mississippi Delta in search of unsanctioned Mexican immigrants. By October, Commissioner Swing proudly proclaimed that more than one million unsanctioned immigrants, mostly Mexican nationals, had been removed from the United States. The "era of the wetback," he declared, was over. As described here, however, Operation Wetback of 1954 never really happened.

At the heart of the Border Patrol's "big push" of 1954 was what Swing described as a detail of 750 specially trained officers. The 750 officers reported to have taken part in Operation Wetback of 1954, however, were actually only a group of about 378 officers assigned to overtime.[1] Further, in contradiction to the descriptions of the detail as a group of well-trained paramilitary men, the officers received no special training for the campaign and used no new techniques. As one officer with many years experience in the patrol explained to Commissioner Swing, the "special operation . . . employed no novel plans of operation. Line operations, roadblocks, mop-up crews, and removal of aliens from the border were means that have been employed in this district throughout the years."[2] Operation Wetback of 1954, therefore, was little more than a larger than usual deployment of the Border Patrol's familiar and failing tactics of migration control.

TABLE 4 Principal activities and accomplishments of the U.S. Border Patrol for the years ended June 30, 1945–1954

	1945	1946	1947	1948	1949	1950	1951	1952	1953	1954
Total number of persons apprehended	70,639	100,785	194,954	193,852	289,400	469,581	510,355	531,719	839,149	1,035,282
Number of deportable aliens located	69,164	99,591	193,657	192,779	288,253	468,339	509,040	528,815	835,311	1,028,246
Number of Mexican nationals apprehended	N/A	N/A	N/A	N/A	N/A	N/A	N/A	N/A	N/A	1,022,267
Number of persons apprehended, Mexican border region	64,368	92,107	183,832	180,774	279,379	459,289	501,713	517,805	827,440	1,022,374
Total number of persons questioned	4,161,571	4,112,966	4,826,442	5,529,685	6,618,056	7,223,069	8,606,693	8,777,886	9,543,005	8,949,130
Number of persons questioned, Mexican border region	2,563,481	2,674,943	3,502,212	4,354,301	5,487,811	6,248,387	7,707,394	7,958,225	8,800,379	8,262,268
Value of all seizures	$78,725	$111,213	$153,299	$234,125	$222,022	$171,439	$261,160	$323,718	$416,903	$952,715

SOURCE: Data compiled from principal activities and accomplishments of the U.S. Border Patrol, *Annual Reports of the Immigration and Naturalization Service, Fiscal Years Ending June 30, 1945–1956, 1962* (Washington, DC: GPO).

Most important, though, is the issue of the more than one million deportations that Commissioner Swing credited to the summer of 1954. Scholars have rightly questioned the veracity of Border Patrol statistics during the summer of 1954.[3] Swing and others generously rounded up the Border Patrol's daily and monthly apprehension reports during the summer of 1954. But the statistical sleight of hand was also a matter of periodization. The one million deportations attributed to Operation Wetback of 1954 occurred during fiscal year 1954, which ran from July 1, 1953, to June 30, 1954. Only twenty days of Operation Wetback of 1954 took place during that year. In those twenty days, the Border Patrol apprehended, at most, 33,307 persons.[4] The more than one million apprehensions recorded for fiscal year 1954, therefore, were actually made before Operation Wetback of 1954 began on June 10 of that year. Fiscal year 1955, which included the largest portion of the 1954 summer campaign, registered only 221,674 apprehensions of Mexican nationals— the smallest number since 1948. Rather than a surge in apprehensions, the summer of 1954 saw a massive drop in U.S. Border Patrol activities (see table 4).

Understanding that Operation Wetback of 1954 was not the "big push" that Commissioner Swing proclaimed it to be does not diminish the importance of the campaign. During the summer of 1954, the U.S. Border Patrol triumphed over the crises of control and consent that had erupted along the U.S.-Mexico border during the mid-1940s. Since 1944, apprehensions along the U.S.-Mexico border had increased exponentially, which suggested that the Border Patrol had lost control over the volume of unsanctioned Mexican immigration. Further, the Border Patrol had lost the support of south Texas ranchers and growers who objected to the patrol's new, aggressive tactics along the border. In the years after 1954, however, apprehensions dropped dramatically, and the rebellious south Texans quieted down. These were the triumphs of 1954, and they were not won with the raids, deportations, and demonstrations of force so often attributed to that summer. Instead, the U.S. Border Patrol ultimately triumphed over the crises of control and consent through negotiation, compromise, and, most important, retreat. This chapter explores how the end of the so-called wetback era had less to do with deporting unsanctioned Mexican immigrants and more to do with how the Border Patrol enforced U.S. immigration laws. The chapter highlights the critical importance of immigration law-enforcement practices in the making and unmaking of the problem of illegal immigration in the U.S.-Mexico borderlands.

ILLEGALS, ILLEGALITY, AND AMERICAN SOCIETY

The summer of 1954 had been in the making for many years. The U.S. Border Patrol had begun its aggressive campaign against undocumented Mexican immigration ten years earlier. Task forces, roadblocks, and an uncompromising focus upon deporting undocumented Mexican immigrants had characterized its work since the early 1940s, and apprehensions of unsanctioned Mexican immigrants sky-rocketed. The farmers' rebellion began when the Special Mexican Deportation Parties first arrived at their gates in the spring of 1944. The U.S. Border Patrol fought back against both the rising numbers of illegal crossings and the farmers' rebellion. The Border Patrol combated the crises of control and consent that emerged from aggressive immigration law enforcement in the U.S.-Mexico borderlands by tightening the screws and, in 1950, introduced the Operation Wetback strategy throughout the southwest. The result was nothing but constant conflicts with farmers who challenged the validity of Border Patrol practices, migrants who resisted arrest, and a mushrooming apprehension rate that seemed to have no foreseeable limit. Against charges of inhumanity and indications of failure, Border Patrol officials and officers engaged in a battle to define the meaning of migration control in the U.S.-Mexico borderlands.

To construct a counternarrative of migration control, Border Patrol officers drew upon a dependable source of support, the Mexican American middle class. In recent years, social conditions for middle-class Mexicanos in the borderlands had improved, but the struggle for full economic and social integration was far from over.[5] Their newly won advances were tentative, and Mexican American civil rights organizations continued to fight to secure additional rights and protect those already won. Employment, housing, and health care were important issues to leading Mexican American civil rights organizations, but few issues eclipsed the centrality of illegal immigration. Key Mexican American political leaders continued to believe that Mexican immigration, particularly unauthorized Mexican immigration, "materially retarded our assimilation."[6] With their continued opposition to the "most serious effects of the wetback invasion upon the life of the American of Mexican descent," representatives of leading Mexican American civil rights organizations supported the Border Patrol's efforts to end unsanctioned Mexican immigration.[7] The patrol found few reservoirs of support as deep and constant as the growing Mexican American middle-class, for whom the new aggressiveness without direct physical brutality was a long-awaited development in U.S. immigration control.

Like the middle class, members of the Mexican American working class could often support increased border enforcement and immigration control. "The legal residents can not live under the wetback wages and compit [sic] with them," explained Drineo González in a 1952 letter to President Lyndon B. Johnson.[8] And the National Farm Labor Union (NFLU) had stepped up its opposition to unsanctioned Mexican immigration after managers used both braceros and undocumented workers to break a strike at the Di Giorgio Fruit Farm in California in 1947. Four years later, during a 1951–52 strike by cantaloupe pickers in the Imperial Valley, union members "went out and arrested the wetbacks who were living in caves and on the ditches and we took them to the border patrol," recalled Juanita

García of the NFLU.[9] Union members also patrolled the border and turned back an estimated three thousand unsanctioned border crossers.[10] But the NFLU was an unpredictable ally because its members' loyalties lay explicitly with U.S. workers rather than with U.S. law enforcement. Dr. Ernesto Galarza headed the NFLU in California and balanced a vigorous opposition to unsanctioned Mexican immigration with advocacy for all migrant workers, regardless of immigration status. Galarza was quick to defend undocumented workers who had been swindled or unfairly treated by employers, coyotes, or the U.S. Border Patrol. Although Galarza worked with the patrol by supplying information regarding which farms employed unsanctioned migrant workers, he did not hesitate to report incidents of abuse on the part of Border Patrol officers. For example, in March 1954 Galarza informed the Mexican consul in Calexico, California, that construction at the INS detention center in nearby El Centro, California, was being completed by detainees without remuneration.[11]

In contrast to the support of farm workers and union members, the support offered by the Mexican American middle class was grounded in the politics of whiteness, nationalism, and citizenship rather than class, and, overall, it offered a more steadfast source of support for the Border Patrol's project of policing unsanctioned Mexican immigration. As the farmers disparaged the Border Patrol, leading Mexican American activists defended the agency as "maligned, misunderstood, and underappreciated" and described its officers as "conscientious and interested in doing a good job."[12] The Border Patrol welcomed their support and confidently asserted that "their interests and our interests are mutual."[13] The barrage of farmers' complaints had forced the Border Patrol to cultivate support from any person or organization that would champion their cause, even from those they did not hire. Of the 331 new recruits attending the Border Patrol Training School during the summer of 1941, none had a Spanish surname. The Spanish-surnamed officers listed on Border Patrol rosters in 1942 were Pete Torres, Manuel Uribe, and Thomas García, the same officers who had joined the organization in the 1920s. Although Torres, Uribe, and García had been in the Border Patrol for many years and were earning the maximum salary, not one of these old-timers served in an official supervisory position. Almost a decade later, in 1951, probationary Patrol Inspectors Joseph J. Samora and Martin S. Doria filed complaints against the Border Patrol. Doria argued that "prejudices of officers with whom, and under whom, he worked in the Laredo Sector of the San Antonio District" prevented him from being able to "perform satisfactorily as an officer."[14] Although Mexican American political organizations typically aggressively opposed employment discrimination against Mexican Americans, they avoided antagonizing the organization that held the authority to deport unwanted and undocumented Mexican nationals and, instead, helped the Border Patrol to craft a counternarrative to the ranchers' and farmers' accusations of racism.[15]

In the early 1950s, one of the Border Patrol's most vocal partners was the American G.I. Forum, a Mexican American veterans' organization. In 1953, the American G.I. Forum published, *What Price Wetbacks?* an investigative study coauthored with the Texas State Federation of Labor (AFL) that examined the economic and social costs of illegal labor and the Bracero Program in Texas. Ed Idar Jr. and Andrew McClellan conducted the study with the cooperation of U.S. Border Patrol officers, who convoyed the investigators to migrant camps and farms along the Texas-Mexico border. With the Border Patrol's assistance, Idar and McClellan gathered evidence to challenge the Texas growers who exploited Cold War rhetoric, paranoia, and anxiety to defend their extralegal employment practices.[16]

Idar, McClellan, and the Border Patrol revealed the oppressive underside of the growers' democracy and free-labor theory. By revealing the crowded "squalor" of migrant housing, the contaminated drinking wells of migrant camps, and the poverty wages paid by Texas employers, they punctured the farmers' narrative of democracy, freedom, and labor in the borderlands. "One moment they were free citizens of the Republic of Mexico," explained Idar and McClellan, but after crossing illegally into the United States, Mexican nationals became "fugitives without recourse to the protection of the laws of either of the two great neighbor nations on the Rio Grande."[17] The historical synonym for the conditions of illegality in the United States, they argued, was the problem of slavery that many Americans thought had been abolished a century earlier. The "threat of deportation hanging over the worker's head," Idar and McClellan explained, turned migrant workers into "virtual slave[s]."[18]

The officers of the U.S. Border Patrol agreed with Idar and McClellan's assessment. Farmers accused officers of being heartless law enforcers with neither pity nor compassion for the people that they deported, but, according to the officers, it was the farmers themselves who lacked humanity. In pursuit of unsanctioned migrants, officers of the Border Patrol found men, women, and children living in wretched conditions. "Wets were housed in every conceivable kind of shelter; ramshackle abandoned old houses, barns, sheds, chicken coops, abandoned automobile bodies, caves dug into canal banks, and tents," explained one officer.[19] If workers complained, employers "kept these people in line by threatening to report them to La Patrulla or La Migra."[20] In one case, officers raided a farm and found migrants who "told us of having been forced to stay there and to work even though they had been abused and underpaid."[21] The migrants, one officer recalled, "wanted to go home, wanted to quit, wanted to leave, and were not allowed to."[22] The arrival of the Border Patrol and the migrants' arrest for the crime of illegal entry into the United States, therefore, served as a back-handed liberation from an abusive employer who was later convicted of "some statute relating to slavery."[23] In response to the farmers' characterization of the Border Patrol as a "nasty sprawling weed" of Gestapo tactics and racist intentions, the officers argued that aggressive migration control was all that stood between slavery and freedom. Force, they argued, was necessary to free slaves from masters in the U.S.-Mexico borderlands. In this, Border Patrol officers imagined undocumented Mexican workers as poor, abused, and systematically oppressed workers and considered themselves to be liberation fighters—aggressive, efficient, and uncompromising—justified by their contributions to American democracy.

The narrative of democracy and deliverance littered Border Patrol correspondence records during the early 1950s. In memo after memo, officers shared stories about abuses by farmers, who held migrants captive, paid poverty wages, and provided unsanitary living conditions. Although officers increasingly noted the rebelliousness of those they apprehended, officers generally agreed that the typical illegal immigrant was an unauthorized Mexican worker, quite often arriving in a family group that was simple-minded, backward, pathetic, and oppressed. The Border Patrol's job rested somewhere between protecting the simple-minded and exploited workers from abusive farmers and protecting American society from the dangerously backward "wetback."

In Border Patrol correspondence records, the archetype of the unsanctioned migrant was represented by a composite character referred to in a press release as José García. García was a twenty-five-year-old man from a "small town" in Zacatecas, Mexico, who had heard stories of the "marvels of life in Yankee land."[24] Needing work, José resolved to go north. He walked forty miles to the nearest railroad, which delivered him to Ciudad Juárez, where he joined a group of men who were planning to cross illegally into the United States "in the desert above the Mtn with the cross."[25] The group left Juárez just before dark and walked for hours out into the desert until they saw the border. After they had stepped across the border, "suddenly from out of the sands bounds a little jeep."[26] The Border Patrol had detected their entry. The immigrants were "herded" into the jeep and returned to Juárez. José was left without any money and alone, but felt lucky that he had escaped forced return to the interior of Mexico.[27]

Back in Juárez, the press release continued, José heard rumors of easy entry and plentiful work in the Lower Rio Grande Valley, so he spent his last few pennies on bus fare to a Mexican town across from the Rio Grande Valley. The bus driver directed José toward the Rio Grande at the border and suggested safe places to cross. When darkness fell, José carefully crossed the river, then walked for miles until he saw "a light on a high pole in a farm yard."[28] Back in Mexico, someone had told him "the light is a sign that the farmer is looking for cotton pickers."[29] He slept in the grass and awoke early in the morning to pick cotton.

The Texas farmer offered to pay José $1 for every hundred pounds of cotton, but first José had to buy a cotton sack and some food from the farmer. One dollar per hundred was about half of what José had expected to earn; he had heard that pickers earned $2 to $2.50 per hundred in New Mexico. However, he was told that he could not leave the farm without the risk of running into the Border Patrol and being deported to the interior of Mexico. Without no money and few options, José stayed with this farmer and quickly plummeted into debt before ever beginning to pick.[30]

The farmer only allowed the workers to pick the bolls that were "fully opened."[31] The field was packed with other undocumented workers from Mexico, and that day José only picked 160 pounds of cotton. This amount earned him $1.60 for his labor—not enough to pay for the cotton sack or the food. That night José went to sleep with 20–25 other workers in a "dilapidated adobe shack" that was a safe distance from the "big white ranch house." During the night, a migrant mother gave birth "in a corner of one of the rooms." Over the next days and weeks, José and the other workers returned to the field to pick cotton. Those who fell behind in picking were taken by the Border Patrol, and the foreman "warn[ed] that the same fate [would] happen to them if they [did] not work hard and grumble[d] at the wages."[32]

For many officers, José García represented the thousands of Mexicans that they encountered during their raids upon farms, ranches, and migrant camps. He was a pitiful character whom they freed from the oppressive grasp of borderland farmers and ranchers. Alongside him were women and children, mothers and babies born into the tight corners and dark shadows of illegality. Against the farmers' indictments and despite their complaints, the Border Patrol slowly developed "liberating José" into a new philosophy of immigration law enforcement in the borderlands. Every day officers used raids and airlifts, fences and concertina wire, and deportations and boatlifts to keep recalcitrant farmers and ranchers from thrusting the southwest into a slave past. "Whatever the total answer may be," explained one Border Patrol officer, "know that the chronic user of this labor will recognize no authority as regards illegal immigration unless he is forced to do so."[33] As the troubles of the early 1950s demonstrated, the battle would be difficult because "the chronic user has a conscience similar to that of the pre-civil war slave owner. He is a overlord of all that he surveys and considers his right to the peon labor as practically a divine one."[34] Farmers may have opposed them, and Mexicans may have resisted them, but Border Patrol officers felt that their mission justified them because—as was true during the struggle against southern slave owners—only force would bring an end to the resurrection of slavery in the fields.

The Border Patrol's abolitionist narrative directly confronted the farmers' public accusations that by aggressively policing unsanctioned Mexican immigrants, the Border Patrol committed racism at home and fostered communism abroad. According to the Border Patrol, undocumented Mexican immigrants were not refugees but slaves, and their deportation closed a dangerous loophole to the past— one that farmers denied in public but often embraced in private. The Border Patrol's response to the farmers' challenge framed migration control as a site of interrupting discredited, undemocratic, and illegal labor relations and emphasized a depiction of unsanctioned Mexican immigrants as oppressed workers rather than unwanted foreigners or even criminals. The Border Patrol defended its practices by arguing that the problem of illegal immigration in the borderlands was, at heart, a social problem that threatened American democracy through its creation of labor conditions and relations similar to those of southern slavery. Rather than turning to a discourse of national sovereignty, nativism, or law and order—all of which sim- mered beneath the surface—the officers of the Border Patrol privileged an under- standing of migration control as a matter of workers, employers, and the unequal social relations between them when laborers illegally crossed into the United States.

Still, in their efforts to defend aggressive migration control in the U.S.-Mexico borderlands, Border Patrol officials did not rely solely upon their abolitionist nar- rative. At the same time that officers wrote about the poor and oppressed workers that they arrested in the fields of south Texas, officials in California argued that the unsanctioned Mexican immigrant was a drain upon public resources and, at times, a menace to public safety. Border Patrol officials, for example, worked with sher- iffs, district attorneys, and city police to compile information on the number of crimes committed by unsanctioned Mexican immigrants. In 1953, the U.S. Bor- der Patrol assisted the district attorney of Imperial County in southern California in preparing a study for U.S. Attorney General Hebert Brownell entitled, "Wet- back Mexican Problems in California."[35] Bitler argued that the desperate and des- titute migrants who entered the United States illegally committed crimes of need and want.[36] In search of food and shelter "they commit various depredations throughout the county . . . such as burglarizing farm houses, stealing fruits and veg- etables to survive."[37] Further, he explained, "upon the heels of the vast army of wet- backs . . . is the problem of prostitution" because "destitute females from Mexico" crossed into the United States to service migrant Mexican workers.[38] Among them, venereal disease spread rampantly. While Bitler believed that "the Mexican labor- ers are, as a whole, law-abiding, tractable, docile persons, and as a class, not in- herently criminal," he argued that unsanctioned Mexican immigrants threatened the homes and health of American communities along the border.[39] Hidden among the poor workers, in other words, were social threats that demanded ag- gressive policing by the U.S. Border Patrol.

Similar to the collaboration between Border Patrol officers and local law-en- forcement officials in southern California, Border Patrol officers working out of the San Antonio and McAllen stations assisted Lyle Saunders and Olen Leonard to conduct research for their 1951 publication, *The Wetback in the Lower Rio Grande Valley*, a project dedicated to exploring the negative social impacts of unsanctioned Mexican immigration into south Texas. Officers guided the authors on tours of the Lower Rio Grande region, showing them where and how unsanctioned migrants lived and demonstrating the difficulties of migration control by allowing the authors to witness raids. In their study, Saunders and Lyle provided a well-researched examination of the process of unsanctioned migration, the profile of Mexican nationals who engaged in unsanctioned migration, and an analysis the social, political, and economic impact upon south Texas of hosting a large population of illegal immigrants. On the basis of an extensive review of INS and Border Patrol records, interviews with migrants detained at INS detention facilities, and a historical analysis of the problem of poverty in Mexico, Lyle and Saunders provided a detailed examination of who migrated illegally from Mexico and why, creating what they called "the profile of the wetback."[40] Most unsanctioned Mexican migrants, they concluded, were male, poor, rural, unskilled, and abused workers.

Saunders and Leonard's profile corresponded with the public position that the Border Patrol had taken in defense of its aggressive deportation of Mexican nationals from the borderlands. Border Patrol work, they argued, liberated the virtual slaves and thus salvaged American democracy. But Border Patrol officers had their own stories to tell, even if only to each other, about the profile of the wetback and the meaning of their work. After the publication of *The Wetback in the Lower Rio Grande Valley*, Patrol Inspector Earl Garrison translated the study into a series of cartoons. Garrison was an amateur sketch artist who shared his creations with his fellow officers. Throughout the years, patrol officers posted his cartoons in their lockers, shared them in their correspondence, and (in recent years) published them in a newsletter for retired officers. Garrison's sketches provide unique insight into the ways that Border Patrol officers understood their work and the people that they policed because, as one officer recalled, the cartoons "captured the frustrations, joys, and philosophies of journeymen patrol inspectors."[41]

Garrison's *Illustrated Version of the Wetback in the Lower Rio Grande* opens with a caricature entitled "The Profile of the Wetback," showing the facial profile of a bronze-skinned male with a large nose and scruffy hair. What Garrison's rendering of Leonard and Saunder's research exemplifies is that while much had changed since the early years of the Border Patrol—the old-timers had lost their dominance, and new national and cross-national concerns shaped everyday practices—the journeymen officers' specific focus upon policing poor, male, and markedly brown-skinned Mexican workers remained. Border Patrol officers, in other words, continued to police a nuanced bundle of class, complexion, gender, and national origins. But Garrison's sketches did mark an important shift in the patrol's policing of Mexican Browns in the early 1950s. Most important, Garrison's "Profile of the Wetback" is followed by a series of images that focused upon the women, children, and families that Border Patrol officers increasingly encountered while on patrol in the bracero era. In sharp contradiction to the farmers' characterization of unsanctioned Mexican workers as industrious and much-needed male laborers and despite the Border Patrol's official narrative of liberating abused workers, Garrison's cartoons captured them in idle moments—drinking with friends, sitting by the road-side, and gathering in family groups. For example, one image from the *Illustrated Version of the Wetback in the Lower Rio Grande* portrays a family unit of a mother, father, and three children with their dog and chicken and towers of household goods. Contradicting the notion that Mexico's unsanctioned labor migrants were male so-journers who quickly, quietly, and easily returned to Mexico either voluntarily or through forced removal and deportation, this image sits above a quotation drawn from Saunders and Leonard's original text: "The return of entire families, particu-larly those with children, was often complicated by the fact that the family unit, par-ticularly if it had been here for some time, had acquired dishes, utensils, bedding, and other household articles too awkard [sic] or too heavy to be easily carried."[42]

While farmers and the Border Patrol engaged in a heated public debate regarding Mexican workers hanging in the balance between communism and liberation, such images revealed the untidy world of families and forced removal that officers con-fronted on a daily basis. Here, the abstractions of communism and liberation failed to register against the challenges of organizing the mass removal of family units and household goods instead of the seemingly simple return of sojourners to their homes south of the border. Still, as Garrison's caricatures of unsanctioned Mexi-can women as bare-footed and brown-skinned mothers with large breasts, wide hips, bright red lips, and long noses suggest, Border Patrol officers regarded fam-ily migration as a social problem, and experience taught them that their forced re-moval from the United States would not be easy.

Further, Garrison's cartoons explored the many facets of the varied interests in unsanctioned Mexican migrants that made it so difficult to catch them. In addi-tion to the farmers and ranchers who hired them, there were the numerous mer-chants and small-business owners who catered to unsanctioned migrants and the family members who protected their own when the legal distinctions between cit-izens, legal residents, and illegal immigrants zigzagged through their families. Ac-cording to Garrison's sketches, the targets of Border Patrol aggression were nei-ther deserving refugees, as represented by the farmers, nor the abused workers most often represented in the Border Patrol's abolitionist narrative. Rather, according to the journeymen officers, Mexico's unsanctioned migrants were more pathetic than pitiful and more socially embedded than suggested by widely held notions of temporary migrant workers. Border Patrol work was not so much a matter of reflex-ive law enforcement but a difficult job centered upon policing the complex social world in which unsanctioned Mexican immigration unfolded.

The Border Patrol's official and locker-room narratives of unauthorized immi-grants and migration control sustained officers against constant assaults from farm-ers and migrants alike. The farmers who opposed them were little more than slave drivers. The migrants who rebelled against them were not productive workers, but abused workers or idle families that comprised a social threat. Regardless of mounting resistance, in other words, aggressive migration control was a difficult—if not thankless—job that benefited American society and protected American communities. Yet few could deny that the Border Patrol seemed to be losing its battles in the borderlands. Border Patrol statistics suggested that each year more migrants crossed the border illegally. Overlooking the Border Patrol's greater efficiencies and capacities that resulted in the rising number of apprehensions, simplistic interpretations of Border Patrol statistics suggested that the ever-increasing number of apprehensions signaled the patrol's failure to effectively control the U.S.-Mexico border. At the same time, the south Texas rebels grew more agitated and vocal. The relationship between the patrol and the south Texas growers was, as one farmer described it, a "nightmare."[43] In 1953, U.S. Border Patrol officials made plans to bring the nightmare to an end: they would use military force to bring the belligerent farmers to their knees, eject the virtual slaves from the United States, and seal the border against all of the Mexican Browns that tried to return.

OPERATION CLOUD BURST OF 1953

On July 15, 1953, Harlon B. Carter of the U.S. Border Patrol sat down with Lieutenant General Joseph Swing and Adjunct General Jones. More than two decades had passed since Carter had killed young Ramón Casiano on the streets of Laredo. Unlike many old-timers who struggled to adjust, Carter adapted to the new patrol and thrived. By 1953, Carter was leading Border Patrol operations throughout the U.S.-Mexico borderlands.

Carter had convened the meeting with Generals Jones and Swing to request the assistance of the U.S. military and the National Guard to purge the nation of undocumented Mexican nationals and seal the U.S.-Mexico border. The Border Patrol's proposal was titled Operation Cloud Burst and consisted of three basic steps. First, an "anti-infiltration operation on or near the border" would seal the border with the assistance of 2,180 military troops. In addition to stationing troops along the border line, the Border Patrol planned to build fences along the areas of heavy illegal traffic. "Two metal picket barbed wire fences, eight feet high and eight feet apart, with rolls of 'concertina' wire in between and one roll of 'concertina' wire on top fence nearest Mexico," built several miles along the border, would form the fence. But previous experience had taught the Border Patrol that fenced areas still needed additional security. Therefore, the concertina fence would be reinforced by "officers in jeeps who will be directed to the scene of any attempted fence or canal crossing by observers in radio-equipped towers."[44]

Second, a "containment operation" would maintain roadblocks on all major roads leading from the southwest to the interior of the United States. These roadblocks would be used "to inspect traffic, including railroad traffic, for the purpose of detecting illegal entrants and to maintain safety patrols around the check points." The roadblocks were planned for strategic locations that would prevent aliens from fleeing to the interior of the nation when the "mopping up" operations— the third phase—began. The "mopping up" operations would be conducted in northern areas, such as San Francisco, where the task forces would raid designated locations, such as migrant camps or places of business. In the final phase of Operation Cloud Burst, officers would work with the Mexican government to airlift or trainlift apprehended Mexican nationals to the interior of Mexico.[45]

General Jones agreed to provide "500 to 900 adequately equipped National Guard troops" to patrol the border and transport apprehended illegal aliens to deportation centers. General Swing offered more. He guaranteed "3,500 to 4,000 troops on the job by August 15th" and showed "enthusiastic interest in the operation," because, while Swing was busy supplying troops for "the Korean campaign," he believed that assigning new military recruits to Operation Cloud Burst could provide "training advantages . . . over and above any training programs . . . that they could set up at any conventional training center." According to Swing, the opportunity for troops to work with the U.S. Border Patrol in a massive purging of the southwest was an ideal "training project" to prepare military recruits for the police action in Korea.[46]

The only problem that stood between the plans for Operation Cloud Burst and its implementation was *Posse Comitatus*, an 1878 law that prohibited the use of the U.S. Army for domestic law enforcement unless granted the authority to do so by Congress. The U.S. Army was a weapon of war, requiring congressional approval for its deployment. General Swing, however, "indicated that this could be overcome by a Presidential Proclamation" and "made it quite clear that in his opinion there is no absolute bar to the use of Army personnel in the manner contemplated."[47] By July 30, Harlon Carter was corresponding with President Eisenhower's assistants and preparing for the presidential order to be issued allowing the U.S. Army to assist the Border Patrol in ending the nightmare along the U.S.-Mexico border. Carter quickly detailed sixty-five Border Patrol officers to California in preparation for Operation Cloud Burst, but Eisenhower never signed the requisite proclamation.[48] The preparations and the expectation that military action would crush the borderland rebellion, liberate and deport the virtual slaves, and seal the border were foiled. Eisenhower refused to deploy troops within the United States, though he supported the Border Patrol's goals. In place of a presidential order to use the military, Eisenhower gave the U.S. Border Patrol General Swing.

In May of 1954, President Eisenhower appointed his old West Point friend, General Joseph Swing (retired), as commissioner of the Immigration and Naturalization Service. Before joining the INS, General Swing's long career with the military had included service with General John Pershing in Mexico and an appointment as commanding general of the U.S. Sixth Army in South Korea. If the Border Patrol could not use troops, at least they could have the leadership and guidance of a seasoned officer in the borderland battles to come.

When General Swing took command of the INS in May of 1954, the U.S. Border Patrol already had one decade of experience in aggressive immigration law enforcement. For years, officers had been battling with Special Mexican Deportation Parties, fences, airlifts, train lifts, boat lifts, buslifts, cross-border raids, head-shavings, and more. Nothing had worked. Each year, in fact, Border Patrol officers apprehended increasing numbers of unsanctioned Mexican immigrants. Many hoped that the arrival of General Swing would lead to a militarization of the Border Patrol that would enable it to take the upper hand in the borderlands.

OPERATION WETBACK OF 1954

As promised, one month after joining the INS, Swing announced that he would lead the U.S. Border Patrol in an intensive, innovative, and paramilitary law-enforcement campaign designed to end the problem of illegal Mexican immigration along the U.S.-Mexico border. No one questioned how in four short weeks he had prepared the officers of the Border Patrol for such a massive campaign. Had Border Patrol officers been rushed through an intensive, military-style training program? No, they had not. Were they instructed in new techniques of migration control? No, they were not. Had they received new equipment? No, they had not. Still, the flashy press releases and the quick start of the campaign prevented critics from asking basic questions about the actual mechanics of a drive that Commissioner Swing promised would make the many problems of illegal Mexican immigration disappear.

On the evening of June 9, 1954, hundreds of Border Patrolmen from the Canadian border and the Florida Gulf Coast region reported for duty in southern California. All they carried with them was a letter from General Swing instructing them to purge the nation of unsanctioned immigrants by "removing the huge number of Mexican nationals who were in this country in violation of the immigration laws."[49] At dawn the next morning, they began their work by erecting roadblocks on routes that led from the U.S.-Mexico border to the interior of the United States. Between June 10 and June 17, 1954, Border Patrol officers working at roadblocks in California and western Arizona apprehended 10,917 undocumented immigrants.[50] On the June 17, the officers were organized into Special Mobile Task Forces and began sweeping from north to south in California and western Arizona. Each Special Mobile Task Force was a self-contained "command unit" of twelve men. Just as they had been doing since Albert Quillin's innovations of 1950, the officers used jeeps, planes, trucks, and mobile immigration stations to apprehend, process, and deport large numbers of migrants each day.[51]

Undocumented Mexican
workers board buses for
deportation in Elysian
Park, 1954. Los Angeles
Times Photographic
Archive, Department
of Special Collections,
Charles E. Young
Research Library, UCLA.

Often, the patrolmen arrested more Mexicans than they could handle. To hold
the detainees, the officers turned public spaces into temporary detention facilities.
For example, in Los Angeles, the Border Patrol transformed Elysian Park, a popular public park, into a temporary holding station, where apprehended Mexican
nationals were processed for deportation. In countless fields and along many country roads, Border Patrol officers set up mobile immigration stations to process unsanctioned Mexican immigrants for official deportation. They used trucks on loan
from the armed services to transport the apprehended immigrants from California to Nogales, Arizona, for deportation into Mexico.

As in the past, cross-border collaboration extended the process of deportation
far south of the U.S.-Mexico border. In the months before the campaign of 1954,
INS and U.S. Department of State officials had worked with the Mexican secretary
of foreign relations and the Mexican Department of Migration to coordinate trainlifts of deportees to the interior of Mexico. In contrast to the years when they first
began their collaborations, however, U.S. officials were less compromising than they
had once been. In the years since the end of World War II, U.S.-Mexico relations
remained marked by a measure of cooperation and accommodation. Still, without
the threat of Axis attacks from across the southern border, U.S. authorities afforded

Mexican officials far less influence in U.S.-Mexico relations. In terms of migration control, Mexico's loss of influence transformed the nature of cross-border collaboration. On May 20, 1954, the U.S. secretary of state asked the U.S. ambassador in Mexico to inform the Mexican secretary of foreign relations of the U.S. Border Patrol's impending campaign. When the campaign began in California, he explained, Mexican officials should expect to receive and process a thousand deportees daily at the port between Nogales, Arizona, and Nogales, Sonora.[52] From there, U.S. authorities expected that Mexican officials would conduct daily or weekly trainlifts of deportees to interior locations.

Two days later, the U.S. ambassador in Mexico City forwarded a memo addressing Mexican concerns about U.S. plans. First, Mexican officials informed the U.S. Department of State that all Mexican government offices would be closed in the week to come. It would be difficult, therefore, for Mexican officials to prepare for the arrival of deportees through the small immigration station at Nogales, Sonora. Instead of coordinating interior deportations through Nogales, the Mexican authorities requested that deportees be airlifted directly from the United States to the interior of Mexico. Responding to the Mexican requests, the U.S. Department of State informed Mexican officials that there were no funds available for an airlift and that, regardless of the difficulties, Mexican officials should prepare to train lift deportees from Nogales to the interior of Mexico. The only accommodation that the U.S. could make would be to remove deportees through Mexicali if Nogales became overcrowded.[53]

Again, Mexican officials raised concerns regarding the details of the proposed campaign. They had long been active participants in cross-border migration control and had recently established the Mexican Border Patrol, but the U.S. Border Patrol's plan to deport one thousand persons daily through Nogales would require that they borrow more than 2.5 million pesos from emergency funds to process the deportees and, as they informed U.S. officials, Nogales had neither adequate detention facilities nor rail lines to receive and remove one thousand deportees per day. In search of a compromise, the Mexican secretary of foreign relations requested that no more than five hundred deportees daily be returned through Nogales. U.S. officials, however, reiterated their plan to deport a thousand Mexicans per day through Nogales and, if necessary, to deport Mexicans through Calexico, California as well.[54] With little influence over the rhythm of deportations, Mexican officials in Nogales, Arizona, received 23,222 of the 33,307 unsanctioned Mexican immigrants that the U.S. Border Patrol task forces had apprehended in California and western Arizona between June 17 and June 30, 1954.[55]

To showcase the large numbers of migrants being processed for forced removal into Mexico, officers were directed to raid Mexicano communities, leisure spots, migrant camps, ranches, farms, and parks. They also paid close attention to urban industries known to employ undocumented Mexican immigrants. Between June 17 and July 26, 1954, 2,827 of the 4,403 migrants apprehended by the task force assigned to Los Angeles area had worked in industry. After Border Patrol raids during the summer of 1954, three Los Angeles brickyards were left without sufficient numbers of workers and temporarily closed down their operations.[56] Similarly, Border Patrol officers paid close attention to the hotel and restaurant business, which routinely hired undocumented Mexican immigrants as "bus boys, kitchen help, waiters, etc."[57] Officers reported apprehending such workers at well-known establishments, such as the Biltmore Hotel, Beverly Hills Hotel, Hollywood Roosevelt Hotel, Los Angeles Athletic Club, and the Brown Derby. At times, Border Patrol raids created moments of chaos at popular restaurants when migrants attempted to escape by running through the serving area.[58]

Everywhere they went, the officers were chased and photographed by journalists who had come to witness what General Swing had promised would be a spectacular show of U.S. immigration law enforcement. Swing pledged that the U.S. Border Patrol would deport or otherwise purge the one million undocumented Mexican nationals estimated to be living in the United States at the time. As the special details headed out into the field during the summer of 1954, Swing certainly seemed to be making good on his promise. The press snapped shots of officers apprehending dozens and hundreds of undocumented Mexican nationals at a time. By raiding popular restaurants and turning public parks into detention facilities, the INS was able to create a constant buzz that kept the summer campaign in the headlines of regional and national newspapers throughout June of 1954.

The very public campaign in California was a strategy designed as a warning to the rebels in south Texas. As the task forces worked in California, Border Patrol officers took the newspaper coverage of the California campaign and visited ranchers in south Texas. Resistance was futile, advised Border Patrol officers, who warned that the coming task forces would be nothing like the south Texans had ever experienced. In south Texas, Harlon Carter and others arranged special meetings with influential ranchers and farmers to outline their options. Either south Texas growers could continue to hire undocumented Mexican laborers and suffer from relentless raids, or they could meet their labor needs through the Bracero Program. The growers typically responded that they would never submit unless the program was dramatically simplified. One farmer argued that the provisions of the program should have been stripped down until they could be "squeezed onto a 3 × 5 card."[59] In particular, the farmers vehemently objected to the Bracero Program's requirements that employers provide contracts regulating adequate housing, sanitation, and disability insurance. Why, they asked, should American employers providing jobs for unemployed Mexicans be required to provide Mexican workers with facilities, protections, and guarantees that were routinely unenforced for Mexican workers in Mexico and systemically denied to all other agricultural workers in the United States according to the occupational limitations of U.S. labor law? Further, they cringed, bracero employers were required to provide all these comforts for workers whom they did not individually select. According to the growers, the employers should have been allowed to select workers rather than having them randomly assigned. In response, INS and Border Patrol officers explained, in great detail, that recent changes in the Bracero Program would satisfy some of their demands.

The INS instituted the I-100 and Specials Programs during the summer of 1954. The I-100 Program worked by providing braceros who had satisfactorily completed their contracts with laminated certificates called I-100 cards. Workers with I-100 cards could be recontracted for work in the United States without having to return to recruitment centers in Mexico. The I-100 program, therefore, saved employers from having to pay for a worker's for transportation from the interior of Mexico to the border. Further, in 1955, Commissioner Swing declared that all workers with I-100 cards should be offered bracero contracts before those without I-100 cards. Privileging workers with I-100 cards effectively provided employers the opportunity to exert greater control over the bracero workforce because workers with negative reports from employers were denied I-100 cards. Future bracero contracts, in other words, were directly linked to favorable reports provided by employers in the United States. The Specials Program offered employers additional control over the bracero workforce by allowing them to select bracero workers. Together, the I-100 Program and the Specials Program assuaged many of the growers' complaints by offering them a way to discipline and select the bracero workforce independently.[60]

When the special mobile task forces arrived in south Texas in the middle of July, Border Patrol officers brought both threats of deporting workers from the fields and promises to allow farmers more control over the selection and discipline of braceros. During the course of farm checks and raids, officers would speak with ranchers and farmers about the benefits of the I-100 and Specials Program.[61] If a grower seemed unconvinced, Border Patrol officials followed up with an offer to station a two-man Border Patrol team on the grower's farm until he signed a pledge to use braceros instead of illegals. By the end of July, the Border Patrol reported apprehending 41,951 Mexicans in the Lower Rio Grande Valley and noted the dramatic increase in the number of braceros contracted in the state of Texas from 168 in July 1953 to 41,766 in July 1954.[62]

The jump in bracero contracts during the summer of 1954 suggested that a combination of coercion and compromise had finally convinced the rebellious south Texans to replace the illegals with braceros. Keeping braceros in the fields, however, depended upon the growers' continued compliance after the summer of 1954. During the fall of 1954 and 1955, therefore, the U.S. Border Patrol conducted a public opinion survey in the Lower Rio Grande Valley to gauge the long-term commitment of employers to the Bracero Program. The survey indicated that the Border Patrol's most vocal opponents were now using the new Bracero Program. Carl

Schuster, for example, had been "one of the most critical and openly opposed men to the Service" and tried "every means possible to hinder the work of the Service and to embarrass the individual officers."[63] In the years leading up to Operation Wetback of 1954, Schuster had placed booby-traps at his farm gates, cursed officers, and lobbied congressmen for reduced Border Patrol appropriations. But after participating in the modified Bracero Program for several months, Schuster testified, "I am very pleased with the Bracero Program" and "intend to cooperate in every way possible with the Immigration Service and its officers."[64] Echoing the remarks of Schuster were many others who vowed to continue using braceros in place of undocumented workers. The El Paso Valley Cotton Association, for example, had long opposed the Bracero Program and spearheaded much of the campaign against the U.S. Border Patrol during the early 1950s. In November of 1955, however, the chairman of the association stated that "although you can still hear reports that the farmers would like to go back to 'the good old days of the wetback,' with no worries about processing, wage scales, and insurance, I believe that we are all convinced that time is gone and the best solution to our problem is the present bracero program."[65] That year, for the first time, the El Paso Valley Cotton Association supported the Bracero Program.

For the U.S. Border Patrol, the growers' acceptance of the Bracero Program marked a turning point in the troublesome south Texas region. As one officer remarked, 1954 was the summer when "deportable aliens became contract laborers," and "the assurance of a plentiful supply of labor at a reasonable cost, though a little higher than before, quieted the farmers and their organizations."[66] The modified Bracero Program undoubtedly addressed the crisis of consent among south Texas farmers that had destabilized and undermined the practices and priorities of the Border Patrol in the U.S.-Mexico borderlands for nearly a decade. But Commissioner Swing and many others also credited the modified Bracero Program with ending the crisis of control along the U.S.-Mexico border.

After the summer of 1954, apprehensions of Mexican nationals dropped to a fraction of what they had been. In 1954, the U.S. Border Patrol apprehended 1,075,168 Mexican nationals. The following year, that number plunged to 242,608, and in 1956, it plummeted to 72,442. The number of Mexican nationals apprehended remained under one hundred thousand until 1967. Further, the number of Mexican nationals as a percentage of the total number of apprehensions dropped from 98 percent in 1954 to 46 percent in 1959.[67] Mass deportation and the shift from illegals to braceros, Swing argued, had dramatically reduced unsanctioned Mexican border crossings. Yet Swing's assessment that modifications within the Bracero Program or the process of making legals out of illegals had reduced Border Patrol apprehensions after 1954 is deeply flawed because significant numbers of the Mexican nationals who had been apprehended for illegal entry were categorically ineligible for bracero contracts. Women and children, for example were ineligible. Further, industrial and service workers were also ineligible for bracero contracts. The gendered and industry limitations of the Bracero Program denied the opportunity for legalization to large numbers of unsanctioned Mexican immigrants. Swing's analysis that the Border Patrol's plummeting rates of apprehension were directly related to the rising number of braceros fell apart in his disregard of the gender dynamics of unsanctioned labor migration and in his dismissal of evidence that unsanctioned Mexican workers worked in manufacturing and service industries. Just as the dramatic increase in Border Patrol apprehension statistics between 1944 and 1954 was a reflection of border-crossing trends and law-enforcement strategies, the post-1954 decline was also the result of a combination of factors.

THE POST-WETBACK RETREAT

In terms of law enforcement, the demobilization of the special mobile task forces significantly reduced the number of apprehensions made each year. First launched as the Special Mexican Deportation Parties, the task force model had functioned as a part of the U.S. Border Patrol's operations along the U.S.-Mexico border since 1944. The Special Mexican Deportation Parties headed out from local offices with the sole purpose of apprehending unsanctioned Mexican immigrants. Accordingly, between 1943 and 1944, the raw number of Mexican nationals apprehended increased along with the percentage of Mexican nationals among the total number of apprehensions nationwide. In 1950, Patrol Officer Quillin of south Texas integrated new radio technology with the Special Mexican Deportation Parties to create the Operation Wetback model of teams of officers with trucks, buses, and planes conducting coordinated raids upon border farms, ranches, and communities. By late 1950, the Operation Wetback model was in use at stations throughout the U.S.-Mexico borderlands and was, as Fletcher Rawls stated, "poundin' away at these wets" throughout the region. But in 1955 U.S. Border Patrol officials reimagined the use of task forces. Rather than using them as a day-to-day strategy, upper officials established regional task forces to be deployed by district authorities to designated pressure points on a case-by-case basis.[68]

The task forces were replaced by seventy-three two-man teams of officers assigned primarily to work along the border and wait for unsanctioned migrants to step across the line.[69] In contrast to the task forces that routinely arrested thousands of people within just a few hours of work, the best that the two-man teams could do was, as one office noted, to "just grab somebody" as they attempted to cross illegally into the United States.[70] Thinly dispersed along the two-thousand-mile border, officers often spent more time lying in wait than arresting unsanctioned migrants. Further, officers had to "wrestle" migrants who tested the ability of two-man patrols to simultaneously contain a large group of migrants while tussling with an individual. "You didn't sit 50 down and expect them to sit there," explained officer Arthur Adams.[71] Without the support of twelve-man teams, buses, and aerial patrols, officers struggled to "grab one or two and hang on to 'em."[72] Unlike the officers involved in the rush and scramble of task force operations during the wetback decade, officers working line patrols in the post-wetback era encountered fewer unsanctioned migrants and struggled to hold onto those they found. The shift in strategies from task forces striking throughout the region to two-man teams watching the line, therefore, reduced the number of apprehensions that officers could make.[73]

Despite the 1955 changes in Border Patrol strategy, Commissioner Swing and many others actively promoted a simple reading of the relatively low number of apprehensions after the summer of 1954. Fewer apprehensions, they argued, were a clear indication that fewer Mexican nationals were attempting illicit entry into the United States. As Commissioner Swing reminisced during the INS appropriation hearings for 1961, the triumphs of 1954 had led to an enduring, "hard-fought conquest of the Mexican border situation."[74] But beneath the propaganda suggesting that deportations, coercive force, and a general militarization of the border had turned back the tides of unsanctioned Mexican migrants, the Border Patrol's triumph along the U.S.-Mexico border was guarded and sustained by changes in day-to-day operations that pulled officers off task forces, put them in two-man teams, and, thereby, limited the number of apprehensions.[75] The Border Patrol's triumph of 1954, therefore, rested on retreat rather than effective force.

THE COMPROMISE OF '55

The Border Patrol's post-1954 retreat frustrated leaders of the Mexican American middle class who had actively supported aggressive immigration law enforcement against unsanctioned Mexican immigration. They had defended the U.S. Border Patrol against the south Texas rebels. Most important, when the patrol began planning Operation Cloudburst of 1953 and Operation Wetback of 1954, members of influential Mexican American political organizations had submitted to their own harassment, hoping that the mass deportation of unsanctioned Mexican immigrants would improve the job security and living conditions of Mexican American workers. For example, in anticipation of Operation Cloud Burst of 1953, representatives and members of the American G.I. Forum had flooded Attorney General Brownell's office with letters requesting that the "entire U.S. Mexican border be closed against illegal entry of aliens; . . . mass invasion by hordes of illegal aliens at will poses great economic educational and social problem in Texas and certainly undermines the security of our country in these dangerous times."[76] Although Operation Cloud Burst was derailed for lack of a presidential executive order, when Operation Wetback began in 1954, representatives of the American G.I. Forum and the League of United Latin American Citizens (LULAC) worked with Border Patrol officials to ensure the campaign's success.

Recognizing that racial profiling would entangle Mexican Americans in the campaign to purge the nation of "the huge number of Mexican nationals," the INS district director of San Antonio, J. W. Holland, addressed a letter to the heads of the American G.I. Forum and LULAC. As he had explained to Swing, "Inasmuch as these gentlemen are very influential among the Spanish-speaking people in Texas, . . . it would be a good gesture on my part to inform them of our contemplated action in order to obviate some complaints from Spanish-speaking people."[77] Holland informed the heads of the American G.I. Forum and LULAC that the U.S. Border Patrol would soon "commence an intensive drive to apprehend and evict thousands of aliens illegally in this country."[78] That campaign would benefit Mexican Americans because, "as you well know," he explained, "the thousands of aliens who have entered this country illegally from Mexico during the past decade have caused serious economic problems for thousands of Spanish-speaking American families residing near the border."[79] Echoing the position of many LULAC and G.I. Forum members, Holland argued that unsanctioned Mexican immigration forced Mexican Americans out of work. "It would be difficult to estimate the number of such families who have given up their homes, taken their children out of school, and moved elsewhere in search of new homes and employment," he explained. Mexican American jobs and homes were endangered by unsanctioned Mexican immigrants who worked for wages and under conditions that citizen workers refused. "The irony of it all," he sympathized, "is that some of the victims of the influx of illegal aliens have been forced to leave their very homes, in which their families have lived for several generations."[80] By deporting unsanctioned Mexican immigrants, therefore, Holland argued that the U.S. Border Patrol and INS were "working on their [Mexican Americans] behalf."[81]

Holland played to the strategic choice of Mexican American organizations such as LULAC and the American G.I. Forum to forge Mexican American inclusion through Mexican exclusion. His approach reaffirmed the mutual desire of the U.S. Border Patrol and Mexican Americans to "evict" the undocumented Mexican nationals living in the borderlands. While he made no promises, Holland suggested that Mexican Americans would no longer have to leave the borderlands to find work if the Border Patrol's upcoming campaign was successful. He also reminded Mexican American leaders that the difference between past Border Patrol failure and future success was the appointment of General Swing as Commissioner of the INS. "After many years of what appear to have been fruitless efforts on the part of the Immigration and Naturalization Service," he admitted, "the guidance of our newly appointed Commissioner, Lt. General Joseph Swing (retired), is taking active steps to combat it."[82] To serve their interests, however, Mexican Americans first had to accept the surveillance and suspicions of U.S. Border Patrol officers who, in the pursuit of deporting unsanctioned Mexican nationals, would mistakenly question Mexican Americans regarding their citizenship. "With that in mind," Holland wrote, "I respectfully solicit your aid in bringing this matter to the attention of your many members and their friends, in order that they will know that we are work-ing in their behalf, and if they are questioned regarding their citizenship, they will understand the motive behind our actions."[83]

Without delay, Ed Idar instructed all "South Texas Forums, Auxiliaries, and Jun-ior Forums" to "call special public meetings and to use the newspapers and the ra-dio to alert our people to this drive and to request that they cooperate with the Im-migration and Naturalization Service in order to minimize the possibility of misunderstandings."[84] He reminded members of the American G.I. Forum that al-though "there may be occasions when some of our legal residents and American citizens may be asked to present identification, . . . our people must be made to re-alize that the officers not only will be discharging a duty imposed on them by law but the successful discharge of that duty in cleaning out the wetbacks will react to the betterment of employment and economic opportunities for our people."[85] It was a Faustian bargain for Mexican Americans: full incorporation into the Amer-ican dream was just around the bend if only they could sacrifice a bit to get there. But, for the Border Patrol, Idar's defense of the coming campaign inverted the south Texas rebels' claims that racial profiling was a form of discrimination that com-promised American justice and equality. Rather, as Idar argued, Border Patrol prac-tice would ultimately uplift Mexican Americans in their quest for economic secu-rity, social inclusion, and upward mobility within the borderlands.

Both anticipating and accepting that racial harassment of Mexican Americans by Border Patrol officers would escalate during the upcoming campaign, Idar set up a process for facilitating complaints that would not interrupt the Border Pa-trol's efforts. Idar instructed all members and officers of the American G.I. Forum to "IMMEDIATELY" refer any complaints to Virgilio Roal and Robert Sánchez, at-torneys in McAllen, Texas, who would "look into the situation and clear with the Austin office if any action has to be taken."[86] Idar and the American G.I. Forum were committed to help Operation Wetback run smoothly. They firmly believed that the removal of undocumented Mexican nationals would improve the life and labor conditions of Mexican Americans. Later that summer, Idar welcomed the chief supervisor of the Border Patrol, W. F. Kelly, as a "guest of honor and the prin-cipal speaker" at the American G.I. Forum's annual conference.[87] Idar took the op-portunity to publicly thank Border Patrol officers for their "extraordinary efforts" during the summer of 1954.[88] Similarly, Frank Piñedo, the president of LULAC, wrote in *LULAC News* that "the Immigration Service is to be highly commended for their careful planning for this drive, not only in South Texas, but in California as well. . . . It is important that all members of LULAC should represent to the people of Texas that the League whole-heartedly supports this drive, and any incidents, if any occur, should be carefully analyzed before hasty judgment is passed and harmful criticism is made."[89]

Piñedo, Idar, and others worked diligently to ensure that Operation Wetback would succeed. In the process, they developed friendly alliances with Border Patrol officers and officials. Holland cultivated that support. When in Austin, he stopped by Piñedo's office. Although Piñedo was out of town, Holland left him a note saying that he was "sorry that I missed seeing you."[90] Yet, beyond the immediate goal of mass deportations, the political convergence of the Border Patrol and Mexican American civil rights organizations diverged. In the years after their shared triumph over unsanctioned Mexican border crossings, the once mutual interests of the U.S. Border Patrol and Mexican American middle class disintegrated.

In early 1955, Idar noted that "although the wetback has been cleaned out in large measure, due to poor administration of the provisions of the international bracero agreement, there is increasing displacement of our domestic agricultural workers by legally imported labor."[91] Many scholars confirm Idar's suspicions that the Bracero Program was marked by systemic corruption and willful mismanagement after 1954. Employers regularly violated the bracero contract after 1954—"I know that we can't live up to the contract 100 percent. It's just a piece of paper," one grower admitted—and the lack of enforcement allowed farmers to participate in the simplified Bracero Program without providing minimum wages or adequate housing.[92] As Manuel García y Griego has written, although the Border Patrol helped switch southwestern growers from illegal practices to a legal labor system, after Operation Wetback, "the cost and attractiveness of bracero labor was not very different from what the same had been for 'wetback' labor."[93]

For the Mexican American leaders who had hoped that the mass deportation of unsanctioned Mexican immigrants would deny employers access to a highly exploitable labor force, the perversions of the Bracero Program were disturbing. Ed Idar, for example, wrote to Walter Sahli, the new district director of the INS in San Antonio, Texas, that he was "quite concerned" over the new predicament in which he found Mexican American workers who had to compete with underpaid and poorly treated legal bracero workers.[94] He and other leaders of the American G.I. Forum turned to their friends in the U.S. Border Patrol for help. Idar and the national chairman of the American G.I. Forum, Dr. Hector García, requested that when conducting routine farm checks, officers report violations of the Fair Labor Standards Act of 1950, which prohibited children under the age of sixteen from working in agriculture during school hours.[95] García suggested that if officers found children working during school hours, they could forward information to the Department of Labor for follow-up and enforcement of the law. But Harlon Carter of the U.S. Border Patrol responded by accusing Dr. García of "misunderstanding . . . the scope and limited purpose of the Fair Labor Standards Act" and refused to collaborate on this project because "the projection of our Service into this field would hinder a number of our efforts to promote good immigration law enforcement through the cooperation of farmers and the press" and "incur the ill-will of employers now won to our side."[96]

Only a few years earlier, Border Patrol officials had stood with Mexican American activists to combat the rise in undocumented Mexican immigration. Mexican American leaders had envisioned the mass deportations promised during Operation Wetback of 1954 as protecting Mexican American interests. With this in mind, they encouraged Mexican Americans to submit to their own harassment and steadfastly supported the effort to deport unsanctioned Mexican workers. Officials of the U.S. Border Patrol entered the summer of 1954 with wholly different objectives in mind, however. In particular, Border Patrol officials sought the return of consent and control along the U.S.-Mexico border, neither of which, once won, they were willing to sacrifice to the aggressive law-enforcement initiatives requested by Dr. Hector García. Dismissed by leadership within the INS and the Border Patrol, Idar, García, and Mexican American community leaders would have to find another way to influence the development of U.S. immigration law enforcement. They would have plenty of time to do so as U.S. immigration law enforcement entered into a period of relative calm in the years after Operation Wetback of 1954.

The Border Patrol's triumphs of 1954 rested on a broken Bracero Program and a retreat from aggressive migration control, each of which quickly diminished Border Patrol activity in the U.S.-Mexico borderlands. Apprehensions plummeted, and officers in the field reported being more bored than busy. The quiet within the patrol was matched by the disappearance of the topic of migration control from the popular press. Drug control was quickly replacing immigration control as the primary line item in U.S.-Mexico relations. Still the U.S.-Mexico borderlands remained the primary theater for U.S. immigration law enforcement, and Border Patrol officers continued to prioritize the policing of unsanctioned Mexican immigration. Chapter 9 examines why the substance of the patrol's project changed so little in the post-wetback era by recounting how Border Patrol officials reimagined their project of policing unsanctioned Mexican immigrants in the quiet years after Operation Wetback of 1954. In particular, Chapter 9 examines how the U.S. Border Patrol made a strategic shift away from liberating José and toward chasing criminals. The switch from migration control to crime control recast the problem of unsanctioned Mexican immigration as a matter of quality not quantity, thereby sustaining and rationalizing the Border Patrol's continued concentration upon the U.S.-Mexico border and persons of Mexican origin despite the reduction of apprehensions that continued into the early 1970s.

9

"The Day of the Wetback Is Over"

"The day of the wetback is over," declared Commissioner Swing in January 1955. Swing's proud victory rested on a broken Bracero Program, changes in U.S. Border Patrol practice, and a statistical sleight of hand, but his proclamations of triumph along the U.S.-Mexico border announced an end to the crises of consent and control that had consumed U.S. Border Patrol practice for a decade. For all the smoke and mirrors, Swing and the triumphs of 1954 closed a chapter in the history of the Border Patrol and opened a series of questions regarding the future of migration control in the United States. What would be the practices and priorities of U.S. migration control in the years after the "wetback crisis"? This chapter examines why the U.S. Border Patrol continued to concentrate upon policing unsanctioned Mexican immigration despite confident pronouncements that the "the so-called wetback problem no longer exists. The southern border has been secured."[1] In many ways, the Border Patrol's continued focus on the U.S.-Mexico border emerged from a deeply rooted infrastructure and an unquestioned goal of deporting Mexican nationals. Most important, however, the patrol's dogged dedication to policing unsanctioned Mexican immigration in the post-wetback era is a story about how officers, officials, and the shifting conditions of border enforcement redefined the need to control unsanctioned Mexican border crossings as an issue of crime control rather than as a matter of migration control. This chapter explores how the politics and practices of crime control breathed new life into Border Patrol's concentration in the U.S.-Mexico borderlands during the quiet years that followed Operation Wetback of 1954.

IMMIGRATION CONTROL IN THE POST-WETBACK YEARS

Regardless of how it was won, Swing's victory at the Mexican border opened space to consider new possibilities for the priorities and practices of migration control in the post-wetback era. As early as December 1954, Swing discussed turning attention toward the forgotten Canadian border. There, he argued, unwanted immigrants, dangerous saboteurs, and "restless Canadian immigrants" had long taken advantage of an ignored border to gain illicit entry into the United States.[2] In 1957, Swing transferred fifty-three officers from the Southwestern Region to the northern border.[3] When Fidel Castro seized Havana, Cuba, in January of 1959, Swing moved one hundred Border Patrol officers to the Florida Gulf Coast region to prevent "hostile flights from the U.S. mainland to Cuba."[4] Officer Bob Salinger attributed his many details to Florida to Commissioner Swing's efforts to insert the INS within the broader apparatus of federal law enforcement. "General Swing," explained Salinger "jumped in and volunteered the Border Patrol for any shitty job that came along [because] Swing, he'd jump in on anything to make points with the Attorney General."[5] While it is doubtful that Swing assigned Border Patrol officers to additional duties without requests or instructions from the Attorney General, Salinger certainly recalled the Swing years as a period of integrating the U.S. Border Patrol into a broad spectrum of federal law-enforcement projects. Most notable, in addition to patrolling the Florida border region, a project at least tangentially related to immigration control, Swing sent Border Patrol officers to quell civil rights disturbances in the south. Once again, Salinger was assigned to take on an extra duty.

On a Sunday morning in May 1961, Salinger received a call instructing him to "alert fifty men to go to Montgomery, Alabama." Thirty minutes later he received another call increasing the detail to seventy-five men. Another half-hour passed and Salinger received a third call: one hundred men were needed immediately in Montgomery, Alabama. "Well, if you're going to take the whole sector, I don't think we can get them all up there," protested Salinger, but the call was from James P. Greene, the assistant commissioner of enforcement in the Southwest Region, and refusal was not an option. Instead, Greene authorized Salinger to "take the pilot. [We had a Cessna 310.] Take the 310 and take the radio tech [and] . . . get on it right now."[6] When the officers arrived in Montgomery, they learned that "Old Martin Luther King was going to preach downtown at one of the churches, and all we were doing at the time was finding out if any riots were going to go on." The Border Patrol officers, however, were not alone. When they entered their detail headquarters at the Maxwell airfield in Montgomery, Alabama, officers from other agencies within the Department of Justice were already there. "They had Alcohol, Tobacco and Tax people, U.S. Marshalls, prison guards, and I think Post Office people" recalled Salinger.[7] This detail was emblematic of the Border Patrol's increasing involvement in federal law enforcement and, in particular, its use as a "go-to" force for on-the-ground federal police activities in the years to come. Throughout the turbulent 1960s, Border Patrol officers would participate in some of the era's most significant federal law-enforcement efforts. In 1962, for example, Border Patrol officers were assigned to stand guard outside of the University of Mississippi when white students and community members rioted to prevent an African-American student named James Meredith from integrating the university. And, in 1973, Border Patrol officers assisted the Bureau of Indian Affairs and an assortment of federal officers when members of the American Indian Movement occupied Wounded Knee, South Dakota.

While these episodes clearly indicate the Border Patrol's integration into the multiple and scattered projects of federal law enforcement, Border Patrol operations still remained centered on patrolling the U.S.-Mexico border and policing persons of Mexican origin. In part, the patrol's continued concentration upon the U.S.-Mexico borderlands was the result of an institution with strong roots in the region. The U.S. Border Patrol emerged from the wetback decade with a massive infrastructure that had been built around the singular focus of apprehending and deporting unsanctioned Mexican nationals. In addition to assigning the majority of Border Patrol officers to offices in the U.S.-Mexico border region, by 1953, the INS had built and staffed three new, large detention facilities in south Texas and southern California. Located within several miles of the U.S.-Mexico border, these detention centers were oriented toward deporting large numbers of people into Mexico. A fleet of transport aircraft based in El Paso, Texas, moved migrants to and from these detention centers.[8] Further, Commissioner Swing insured that El Paso would continue to be a hub of Border Patrol activity by establishing a permanent home for the Border Patrol Training School at the Fort Bliss military base just outside of the El Paso city limits. The proliferation of Border Patrol buildings, personnel, and institutional resources along the U.S.-Mexico border gave the organization deep roots in the region.

Perpetuating the imbalance of U.S. Border Patrol resources in the U.S.-Mexico borderlands were changes that Commissioner Swing instituted in INS administration. In 1956, Swing split the INS into four independent regional units: Southwest Region, Northwest Region, Northeast Region, and Southeast Region. Each region had two main divisions, Immigration and Enforcement. The Enforcement Division comprised the U.S. Border Patrol and Immigration Investigators. The regional model discouraged redistribution of officers and resources across regions because it encapsulated each region as a nearly autonomous unit of operations, authority, strategic planning, and resource sharing.[9] Regionalization, in other words, gave the institution sticky feet in the U.S.-Mexico border region, where more officers, more resources, and more facilities were located when Swing split the national police force into four unequal parts.

THE MIND-SET OF MIGRATION CONTROL

The Border Patrol's concentration in the U.S.-Mexico border region did not necessitate a focus on policing unsanctioned Mexican immigrants. Confirming Swing's suspicions that the post-wetback era would bring new challenges to migration control, officers working along the U.S.-Mexico border routinely reported in the late 1950s and early 1960s that there was no "large build up of potential illegal [Mexican laborer] entrants adjacent to the border area."[10] Officers working the traffic checks along roads and highways leading from the border to the interior reported that apprehensions of unsanctioned Mexican immigrants "were few and far between."[11] As one officer recalled, "more often than illegal aliens," officers found cars carrying unexpected contraband such as fireworks, liquor, and parrots.[12] At the same time, Border Patrol intelligence reports warned that nontraditional groups such as British Hondurans and Cubans were arriving in Mexican border towns and trying to cross illegally into the United States.[13] As the number of Mexican nationals removed from the United States plunged to a post-wetback low of only 29,651 in 1960, new possible targets for migration control emerged. But officers in the southwestern region continued to focus their attention upon policing unsanctioned Mexican immigrants.

Border Patrol officers working during the post-wetback era often described their focus upon policing Mexican nationals as a "mind-set." Recounting a 1957 raid in the Sacramento, California, area Border Patrol officer Ralph Williams explained that "we went in a bar and . . . we cleaned the bar out . . . except for one albino." Williams had walked right by the albino and intended to leave him sitting there, until another officer asked, "What about this guy here?" In a crude example of the very narrow intersection of class, color, and national origins that U.S. Border Patrol officers policed, Williams responded "Ah, hell, he's just an albino!" Like many other officers, Williams had narrowly focused his suspicions upon brown-skinned Mexicanos. His colleague, however, wondered, "An albino in here with a bunch of Mexicans?" and walked up to the man. "Where are you from?" he asked, and when the albino answered "I'm from Mexico," he was quickly arrested for illegal entry into the United States. Many years later, Williams was still amused by the incident and laughed about how "we caught us an albino wetback." The idea of a white-skinned illegal was ludicrous and illogical to Williams, who admitted that "I think I would have passed him up, as I recall."[14]

In striking similarity to the officers working in the 1920s, Williams considered any connection between whiteness and illegality to be laughable because, as Patrol Inspector Chester Courtney had explained in 1927, it was "absurd to say they believed the [white] Americans to be aliens."[15] The bonds between whiteness and American citizenship reached back to the Naturalization Act of 1790, which restricted the right to naturalization to whites, but the particular linkages between

TABLE 5 Principal activities and accomplishments of the U.S. Border Patrol for the years ended June 30, 1955–1964

	1955	1956	1957	1958	1959	1960	1961	1962	1963	1964
Total number of persons apprehended	227,380	70,846	48,433	41,956	34,218	29,881	30,209	30,686	39,885	43,993
Number of deportable aliens located	225,186	68,420	46,225	40,504	32,996	28,966	29,384	29,897	38,861	42,879
Number of Mexican nationals apprehended	221,674	62,625	38,822	32,556	25,270	22,687	23,109	23,358	31,910	35,146
Number of persons questioned	7,713,858	9,890,424	8,882,563	13,033,167	6,715,787	6,189,817	6,267,642	6,808,638	6,331,404	5,433,546
Value of narcotics seizures[a]	$678,532	$682,742	$763,859	$172,085	$144,883	$52,083	$26,416	$13,408	$11,930	$251,692

SOURCE: Data compiled from principal activities and accomplishments of the U.S. Border Patrol, *Annual Reports of the Immigration and Naturalization Service, Fiscal Years Ending June 30, 1955, 1956, and 1967* (Washington, DC: GPO).

[a] Value of narcotics seizures is not available prior to 1958. All data for seizures prior to 1958 indicate total value, and all data for seizures for 1958 and after indicate only the value of narcotics seized.

Mexican Browns and the caste of illegals were constructed across three distinct generations of Border Patrol work. In the first generation, local boys who had become federal officers enforced U.S. immigration restrictions according to the customs of borderland communities built upon and around the interests of the agribusiness economy. During the second generation, Border Patrol officers developed practices of aggressive migration control in conversation and coordination with the Bracero Program as a cross-border system of managing labor migration. By the late 1950s, the patrol's narrow focus upon policing poor and brown-skinned Mexicans operated according to an unquestioned logic of migration control that, many believed, had been naturalized by the test of time. As one officer explained, "after 13 years of doing this, I can't really describe, it's a gut feeling, a hunch. I can walk downtown El Paso and walk by a lot of people and know they are legal," he explained, and "all of a sudden, one will be by me or passing in front of me, that I just know doesn't have documents."[16]

DETENTION AND DEPORTATION CAPACITIES

The racialization and regionalization of U.S. Border Patrol work did not persist into the post-wetback era on hold-overs and hunches alone. In these years, the officers' focus upon policing persons of Mexican origin was also structured by new and old migration control strategies. The ongoing lifts into the interior of Mexico, for example, continued to place a premium upon apprehending unsanctioned Mexican nationals. The buslifts and trainlifts operated with rare breaks during the 1950s, 1960s, and 1970s. When the boatlift was cancelled after the riot aboard the *S.S. Mercurio* in August of 1956, the INS reintroduced the airlift program from Reynosa, Tamaulipas, to León, Guanajuato. At times, the airlift also ran between Mexicali, Baja California, and León. Between November 29, 1957, and June 30, 1964, U.S. and Mexican officials airlifted 56,301 adult Mexican males to León and trainlifted another 53,914 Mexican nationals, including men, women, and children, to Chihuahua City, Chihuahua.[17] These 110,215 Mexicans lifted into the interior of Mexico represented 38.7 percent of the total number of Mexicans returned to Mexico between fiscal years 1957 and 1964. Men, however, experienced higher rates of removal to the interior because of the gendered restrictions that generally prohibited women and children from being removed via planelift. For example, of the 18,901 adult Mexican males apprehended during fiscal year 1964, 83.5 percent of them were relocated to the interior via plane or train: 11,200 were airlifted to León, and another 4,579 were removed via the bus-trainlift from Presidio, Texas, to Chihuahua, Mexico.[18] In an era when unsanctioned Mexican immigrants were difficult to find and hard to hold onto, officers struggled to fill the planes, trains, and buses waiting to take them to the interior of Mexico. In January 1959, the Mexican airline that was contracted by the INS to carry male deportees from Reynosa to León complained that, although they had been hired to conduct daily flights, the pilot and staff were routinely stranded in Reynosa for up to a week at a time while waiting for sets of deportees to be ready for removal.[19] Officers were under pressure to supply the cross-border system of deportation that moved Mexican deportees across the U.S.-Mexico border. One inspector recalled taking unusual measures to fill the buses. "We usually only worked the skid row to fill up the buses when we [came] in with half a busload; . . . we would go down and work skid row and get up enough to fill the bus," he explained of his work in the Sacramento, California, area.[20] Still, INS supervisors and Border Patrol officials often reminded officers in the field that they should not equally police all unsanctioned Mexican immigrants. Women and children, they instructed, were not priorities for the U.S. Border Patrol and should be let alone, notwithstanding extenuating circumstances.

Arresting women and children was as politically unsavory as always, and gender segregation with INS detention facilities and the gendered systems of cross-border deportation limited the INS' institutional ability to handle female and juvenile deportees. Further, the gender and age limitations of the Bracero Program prohibited the option of turning unsanctioned women and children into legal bracero workers. Arresting women and children, therefore, would only drive up Border Patrol apprehension rates and bring unfavorable media attention at a time when Commissioner Swing was busy boasting about having brought calm and conquest to the U.S.-Mexico border. Accordingly, Border Patrol officials actively discouraged officers from apprehending women and children. For example, when INS officials in the Central Office received reports that women and children represented 63 percent of the total number of apprehensions in the El Paso region during January of 1956, the assistant commissioner of the Enforcement Division inquired as to the reason for the high number of apprehensions of women and children. The chief enforcement officer (CEO) of the Southwest Region explained that more women and children had recently been apprehended in the El Paso sector because the El Paso Border Patrol office had begun to pay rewards of one to two dollars to El Paso City Police officers for each undocumented Mexican woman or child that they delivered to the U.S. Border Patrol office in El Paso.[21] The incentive caused a spike in the number of undocumented women and children arrested by the El Paso Police Department. The CEO of the Southwest Region assured the anxious Central Office officials that the number of women and children being apprehended would soon drop. The El Paso Border Patrol was deporting two large groups of women and children each day, and the officers expected that the El Paso police would soon clear out the area. Further, the head of the Mexican Immigration Service in Ciudad Juárez had recently renewed his efforts south of the border to "reduce the number of illegal entries of women and children."[22] By February of 1957, women and children represented only 22 percent of the persons arrested for illegal entry in the El Paso region, and the Central Office applauded the reduction.[23]

When apprehensions of Mexican women and children began to rise in the Lower Rio Grande Valley region during the early 1960s, the new assistant commissioner of enforcement in the Southwest Region, James Greene, repeated the concern regarding the large number of women and children being apprehended. To address the issue, he reminded officers that "the Border Patrol . . . is not concentrating on maids and children" and instructed them that "maids should be worked only on a complaint basis, and crews should not be assigned to a 'maid detail.'"[24]

The hands-off policy regarding maids and children exemplifies how law enforcement is negotiated. In this case, law-enforcement practices focused on persons of Mexican origin split upon an axis of gender according to the gendered limitations of INS detention space and deportation policies. Overlooking the daily crossings of domestic workers who lived in Mexico but worked in homes north of the border most likely dampened the number of apprehensions that Border Patrol officers made in the post-wetback era, when a good number of the men who had been illegals became braceros, but the women and children excluded from the Bracero Program continued to cross illegally. As the chief patrol inspector in El Centro, California, noted, "The wives and children of contract laborers . . . are attempting to enter the United States in increased numbers to join their husbands on farms in the area."[25]

Still, instructions to let women and children alone and the general retreat from aggressive migration control in the post-wetback period were not part of a transition from concentrating upon policing persons of Mexican origin. At the same time that Border Patrol officials directed officers to not apprehend Mexican maids and children, they warned that a new level of vigilance was needed along the U.S.-Mexico border. In countless memos and agency publications, officials of the Enforcement Division of the INS explained, analyzed, and proffered evidence that Mexican nationals had developed new techniques of illegal entry since the conquest of 1954. Soon after the close of Operation Wetback, one immigration investigator in the Los Angeles area explained, "The most difficult problem we have encountered is the detention of illegal Mexican aliens who have assumed the identity of United States citizens and have acquired documents showing birth in the United States."[26] Illegal Mexican immigrants, he cautioned, had switched from illicit border crossings between official ports of entry to legal entries on the basis of fraudulent documents.[27]

FRAUDULENT CITIZENS

In July 1960, Edgar C. Niehbur, once an anthropology student at the University of Texas, was the assistant chief of the Border Patrol, and he used his research skills to improve immigration control. On the basis of research conducted with birth and immigration records, Niehbur informed officers that in the state of Texas alone, one in four filings for birth certificates between May of 1954 and April of 1957 were fraudulent claims to American birth or citizenship. Considering that between 1940 and 1960 the state of Texas issued one hundred and ninety thousand birth certificates to persons of Mexican origin, Niehbur argued that a considerable number of persons claiming to be Mexican Americans were actually false claimants and, thereby, fraudulent citizens. Niehbur examined the consequences of such false claims for migration control efforts in the U.S.-Mexico borderlands. Citing a recent case of a false claimant who had gained legal entry for his wife, eleven children, and twenty-five grandchildren, Niehbur provided a dramatic example of how one false claimant to U.S. citizenship could open the pathway to illegal entry and fraudulent citizenship for an unlimited number of family members.[28]

The Border Patrol's identification of illegal entry by fraudulent documentation provided a new way to interpret the quiet along the U.S.-Mexico border in the post-wetback years. According to INS and Border Patrol analysis, the drop in apprehensions of Mexican nationals was not a reflection of the Border Patrol's retreat from task forces, nor did it necessarily indicate a decrease in the number of Mexican nationals effecting illegal entry. The illegals who once swam, climbed, and hiked across the border had not vanished. Instead, they slipped through official ports of entry under the cover of false documents. Border Patrol officials, in other words, interpreted the low number of apprehensions in the post-wetback period as a reflection of the U.S. Border Patrol's failure to detect and deport the illegal immigrants masquerading as U.S. citizens of Mexican origin.

The Border Patrol's identification of the "fraudulent citizen" problem after Operation Wetback of 1954 carried implications for Border Patrol work. In particular, officials instructed officers to find the frauds who were hiding among the citizens and legal immigrants. Officers in the field, however, were struggling with this objective. In April 1957, officers in Los Angeles reported difficulties in finding undocumented Mexican immigrants among the city's large resident Mexican American population.[29] Officials instructed them to look again. Still, in 1957 Border Patrol officers arrested a total of only 181 persons making false claims to U.S. citizenship. In 1958, to address problems in locating false claimants, the INS established the Fraudulent Document Center in Yuma, Arizona, to collect and analyze information regarding individuals using or trafficking in false immigration papers and citizenship records, such as birth certificates. In particular, the Fraudulent Document Center was established as "a reservoir for data relating to documented false claims to United States citizenship by Mexican nationals." Beginning in 1964, all officers were trained in document analysis.[30] With special training and incredible diligence, therefore, the Border Patrol continued to find unsanctioned Mexican immigrants in the years after Operation Wetback of 1954.

In the post-wetback years, the concentration of Border Patrol personnel and resources in the U.S.-Mexico borderlands positioned the national police force to focus most of its attention upon the problems of migration control that were particular to the southwestern United States. There, the racialization of U.S. migration control was carried into the post-wetback era by the combination of the officers' mind-set that illegal immigrants were persons of Mexican origin with instructions to find the false claimants of Mexican origin and demands to supply the ongoing systems of deportation into the interior of Mexico. At the same time, however, enforcement officials warned Border Patrol officers against apprehending too many unsanctioned Mexican women and children, who could easily swell the ranks of deportees and end the impression of victory along the U.S.-Mexico border.

FROM WETBACKS TO CRIMINALS

Other than the explicit search for fraudulent citizens and the demobilization of the task forces, the bulk of Border Patrol practices in the post-wetback period were scaled-down versions of what officers had been doing for many years along the border. Line watches complemented by traffic checks, city patrols, and the lifts into the interior of Mexico were all familiar tactics. But from the earliest days after the close of Operation Wetback of 1954, Border Patrol officials began to script a new meaning for the familiar practices of migration control in the post-wetback era. In particular, officials embraced the politics and practices of crime control along the U.S.-Mexico border. Linking the Border Patrol's mandate for migration control with a more generalized objective of crime control infused the racialization and regionalization of Border Patrol practices with a renewed urgency, despite the apparent end of the crisis of control along the U.S.-Mexico border.

Leading up to Operation Wetback of 1954, Border Patrol officers had spun sympathetic tales of the undocumented Mexican immigrant. José García, a poor and pitiable character, was the archetype of the so-called Mexican wetback. Against the farmers' accusations that they fomented communism, officers of the U.S. Border Patrol mustered evidence from the living and working conditions of unsanctioned Mexican immigrants to argue that the conditions on southwestern farms approximated those of slavery. Accordingly, aggressive migration control was a liberation movement that did not deport workers so much as free the enslaved. In 1954, the patrol triumphed over the problem of slavery in the fields by deporting the virtual slaves from the borderlands, making braceros out of the remaining illegals, and securing the U.S.-Mexico border against the hordes of unsanctioned Mexican workers that had once flooded the southwest. Those who dared to return, argued Border Patrol officials, were members of a new breed.

In November of 1956, the chief enforcement officer of the Southwest Region instructed officers in his region that "the word 'wetback' . . . should be deleted from the vocabulary of all Immigration officers." As he explained, "We have been aware for sometime that the name 'wetback' creates a picture in the minds of the public and the courts of a poor, emaciated, Mexican worker, entering the United States

illegally to feed a starving family at home. . . . There may have been some justification to this view a few years ago when we were invaded by hordes of just such people,
but today it is no longer true." He asserted that "today's apprehensions consist in
the main part of criminals, often vicious in type, and of hardened and defiant re-
peaters." To defeat the sympathetic attitude engendered by the term *wetback,* the
officer suggested that "in its place a true designation should be used, both orally
and otherwise, in our contacts with each other, the public, and the press." His recommendation was that "whenever a criminal record exists, we use the words, 'criminal alien', and when no criminal record exists, the words, 'deportable alien.' I feel
this change will have a psychological effect on the public and courts that will benefit
the Service." National and local level officials agreed with his assessment, but replaced *deportable alien* with the term *border violator.*[31]

The terms *criminal alien* and *border violator* indicated that the Border Patrol
was assuming new responsibilities. The patrol's mandate may have been migration
control, but its mission was crime control in general by preventing the entry of criminal aliens and deporting border violators. The Border Patrol disseminated the new
terminology to the general public via a network of public information officers assigned to individual stations beginning in 1955. While Public Information Officers
stationed throughout the country collected stories and tidbits for the local press
regarding Border Patrol achievements (with an emphasis on anti-smuggling and
narcotics activities), Robert J. Seitz of the Central Office launched an effort to "give
the American youth a new American hero—the Border Patrol."[32] Seitz pitched the
idea that "one possible means of obtaining nationwide publicity and good will for
the Border Patrol would be through the huge give-away programs conducted by
cereal manufacturers." Seitz believed that General Mills would have an interest in
promoting the Border Patrol by "having children send in box tops to receive a 'Junior Border Patrol badge' and whatever accompanying toys or articles might be
appropriate." Excited about the possibilities, Seitz argued that "there [was] no limit
to which such a program could be carried." For example, "a boy who receives his
Junior Patrol Inspector badge could, by organizing a group of 5 or 6 others, then
become eligible to send in another couple of box tops and receive a Senior Patrol
badge and, after organizing 2 or 3 such groups, would then be eligible for a 'Sector
Chief badge.'"[33]

Hoping to build admiration and goodwill among the next generation, the INS
took Seitz's idea to General Mills, but the company declined to include the Border
Patrol in its bonanza and box-top programs. "The turn-down has not discouraged
us in the least," wrote Richard A. Golling, an INS regional commissioner. "There
are many other ways and means of focusing attention on the objectives of the Border Patrol and its fine record of accomplishments."[34] One of the methods was to
establish Junior Patrol Clubs for boys in communities with Border Patrol stations.
The basic objective of the Junior Patrol Clubs was to promote the Border Patrol

and its many crime-control activities and thereby to preserve the goodwill of the communities in which officers worked and lived. As its recruitment materials advised, the Border Patrol was America's first line of defense against crime because "the alien who violates our border is breaking the laws of this country and his own. Having broken one law, it is easier for him to break another."[35]

The Border Patrol's new law-enforcement image was accompanied by a dramatic shift in Border Patrol activities toward a more generalized program of crime control along the U.S.-Mexico border. In August 1956, the Southwestern Region launched the Criminal, Immoral, and Narcotics (CIN) program. The basic objective of the CIN program was the "identification and location of persons excludable from the United States under those sections of the Immigration and Nationality Act dealing with the Criminal, Immoral, and Narcotic classes."[36] Targeted persons were immigrants, namely Mexican nationals, already living within the United States, and "persons residing in contiguous territory who are likely to be applicants for admission."[37] The adoption of the CIN program altered Border Patrol objectives and operations in the U.S.-Mexico border region.

The CIN program was, at heart, a system of information-gathering and sharing. Immigration investigators and Border Patrol officers were charged with recording the illicit activities of persons living in Mexico who were expected to apply for entry into the United States. The officers worked with Mexican police officers and judicial officials to gain access to the arrest and court records of suspected persons. They perused Mexican newspapers for crime reports. They monitored the movements of prostitutes working in bordertown brothels. Above all, Border Patrol officers depended upon a cadre of immigrant informants for information on the activities and whereabouts of potential immigrants engaged in criminal activities south of the border. In exchange for information, the patrol either paid the informants or, as one report explained, offered them "entry into the United States as parolees . . . as an inducement to obtain and insure the continuous cooperation of certain informants who may not otherwise be permitted to enter the United States."[38]

Among the primary targets of the CIN officers were drug smugglers and persons convicted of violent crimes, yet the officers seemed to spend most of their time gathering information on prostitutes working south of the border. "Normally" remarked one officer, "the operators of the houses furnished the Border Patrol a current list each month of the girls in their employ, and kept the Border Patrol advised of the girls' activities (plans on leaving, for how long, where they [were] going, and new girls coming in)."[39] In Naco, Sonora, brothel owners worked with the local chief of police to "fingerprint the girls, identify, and mug them." Copies of the prostitutes' fingerprints and mug shots were shared with the U.S. Border Patrol office in Douglas, Arizona. North of the border, officers kept an eye out for the women identified as prostitutes by immigrant informants, brothel owners, and

Mexican police officers. The CIN program, therefore, demonstrates that the gendered discretions of Border Patrol practices were negotiable according to the varying moralities of women's work along the U.S.-Mexico border. Not all Border Patrol officers were assigned to conduct investigations for the CIN program, but its establishment shifted Border Patrol operations toward arresting criminal aliens rather than apprehending undocumented immigrants. By 1958, the El Centro, California, CIN unit alone held "10,000 cards containing the correct names and aliases, and usually a photograph, of persons of the immoral classes in Mexico . . . approximately 1,000 cards pertaining to known criminals, and 1,300 cards pertaining to known narcotic or suspected narcotic violators in Mexico."[40]

The switch to looking for criminals instead of migrants had consequences for a wide range of practices and policies. On patrol, officers assigned to the CIN program searched for criminal aliens instead of undocumented workers. Although the INS detention centers along the U.S.-Mexico border had been established to function as staging centers to prepare detainees for either voluntary departure or deportation, the turn toward crime control sparked the invention of new tactics to handle criminals rather than migrants. In April 1956, the INS instituted a new policy of strip-searching all detainees upon entrance to the immigrant detention facilities, because, as officer Don Coppock advised all chief patrol inspectors, "they were not dealing with docile aliens as in the past, but were dealing with an increasing number of desperate criminals."[41] Further, instead of simply prepping migrants for departure, INS facilities began to function as holding centers where migrants were kept until investigations into their possible criminal backgrounds could be completed. In the late 1950s, the INS began to fingerprint detainees with repeat immigration offenses. The fingerprints were forwarded to the FBI.[42] If within fifteen days the INS did not receive a "kick-back" from the FBI—a positive identification of an immigrant with a criminal record—then the detainee would be processed for deportation. If the FBI positively identified a detainee as having a criminal record, INS and Border Patrol officers at the detention facilities initiated prosecution proceedings. This practice linked the relatively marginal and underfunded efforts of U.S. immigration control to the institutional heart of U.S. federal law enforcement, the FBI. Collaborating with the FBI to identify felons and miscreants among the undocumented not only emphasized the importance of migration control in the quiet post-wetback period but also further integrated the U.S. Border Patrol into a broader fabric of federal law-enforcement initiatives. In January 1965, the process of searching for criminals among detainees intensified when the associate deputy regional commissioner of operations in the Southwest Region extended the policy to first-time immigration offenders along the Mexican border.[43] The changes in INS detention practices and policies meant that Border Patrol officers spent increasingly more time working criminal cases because, as Commissioner Swing explained, since the close of Operation Wetback, the INS had a role to play in identifying unsanctioned migrants with criminal records "so that the orderly and vigorous campaign for law enforcement on the border can be further improved."[44]

The INS identified few persons with criminal records among the detainees being held along the border. A 1957 internal report suggested that only three people per day qualified for criminal prosecution.[45] But in his budget request for fiscal year 1958, INS Commissioner Joseph Swing argued that the criminal threat within the undocumented Mexican community demanded that U.S. Border Patrol efforts along the U.S.-Mexico border be adequately funded as a form of crime control. "I would like to read carefully this next paragraph. I am still talking about Mexicans, Mr. Chairman," he began his testimony before the Subcommittee of the Committee on Appropriations in the House of Representatives (John J. Rooney–NY, chair). Then, drawing upon an unarchived study, Swing stated that "of the aliens currently apprehended, over 50 percent have been previously arrested for various crimes. For example, a survey of results obtained from fingerprint records of aliens apprehended during the period July 8 to October 31, 1956, disclosed that out of 14,980 records examined, prior arrest records existed as follows: 1,022 for crimes involving moral turpitude—and they went all the way from rape to carnal knowledge of young girl children—136 for violation of the narcotics laws; 16 for prostitution; 50 for alien smuggling; 91 for false claims to citizenship; 6,131 for previous expulsion, and 1,278 for other crimes."[46] Setting aside the Swing-era tendency to inflate Border Patrol statistics, Swing's testimony before the appropriations subcommittee argued that Border Patrol work should be considered as an arena of crime control. When placed alongside the procedures developed at INS detention centers, the practices of Border Patrol officers and the emergent priorities such as the CIN program, along with the various details to Florida and the American South made it clear that, in the post-wetback years, the Border Patrol had retired its limited mandate for migration control at the nation's margins and had remade itself into a full participant in crime control and federal law enforcement.

For Border Patrol officers, the rise of crime-control discourses and initiatives offered a new way to analyze what some explained as the moral tensions in their work. "If you look at the humane aspects, we are stopping starving people from coming in to work, [and] it is not pretty to look at," explained officer Joe Aubin, who described his job as "not too great" because "I'm really the go-between that prohibits this poor man from finding work to take groceries home."[47] Like many officers, Aubin still understood the problem of unsanctioned Mexican immigration to be an economic issue, and he empathized that "if I had a wife and five or six, seven, eight, nine, 12, 15 kids to support, and could only make a dollar in my own country, I would do the same thing. All they really want to do is come in and earn enough money to feed their families."[48] On the literal front line between underemployed Mexican workers and jobs in the United States, Border Patrol officers often struggled with being in the business of policing workers and families whose crimes of unsanctioned migration were driven by poverty and want. Out on the line, Aubin admitted, he "sympathize[d] . . . with the poor man . . . who simply [wants to] cross over here to pick cotton and support his family." But, Aubin explained, "We have a job to do. I'm paid to do a job in the U.S." His own livelihood was predicated upon stopping unsanctioned migration to the United States, regardless of the plight of Mexico's migrants. Still, if preventing a hungry migrant from reaching work and wages north of the border was difficult, the intersection of migration control and crime control provided officers with a new way of understanding their work. In routine comparisons made between the wetback and post-wetback years, officers commented that in the earlier period the unsanctioned Mexican immigrant was "an honest, easygoing guy (and that was true in the earlier days, there was a lot of people like that), [but] in later years, you ran into a more militant type of people."[49]

For officers in the field, the new militant character of unsanctioned Mexican immigrants was manifested in the escalating hostility of migrants toward Border Patrol officers. "They gradually became more defiant and gave you a little more run for your money," explained officer Walter Bradley about his work in Chula Vista, California. The poor workers continued to cross, and, as they had increasingly done since the early 1950s, they ran to escape arrest. But with the easygoing laborers, he explained, arrived an increasing number of militants and criminals who flipped the dynamics of the border by placing the officers under siege.[50] "Here in El Paso," explained Aubin, "I've had people throw rocks and bricks at me from the Mexican side. I was hit in the head about two years ago. It all started when they took sling shots away from the Border Patrol. It was declared an unprofessional weapon. . . . Now they have the sling shots, David and Goliath slings, and we are bombarded with rocks and bricks on a daily basis." Aubin described line-watches along the levy as "running a gauntlet. If you get 20 or 30 Mexicans with slings, chunking rocks at you, you got your hands full just getting out of there."[51] For Aubin, the brick-lobbing Mexicans confirmed that a new generation of border crossers had arrived. Among the workers walking through the deserts, scaling the fences, and wading across the increasingly toxic New River was a cast of dangerous individuals. These were the criminal aliens that his senior advisors had warned him about.

The rise of the criminal alien within Border Patrol rhetoric, the explicit search for unsanctioned migrants engaged in illicit activities, and the adoption of safety procedures designed to handle criminals in INS detention facilities all indicate the evolution of U.S. migration control toward a more generalized program of crime control in the U.S.-Mexico borderlands. Undoubtedly, Border Patrol and INS attempts to refashion migration control as a means of preventing crimes other than unsanctioned migration was a strategy designed to defend the relevance of the bloated Border Patrol bureaucracy in the post-wetback era. The Border Patrol's budget had jumped from $7,114,147 in 1954 to $11,530,947 in 1955 and increased again to $12,168,698 in 1956. The more generalized crime-control strategies and priorities emerged from within the patrol as a matter of self-preservation after Swing's triumphant declaration of victory at the U.S.-Mexico border. Yet the Border Patrol's turn toward crime control at the U.S.-Mexico border complemented and occurred in the context of a rising urgency regarding drug control.[52]

DRUG CONTROL, MIGRATION CONTROL

Since the 1930s, Harry Anslinger had led the Federal Bureau of Narcotics and directed a powerful publicity campaign regarding the many threats of the domestic and international drug trade. In the 1930s, he reached beyond public health arguments regarding the dangers of individual drug use and highlighted the role of organized crime in the drug trade. Drug control, Anslinger argued, was a critical component of policing mafiosos and organized crime.[53] His campaign played a pivotal role in shaping the Marijuana Tax Act of 1937, which placed the first tax on the sale of cannabis, hemp, and marijuana. In the early years of the Cold War, Anslinger consolidated his campaign into a deeply consequential and widely accepted social project. These years, as David F. Musto has argued, represent "the high point of federal punitive action against narcotics."[54] In particular, Congress aggressively took up the project of punishing drug users and suppliers. For example, between 1947 and 1950, changes in the Uniform Narcotic Drug Acts created mandatory minimums for drug convictions. In 1951, the Boggs Act applied a mandatory minimum penalty of two years in prison for first-time drug offenders. The ascent of drug control climaxed with the passage of the Narcotics Control Act of 1956, which imposed life imprisonment or even the death penalty for certain drug offenses that involved minors.[55] Further the Narcotics Control Act of 1956 translated the increasingly punitive dimensions of drug control to migration control by establishing drug addiction and drug-law violations as grounds for deportation. Drug control, therefore, applied the state's ultimate sanctions—life in prison, death, or banishment—to drug violations.

The U.S. Border Patrol was deeply affected by the rise of drug control as a federal law-enforcement initiative. Although the U.S. Customs Service had long led interdiction efforts along U.S. land borders and coastlines, in 1955, all U.S. Border Patrol officers were officially cross-designated as customs inspectors.[56] As such, Border Patrol officers were granted the authority to include drug interdiction among their top priorities while policing the crime of unsanctioned entry.[57] By the mid-1950s, therefore, drug control was no longer a side issue in migration control. Accordingly, in 1958, the Border Patrol began to keep detailed records of the volume and value of narcotics seized by its officers. The patrol's official participation in drug interdiction deepened its roots in the U.S.-Mexico borderlands as the illicit drug trade moved progressively toward the border after World War II.

DRUG INTERDICTION AT THE U.S.-MEXICO BORDER

Prior to World War II, most of the opium and heroin consumed in the United States came from Italy, France, and the Middle East. When World War II cut off licit and illicit European trade routes with the United States, Mexico emerged as a core producer of opium and heroin. The increased production of opium poppies in Mexico was a response to the vacuum created in the illicit international market, but it also developed because the U.S. government encouraged Mexico to produce opium and hemp for the war effort. The United States wanted opium to make morphine for medical purposes and hemp to make strong fibers and ropes. Production increased rapidly; by 1943, opium had become the primary cash crop in Mexico's northern state of Sinaloa. After the war, the United States called for an end to opium and hemp production in Mexico, and the Mexican government obeyed these demands. In 1948, the Mexican military began chopping down poppy plants and marijuana fields in the "critical triangle" of Sinaloa, Sonora, and Durango—the three northern states where heroin and marijuana production was most intense. The eradication campaign was slow and limited as soldiers hacked away at thousands of acres of illicit crops, but the United States was satisfied with Mexico's progress, given that its share of the heroin market in the United States remained at 10–15 percent throughout the 1950s and 1960s. Mexico, however, continued to be a primary source of marijuana destined for the United States, and Mexico emerged as the primary thoroughfare between the United States—the world's largest drug consumer—and burgeoning drug cartels in South America.[58] The shift of the drug trade to the U.S.-Mexico border (a shift that would only deepen over time), the rise of drug control as a federal crime-control priority, and the official cross-designation of U.S. Border Patrol officers as a federal interdiction agents reinforced the Border Patrol's concentration in the U.S.-Mexico borderlands.

In the late 1960s, Richard Nixon elevated federal drug control to a new high. Whereas crime control had yet to operate as a core issue in national politics, Richard Nixon's 1968 presidential campaign focused on "law and order" issues and promised to increase the federal involvement in crime control. Once in office, Nixon began his confrontation with crime by targeting drug trafficking at the U.S.-Mexico border. In particular, to reduce the amount of marijuana available within the United States and to strong-arm Mexico into doing more to eradicate marijuana fields, President Nixon launched Operation Intercept on September 21, 1969. During Operation Intercept, U.S. officers stopped all pedestrian and vehicular traffic at the U.S.-Mexico border to check for drugs being smuggled into the United States. The U.S. Border Patrol only seized sixty-nine hundred pounds of marijuana, three hundred and fifty thousand dangerous pills, and a half ounce of heroine, but the seven-week campaign confirmed the U.S.-Mexico border as a primary site of the war on drugs and affirmed the general broadening of Border Patrol operations to include crime control in the post-wetback years.[59]

By the early 1970s, U.S. Border Patrol officers reported that the line between drug interdiction and migration control had become almost too difficult to decipher as it became increasingly difficult to distinguish between illegal immigrants and drug smugglers. Border Patrol officers, for example, would often find unsanctioned border crossers "carrying big sacks of marijuana."[60] The men carrying the sacks of narcotics across the border were officially categorized as drug smugglers, but, as officer Mario Chamberlain explained, "They're just what we call mules. They're usually not really the guy who's the smuggler, so to speak."[61] The smugglers made the deals north and south of the border, he explained, while the person bringing the drugs across was "just an old working man, really what he is, usually trying to make a few bucks."[62] But in his official capacity, he arrested the old workingmen as both unsanctioned immigrants and drug smugglers.

Crime control and, in particular, drug control were thus critical dimensions in the making of U.S. Border Patrol policy and practice after Operation Wetback of 1954. The Bracero Program and the Border Patrol's participation in the mismanagement of Mexican labor migration to the United States remained important factors, but in an era when the Bracero Program swept an increasing number of Mexico's male labor migrants into legal migration streams, Border Patrol officials were forced to think in new ways about their efforts in the U.S.-Mexico borderlands. While U.S. Border Patrol officers were not busy enforcing international labor agreements or domestic labor law, they expanded their practices, policies, and priorities to participate in projects of federal law enforcement and crime control, especially drug control. The post-wetback period, therefore, was a period of quiet but dramatic transformation in which Border Patrol officials and the dictates of the emerging war on drugs shifted the orientation of U.S. immigration law enforcement toward a broader program of crime control. In this period, the Border Patrol devised new practices and policies to police unsanctioned migration as a crime committed by drug smugglers, prostitutes, and fraudulent citizens. The post-wetback era, in other words, was a regenerative period during which the fusion of migration control with crime control altered the basic mechanics and meaning of Border Patrol work, but the racialization and regionalization of U.S. migration control remained the same.

THE END OF THE POST-WETBACK ERA

Many INS officials believed that the quiet post-wetback era would come to an end with the termination of the Bracero Program on December 31, 1964. The Border Patrol prepared for an onslaught of unsanctioned Mexican migrants in the months after the doors shut at bracero recruitment centers south of the border. In antici-pation of a quick and dramatic return to the days of the wetback, the Southwest-ern Regional headquarters in San Pedro, California, distributed a document enti-tled "A Plan to Bolster the Border" to all Border Patrol offices along the U.S.-Mexico border. The plan outlined a program for detailing 216 additional officers to the Cali-fornia border region in the case of an emergency. When the Bracero Program ended, however, there were only minor increases in unsanctioned border crossings. U.S. Department of State officials in Baja California forwarded memos regarding a large number of ex-braceros and their families waiting and hoping for new contracts, and some crossed illegally into the United States.[63] But apprehensions of Mexican nationals did not spike as expected. Without signs of a crisis, the regional office never dispatched the special detail of officers. The post-wetback era did not begin to unravel until the late 1960s, when the Mexican economy headed into a tailspin, and the U.S. Border Patrol returned to using aggressive migration control tactics.

The underside of Mexico's postwar industrialization program began to show during the late 1960s. Although the Mexican economy had grown an average of 3.2 times annually between 1940 and 1960, and another 2.7 times between 1960 and 1970, the distribution of wealth was negligible.[64] The percentage of income available to the poorer half of society fell from 19 percent in 1950 to 16 percent in 1957. It dropped again to 15 percent in 1963 and 13 percent in 1975. The wealth-iest 20 percent of Mexican society, however, claimed a near steady 60 percent of the available income.[65] What had been dubbed the "Mexican Miracle" of economic expansion after World War II was not a miracle for all. When the global recessions and panics of the mid-1970s hit the Mexican economy, Mexico's poor suffered enor-mous losses. In 1975, the Mexican economy experienced zero per capita growth, real wages fell, and underemployment plagued 45 percent of workers.[66] At the same time, the country was experiencing another population boom. Beginning in 1940, Mexico's population had increased at the rate of 3 percent per year. Whereas the population was only 19.6 million in 1940, by 1977 it had increased to 67 million. By 1980, the Mexican population stood at 70 million.[67] So just as the Mexican econ-omy was contracting, more Mexicans were entering the workforce.

For many of Mexico' poor, migration was a strategy for economic survival, but as the Mexican Miracle unraveled, changes in U.S. immigration law closed more options for legal Mexican immigration. In 1965, the United States Congress passed the Immigration Reform Act, which ended the era of racially restrictive national quotas launched by the National Origins Act of 1924 and placed the first numeri-cal limit upon legal immigration into the United States from Mexico. According to the Immigration Reform Act of 1965, immigration from the Western Hemi-sphere, including Mexico, was capped at 120,000 annually (excluding quota ex-emptions). The 120,000 cap was too low to accommodate the volume of Mexican labor migration to the United States.[68] In fiscal year 1967, 43,034 Mexican nationals were legally admitted to the United States, and another 86,845 were apprehended by the Border Patrol, and a total of 108,327 were forcibly returned to Mexico.[69] The Immigration Reform Act of 1965 became effective on July 1, 1968, meaning that as the end of the Mexican Miracle began to move through the Mexican countryside and urban areas, the opportunities for Mexican nationals to legally enter the United States were capped by quota limitations. Mexicans fleeing the collapse of the Mexican Miracle crossed the border without inspection or entered with false documents. Accordingly, U.S. Border Patrol apprehension rates along the U.S.-Mexico border began to climb out of their post-wetback lows. The number of Mexican nationals apprehended by the U.S. Border Patrol crossed the 100,000 mark in 1968 and inched toward 500,000 in 1973.

Yet, as always, the rising apprehension rate along the U.S.-Mexico border resulted both from trends in unsanctioned Mexican migration and from changes in Border Patrol practice. Unfortunately, precisely what happened in terms of Border Patrol practice is less clear. Many U.S. Border Patrol correspondence records for the post-1965 period remain closed to public inquiry. But public documents, such as INS annual reports, congressional appropriations hearings for the U.S. Department of Justice, and published ethnographies conducted with Border Patrol assistance all indicate a return to aggressive migration control tactics directed toward detecting and deporting unsanctioned immigrants of Mexican origin during the late 1960s.

In 1967, the INS expanded the capacity for cross-border deportations into the interior of Mexico by supplementing the ongoing trainlifts to Chihuahua City and the airlifts to León, Guanajuato, with buslifts that ran from Ciudad Juárez to Jiménez, Chihuahua.[70] Two years later, the INS opened new staging centers for deportation along the U.S.-Mexico border. The new lifts and staging centers allowed the INS to process and deport greater numbers of unsanctioned Mexican immigrants, and the Border Patrol resumed regular raids that again had the singular objective of apprehending unsanctioned Mexican immigrants. By the early 1970s, the patrol had returned to conducting mass raids on farms and ranches throughout the southwest, but Border Patrol officials also intensified the search for fraudulent citizens assumed to be hiding in urban areas with large Mexicano communities, such as Los Angeles, California, and San Antonio, Texas.[71] In 1972, the urban raids produced at least one-quarter of the apprehensions made that year in the Southern California region.[72] The next year, the INS annual report boasted that "in a single operation of 20 workdays in the Los Angeles area, a special force of 75 Service officers located and processed 11,500 deportable aliens."[73] In 1973, raids in the Los Angeles area escalated as immigration investigators and officers of the U.S. Border Patrol conducted raids on factories and Mexicano residential communities.[74] The massive jump in apprehensions of Mexican nationals from just 44,161 in 1965 to 616,630 in 1974, therefore, was largely due to the wave of unemployed Mexican

TABLE 6 Principal activities and accomplishments of the U.S. Border Patrol for the years ended June 30, 1965–1974

	1965	1966	1967	1968	1969	1970	1971	1972	1973	1974
Total number of persons apprehended	53,279	80,701	96,021	124,908	174,332	233,862	305,902	373,896	503,936	640,913
Number of deportable aliens located	52,422	79,610	94,778	123,519	172,391	231,116	302,517	369,495	498,123	634,777
Number of Mexican nationals apprehended	44,161	71,233	86,845	113,304	159,376	219,254	290,152	355,099	480,588	616,630
Number of persons questioned	5,285,157	5,582,551	5,606,549	5,281,193	6,086,775	6,805,260	7,663,759	9,023,631	9,506,719	10,201,915
Value of narcotics seizures	$393,474	$382,185	$1,718,937	$688,205	$1,208,040	$3,864,903	$5,379,189	$11,708,554	$23,464,030	$45,056,331

SOURCE: Data compiled from principal activities and accomplishments of the U.S. Border Patrol, *Annual Reports of the Immigration and Naturalization Service, Fiscal Years Ending June 30, 1965–1974* (Washington, DC: GPO).

workers heading to jobs north of the border, but it also reflects an increase in INS capacities along the U.S.-Mexico border, marks the U.S. Border Patrol's return to aggressive migration control practices, and signals the adoption of urban raids as a key method of increasing apprehension rates. These were the days when Jorge Lerma sang his song, "Superman Is an Illegal Alien," protesting the aggressive enforcement of U.S. immigration restrictions against Mexicanos in the U.S.-Mexico borderlands.

After twenty years of relative quiet along the U.S.-Mexico border, the steady increase in the number of apprehensions of unsanctioned Mexican nationals prompted the new commissioner of the INS, Leonard F. Chapman, to declare that 1974 was the year when the post-wetback era officially ended. Chapman confessed that "the virtual flood of illegal entries across the Southern Border" had returned, and the crisis of control was worse than it had ever been. Chapman estimated that an estimated six to twelve million illegal immigrants lived in the United States, more than 90 percent of whom were Mexican nationals.[75] Other sources disputed his claim. The U.S. Census Bureau estimated that, by the end of the 1970s, only five million undocumented immigrants lived in the United States, with Mexican nationals comprising less than one-half of the total.[76] But Chapman maintained that illegal immigration was again at crisis levels and that, this time, the immigrants were criminal aliens, prostitutes, and drug smugglers rather than the simple and easygoing "wetbacks" of the past.[77]

At the close of the post-wetback period, the primary targets of U.S. migration control remained the same. What had changed was the expansion of Border Patrol's mandate for migration control to include the broader objective of crime control. From this process of transformation, the U.S. Border Patrol emerged more closely interwoven with federal law-enforcement institutions and initiatives. The patrol was no longer an outlier with a narrow agenda along the nation's borders; its new focus on drug control and crime control folded the Border Patrol into the expanding systems of federal law enforcement. In the years after Richard Nixon unleashed an era of strategic consolidation of federal law enforcement operations, Border Patrol work routinely included policing immigrants, policing criminals, and policing drugs. Officers experienced dissonance in their simultaneous efforts to police the U.S.-Mexico border as a pathway for illegal migrants seeking escape from poverty in Mexico and as a theater of drug interdiction in the United States. However, the chaotic intersections of migration control and drug control along the border would increasingly structure the making and meaning of U.S. Border Patrol work in the last decades of the twentieth century.

Epilogue

On May 28, 1974, the U.S. Border Patrol celebrated its golden anniversary. Established fifty years earlier as a small outfit of officers, the patrol had seen many changes since those early days. Amid the chaos of the wetback's return and the constant escalation of America's war on drugs, Border Patrol officials paused to revel in a commemorative understanding of their past. In countless speeches, presentations, and publications, Border Patrol officials told epic tales of rising from obscurity to defend the nation by aggressively enforcing U.S. immigration laws. Except for a brief moment during World War II, national security was a new language for the U.S. Border Patrol, but in a decade marked by stagflation and various challenges to postwar U.S. global dominance, nation-centered narratives of border enforcement and immigration control abounded. "Composed from the very beginning of hard-working and dedicated officers enforcing unpopular laws," explained public information officer Samuel Tidwell, "the Border Patrol has fought an up-hill battle all the way to insure each American citizen and legal resident alien the right to economic security, and the right to be free from undesirable alien forces that would sweep the boundaries that demarcate the greatest nation on earth."[1]

In the summer of 1974, the *I and N Reporter* consolidated the many stories that the officers had told during the year and published a short history of the Border Patrol. With the simple title, "The First Fifty Years," this official history was a sweeping document that touched upon key moments in the development of the Border Patrol but expunged many of the social and political dimensions that so deeply shaped the patrol's translation of U.S. immigration law into a social reality of policing mexicanos in the U.S.-Mexico borderlands.

To begin, "The First Fifty Years" described the first generation of patrol officers as "former mounted guards, policemen, sheriffs, gunslingers of various types, and appointees from the Civil Service Register of Railway Postal Clerks and Immigrant Inspectors" and profiled E. A. "Dogie" Wright as a typical hire in the early years. Dogie, as the story goes, had been a Deputy U.S. Marshal and a Texas Ranger before joining the U.S. Border Patrol, but "The First Fifty Years" made no mention of the many other jobs he held before joining the patrol. By choosing to profile Dogie as nothing more than lawman rather than as a man with an eclectic past—as a clerk, chauffeur, construction worker, and ticket-taker at a movie theater—Border Patrol officials refused to recognize their predecessors as men and workers with a wide range of social entanglements that influenced their enforcement of U.S. immigration restrictions. Disregarding such entanglements made the Border Patrol's turn toward policing Mexican nationals in the U.S.-Mexico borderlands emerge as the certain and inevitable product of impartial law enforcement rather than as the messy result of the uneven politics, possibilities, and limitations of policing illegal immigration in the 1920s and 1930s. Further, erasing the connections between the officers' lives and work buried the social history of Border Patrol violence, which swung almost indecipherably between the officers' enforcement of U.S. immigration restrictions and their lives as men, brothers, and community members. According to "The First Fifty Years," all violence related to the Border Patrol's enforcement of U.S. immigration restrictions was rooted in the officers' mandate for federal law enforcement, namely, in the "nightly gun battles" of the Prohibition Era. Never mentioned were the names of Samuel Askins, who "was really in favor of banging a suspect over the ears with a sixshooter," or Jack Cottingham, who shot randomly into Mexico to avenge the wounds of his brother. Also unmentioned was Harlon B. Carter, who led Operation Wetback of 1954 and had shot and killed Ramón Casiano on the streets of Laredo before joining the Border Patrol. The patrol of the mid-1970s, therefore, refused to acknowledge the ways in which the borderland's history of racial violence lived within the Border Patrol and how, in turn, the patrol's history lived within the violence of the borderlands.[2]

"The First Fifty Years" also obscured the development of key strategic innovations in U.S. immigration law enforcement by hiding the role of Mexican officials in the accumulation of U.S. immigration law enforcement in the broader U.S.-Mexico borderlands and by denying the significance of gender in the rise of the border fence as a method of migration control. But filed among Border Patrol correspondence records and monthly apprehension reports during the mid-twentieth century lay the both records of Mexican officials who championed the policing of unsanctioned Mexican immigrants and the notable presence of Mexican women and children who confronted the tightening regime of migration control along the U.S.-Mexico border. Mexican authorities encouraged the Border Patrol's national turn toward the U.S.-Mexico border and expanded the field for enforcement by providing new opportunities to conduct migration control on the Mexican side of the border, and the unruly resistance of women, children, and families increased the urgency of fencing the border because Border Patrol officers' uncomfortable encounters with unsanctioned Mexican women and children led officers to avoid the physical confrontations and coercions required to stop illegal migrants from crossing the border. In part, therefore, the development of the enforcement strategies that pushed unsanctioned Mexican immigrants to the dangerous backlands of the U.S.-Mexico border region emerged as a process of resolving the gendered problems posed to the use of violence when women, children, and families illegally crossed the border.

Written during an era of the "wetback's return," "The First Fifty Years" recalled 1954 as a year of triumph along the U.S.-Mexico border. Honoring Commissioner Swing's 1954 campaign as the innovative act that restored "control of the border," "The First fifty Years" marked Operation Wetback as a turning point in the policing of unsanctioned Mexican immigration. Before and after the triumph of 1954, many changes in Border Patrol practice contributed to the rise and fall of the problem of unsanctioned Mexican migration, but "The First Fifty Years" erased the decade-long increase and decrease in the use of aggressive immigration law-enforcement tactics, which defined the Border Patrol's victory of 1954. In their lament for a triumph long gone, Border Patrol officials of the mid-1970s denied the recent intensification in U.S. immigration law enforcement in the U.S.-Mexico borderlands. The emergence of urban raids in Mexicano communities might best be described as Operation Wetback II, but the Border Patrol declined to name it; instead, it buried increased migration control in recent years beneath nostalgia for Swing's conquest of 1954.

In everything that it left untold, "The First Fifty Years" buried the many histories embedded in the Border Patrol's rise in the U.S.-Mexico borderlands. Of course, it was never intended to serve as anything more than a propaganda piece for the patrol, but as the debates regarding U.S. immigration control and the "wetback problem" began to explode during the 1970s, such a narrow construction of the Border Patrol's past meant that few people really understood all of the Border Patrol's project in the U.S.-Mexico borderlands. Unspoken histories, however, clearly reverberated within everyday Border Patrol practice.

UNSPOKEN HISTORIES

On the evening of June 11, 1973, two Border Patrol officers sat in a parked car on the northbound side of Highway 5 in southern California. Sometime after dark, the officers saw in their headlights Felix Humberto Brignoni-Ponce, his two friends, and the evidence of crimes that had gone unseen. According to the officers, the three men appeared to be of "Mexican descent," which was sufficient evidence to suspect them of illicitly crossing the U.S.-Mexico border. The officers pulled the men over after a short pursuit and questioned them about their citizenship status. Brignoni-Ponce was a U.S. citizen, but his two passengers both admitted that they had illegally entered the country. The officers arrested all three men: the two passengers for illegal entry, and Brignoni-Ponce for "knowingly transporting illegal immigrants," a felony punishable by a fine of five thousand dollars and up to five years in prison for each violation.[3]

Much as Mariano Martínez and Jesús Jaso had done after their arrest by Officers Pete Torres and George W. Parker Jr. in March 1927, Brignoni-Ponce challenged his arrest on the grounds that Border Patrol officers had no reason to suspect him of violating U.S. immigration restrictions. According to Brignoni-Ponce and his lawyers, "Mexican descent" was insufficient evidence of the crime of illegal entry and, therefore, the Border Patrol officers had violated Brignoni-Ponce's Fourth Amendment protections against unreasonable search and seizure. This time, one full decade after the legislative victories of the civil rights movement had prohibited the explicitly racialized distribution of rights, resources, and protections in American public life, the legal battle ended in the U.S. Supreme Court.

The Supreme Court recognized the broad social importance of the Brignoni-Ponce case. If Brignoni-Ponce's interrogation, arrest, and conviction arose from discriminatory discretions in Border Patrol practice, then the officers were guilty of subjecting Brignoni-Ponce and his two passengers to undue suspicion, surveillance, and state violence. When multiplied by the millions of interrogations that Border Patrol officers made each year, Border Patrol practices potentially represented a massive site of targeting persons of "Mexican appearance" for undue, unequal, and unjust police action. Therefore, Brignoni-Ponce's case raised serious questions regarding the persistence of racialized governance in the post–civil rights era. In particular, the *Brignoni-Ponce* case suggested that race continued to determine the degrees of freedom that state officials afforded to those living within the United States. Brignoni-Ponce and his passengers had been pulled over, detained, questioned, arrested, and threatened with imprisonment or deportation (plus all of the collateral pecuniary, social, personal, and political consequences that each form of punishment carries). The question before the Court was not whether they had broken the law, but whether race was a legitimate tool of discretion when policing the crime of illegal immigration.

Despite the social consequences of subjecting persons of Mexican appearance to high levels of state surveillance and force, the Supreme Court found U.S. Border Patrol statistics to be a persuasive. In 1973, 85 percent of the persons arrested for the crime of illegal entry were persons of Mexican origin. Assuming that Border Patrol statistics accurately reflected trends in the crime of illegal immigration, the Court reasoned that "85% of the aliens illegally in the country are from Mexico."[4] The justices translated Border Patrol statistics into a profile of the illegal immigrant and thereby held that Border Patrol officers' use of Mexican appearance as an indicator of the crime of illegal entry was both reasonable and legitimate. According to the Court's decision in *United States v. Brignoni-Ponce,* Mexicanos were the unfortunate but appropriate suspects of the crime of illegal immigration and the legitimate subjects of unequal levels of state violence in the pursuit of immigration control.

Certainly, hundreds of thousands of Mexican nationals illicitly crossed the U.S.-Mexico border during the twentieth century and continue to do so into the twenty-first century. Scholars, politicians, and activists debate the actual volume of unsanctioned Mexican immigration but, if nothing else, the bodies pulled from the Rio Grande and dragged from the deserts have long revealed the reality of unsanctioned Mexican migration across the U.S.-Mexico border. There is no doubt that the high volume of such immigration influenced the Border Patrol's turn toward the southern border. More specifically, the politics of controlling the labor migration of Mexican workers back and forth across the U.S.-Mexico border undoubtedly shaped the making of the Border Patrol. But the history of the U.S. Border Patrol is much more than a chapter in the story of Mexican labor migration to the United States.

In the early years, officers interpreted their mandate for federal immigration law enforcement according to local histories and interests in the management of Mexican immigrant labor. At that time, Border Patrol violence was far from unique in a region dominated by ranchers, farmers, and their guns. But Border Patrol violence was tied to the category of the illegal immigrant, which gave new meanings to familiar acts. Border Patrol violence introduced a new way of marking the meaning of race in the U.S.-Mexico borderlands. In particular, whereas discourses of the differences between blackness and whiteness continued to dominate the logic of racial inequity in the United States, the danger, dislocations, damage, and death that touched Mexicano lives and communities through U.S. immigration law enforcement linked Mexicanos in the borderlands to the crimes and consequences of being illegal in the United States. The Border Patrol's narrow focus upon policing unsanctioned Mexican immigration, therefore, drew a very particular color line around the political condition of illegality. Border Patrol practice, in other words, imported the borderlands' deeply rooted racial divides arising from conquest and capitalist economic development into the making of U.S. immigration law enforcement and, in turn, transformed the legal/illegal divide into a problem of race.

This problem of race began as a local interpretation of federal immigration laws, but it evolved upon the cross-border foundation of U.S. and Mexican collaboration during the 1940s. By the late 1960s, it had taken root in national initiatives for crime control and drug interdiction along the U.S.-Mexico border. This history of the U.S. Border Patrol's evolving dedication to the project of policing unsanctioned Mexican immigration complicates any easy equations between Mexicanos and the crime of illegal immigration by providing a detailed examination of the social and political ruptures that lay beneath the Border Patrol's seemingly unbroken focus upon policing unsanctioned Mexican immigration. The U.S. Supreme Court, however, swept aside the intrinsic and historically rooted complexities of the Border Patrol's uneven enforcement of U.S. immigration restrictions and, instead, effectively legitimated U.S. Border Patrol practice as a site of state violence in which the differences between being legal and being illegal could be legitimately policed by targeting Mexicanos—namely, Mexican Browns—in the United States.

Sanctified by the Supreme Court, the Border Patrol moved into the late twentieth century with no interruption to its project of policing Mexicans in the U.S.-Mexico borderlands. Still, mass arrests and targeted enforcement against Mexicanos did not persist uncontested. Mexico's unsanctioned migrants continued to lob bricks, evade arrest, and taunt Border Patrol officers from the other side of the line, while a new generation of immigrant rights advocates and civil liberties groups forcefully protested the new wave of aggressive migration control and its impact upon Mexicano communities in the United States. In particular, these groups protested the Border Patrol's searches for fraudulent citizens by raiding Mexican American communities. During the 1973 surge in raids in the Los Angeles area, for example, the Los Angeles branch of the American Civil Liberties Union filed for an injunction against INS raids targeting "Hispanic" neighborhoods, charging that among those apprehended for deportation were U.S. citizens.[5] As the raids pushed deeper into residential communities, priests and leaders of the clergy advocated for parishioners. "It shouldn't be a crime to have brown skin," charged Reverend Mark Day of St. Joseph's Church.[6] The next year, Mexican American community leaders in Chicago launched a campaign against Border Patrol raids and forced the INS to establish the Concerned Citizens Committee on Immigration to broker charges of harassment and undue surveillance.[7] But tensions only mounted between the Border Patrol and Mexicano communities in the southwestern United States. In 1978, the U.S. Commission on Civil Rights launched an investigation into the impact of U.S. immigration law enforcement upon the civil rights of citizens and immigrants.[8] The commission exposed corruption within the INS and affirmed the critics' charges of discrimination and use of excessive force by the Border Patrol. In particular, it confirmed the harassment of Mexicano communities in the southwestern United States. The commission's report and the exposé of a crooked and brutal task force comprised of San Diego Police officers and Border Patrol officers working undercover along the San Diego-Tijuana border each helped to push criticism of U.S. immigration law enforcement into the spotlight. Signaling a new age of public cynicism, Universal Studios released *The Border* (1982), which portrayed the U.S. Border Patrol as awash in corruption and violence.

While public scorn mounted, it was the emergent generation of Chicana/o activists who formed the epicenter of the resistance against Border Patrol practices. Chicana/o activism during the late 1960s dramatically reshaped the politics of migration control in the U.S.-Mexico borderlands. Unlike the middle-class Mexican American activists of their parents' generation, Chicana/o activists embraced Mexican immigration and thereby reimagined their community's interests in immigration law enforcement. Rather than rejecting Mexico's labor migrants and demanding increased migration control, Chicana/o activists tended to mobilize on behalf of migrants—legal and illegal—while challenging state systems that continued to marginalize the Mexicano community within the United States.[9] On the streets, Chicana/o activists forced Border Patrol officers to operate under intense counter-surveillance by closely monitoring Border Patrol activities. "I've had Mexican people stand by and . . . check me, to see if I am checking everybody," explained Officer Joe Aubin in 1978.[10]

In 1987, the American Friends Service Committee sponsored the consolidation and institutionalization of counter-surveillance over U.S. immigration law enforcement officers by establishing the Immigration Law Enforcement Monitoring Project (ILEMP). Led by veteran activists María Jiménez (Houston, Texas) and Roberto Martínez (San Diego, California), ILEMP solicited, received, and investigated complaints from immigrants and citizens regarding violence and mistreatment by U.S. immigration officers. Between 1987 and 1990, ILEMP documented more than 380 cases of excessive force, racial harassment, and sexual assault, most of which they charged to the officers of the U.S. Border Patrol.[11] In 1990, the work of ILEMP encouraged the Committee on Foreign Affairs in the U.S. House of Representatives to hold hearings entitled *Allegations of Violence along the United States-Mexico Border*. At the hearings, Jiménez protested the racialization of U.S. immigration law enforcement. As Jiménez testified, "Residents of the southern border, including U.S. citizens, whose language, culture, and skin color make them appear 'foreign' are considered suspect. Incidents of exclusion, illegal arrest, and illegal deportation of citizens and immigrants legally in the country are frequently reported."[12]

Understanding Border Patrol work as a site of racialized state violence, Jiménez and a growing circle of scholars and activists articulated powerful historical genealogies for policing Mexicanos in the U.S.-Mexico borderlands. Jiménez, for example, compared the Border Patrol to the slave patrols of the American south.[13] Historian David Montejano argued that the racial violence of immigration law enforcement stemmed from the history of conquest in the U.S.-Mexico borderlands.[14] In stark contrast to the Border Patrol's attempts to expunge the past from U.S. immigration control, these scholars and activists interpreted Border Patrol work as intimately bound to histories of race, labor control, and conquest across four centuries of the American past. Jiménez and Montejano were correct to insist that policing Mexicans stemmed from these deeper histories, but they also oversimplified the Border Patrol's rise in the U.S.-Mexico borderlands. Mexican elites had played important roles in crafting U.S. migration-control practices; Mexican American leaders had protected the project of policing unsanctioned Mexican immigrants; and an expansion in federal law enforcement defined the phenomenal growth of the U.S. Border Patrol in the post-wetback era. Therefore, in their own particular ways, U.S. Border Patrol officials, the U.S. Supreme Court, and critics of U.S. immigration law enforcement all embraced a limited understanding of the Border Patrol's project of policing Mexicans in the U.S.-Mexico borderlands.

THE MEN AND WOMEN OF THE PATROL

Against the many efforts to promote a simple history of the U.S. Border Patrol, no one more doggedly held onto the untold complexities of U.S. immigration law enforcement than the members of the Fraternal Order of Retired Border Patrol Officers (FORBO). Established on October 25, 1978, the FORBO took shape during another period of major transition in the U.S. Border Patrol. After almost two decades of slipping into near political oblivion, U.S. immigration law enforcement had reemerged on the political landscape in the 1970s. Although many advocated greater border control and immigration enforcement, immigrant activists increasingly challenged immigration law enforcement as excessive and racially discriminatory toward Mexicanos in the borderlands. Others cared little for immigration politics but decried what seemed to be rampant ineptitude and corruption within the INS.[15] By 1977, immigration control was at center stage in American politics. That year, President Jimmy Carter proposed comprehensive immigration reform to address the problem of illegal immigration and appointed Leonel Castillo to lead the Immigration and Naturalization Service through this difficult and divisive period.[16] As commissioner of the Immigration and Naturalization Service, Castillo attempted to build a more efficient and less corrupt organization that equitably enforced U.S. immigration restrictions. Among the many changes he oversaw was a massive turnover in Border Patrol personnel when new federal regulations required the retirement of all Border Patrol officers upon reaching the age of fifty-five.[17] FORBO members recall this period as the "mandatory exodus of January 1, 1978."[18]

The wave of officers exiting the patrol understood that "as the number of retirees continued to grow and scatter out across the country, it became evident that the friendships and shared experiences of a quarter century were in jeopardy." Hoping to "preserve the friendships and associations that might otherwise be lost in retirement—with no commercial, political, or other controversial commitments to muddy the cause," thirty-four retirees organized a meeting in Denver, Colorado, and established the Fraternal Order of Retired Border Patrol Officers on October 25, 1978. Since then, the FORBO has organized annual retreats for retirees to reminisce on the past and maintain old friendships.[19]

In 1981, the FORBO broke ground for the National Border Patrol Museum in El Paso, Texas. Founded as a place to "capture our memories" and "to tell our story and do it our way," the retirees of the U.S. Border Patrol made a place of their own.[20] The records that retirees deposited at the NBPM and the oral histories they have collected from one another capture the officers' everyday experiences with the making of U.S. migration control and thus highlight the social and political life of U.S. immigration law enforcement. This is a story that the "The First Fifty Years" declined to tell. It is a story that the U.S. Supreme Court refused to acknowledge. And it is a story that the Border Patrol's critics dismiss. But it is the story that the retired officers of the U.S. Border Patrol preserved by establishing a place where the social world of U.S. immigration law enforcement is not forgotten, suppressed, or disregarded.

In 1987, retired officer David Burnett authored his own fifty-three-page story for deposit at the National Border Patrol Museum. Breaking from the celebratory mold of many personal narratives, Burnett had the courage to tell all that he knew of the patrol, and, in particular, he recounted troubling stories of old-timers' actions. It was Burnett, for example, whom Jim Cottingham had admonished for not killing an immigrant when confronted with his unruly behavior. Burnett closed his narrative with a request. "I've always had this one reservation about the Museum; I hope that in the future, five years, twenty-five years, whenever, that people come back to read reports, listen to tapes, or research the past . . . [and] that they won't judge the Border Patrol and its officers by standards that are then current." As Burnett explained, "It is easy to read of things that happened, and conclude [that] officers' actions were just unreasonable, but many of those things were reasonable under the circumstances and under the guidelines and the policies of the time. I just hope that any one who does research and looks into these things will keep that in mind."[21] This book offers no leniency to the old-timers or, as Burnett explains, "the things that happened, gun fights for example or beatings, or a lot of other things that happened."[22] But it does place the old-timers and their actions within the context of the times by chronicling the social history of U.S. immigration law enforcement in the U.S.-Mexico borderlands. As Burnett well understood, "They [the old-timers] built the Border Patrol, they made it what it was."[23]

In the years after the exodus of 1978, a new generation of U.S. Border Patrol officers took their place to enforce U.S. immigration law. Among them were women and African Americans, both formerly excluded from employment as Border Patrol officers.[24] From the outside, the old-timers watched the changes and complained that Border Patrol work was "strictly a man's job."[25] Men hired well into the 1990s expressed that they "did not like it, but that was the new way, the accepted way. It was the law."[26] Still the pressure for gender equity in federal government employment did not ultimately translate into gender parity among Border Patrol personnel. By the mid-1980s, eighty-four women comprised only 3.1 percent of Border Patrol officers, and by 2007, the percentage of female officers had jumped nominally to 5.4 percent of all officers.[27]

Although women had been categorically excluded from employment as U.S. Border Patrol officers, African Americans were more carefully prevented from taking jobs as patrolmen until the 1970s. As one retired Border Patrol officer recalled of a recruitment trip that he had taken to the South during the 1920s, "The colored people were trying to get their students in to break the barrier," but Border Patrol recruiters were "very fortunate" to have the assistance of a "civil service employee in the south."[28] The civil service representative "could tell from the application. Usually the name or the schools he attended" and helped the recruitment officer to discard African American applicants.[29] When asked, "You didn't like to hire colored people back then?" the officer responded, "Oh, no. We could have been accused of discrimination, there is no question at all about it."[30]

The movement for equity in federal employment produced a small but steady cohort of African American officers during the mid-1970s. The tenor of their reception is suggested by the response that Kellogg Whittick received when he was promoted as the first African American to hold a senior position within INS: employees rubbed excrement on Whittick's car.[31] Retiring in 1983, Whittick described incidents in which "[INS] bosses refer[ed] to blacks as 'niggers' and 'porch monkeys,' or their colleagues [made] nasty jokes about deporting them back to Africa."[32] With such internal hostility toward black officers within the INS, it is not surprising that the number of African American Border Patrol agents only increased from eleven in 1977 to twenty-eight in 1988 and to only forty-four in 1994.[33]

But the most significant change in Border Patrol personnel has been the dramatic rise in the number of Latino officers. Since 1924, Mexican Americans had consistently represented a small fraction of Border Patrol officers. By the 1960s, in the context of Chicano/a activism and brick-lobbing Mexican border crossers, Mexican American Border Patrol officers were often derided as traitors to their ethnic community, but the number of Latino officers continued to rise. By 1977, the Border Patrol maintained three hundred and twenty-one Latino officers, and by 2008, 51 percent of all Border Patrol officers were Hispanic—primarily Mexican Americans.[34]

According to sociologist-historian Josiah C. Heyman, this new generation of Latino officers "var[ies] on the question of [self-identified] ethnicity, but with striking consistency they emphasize their standing as U.S. citizens, with specific rights to jobs and public distributions."[35] Latino officers and their political commitments to the rights of citizens pioneered dramatic changes in Border Patrol strategy in the late twentieth century. Among the most influential of this new generation of Border Patrol officers was Silvestre Reyes. Born in 1944 in Cantuillo, Texas, Reyes grew up as the oldest of ten children on his family's farm five miles outside of El Paso, Texas.[36] He was a third-generation Mexican American, but Spanish was his native tongue, and he learned English when he entered school.[37] As a child, one of Reyes's jobs on his family's farm was to watch for the U.S. Border Patrol and sound an alarm in the event of a raid.[38] But by the time Reyes was ten years old, the Border Patrol had begun its post-1954 retreat from aggressive immigration law enforcement. Reyes would have known the quieter times of the post-wetback era until he joined the U.S. Army and left Texas to fight in the Vietnam War. When he returned from Vietnam in 1969, he joined the U.S. Border Patrol. At the leading edge of the rising Mexican American generation within the Border Patrol, Reyes sparked a dramatic shift in Border Patrol strategy in the U.S.-Mexico borderlands.

Toward the end of the 1980s, Mexican American community leaders in El Paso, Texas, began to complain that Border Patrol practices were damaging city life. Harassment of Mexican Americans and legal immigrants along with the pursuit of immigrants in business districts and residential areas had created a sense of surveillance, chaos, and danger that negatively affected the broader civic, social, and economic life of El Paso. Finally, in November of 1991, the tensions between the Border Patrol and Mexican Americans in El Paso erupted at Bowie High School.

Bowie High was a predominately Mexican American and working-class high school located on the border between El Paso and Ciudad Juárez, Chihuahua. Border Patrol officers routinely patrolled the vicinity of the school and entered school property to question students, staff, and visitors. On November 9, 1991, the football coach, Benjamin Murillo, and two of his varsity players were driving to a game when Border Patrol officers stopped their car. One officer approached the car and pointed his pistol at Murillo's head. Jaime Amezaga, the assistant football coach drove past and stopped to inform the officers that the man they had stopped was the Bowie High head football coach. The officer turned the gun on Amezaga and told him to mind his business. The officer then searched Murillo while his partner searched the two student athletes, Isaac Vallalva and Cesar Soto.

Murillo led Vallalva and six other Bowie High students in filing for a restraining order and injunction against the Border Patrol. The judge decided in favor of the plaintiffs, allowing the injunction and restraining order to transform Bowie High into a sanctuary free from Border Patrol activities. The Bowie High case signaled a new era of political organizing among Mexican Americans in El Paso that would force changes upon Border Patrol activity. Bowie High was off-limits to the patrol, and compromises would have to be reached with the broader Mexicano community regarding the future of U.S. immigration law enforcement.

In 1993, the INS moved Silvestre Reyes to El Paso, where he addressed the concerns of Mexican Americans by launching Operation Hold the Line. Reflecting the citizenship politics of the emergent generation of Mexican American Border Patrol officers, Reyes ended the raids and harassment that ensnared Mexican Americans in the Border Patrol's pursuit of immigration control. Instead of assigning officers to chase fraudulent citizens, conduct raids in Mexicano-dominated communities, and run down suspects on city streets, Reyes moved officers to the international boundary. Stationed every several hundred feet directly along the border, Operation Hold the Line effectively built a human wall between El Paso and

Ciudad Juárez.[39] Reyes attempted to protect the citizenship rights of Mexican Americans by focusing Border Patrol resources on the physical boundary between the
United States and Mexico. As a direct result of the new strategy, complaints by Mexican Americans declined, and Reyes was honored by the leading Mexican American organizations for his contributions to the protection of Mexican American citizenship rights and community life.[40]

INS supervisors looked at Operation Hold the Line and saw the future of immigration law enforcement in the U.S.-Mexico borderlands. Beyond improving
community relations, Operation Hold the Line reduced apprehensions in the historically busy El Paso area by 76 percent during fiscal year 1994.[41] Interpreted as
reducing the overall volume of unsanctioned migration, Reyes's local strategy
gained national recognition and was implemented in other busy crossing zones
along the U.S.-Mexico border. On October 1, 1994, the San Diego sector of the U.S.
Border Patrol implemented Operation Gatekeeper. By 1999, the line patrols had
been extended across south Texas and from the Pacific Ocean to Yuma, Arizona.[42]

Numerous scholars have examined the impact of this strategy.[43] In particular,
they have critiqued the Border Patrol's assessment that declining apprehensions
in historically busy crossing zones signified a reduction in the volume of unsanctioned migration. Instead, many scholars have argued that border enforcement
strategies only redirected unsanctioned border crossers away from blockaded
areas and into the deserts, resulting in an overall rise in the number of migrant
deaths in the harsh deserts of the U.S.-Mexico borderlands. The Mexican Consulate
recorded nearly seventeen hundred migrant deaths along the border between 1994
and mid-2000. Some drowned in the Rio Grande, the All-American Canal, or in
the toxic New River, but most died while attempting to cross the desolate deserts
of Arizona, where they succumbed to dehydration, hypothermia, or heat stroke.[44]

Harshly criticized for the impact of the Hold the Line strategy on unsanctioned
border crossers, INS Commissioner Doris Meisner defended strategic border control as a legitimate deterrence method. "We did believe geography would be an ally,"
she explained.[45] But Meisner miscalculated. More than one hundred years of economic and social integration between the United States and Mexico had linked displaced workers in Mexico with jobs in the United States. Mexican workers traveled along corridors forged by processes far beyond the border. Geography would
not be enough to stop a migration that violated U.S. immigration law but conformed
to the strictures of U.S.-Mexico integration.

As the Border Patrol was extending Operation Hold the Line along the U.S.-
Mexico border, the economic integration of the two countries deepened with the
implementation of the North American Free Trade Agreement (NAFTA) on January 1, 1994. NAFTA eliminated many trade barriers between the United States,
Mexico, and Canada, creating a North American free-trade bloc that encouraged
the mobility of capital, production, and manufacturing throughout the region. U.S.-

financed businesses rushed into Mexico. Competition from transnational corporations for land, profits, and market shares drove increasingly large numbers of Mexican campesinos from the countryside into cycles of migration or into manufacturing jobs along Mexico's northern border region. Wages for these jobs were higher than elsewhere in Mexico and drew migrants to the border region. Still, many of the transnational corporations, which located their factories in Mexico to take advantage of cheap labor and minimal trade barriers, did not pay a living wage, and working conditions for the overwhelmingly young and female factory workforce were often dangerous, if not outright lethal. Displaced campesinos, border factory workers, and their families often weighed the risks of their employment and unemployment options in Mexico against the dangers of crossing into the United States, where daily wages continued to dwarf those available in Mexico. At some time in their lives, particularly when they were young, a good number of Mexico's poor, both male and female, made the trek north to earn enough to live in Mexico.

Since 1994, the exodus of Mexico's poor along the corridors of migration into the United States has confronted an increasingly barricaded border. The barricades began as a sector project responding to the concerns of Mexican Americans in El Paso, Texas, but they also complemented political quests for a semblance of national order and authority in an era of globalization and drew resources from funds dedicated to drug interdiction, which, by the late 1970s, was thoroughly entangled with the project of migration control. The mixing of migration control and drug interdiction profoundly shaped the working lives of Border Patrol officers. Whereas many officers said that joining the patrol allowed them to pay offs old debts, buy houses, support their families and, overall, reach a place where their "troubles were not about money," drug control transformed the U.S.-Mexico border into an increasingly unpredictable, militarized, and violent worksite.[46] "Remember: You are a target," reads a poster in the McAllen, Texas, Border Patrol station warning of the well-armed drug smugglers that officers might encounter during their shifts.[47] With officers and smugglers squaring off at the U.S.-Mexico border, heavily armed and watching anxiously for each other, the most extreme incidents of Border Patrol violence—as during the era of Prohibition—unfold at the intersection of drug control and migration control.

Unsanctioned migrants had long run from patrol officers, but Timothy Dunn, in *Militarization of the U.S.-Mexico Border*, writes that, by the 1990s, "seasoned agents say that when a suspect runs from agents along the border, it is likely he is a drug smuggler."[48] On March 18, 1992, this logic proved faulty when a Border Patrol officer opened fire on 25–30 unarmed, undocumented immigrants walking near the Nogales, Arizona, border. Three months later, Border Patrol officer Michael Elmer shot an unarmed Mexican resident of Nogales, Sonora, twice in the back with an AR-15 rifle, and killed him. The shooting occurred during a drug interdiction operation. Elmer attempted to conceal the shooting by burying the body, but another agent resisted Elmer's threats and reported the murder several hours later. Elmer, however, successfully defended himself against manslaughter charges by imploring jurors to understand the stress, danger, and confusion of Border Patrol work in the era of the war on drugs. The war on drugs, therefore, simultaneously created an increasingly dangerous and stressful worksite for Border Patrol officers and provided a new logic of impunity that justified even the most egregious acts of violence committed by Border Patrol officers.

The expansion of the war on drugs also affected the U.S. Border Patrol by fostering a national culture that invested in police and prisons as core mechanisms of social control. For example, when Congress addressed the problem of illegal immigration with the passage of the Immigration Reform and Control Act (IRCA) of 1986, policing immigration functioned as the lynchpin of future efforts to control unsanctioned migration. The IRCA offered amnesty to undocumented immigrants who had continuously resided in the United States since January 1, 1982, penalized the employers of unsanctioned workers, and dramatically expanded the U.S. Border Patrol. Amnesty allowed more than three million undocumented immigrants to legalize their status, but no system was established for handling changes in immigration status for future generations of unsanctioned immigrants, and the enforcement of employer sanctions was a seriously underfunded project, leaving the expansion of the Border Patrol as the bedrock of immigration-control efforts. Immigration reform, in other words, depended upon immigration policing. Despite increased police efforts, unsanctioned migration continued. Congress took up the question of immigration reform once again in the mid-1990s. The passage of the 1996 Illegal Immigration Reform and Immigrant Responsibility Act (IIRIRA) provided for five thousand additional Border Patrol agents. The IIRIRA also increased penalties for immigration violations, lowered the threshold for crimes that triggered deportation for legal immigrants, retroactively applied the triggers for deportation, and required imprisonment or detention for immigrants awaiting deportation hearings. Again Congress approached immigration control as a matter of crime and punishment. Then, on September 11, 2001, the attacks on the Twin Towers and the Pentagon promised to dramatically reshape and expand U.S. immigration law enforcement and border control. In the immediate aftermath of the attacks, U.S. federal authorities were jolted from their single-minded focus on policing unsanctioned Mexican immigration in the U.S.-Mexico borderlands. New targets were found in persons of "Muslim appearance," and immigration-control responsibilities were dispersed among a wider net of law-enforcement agencies.[49] Yet the expansion of targets failed to dislodge the U.S. Border Patrol from its concentration on policing unsanctioned Mexican immigration in the U.S.-Mexico borderlands, while the urgency of anti-terrorism fueled additional fiscal and political resources for immigration control and border enforcement. On March 1, 2003, the U.S. Border Patrol was transferred to the new Department of Homeland Security.

On May 15, 2006, President George W. Bush promised to further militarize immigration control by deploying 6,000 National Guard troops along the U.S.-Mexico border. And although the U.S. Border Patrol began the twenty-first century with slightly more than 4,000 officers on duty, by 2006, the Border Patrol fielded more than 12,000 officers, and President Bush mandated that the United States Border Patrol increase its patrol force to 18,319 officers by the end of 2008.[50]

POLICING MEXICANS IN THE CARCERAL ERA

In its two decades of expansion, the Border Patrol has failed to stop or significantly curtail unsanctioned immigration. What more officers, fences, guns, and technology have effectively produced is a steady stream of apprehensions. Without enough detention space to hold all of the persons held for immigration violations, immigrant inmates are often transferred to await trial or serve time in one of the nation's many jails or prisons. The U.S. Border Patrol is not the only agency delivering immigrants to the many houses of incarceration in the United States, but the rise of the U.S. Border Patrol as a story of race and inequity is powerfully signified by the increasing number of undocumented immigrants joining African Americans in jails and prisons across the country.

African Americans comprise 7 percent of the U.S. population but represent more than half of the prison and jail population. The over-representation of African Americans in America's growing prison population inspired novelist Edgar Wideman to describe prisons as "the dark places where only blacks reside."[51] The number of black men and women in prison has had far-reaching negative consequences for the African American community.[52] Imprisonment not only removes people from their families but also imposes an expanding matrix of "invisible punishments" that strips parolees and ex-convicts of their basic citizenship entitlements and rights.[53] For example, the Anti-Drug Abuse Act of 1988 prohibits tenants (or their guests) of public housing from engaging in "criminal activity, including drug related criminal activity, on or near public housing." Under this 1988 law, an individual's conviction for a drug crime could lead to eviction for an entire family. In addition, the 1996 Personal Responsibility and Work Opportunity Reconciliation Act established a lifetime ban on welfare benefits for persons with drug convictions. Drug convictions thus have the potential of thrusting families into homelessness and destabilizing communities. The social dislocations rooted in these invisible punishments are compounded by disenfranchisement laws that deny the right to vote to prisoners and ex-convicts. According to the Sentencing Project, 13 percent of African American men are currently disenfranchised by the felony disenfranchisement laws of various states, and if the current rates of imprisonment persist, 30 percent of "the next generation of black men will be disenfranchised at some point in their lifetime."[54] The effect of the prison system, therefore, has been to strip a growing percentage of the African American population of their basic citizenship rights and to restrict their access to basic needs such as housing, social services, family, and employment.

Black lives behind bars and the various long-term penalties that ex-convicts and their families pay for their crimes are the material evidence that crime and punishment operate as a broad-reaching system of racialized social organization in the United States.[55] Loïc Wacquant argues that mass imprisonment in the carceral era operates as a "peculiar institution" that extends the history of black slavery and Jim Crow in the United States by withholding full citizenship status from prisoners and ex-convicts, despite the many accomplishments of the civil rights movement.[56]

What many scholars of race and inequity in the carceral era are now examining is the rapidly growing number of immigrants (overwhelmingly Mexican nationals) serving time for immigration offenses and drug violations prior to deportation.[57] Between 1985 and 2000, the percentage of noncitizens in federal prison increased from 15 percent to 29 percent, making immigrants (along with black women) one of the most rapidly growing sectors of the federal prison population.[58] In addition to the growing number of immigrants in U.S. prisons and jails, increasing numbers of persons are being held in INS, now known as ICE (Immigration and Customs Enforcement), detention centers. When added to the more than one million persons per year who are processed at U.S. Border Patrol stations, immigrants are a significant portion of America's carceral population, and thus prisons are an increasingly important dimension of U.S. immigration control. The rising number of undocumented immigrants held in U.S. jails and prisons clarifies the story of race at the heart of policing Mexicans in the U.S.-Mexico borderlands. For African Americans, the arrival of undocumented immigrants in the prison system magnifies and strengthens the prison's function as a special reserve for those without full citizenship rights within the United States. For the caste of illegals, their arrival in U.S. jails and prisons—"the dark places where only blacks reside"— confirms that U.S. systems of migration control are busy not only in returning Mexicans back to Mexico but also in delivering Mexico's poor to peculiar institutions north of the border where broad-reaching and racialized social, political, and economic inequities are now defined within the United States. Therefore, chronicling the Border Patrol's rise in the U.S.-Mexico borderlands as a matter of policing in modern America reveals how the paths of Mexican Browns and black Americans cross in the carceral era.

When Jorge Lerma sang of Superman as America's forgotten illegal immigrant, he could hardly have known of the ways in which the coming of the carceral age would force him to dig deeper to understand the Border Patrol's policing of Mexicans. But by evoking the image of Superman, Lerma provided his own example of Gramsci's call to take an "inventory" of the many pasts buried within the present.[59] Superman, after all, was crafted by communist-leaning cartoonists who based their new American hero upon the life and legend of John Henry. An African American convict leased out as a railroad worker on the lines of the Chesapeake & Ohio Railroad in West Virginia during the 1870s, John Henry was a stout but powerful and proud man. When his employer brought a steam-powered drill to the line, he challenged the machine to a steel-driving race. Man against machine, John Henry drove steel faster and deeper than the steam-powered drill. His triumph inspired generations of workers who struggled against the dehumanization of work in industrial America. They carried his legend forward in song. As the legend's most recent biographer notes, by the 1930s, communists and cartoonists had "morph[ed]" the steel-driving man into the man of steel.[60] Buried deep within the figure of Superman, therefore, lay both the illegal immigrant and the black convict. By evoking the story of a black convict laborer turned American superhero who, through it all, was an illegal immigrant, Jorge Lerma tapped into and smuggled forward a critical socio-historical inventory of the Border Patrol's rise in the U.S.-Mexico borderlands. Policing Mexicans in the pursuit of immigration control, his song suggests, is intimately bound to projects that define the meaning of blackness and whiteness in American life. In America's prisons and jails, the paths of Mexico's poor collide with the paths of poor African Americans, making it clear that, for Mexican Browns, the story of race has tipped away from whiteness and toward blackness partly because of the U.S. Border Patrol's uneven policing of the legal/illegal divide.

The significance of both blackness and whiteness in the development of policing Mexicans is certainly a hidden history but, as records scattered north and south of the border make clear, the U.S. Border Patrol took many peculiar and forgotten paths to its now familiar concentration in the U.S.-Mexico borderlands. Efforts to manage the mobility of Mexican workers were always central and, over the years, anxieties regarding border security increasingly took hold of Border Patrol practices, but the Border Patrol's rise began with the old-timers who built a brotherhood of immigration control. Their story evolved upon Mexican hopes for modernity and Mexican American quests for incorporation and, at the dawn of the carceral era, a subtle turn toward crime control met the emerging concern with drug interdiction to further concentrate U.S. immigration control in the U.S.-Mexico borderlands. All along the way, whether considering the guns of the old-timers, the fences of the new recruits, or the barricades of the neoliberal era, gender was a critical factor in the formation of state violence, while, from Jim Crow to the prison system, the Border Patrol's racialization of the caste of illegals unfolded alongside the evolution of blackness and whiteness in American life. These untold dimensions of the Border Patrol's past were long-ago boxed up and submerged under more simple narratives, but they defined the rise of the U.S. Border Patrol in the U.S.-Mexico borderlands.

NOTES

INTRODUCTION

1. Mae Ngai, *Impossible Subjects: Illegal Aliens and the Making of Modern America* (Princeton, NJ: Princeton University Press, 2004), 58.

2. Peter Andreas, *Border Games: Policing the U.S.-Mexico Divide* (Ithaca, NY: Cornell University Press, 2000); Timothy Dunn, *The Militarization of the U.S.-Mexico Border, 1978–1992: Low-Intensity Conflict Doctrine Comes Home* (Austin: Center for Mexican American Studies, University of Texas at Austin, 1996); Joseph Nevins, *Operation Gatekeeper: The Rise of the "Illegal Alien" and the Making of the U.S.-Mexico Boundary* (New York: Routledge, 2002). See also Jorge Bustamante, "Commodity Migrants: Structural Analysis of Mexican Immigration to the United States," in *Views across the Border: The United States and Mexico*, ed. Stanley P. Ross (Albuquerque: University of New Mexico Press, 1978), 183–203; and Josiah Heyman, "State Effects on Labor Exploitation: The INS and Undocumented Immigrants at the U.S.-Mexico Border," *Critique of Anthropology* 18, no. 2 (1998): 161–80.

3. Kitty Calavita, *Inside the State: The Bracero Program, Immigration, and the I.N.S.* (New York: Routledge, 1992), and *U.S. Immigration Law and the Control of Labor, 1820–1924* (London: Academic Press, 1984); Roger Daniels, *Guarding the Golden Door: American Immigration Policy and Immigrants since 1882* (New York: Hill and Wang, 2004); Juan Ramón García, *Operation Wetback: The Mass Deportation of Mexican Undocumented Workers in 1954* (Westport, CT: Greenwood Press, 1980); Gilbert González and Raúl A. Fernández, *A Century of Chicano History: Empire, Nations, and Migration* (New York: Routledge, 2003); David Montejano, *Anglos and Mexicans in the Making of Texas, 1836–1986* (Austin: University of Texas Press, 1987), 97; Ngai, *Impossible Subjects;* George Sánchez, *Becoming Mexican American: Ethnicity, Culture, and Identity in Chicano Los Angeles, 1900–1945* (New York: Oxford University Press, 1993), 59–60; and Daniel J. Tichenor, *Dividing Lines: The Politics of Immigration Control in America* (Princeton, NJ: Princeton University Press, 2002). See also Alexandra Minna Stern, "Nationalism on the Line: Masculinity, Race, and the Cre-

ation of the U.S. Border Patrol, 1910–1940," in *Continental Crossroads: Remapping U.S.-Mexico Borderlands History*, ed. Samuel Truett and Elliott Young (Durham, NC: Duke University Press, 2004), 299–324; and Eithne Luibhéid, *Entry Denied: Controlling Sexuality at the Border* (Minneapolis: University of Minnesota Press, 2002).

4. Nicholas De Genova, "Migrant 'Illegality' and Deportability in Everyday Life," *Annual Review of Anthropology* 31 (2002): 419–47.

5. I use the term *Mexicano* to refer a social group that includes both Mexican nationals and U.S. citizens of Mexican descent. The term *Mexicano*, in other words, denotes a broad social category inclusive of all persons of Mexican descent, regardless of national citizenship. I use *Mexican-American* when specifically and solely referring to U.S. citizens of Mexican descent. I use the term *Mexican* when specifically and solely referring to Mexican citizens.

6. For a discussion of migration corridors, see González and Fernández, *A Century of Chicano History*, 29–66; Douglas S. Massey, Jorge Durand, and Nolan J. Malone, *Beyond Smoke and Mirrors: Mexican Immigration in an Era of Economic Integration* (New York: Russell Sage Foundation, 2002); and Saskia Sassen, *The Mobility of Labour and Capital: A Study in International Investment and Labor Flow* (Cambridge: Cambridge University Press, 1988).

7. In March of 2003, the INS moved from the Department of Justice to the new Department of Homeland Security and the Immigration and Customs Enforcement Agency. Accordingly, the INS Historical Library was renamed the Citizen and Immigration Services Historical Reference Library.

8. For similar community studies of U.S. police systems, see Sally Hadden, *Slave Patrols: Law and Violence in Virginia and the Carolinas* (Cambridge, MA: Harvard University Press, 2001); Roger Lane, *Policing the City: Boston, 1822–1885* (Cambridge, MA: Harvard University Press, 1971); Eric Monkkonen, *Police in Urban America, 1860–1920* (New York: Cambridge University Press, 1981); Dennis Rousey, *Policing the Southern City: New Orleans, 1805–1889* (Baton Rouge: Louisiana State University Press, 1996); Robert M. Utley, *Lone Star Justice: The First Century of the Texas Rangers* (Oxford: Oxford University Press, 2006), and *Lone Star Lawmen: The Second Century of the Texas Ranger* (Oxford: Oxford University Press, 2007); and William Westley, *Violence and the Police: A Sociological Study of Law, Custom, and Morality* (Cambridge, MA: MIT Press, 1970).

9. Congressional plenary power over immigration control is rooted in both the principle that the national government retains the sovereign power to dictate who may enter the national territory *and* the maxim that the federal government directs international relations. See *Fong Yue Ting v. US*, 149 U.S. 698 (1893), and T. Alexander Aleinikoff, *Semblances of Sovereignty: The Constitution, the State, and American Citizenship* (Cambridge, MA: Harvard University Press, 2002), 151–81. The making and meaning of U.S. immigration control is typically examined in an exclusively U.S.-based context. For example, see Ngai, *Impossible Subjects;* Peter H. Schuck, *Citizens, Strangers, and In-Betweens: Essays on Immigration and Citizenship* (Boulder, CO: Westview Press, 1998).

10. In recent years, scholars have made significant contributions to the study of the way territorially bound police forces negotiate the limits of their authority by engaging in cross-border cooperation. This work makes clear that the mid-century cross-border innovations

of the U.S. Border Patrol occurred alongside the expansion of international policing after World War II. For example, see Malcolm Anderson, *Policing the World: Interpol and the Politics of International Police Co-operation* (New York: Oxford University Press, 1989); Ethan A. Nadelmann, *Cops across Borders: The Internationalization of U.S. Criminal Law Enforcement* (University Park: Pennsylvania State University Press, 1993); J. W. Sheptycki, "Transnational Policing and the Makings of a Postmodern State," *British Journal of Criminology* 35, no. 4 (1995), 613–35, *Issues in Transnational Policing* (New York: Routledge, 2000), and *In Search of Transnational Policing: Toward a Sociology of Global Policing* (Aldershot, U.K.: Ashgate, 2003); and Neil Walker, "The Pattern of Transnational Policing," in *Handbook of Policing*, ed. Tim Newburn (Cullompton, U.K.: Willan Publishing, 2003), 111–35.

11. Kelly Lytle Hernández and Pablo Yankelevich, "An Introduction to the Archivo Histórico del Instituto Nacional de Migración," *Aztlán: A Journal of Chicano Studies* 34 (Spring 2004): 157–68.

12. This book is far from the first account of emigration control within Mexico. John R. Martínez began this work with "Mexican Emigration to the United States, 1910–1930" (PhD diss., University of California, 1957). His work was followed by Mark Reisler, *By the Sweat of Their Brow: Mexican Immigrant Labor in the United States, 1900–1940* (Westport, CT: Greenwood Press, 1976); and Lawrence Cardoso, *Mexican Emigration to the United States: 1897–1931* (Tucson: University of Arizona Press, 1980). In 1994, Moisés González Navarro provided the most comprehensive study to date regarding immigration to and from Mexico. Navarro's book, *Los extranjeros en México y los mexicanos en el extranjero, 1821–1970*, vol. 3 (Mexico City: El Colegio de México, 1994), drew upon an extensive survey of Mexican newspapers, law, and archival records to examine how Mexican state officials have attempted to regulate migration into and out of the national territory. See Jaime Aguila, "Protecting 'México de Afuera': Mexican Emigration Policy, 1876–1928" (PhD diss., Arizona State University, 2000), 96–118; David Fitzgerald, "A Nation of Emigrants? Statecraft, Church-Building, and Nationalism in Mexican Migrant Source Communities" (PhD diss., University of California–Los Angeles, 2005); and Casey Walsh, "Development in the Borderlands: Cotton Capitalism, State Formation, and Regional Political Culture in Northern Mexico" (PhD diss. New School University, 2001).

13. John Mason Hart, *Empire and Revolution: The Americans in Mexico since the Civil War* (Berkeley and Los Angeles: University of California Press, 2002); Stephen R. Niblo, *The Impact of War: Mexico and World War II* (Melbourne, Australia: La Trobe University Institute of Latin American Studies, Occasional Paper No. 10, 1988), and *War, Diplomacy, and Development: The United States and Mexico, 1938–1954* (Wilmington, DE: Scholarly Resources, 1995); Dirk W. Raat, *Mexico and the United States: Ambivalent Vistas* (Athens: University of Georgia Press, 2004).

14. Hart, *Empire and Revolution*, 403–31.

15. There has yet to be written a comprehensive history of federal law enforcement. Works dedicated to aspects of the history of federal law enforcement include Larry Ball, *The United States Marshals of New Mexico and Arizona Territories, 1846–1912* (Albuquerque: University of New Mexico Press, 1978); Frederick S. Calhoun, *The Lawmen: United States Marshals and Their Deputies, 1789–1989* (Washington, DC: Smithsonian Institution Press, 1989); Stephen Cresswell, *Mormons and Cowboys, Moonshiners and Klansmen* (Tuscaloosa:

University of Alabama Press, 1991); Lawrence Friedman, *Crime and Punishment in American History* (New York: Basic Books, 1993); Marie Gottschalk, *The Prison and the Gallows: The Politics of Mass Incarceration in America* (Cambridge: Cambridge University Press, 2006), 41–76; David K. Johnson, *The Lavender Scare: The Cold War Persecution of Gays and Lesbians in the Federal Government* (Chicago: University of Chicago Press, 2004); David R. Johnson, *Illegal Tender: Counterfeiting and the Secret Service in Nineteenth-Century America* (Washington, DC: Smithsonian Institution Press, 1995), and *American Law Enforcement: A History* (St. Louis, MO: Forum Press, 1981); John C. McWilliams, *The Protectors: Harry J. Anslinger and the Federal Bureau of Narcotics, 1930–1962* (Newark, DE: University of Delaware Press, 1990); Wilbur R. Miller, *Revenuers and Moonshiners: Enforcing Federal Liquor Law in the Mountain South, 1865–1900* (Chapel Hill: University of North Carolina Press, 1991); Nadelmann, *Cops across Borders*, 46–55; Carl E. Prince and Mollie Keller, *The U.S. Customs Service: A Bicentennial History* (Washington, DC: Department of Treasury, 1989), 200–216; Mary M. Stolberg, "Policing the Twilight Zone: Federalizing Crime Fighting during the New Deal," *Journal of Policy History* 7, no. 4 (1995): 393–415; Samuel Walker, *Popular Justice: A History of American Criminal Justice* (Oxford: Oxford University Press, 1997).

16. Linda Bosniak, *The Citizen and the Alien: Dilemmas of Contemporary Membership* (Princeton, NJ: Princeton University Press, 2006); Kevin R. Johnson, "The End of 'Civil Rights' as We Know It? Immigration and the New Civil Rights Law," 49 *UCLA Law Review* 1481 (2002); Ngai, *Impossible Subjects*; Schuck, *Citizens, Strangers, and In-Betweens*; Michael Walzer, *Spheres of Justice: A Defense of Pluralism and Equality* (New York: Basic Books, 1983).

17. Susan Bibler Coutin, *Legalizing Moves: Salvadoran Immigrants' Struggle for U.S. Residency* (Ann Arbor: University of Michigan Press, 2000), 28.

18. Ngai, *Impossible Subjects*, 2.

19. Bibler Coutin, *Legalizing Moves*; Bosniak, *The Citizen and the Alien*, 37–76; Kevin R. Johnson, *The "Huddled Masses" Myth: Immigration and Civil Rights* (Philadelphia, PA: Temple University Press, 2004); Daniel Kanstroom, *Deportation Nation: Outsiders in American History* (Cambridge, MA: Harvard University Press, 2007), 15–20; Gerald L. Neuman, *Strangers to the Constitution: Immigrants, Borders, and Fundamental Law* (Princeton, NJ: Princeton University Press, 1996); Walzer, *Spheres of Justice*, 52–63; Aleinikoff, *Semblances of Sovereignty*, 151–81.

20. Bibler Coutin, *Legalizing Moves*, 40.

21. For a general discussion of police practice and labeling theory, see Monkkonen, *Police in Urban America*, 22.

22. Nicholas De Genova, "The Legal Production of Mexican/Migrant 'Illegality,'" in *Latino Studies* 2, no. 1 (2004): 160–85, and *Working the Boundaries: Race, Space, and "Illegality" in Mexican Chicago* (Durham, NC: Duke University Press, 2005); Kevin R. Johnson, "The Case against Race Profiling in Immigration Enforcement," *Washington University Law Quarterly* 78 (2000): 675–736; Erika Lee, *At America's Gates: Chinese Immigration During the Exclusion Era, 1882–1943*, (Chapel Hill: University of North Carolina Press. 2004), 248–50; Ngai, *Impossible Subjects*, 7; Sánchez, *Becoming Mexican American*, 59, and "Face the Nation: Race, Immigration, and the Rise of Nativism in Late Twentieth-Century America," *International Migration Review* 31, no. 4 (1997): 1009–30; Stern, "Nationalism on the Line."

23. Bill Jordan, *Tales of the Rio Grande* (El Paso, TX: National Border Patrol Museum, 1995), 24.

24. Arnoldo De León, *They Called Them Greasers: Anglo Attitudes toward Mexicans in Texas, 1821–1900* (Austin: University of Texas Press, 1983); Neil Foley, *The White Scourge: Mexicans, Blacks, and Poor Whites in Texas Cotton Culture* (Berkeley and Los Angeles: University of California Press, 1997), "Becoming Hispanic: Mexican Americans and the Faustian Pact with Whiteness," in *Reflexiones 1997* (Austin: University of Texas Press, 1998), 53–70, and "Partly Colored or Other White: Mexican Americans and Their Problem with the Color Line," in *American Dreaming, Global Realities: Rethinking U.S. Immigration History,* ed. Vicki L. Ruíz and Donna R. Gabaccia (Champaign: University of Illinois Press, 2006), 361–78; Thomas A. Guglielmo, "Fighting for Caucasian Rights: Mexicans, Mexican-Americans, and the Transnational Fight for Civil Rights in World War II Texas," *Journal of American History* 92, no. 4 (March 2006): 1212–37; Martha Menchaca, "Chicano Indianism: A Historical Account of Racial Repression in the United States," *American Ethnologist* 20, no. 3 (August 1993): 583—604, and *Recovering History, Constructing Race: The Indian, Black, and White Roots of Mexican Americans* (Austin: University of Texas Press, 2001); Montejano, *Anglos and Mexicans,* 181–82. For more general works on the importance of whiteness in the incorporation of immigrants into U.S. social systems, see James Barrett and David Roediger, "Inbetween Peoples: Race, Nationality, and the New Immigrant Working Class," *Journal of American Ethnic History* 16 (Spring 1997): 3–44; Matthew Frye Jacobson, *Whiteness of a Different Color: European Immigrants and the Alchemy of Race* (Cambridge, MA: Harvard University Press, 1998); David Roediger, *The Wages of Whiteness: Race and the Making of the American Working Class* (New York: Verso, 1999), and *Working toward Whiteness: How America's Immigrants Became White: The Strange Journey from Ellis Island to the Suburbs* (New York: Basic Books, 2005).

25. Thomas Borstlemann, *The Cold War and the Color Line: American Race Relations in the Global Arena* (Cambridge, MA: Harvard University Press, 2001); Mary Dudziak, *Cold War Civil Rights: Race and the Image of American Democracy* (Princeton, NJ: Princeton University Press, 2000); Penny Von Eschen, *Race against Empire: Black Americans and Anticolonialism, 1937–1957* (Ithaca, NY: Cornell University Press, 1997), and *Race and Empire During the Cold War* (Cambridge, MA: Harvard University Press, 2004).

26. In doing so, this book contributes to the movement to narrate and examine U.S. history beyond its territorial borders. See Thomas Bender, ed. *Rethinking American History in a Global Age* (Berkeley and Los Angeles: University of California Press, 2002); Samuel Truett and Elliott Young, *Continental Crossroad: Remapping U.S.-Mexico Borderlands History* (Durham, NC: Duke University Press, 2004); and "Rethinking History and the Nation-State: Mexico and the United States as a Case Study," special issue, *Journal of American History* 86, no. 2 (1999).

27. Barbara J. Fields, "Ideology and Race in American History," in *Region, Race, and Reconstruction: Essays in Honor of C. Vann Woodward,* ed. J. Morgan Kousser and James M. McPherson (Oxford: Oxford University Press, 1982), 143–77; Michael Omi and Howard Winant, *Racial Formation in the United States: From the 1960s to the 1990s,* 2nd ed. (New York: Routledge, 1994).

28. Antonio Gramsci, *Selections from Prison Notebooks*, ed. Quinten Hoare and Geoffrey Nowell Smith (New York: International Publishers, 1985), 324.

1. THE EARLY YEARS

1. Dorothy Burns Peterson, *Daughters of the Republic of Texas: Patriot Ancestor Album* (Nashville, TN: Turner Publishing, 1995), 277.

2. List of American settlers in the Colorado District, Austin's colony, March 4, 1823, compiled by John Tumlinson, Robert Kuykendall, Nicholas Clopper, and Moses Morrison, *Manuscripts, Documents and Letters of Early Texans* (Austin, TX: The Steck Company, 1937), 18–23.

3. Bill Stein, "Consider the Lily: The Ungilded History of Colorado County, Texas," Nesbitt Memorial Library, Columbus, Texas.

4. Montejano, *Anglos and Mexicans*, 125–27; Américo Paredes, *"With His Pistol in His Hand": A Border Ballad and Its Hero* (1958; reprint, Austin: University of Texas Press, 2000), 26–29; Utley, *Lone Star Justice,* and *Lone Star Lawmen;* Walter Prescott Webb, *The Texas Rangers: A Century of Frontier Defense* (Austin: University of Texas Press, 1965).

5. Peterson, *Daughters of the Republic of Texas,* 277.

6. Webb, *Texas Rangers,* 87. See also Benjamin Heber Johnson, *Rebellion in Texas: How a Forgotten Rebellion and Its Bloody Suppression Turned Mexicans into Americans* (New Haven, CT: Yale University Press, 2003); Paredes, *"With His Pistol in His Hand,"* 26–59; and James A. Sandos, *Rebellion in the Borderlands: Anarchism and the Plan of San Diego, 1904–1923* (Norman: University of Oklahoma Press, 1992), 89–94.

7. Reginald Horsman, *Race and Manifest Destiny: The Origins of American Racial Anglo-Saxonism* (Cambridge, MA: Harvard University Press, 1981), 79–186, 208–48.

8. Patricia Nelson Limerick, *The Legacy of Conquest: The Unbroken Past of the American West* (New York: W. W. Norton, 1987), 55–62; Douglas Monroy, *Thrown among Strangers: The Making of Mexican Culture in Frontier California* (Berkeley and Los Angeles: University of California Press, 1990), 183–232; George H. Phillips, *The Enduring Struggle: Indians in California History* (San Francisco: Boyd and Frasur, 1981), 42–52, 57–61; Leonard Pitt, *The Decline of the Californios: A Social History of the Spanish-Speaking Californians, 1846–1890* (Berkeley and Los Angeles: University of California Press, 1998), 83–103; Montejano, *Anglos and Mexicans,* 50–74; and James J. Rawls, *Indians of California: The Changing Image* (Norman: University of Oklahoma Press, 1984), 137–201.

9. Cletus Daniel, *Bitter Harvest: A History of California Farm Workers, 1870–1941* (Ithaca, NY: Cornell University Press, 1981), 15–39; Carey McWilliams, *Factories in the Field: The Story of Migratory Farm Labor in California* (1939; reprint, Santa Barbara: Peregrine Publishers, 1971); Donald J. Pisani, *From the Family Farm to Agribusiness: The Irrigation Crusade in California and the West, 1850–1931* (Berkeley and Los Angeles: University of California Press, 1984).

10. McWilliams, *Factories in the Field.*

11. William O. Hendricks, "Developing San Diego's Desert Empire," *Journal of San Diego History* 17, no. 3 (1971); Paul Horgan, *Great River: The Rio Grande in North American History* (New York: Holt, Rinehart, and Winston, 1954), 3–6.

12. For a discussion of irrigation in the American West, see Norris Hundley Jr., *The Great Thirst: Californians and Water; A History*, rev. ed. (Berkeley and Los Angeles: University of California Press, 2001); Pisani, *Family Farm to Agribusiness*; Donald Worster, *Rivers of Empire: Water, Aridity, and the Growth of the American West* (New York: Pantheon, 1985).

13. *Fourteenth Census of the United States (1920)*, vol. 5, *Agriculture* (Washington, DC: GPO, 1922), 699, 710–11.

14. *Fifteenth Census of the United States (1930)*, vol. 1, *Agriculture* (Washington, DC: GPO, 1931), 32, 58, 412, 604.

15. Daniel, *Bitter Harvest*, 40–70; Lawrence J. Jelinek, *Harvest Empire: A History of California Agriculture*, 2nd ed. (San Francisco: Boyd and Frasur, 1982).

16. Sucheng Chan, *This Bittersweet Soil: The Chinese in California Agriculture, 1860–1910* (Berkeley and Los Angeles: University of California Press, 1986).

17. Evelyn Hu-Dehart, "Immigrants to a Developing Society: The Chinese in Northern Mexico, 1875–1932," *Journal of Arizona History* 21 (Autumn 1980): 275–312; María E. Ota Mishima, ed. *Destino México: Un estudio de las migraciones asiáticas a México, siglos XIX y XX* (Mexico City: El Colegio de México, 1997).

18. Benny Joseph Andres Jr., "Power and Control in Imperial Valley, California: Nature, Agribusiness, Labor, and Race Relations, 1900–1940" (PhD diss., University of New Mexico, 2003), 95–98.

19. Roger Daniels, *Coming to America: A History of Immigration and Ethnicity in American Life*, 2nd ed. (New York: Perennial, 2002), 250–58.

20. Roger Daniels, *The Politics of Prejudice: The Anti-Japanese Movement in California and the Struggle for Japanese Exclusion* (Berkeley and Los Angeles: University of California Press, 1977).

21. Daniels, *Guarding the Golden Door*, 40–45.

22. Andres, "Power and Control in Imperial Valley," 118. See also Daniels, *Politics of Prejudice*, 129; Karen Leonard, "Punjabi Farmers and California's Alien Land Law," *Agricultural History* 59, no. 4 (1985): 549–62.

23. Daniels, *Coming to America*, 356–60.

24. Ernesto Galarza, *Merchants of Labor: The Mexican Bracero Story, An Account of the Managed Migration of Mexican Farm Workers in California, 1942–1960* (Santa Barbara, CA: McNally and Loftin, 1964), 34–35; Dawn Bohulano Mabalon, "Life in Little Manila: Filipinas/os in Stockton, California, 1917–1972" (PhD diss., Stanford University, 2004).

25. Senate Committee on Immigration, *Restriction of Western Hemisphere Immigration: Hearings before the Committee on Immigration, United States Senate*, statement of C. B. Moore, 70th Cong., 1st sess., 1928, 64; see also Daniel, *Bitter Harvest*, 67; Paul Schuster Taylor, *Mexican Labor in the United States: Imperial Valley* (Berkeley and Los Angeles: University of California Press, 1930), 33–40.

26. Gilbert G. González, *Mexican Consuls and Labor Organizing: Imperial Politics in the American Southwest* (Austin: University of Texas Press, 1999); Zaragosa Vargas, *Labor Rights Are Civil Rights: Mexican American Workers in Twentieth-Century America* (Princeton, NJ: Princeton University Press, 2005); Emilio Zamora, *The World of the Mexican Worker in Texas* (College Station: Texas A&M University Press, 1993).

27. House Committee on Immigration, *Hearing before the Committee on Immigration*

and Naturalization on H.R. 6741, H.R. 7559, H.R. 9036, testimony of S. Parker Frisselle, 69th Cong., 1st. sess., January 28 and 29, February 2, 9, 11, and 23, 1926, 7.

28. Douglas E. Foley, *From Peones to Politicos: Class and Ethnicity in a South Texas Town, 1900-1987* (Austin: University of Texas Press, 1988), 4-6; Mario T. García, *Desert Immigrants: The Mexicans of El Paso, 1880-1920* (New Haven, CT: Yale University Press, 1981), 43-60; Paul Schuster Taylor, *An American-Mexican Frontier, Nueces County, Texas* (Chapel Hill: University of North Carolina Press, 1971), 100-105.

29. Senate Committee on Immigration, *Restriction of Western Hemisphere Immigration,* testimony of Mr. Smith, 114. Paul Schuster Taylor argued that U.S. farmers provided inaccurate estimates of their labor force: the "racial composition of the cotton labor supply in 1929 [was] as follows: local labor—Mexicans 97 per cent, Negroes 3 per cent, and practically no whites; outside seasonal labor—Mexicans 65%, Negroes 20%, whites 15%" (*American-Mexican Frontier,* 103).

30. Devra Weber, *Dark Sweat, White Gold: California Farm Workers, Cotton, and the New Deal* (Berkeley and Los Angeles: University of California Press, 1994), 37-42.

31. Francisco Balderrama and Raymond Rodríguez, *Decade of Betrayal: Mexican Repatriation in the 1930s* (Albuquerque: University of New Mexico Press, 1995), 5-26. See also Cardoso, *Mexican Emigration,* 1-38; Douglas Monroy, *Rebirth: Mexican Los Angeles from the Great Migration to the Great Depression* (Berkeley and Los Angeles: University of California Press, 1992), 75-83.

32. John Mason Hart, *Revolutionary Mexico: The Coming and Process of the Mexican Revolution* (Berkeley and Los Angeles: University of California Press, 1997); Alan Knight, *The Mexican Revolution,* vol. 1, *Porfirians, Liberals, and Peasants,* and vol. 2, *Counter-Revolution and Reconstruction* (Lincoln: University of Nebraska Press, 1986); Moisés González Navarro, *Sociedad y cultura en el Porfiriato* (Mexico City: Consejo Nacional para la Cultura y las Artes, 1994).

33. García, *Desert Immigrants,* 1-64.

34. Cardoso, *Mexican Emigration,* 34.

35. Ibid., 94-95.

36. Moon-Ho Jung, *Coolies and Cane: Race, Labor, and Sugar in the Age of Emancipation* (Baltimore, MD: Johns Hopkins University Press, 2006), 38.

37. Daniels, *Guarding the Golden Door;* John Higham, *Strangers in the Land: Patterns of American Nativism, 1860-1925* (New York: Rutgers University Press, 2002); Desmond King, *Making Americans: Immigration, Race, and the Origins of the Diverse Democracy* (Cambridge, MA: Harvard University Press, 2000); Hiroshi Motomura, *Americans in Waiting: The Lost Story of Immigration and Citizenship in the United States* (New York: Oxford University Press, 2006).

38. *Page Act of 1875,* 43rd Cong., 2nd sess. (18 *Stat.* 477), March 3, 1875.

39. *Immigration Act of 1882,* 47th Cong., 1st sess. (22 *Stat.* 214), August 3, 1882. See also, Lee, *At America's Gates;* Lucy E. Salyer, *Laws Harsh as Tigers: Chinese Immigrants and the Shaping of Modern Immigration Law* (Chapel Hill: University of North Carolina Press, 1995); and Alexander Saxton, *The Indispensable Enemy: Labor and the Anti-Chinese Movement in California* (Berkeley and Los Angeles: University of California Press, 1971).

40. *Contract Labor Law of 1885,* 48th Cong., 2nd sess. (23 *Stat.* 332), February 26, 1885.

41. *Immigration Act of 1891*, 51st Cong., 2nd sess. (26 *Stat.* 1084), March 3, 1891.

42. *Immigration Act of 1903*, Public Law 57–162, 57th Cong., 2nd sess. (32 *Stat.* 1213), March 3, 1903; *An Act: To establish the Department of Commerce and Labor*, Public Law 57–87, 57th Cong., 2nd sess. (32 *Stat.* 825), February 14, 1903.

43. *Immigration Act of 1907*, Public Law 59–96, 59th Cong., 2nd sess. (34 *Stat.* 898), February 20, 1907.

44. *An Act: To Create a Department of Labor*, Public Law 62–426, 62nd Cong., 3rd sess. (37 *Stat.* 737), March 4, 1913.

45. *Immigration Act of February 5, 1917*, Public Law 64–301, 64th Cong., 2nd sess. (39 *Stat.* 874).

46. Higham, *Strangers in the Land*, 264–330.

47. Ibid.; and Daniels, *Guarding the Golden Door*, 27–58.

48. Higham, *Strangers in the Land*, 316–23.

49. Ngai, *Impossible Subjects*, 25.

50. Quoted in David Gutiérrez, *Walls and Mirrors: Mexican Americans, Mexican Immigrants, and the Politics of Ethnicity* (Berkeley and Los Angeles: University of California Press, 1995), 53–54.

51. House Committee on Immigration and Naturalization, *Seasonal Agricultural Laborers from Mexico: Hearings before the Committee on Immigration and Naturalization*, statement of John C. Box, 69th Cong., 1st sess., 1926, 324.

52. Senate Committee on Immigration, *Restriction of Western Hemisphere Immigration*, statement on Mexican immigration submitted by the Immigration Restriction League, 188.

53. House Committee on Immigration and Naturalization, *Seasonal Agricultural Laborers from Mexico*, testimony of S. Parker Frisselle, 6–7.

54. Ibid, 7.

55. Ibid, 6.

56. Taylor, *American-Mexican Frontier*, 286.

57. Weber, *Dark Sweat, White Gold*, 45.

58. Taylor, *American-Mexican Frontier*, 89.

59. Robert Alvarez Jr. "The Lemon Grove Incident: The Nation's First Successful Desegregation Court Case," *Journal of San Diego History* 32, no. 2 (1986), 116–35; Andres, "Power and Control in Imperial Valley," 187–204, 248–77; Foley, *Peones to Politicos*, 65–66, 82–83; Matt García, *A World of Its Own: Race, Labor, and Citrus in the Making of Greater Los Angeles, 1900–1970* (Chapel Hill: University of North Carolina Press, 2001), 47–78; García, *Desert Immigrants*, 85–126; Montejano, *Anglos and Mexicans*, 157–256; Taylor, *Mexican Labor: Imperial Valley*, 48, 55–61, 75–76, 83–94; Paul Schuster Taylor, *Mexican Labor in the United States: Dimmit County, Winter Garden District, South Texas* (Berkeley and Los Angeles: University of California Press, 1930), 373–432; Taylor, *American-Mexican Frontier*, 215–40.

60. William Leonard, quoted in Montejano, *Anglos and Mexicans*, 82.

61. Statement of Edward B. Tilton, assistant superintendent of schools, San Diego, California, on February 15, 1929, carton 10, folder 5, Mexican Labor in the United States, field notes series B, set 1, Paul Schuster Taylor Collection.

62. Manuel Gamio, *The Life Story of the Mexican Immigrant: Autobiographical Documents* (New York: Dover, 1971), 175–76.

63. Statement of Mr. Henry Allsmeyer, agricultural agent, Cameron County, San Benito, Texas, carton 10, folder 4, unpublished notes, Paul Schuster Taylor Collection. See also Taylor, *American-Mexican Frontier*, 172.

64. Senate Committee on Immigration, *Restriction of Western Hemisphere Immigration*, statement of Fred Bixby, 26. See also in this document the statement by Ralph H. Taylor, executive secretary, Agricultural Legislative Committee of California, 72-74.

65. Senate Committee on Immigration, *Restriction of Western Hemisphere Immigration*, statement of Fred Bixby, 30.

66. Barrett and Roediger, "Inbetween Peoples." See also Taylor, *Mexican Labor: Imperial Valley*, 86-94, and *Mexican Labor: Dimmit County*, 420-23.

67. House Committee on Immigration and Naturalization, *Seasonal Agricultural Laborers from Mexico*, testimony of S. Parker Frisselle, 6.

68. Ibid.

69. Taylor, *American-Mexican Frontier*, 278-92.

70. "A Plan to Establish a Border Patrol." Citizen and Immigration Services, Historical Reference Library. (Washington, DC; hereafter cited as CIS/HRL).

71. Robert Chao Romero, "Transnational Chinese Immigrant Smuggling to the United States via Mexico and Cuba, 1882-1916," *Amerasia Journal* 30, no. 3 (2004/2005): 1-16; Lawrence Douglas Taylor, "El Contrabando de chinos a lo largo de la frontera entre México y Estados Unidos, 1882-1931," *Frontera Norte* 6, no. 11 (1994): 41-55.

72. Teresa Alfaro-Velkamp, *So Far from Allah, So Close to Mexico: Middle Eastern Immigrants in Modern Mexico* (Austin: University of Texas Press, 2007).

73. Records of the United States District Court, Southern District of Texas, Laredo Division, Criminal Records (U.S. National Archives and Records Administration–Fort Worth, Texas, Record Group 21). Hereafter cited as NARA–Fort Worth; Record Group is abbreviated as RG.

74. Records of District Courts of the United States, Central District Court, Southern Division, Los Angeles Criminal Dockets (NARA–Laguna Niguel, RG 21, shelf A3744).

75. *Department of Labor Appropriation Act of May 28, 1924*, Public Law 68-153, 68th Cong., 1st sess. (43 *Stat.* 205).

76. Richard Tait Jarnagin, "The Effect of Increased Illegal Mexican Migration upon the Organization and Operations of the United States Immigration Border Patrol, Southwest Region" (master's thesis, University of Southern California, 1957), 90; *Principal Activities Reports, Fiscal Years 1925-1940* (CIS/HRL); and NARA 55853/300B; copy held at CIS/HRL.

77. David F. Musto, *The American Disease: Origins of Narcotics Control* (New York: Oxford University Press, 1999).

78. National Commission on Law Observance and Enforcement, *Wickersham Commission Report on the Enforcement of the Prohibition Laws of the United States*, 71st Cong., 3rd sess. (Washington, DC: GPO, 1931).

79. *Act of April 2, 1924*, 68th Cong., 1st sess. (43 *Stat.* L. 50). See also Laurence F. Schmeckemier, *The Bureau of Prohibition: Its History, Activities, and Organization* (Washington, DC: The Brookings Institution, 1929), 14.

80. August 19, 1924, letter from Alfred Hampto, District Director of District No. 26 to the Commissioner General of Immigration (NARA 53108/22, box 157, entry 9), 1.

81. Ibid.

82. August 30, 1924, "Memorandum for the Second Assistant Secretary," memo from Commissioner-General of the Bureau of Immigration (NARA 53108/22, box 157, entry 9), 2.

83. Ibid.

84. Wesley Stiles, interviewed by Wesley Shaw, January 1986; interview no. 756 (Institute of Oral History, University of Texas, El Paso), 2.

85. Eric Monkkonen, *Police in Urban America*, 49–64.

86. *Lew Moy et al. v. United States*, 237 Fed. 50 (1916).

87. *Act of February 27, 1925*, Public Law 68–502, 68th Cong., 2nd sess. (43 *Stat.* 1049–1050). See also *Annual Report of the Commissioner General of Immigration, Fiscal Year ended June 30, 1930*, 68th Cong., 1st sess. (Washington, DC: GPO, 1930), 35; *Annual Report of the Immigration and Naturalization Service, Fiscal Year ended June 30, 1941* (Washington, DC: GPO, 1942), 223; and Jarnagin, "Effect of Increased Illegal Mexican Migration," 18—22.

88. Clifford Alan Perkins, *Border Patrol: With the U.S. Immigration Service on the Mexican Boundary, 1910–1954* (El Paso: Texas Western Press, 1978), 2 –3.

89. Ibid, 3.

90. Ibid.

91. Ibid.

92. The Border Patrol began along the U.S.-Mexico border and extended to cover the Florida coast and the Canadian border over the next three years. In January 1932, Mexican Border and Canadian Border districts for BP were established. This plan was terminated on June 1, 1933 and the Border Patrol returned to its original three districts along the U.S.-Mexico border until the regional concept was adopted in 1955.

93. The San Antonio District headquarters were moved to Galveston, Texas in 1934 but returned to San Antonio in 1938.

94. Perkins, *Border Patrol*, 16. See also Jarnagin, "Effect of Increased Illegal Mexican Migration," 23—26.

95. Edwin Reeves, interviewed by Robert H. Novak, June 25, 1974, interview no. 135 (Institute of Oral History. University of Texas at El Paso).

96. Original Border Patrol Officers roster, National Border Patrol Museum (hereafter cited as NBPM).

97. Haley, Obituary of Jeff Milton, Jeff Milton Biography File, Center for American History, University of Texas at Austin (hereafter cited as CAH); H. J. Evetts Haley, *Jeff Milton: A Good Man with a Gun* (Norman: Oklahoma University Press, 1948), and "First Border Patrolman, Jeff Milton, Dies," *Monthly Review*, May 1947 (Washington, DC: Department of Justice), 150.

98. Jeff Milton Personnel File (NBPM).

99. Jeff Milton Biography File (CAH); Jeff Milton Personnel File (NBPM); Haley, *Jeff Milton*.

100. Jeff Milton Personnel File (NBPM).

101. Ibid. See also Mary Kidder Rak, *The Border Patrol* (Boston, MA: Houghton Mifflin, 1938), 6–7.

102. Clement David Hellyer, *The U.S. Border Patrol* (New York: Random House, 1963),

22; Rak, *Border Patrol,* 5–7; John Myers Myers, *The Border Wardens* (Englewood Cliffs, NJ: Prentice-Hall, 1971); Peter Odens, *The Desert Trackers: Men of the Border Patrol,* n.p.

103. *Annual Report of the Commissioner General of Immigration to the Secretary of Labor, Fiscal Year ended June 30, 1925* (Washington, DC: GPO, 1925), 15.

104. "A Plan to Establish a Border Patrol" (CIS/HRL).

105. Notes from an oral history with E. A. Wright, interviewed by Esther Terrie Cornell, November 17, 1985 (Institute of Oral History, University of Texas at El Paso), 11.

106. October 5, 1925, Del Rio Sub-District Report (NARA 55396/22A, 340, entry 9); October 9, 1925, Del Rio Sub-District Inspection Report (NARA 55396/22, 340, entry 9); April 20, 1925, Del Rio Sub-District Inspection Report (NARA 55396/22A, 340, entry 9); September 28, 1925, and September 29, 1925, Brownsville Sub-District Inspection Reports (NARA 55396/22A, 340, entry 9); April 24, 1925, Laredo Sub-District Inspection Report (NARA 55396/22A, 340, entry 9).

107. The following discussion of the early officers of the United States Border Patrol is based upon research I completed with the Border Patrol's 1929 employee roster, which is the only remaining complete roster from the 1920s. I investigated the social background of each of the 290 officers listed on the 1929 roster. Some of the sources I utilized to construct the following social portrait of the U.S. Border Patrol were the U.S. Census records from 1900, 1910, 1920, and 1930, city directories, oral histories, personal memoirs, the social security index, obituaries, death certificates, officer scrapbooks held at the National Border Patrol Museum, and personal and family Web pages.

108. One-half of these officers owned their own ranches or farms; the other half were tenants and farm laborers. This 24 percent includes men who had served as "hired guns" for borderland ranchers and farmers.

109. See information for Horace B. Carter, *Fourteenth Census of the United States: 1920—Population,* Hood County, Texas; Supervisor's District 12, Enumeration District 23, sheet 8A.

110. See information for Don Gilliland, *Fourteenth Census of the United States: 1920—Population,* Floresville, Wilson, Texas; Roll T625_1859, Page 9B, Enumeration District 195, Image 614.

111. See information for Orville Knight, *Fourteenth Census of the United States: 1920—Population,* Lyman, Ford, Illinois; Roll T625_368, Page 14A, Enumeration District 7, Image 172.

112. See information for Emmanuel Avant Wright, *Fourteenth Census of the United States: 1920—Population,* Presidio, Texas, Supervisor's District 16, Enumeration District 163, sheet number illegible.

113. Emmanuel Avant "Dogie" Wright, oral history taken June 14, 1983, by Jim Cullen (Archives of the Big Bend at Sul Ross State University; untranscribed).

114. Hellyer, *U.S. Border Patrol,* 22. For similar characterization of the early Border Patrol see, Myers, *Border Wardens.*

115. Taylor, *American-Mexican Frontier,* 289.

116. Ibid.; see also 138–39; Senate Committee on Immigration, *Restriction of Western Hemisphere Immigration,* statement of Edward H. Dowell, Vice President California State Federation of Labor, 6–16. For a discussion of tension between agribusinessmen and Border Patrol officers, see Taylor, *Mexican Labor: Dimmit County,* 325–30.

117. Foley, *White Scourge*, 5–8.

118. David Bayley, *Patterns of Policing: A Comparative International Analysis* (New Brunswick, NJ: Rutgers University Press, 1985), 189.

119. See information on Manuel Albert Saldaña, *Fourteenth Census of the United States: 1920—Population*, Texas, Cameron County, vol. 15, enumeration 23, sheet 3A, line 8. See also John R. Peavey, *Echoes from the Rio Grande*, 194.

120. See information on Manuel Albert Saldaña, Registration Location: Cameron County, Texas; Roll: 1952400; Draft Board: 0. See also World War I Draft Registration Cards, 1917–1918 (available online from the Generations Network, Provo, UT, at www.ancestry.com). Original data: United States, Selective Service System. World War I Selective Service System Draft Registration Cards, 1917–1918 (Washington, DC: National Archives and Records Administration. M1509, 4,582 rolls).

121. October 5, 1925, Laredo Sub-district investigation (NARA 55396/22A, 340, entry 9).

122. See information on Manuel Uribe, *Thirteenth Census of the United States: 1910—Population*, Justice Precinct 2, Zapata, Texas; Roll T624_1596, Page 10A, Enumeration District 170, Image: 466.

123. See information on Manuel Uribe, *Fourteenth Census of the United States: 1920—Population*. Texas, Zapata County, vol. 176, enumeration 196, sheet 5, line 42.

124. Jeffrey Kirk Cleveland, "Fight Like a Devil: Images of the Texas Rangers and the Strange Career of Jesse Perez" (master's thesis, University of Texas, 1992).

125. Perkins, *Border Patrol*, 96.

126. September 28, 1925, Brownsville Sub-District Inspection Report (NARA 55396/22A, 340, entry 9).

127. Foley, "Becoming Hispanic," 53–70; Gutiérrez, *Walls and Mirrors*, 5; Benjamin Márquez, *LULAC: The Evolution of a Mexican American Political Organization* (Austin: University of Texas Press, 1993).

128. Taylor, *American-Mexican Frontier*, 290–91.

129. Gutiérrez, *Walls and Mirrors*, 5; Taylor, *American-Mexican Frontier*, 290–91.

130. B. J. Parker (pseudonym), interviewed by Terrie Cornell, October 16, 1985 (NBPM), 3.

2. A SANCTUARY OF VIOLENCE

1. Ralph Williams (pseudonym), oral history, untranscribed (NBPM).

2. *Principal Activities of the U.S. Border Patrol Officers, Fiscal Year 1925* (CIS/HRL).

3. Chester C. Courtney, *U.S. Army, Register of Enlistments, 1798–1914*, available online from The Generations Network, Inc., 2007, Provo, UT at www.ancestrylibrary.com. Original data: Register of Enlistments in the U.S. Army, 1798–1914 (National Archives Microfilm Publication M233, 81 rolls); Records of the Adjutant General's Office, 1780s-1917, record group 94; National Archives, Washington, DC. See also information for Chester C. Courtney, *Thirteenth Census of the United States: 1910—Population*, Conway Ward 1, Faulkner, Arkansas; Roll T624_49, Page 28B, Enumeration District 24, Image 1040.

4. Information for Chester C. Courtney. *Fourteenth Census of the United States: 1920—Population*, Justice Precincts 1 and 2, Dimmit, Texas; Roll T625_1796, Page 12B, Enumeration District 42, Image 550.

5. December 16, 1926, letter from Chief Patrol Inspector Chester C. Courtney to District Director of the U.S. Immigration Service, El Paso, Texas (NARA 55609/550, 408, entry 9).

6. *Principal Activities of the U.S. Border Patrol, Fiscal Year 1927* (CIS/HRL).

7. Taylor, *American-Mexican Frontier*, 102–3.

8. March 28, 1929, memo from Acting Chief Patrol Inspector Chester C. Courtney to U.S. Immigration Service District Director, El Paso (NARA 55606/670, 4, 58A734), 1.

9. Ibid.

10. Ibid.

11. Ibid.

12. Rak, *Border Patrol*, 18.

13. February 3, 1926, letter from Patrol Inspector William A. Blundell, Whitefish, Montana, to Alfred Hampton, District Director, Immigration Service, Spokane, Washington (NARA 58A108/22, entry 9), 1.

14. February 9, 1926, from the District Director at Spokane, Washington to Honorable Robe Carl White, Assistant Secretary of the U.S. Department of Labor (NARA 53108/22, box 157, entry 9), 1.

15. March 28, 1929, memo from Acting Chief Patrol Inspector Chester C. Courtney to U.S. Immigration Service District Director, El Paso (NARA 55606/670, 4, 58A734), 1.

16. Ibid., 2.

17. March 28, 1929, memo from Chester C. Courtney to U.S. Immigration Service District Director, 2.

18. Ibid.

19. Jordan, *Tales of the Rio Grande*, 24.

20. Peter Odens, *The Desert Trackers: Men of the Border Patrol* (Yuma, AZ: published by author, 1975), chap. 3.

21. Jordan, *Tales of the Rio Grande*, 24.

22. July 10, 1936, "Memorandum," from G. C. Wilmoth, District Director, El Paso District (NARA 55854/100A, 455, 58A734). José Hernández is a pseudonym.

23. Ibid., 2.

24. Ibid.

25. Ibid.

26. November 5, 1937, letter from Commissioner of Immigration James Houghteling to Honorable R. H. Thomason, Member of Congress, El Paso, Texas (NARA55854/100A, 455, 58A734), 2.

27. Ibid., 1.

28. *Principal Activities of the U.S. Border Patrol, Fiscal Year 1927* (CIS/HRL).

29. *Principal Activities of the U.S. Border Patrol, Fiscal Year 1928* (CIS/HRL).

30. *Principal Activities of the U.S. Border Patrol, Fiscal Year 1929–30* (CIS/HRL).

31. Interview with Chester C. Courtney, Earl Fallis, and E. J. Stovall, by Will R. McLeRoy, August 22, 1968 (Oral History Collection, Southwest Collection at Texas Tech University).

32. Ibid.

33. Ibid.

34. Ibid.

35. Ibid.

36. Julio Santos Coy, oral history, interviewed by Oscar J. Martínez, November 7, 1977, interview no. 699 (Institute of Oral History, University of Texas at El Paso), 20.

37. Ibid.

38. *Principal Activities Report, 1925.*

39. *Fifteenth Census of the United States: 1930—Population,* vol. 3, pt. 2, Texas (Washington, DC: GPO, 1932), 975—990.

40. *Fifteenth Census of the United States: 1930—Agriculture,* Texas (Washington, DC: GPO, 1932), 1469, 1479, 1486.

41. *Fifteenth Census of the United States: 1930—Population,* vol. 3, pt. 2, Texas, 1025—1058.

42. Mexican Labor in US—Field Notes, box 10, folder 7: Series D, set 1, page 133 (Paul Schuster Taylor Collection).

43. Interview with S. Maston Nixon—C. C., August 19, 1929, in Mexican Labor in US—Field Notes, box 10, folder 7: Series D, set 1 (Paul Schuster Taylor Collection).

44. Interview with John Asker, Carrizo Springs, August 1929, in Mexican Labor in US—Field Notes, box 10, folder 7: Series D, set 1 (Paul Schuster Taylor Collection).

45. Interview with G. C. Wilmoth, District Director USIS, April 29, 1929, in Mexican Labor in US—Field Notes, box 10, folder 5: Series B, set 1 (Paul Schuster Taylor Collection). See also February 2, 1938, memo from Walter S. Hunicutt to Herbert C. Horsley, "Edwin Kelly and AH Kelly" (NARA 55854/100A, 455, 58A734); Senate Committee on Immigration, *Restriction of Western Hemisphere Immigration: Hearings before the Committee on Immigration, United States Senate,* testimony of Mr. R. H. Smith, representing South Texas Chamber of Commerce, Corpus Christi Texas, 70th Cong., 1st sess., 1928, 116.

46. Interview with Mr. Ryan, cotton breeder on W. T. Young Ranch, Acala, Texas, El Paso Valley, Nov. 15, 1928, in Unpublished Notes, carton 10, folder 4 (Paul Schuster Taylor Collection).

47. E. A. Wright, oral history, interviewed by Jim Cullen, June 14, 1983, interview no. 86, untranscribed (Archives of the Big Bend, Bryan Wildenthal Memorial Library, Sul Ross State University, Alpine, Texas).

48. Ibid.

49. Ibid.

50. Rak, *Border Patrol,* 23.

51. Charles Askins, *Unrepentant Sinner: The Autobiography of Colonel Charles Askins* (Boulder, CO: Paladin Press, 1984), 49.

52. September 28, 1925, Subdistrict Inspection Report from Brownsville, Texas (NARA 55396/22A, 340, entry 9).

53. Information for John Cottingham and James Cottingham, *Twelfth Census of the United States,* Cameron, Texas; Roll T623_1617, Page 26B, Enumeration District 15.

54. Information for John Cottingham and James Cottingham, *Thirteenth Census of the United States: 1910—Population,* Uvalde, Uvalde, Texas; Roll T624_1593, Page 3A, Enumeration District 132, Image 817.

55. John R. Peavey, *Echoes from the Rio Grande* (Brownsville: Springman-King, 1963), 185–320.

56. January 22, 1939, memo from G. J. McBee to the District Director in El Paso, Texas (NARA 55606/391F, 6, 58A734). See also Cottingham Personnel File (NBPM).

57. David Burnett (pseudonym), Personal Narrative, submitted on May 16, 1987 (NBPM), 46.

58. Ibid.

59. Ibid.

60. June 3, 1929, letter from Chief Patrol Inspector Herbert C. Horsley to Mr. and Mrs. Hill (NARA 55601/670, 4, 58A734).

61. Ibid.

62. "Memorandum in re Officers of the Immigration and Naturalization Service Killed in the Line of Duty. Record Probably Complete as to Those Killed Prior to July 1, 1924" (NARA 55879/710, 715, 58A734).

63. November 12, 1931, memo from N. D. Collear, Asst. Supt. of Border Patrol, to District Director, El Paso, regarding the shooting of Patrol Inspector McCraw (NARA 55606/391B, 6, 58A734), 3.

64. January 22, 1939, letter from G. J. McBee, Chief Patrol Inspector, Alpine, Texas, to District Director, U.S.I.N.S., El Paso (NARA 55606/391f, 6, 58A734), 2.

65. Ibid., 1

66. Rak, Border Patrol, 234.

67. Ibid.

68. Narciso and Domitilio Ochoa are pseudonyms provided by Mary Kidder Rak for this incident. Moore refers to the smugglers as "the Mexican," "the man," and "Sánchez."

69. Alvin Edward Moore, The Border Patrol (Santa Fe, NM: Sunstone Press, 1988), 13.

70. Ibid., 14.

71. Ibid., 13.

72. Ibid., 18.

73. Ralph Williams (pseudonym), oral history, untranscribed (NBPM).

74. Ibid.

75. Robert Moss (pseudonym), interviewed by Terrie Cornell on February 27, 1989 (NBPM), 7.

76. Stern, "Nationalism on the Line," 311–14.

77. Massad Ayoob, "The Gunfights of Col. Charles Askins," American Handgunner, November–December, 1999, 60–65.

78. Ibid.

79. Information for Charles Askins, Thirteenth Census of the United States: 1910— Population, Cimarron, Major, Oklahoma; Roll T624_1262, Page 13B, Enumeration District 169, Image 69. See also Skeeter Skelton, "The Legend of Charley Askins," Shooting Times Magazine, May 1972; available online at www.darkcanyon.net/The_Legend_Of_Charley_Askins.htm.

80. Askins, Unrepentant Sinner, 53.

81. Ibid., 47.

82. Ibid.

83. Ibid., 49.

84. Ibid., 50.

85. Ibid., 53.

86. Ibid., 51.

87. Ibid.

88. Ibid.

89. Ibid.

90. "Border Patrol: Criminal Charges Against Members—Disposition as of 1930" (NARA 55688/876A, 449, entry 9).

91. Burnett, Personal Narrative, 19 (NBPM).

92. August 22, 1932, "Statement made by Senior Patrol Inspector John V. Suul at Brownsville, Texas" (NARA 55601/670A, 4, 58A734), 2.

93. Ibid.

94. Ibid.

95. Ibid.

96. Ibid.. 3

97. August 23, 1932, letter from Edmund H. Levy, Acting Chief Patrol Inspector, Brownsville, Texas, to Director of Border Patrol, El Paso, Texas (NARA 55606/391C, 6, 58A734), 3.

98. Ibid.

99. February 16, 1928, memo entitled "TO ALL IMMIGRATION OFFICERS AND EMPLOYEES," from George J. Harris, District Director of the U.S. Immigration Service in El Paso, Texas (NARA 55494/25, 3, 58A734).

100. October 1, 1929, memo from District Director G. C. Wilmoth to U.S. Immigration Service (NARA 55494/25, 3, 58A734).

101. November 19, 1929, "TO ALL IMMIGRATION OFFICERS AND EMPLOYEES," from G. C. Wilmoth, District Director, El Paso, Texas (NARA 55494/25, 3, 58A734).

102. Welcome letter signed by Nick D. Collaer, Assistant Superintendent, Border Patrol (NARA 55494/25, 3, 58A734).

103. Ibid.

104. Ibid.

105. March 24, 1931, memo from G. C. Wilmoth, District Director in El Paso, Texas (NARA 55494/25, 3, 58A734).

106. Harlon B. Carter, "The Border Patrol Training Schools" (CIS/HRL).

107. Principal Activities of the U.S. Border Patrol, Fiscal Year 1927.

108. Ibid.

109. Perkins, Border Patrol, 113.

110. Archie Quin (pseudonym), addendum to oral history submitted on November 25, 1990 (NBPM), 1.

111. Bruce Lambert, "Harlon B. Carter, Longtime Head of Rifle Association, Dead at 78," New York Times, November 22, 1991. See also John. L. Crewdson, "Hard-Line Opponent of Gun Laws Wins New Term at Helm of Rifle Association," New York Times, May 4, 1981.

112. Lambert, "Harlon B. Carter."

3. THE CALIFORNIA-ARIZONA BORDERLANDS

1. Erika Lee, "Enforcing the Borders: Chinese Exclusion along the U.S. Borders with Canada and Mexico, 1882–1924," *Journal of American History* 89, no. 1 (2002): 54–86; Emily Ryo, "Through the Back Door: Applying Theories of Legal Compliance to Illegal Immigration during the Chinese Exclusion Era," *Law and Social Inquiry* 31, no. 1 (2006): 109–46.

2. Kennett Cott, "Mexican Diplomacy and the Chinese Issue, 1876–1910," *Hispanic American Historical Review* 67, no. 1, (1987): 63–85; Sergio Camposortega Cruz, "Análisis demográfico de las corrientes migratorias a México desde finales del siglo XIX," in Mishima, *Destino México,* 23–54.

3. María Elena Ota Mishima, *Siete migraciones Japonesas en México, 1890–1978* (Mexico City: El Colegio de México, 1982), and *Destino México.*

4. Rosario Cardiel Marin, "La migración china en el norte de Baja California," in Mishima, *Destino México,* 226.

5. Quoted in Martínez, "Mexican Emigration," 36.

6. Kif Augustine-Adams, "Making Mexico: Legal Nationality, Chinese Race, and the 1930 Population Census," *Law and History Review* 27, no. 1 (2009): 113–44.

7. "Wholesale Jap Invasion from Hawaii Checked under New Law," *Calexico Chronicle,* July 16, 1924.

8. "Aliens in Mexicali Seek Entrance to U.S.," *Calexico Chronicle,* July 10, 1924. See also "1,052 Orientals Enter Mexico This Port," *Calexico Chronicle,* July 19, 1924; "Expect Japs to Enter Secretly," *Calexico Chronicle,* July 19, 1924; "Many Aliens in Mexicali Are Expected to Be Turned Away," *Calexico Chronicle,* July 3, 1924.

9. "The Wall against Japan," *Calexico Chronicle,* June 11, 1924.

10. "Meiers Contesting Smuggling Charge," *Calexico Chronicle,* May 1, 1924; "Meiers Guilty, Is Fined $300," *Calexico Chronicle,* May 10, 1924.

11. "German without Passport Held," *Calexico Chronicle,* May 8, 1924.

12. "Italian Aliens and Smuggler Captured," *Calexico Chronicle,* June 2, 1924.

13. "New Immigration Law May Cause Confusion July 1," *Calexico Chronicle,* June 13, 1924.

14. Ibid.

15. "Aliens without Passports Are Turned Back: Stricter Enforcement at Line Ordered to Prevent Illegal Crossings," *Calexico Chronicle,* June 28, 1924.

16. "Many Aliens in Mexicali Are Expected to be Turned Away," *Calexico Chronicle,* July 3, 1924.

17. "New Alien Law Handicap to Ranchers: Head Tax and Visa Fee Required of Mexicans Moving to United States—Shoppers Not Affected—Local Immigration Office Decides on Lenient Interpretation of Act," *Calexico Chronicle,* July 9, 1924.

18. Ibid.

19. "New Immigration Men Start Duties," *Calexico Chronicle,* August 2, 1924.

20. Information for Alfred E. H. Their [Thur], *Fourteenth Census of the United States: 1920—Population,* Castro Valley, Alameda, California; Roll T625_91, Page 8B, Enumeration District 147, and *Fifteenth Census of the United States 1930—Population,* Los Angeles, Los Angeles, California; Roll 156, Page 5A, Enumeration District 598.

21. Information for Ralph Armstrong, *Eleventh Census of the United States: 1900—Population*, Jamestown, Stutsman, North Dakota; Roll T623 1232, Page 4A, Enumeration District 178, and *Twelfth Census of the United States: 1910—Population*, San Diego Ward 7, San Diego, California; Roll T624_95, Page 8B, Enumeration District 158.

22. Information for Ralph V. Armstrong, *Thirteenth Census of the United States: 1920—Population*, San Diego, San Diego, California; Roll T625_132, Page 5A, Enumeration District 327.

23. Information for Frank P. McCaslin, *Fourteenth United States Census: 1920—Population*, Cleveland Ward 24, Cuyahoga, Ohio; Roll T625_1371, Page 1A, Enumeration District 633, Image 60.

24. Interview with Frank Garfield Ellis conducted by Edgar F. Hastings on March 28, 1961 (San Diego Historical Society), 14.

25. "Italian Aliens and Smuggler Captured," *Calexico Chronicle*, June 2, 1924.

26. "Aliens without Passports to Be Sent Back Home," *Calexico Chronicle*, August 1, 1924.

27. "Smuggled Hindus and Smugglers to Be Prosecuted," *Calexico Chronicle*, August 13, 1924.

28. *Principal Activities of the U.S. Border Patrol, Fiscal Year 1925* (CIR/HRL).

29. Ibid.

30. Senate Committee on Immigration, *Restriction of Western Hemisphere Immigration: Hearings before the Committee on Immigration, United States Senate*, statement of C. B. Moore, 70th Cong., 1st sess., 1928, 61–62. See also Reisler, *By the Sweat of Their Brow*, 61–66.

31. Ibid.

32. Ibid.

33. Ibid.

34. March 16, 1927, letter to the U.S. Immigration Service from G. C. Wilmoth, District Director in El Paso, TX (NARA 55494/25, 3, 58A734). For a discussion of earlier efforts to economize deportations to China, see Torrie Hester, "Deportation: Origins of a National and International Power" (PhD diss., University of Oregon, 2008), 77–91.

35. Ibid.

36. Ibid.

37. March 16, 1927, letter to the Immigration Service from G. C. Wilmoth.

38. *Principal Activities of the U.S. Border Patrol, Fiscal Year 1928* (CIR/HRL).

39. *Principal Activities of the U.S. Border Patrol, Fiscal Year 1929* (CIR/HRL).

40. Marin, "La migración china, 232.

41. Ibid.

42. Philip A. Dennis, "The Anti-Chinese Campaigns in Sonora, Mexico," *Ethnohistory* 26, no. 1 (1979): 65–80.

43. Statement of Tan Luk (NARA 55771/718B, entry 9).

44. Statement of Yee Chu Chim (NARA 55771/718B, entry 9).

45. Ibid.

46. Ibid.

47. March 16, 1932, letter from Senior Patrol Inspector Ivan Williams to Chief Patrol Inspector, U.S. Border Patrol, Tucson, Arizona on (NARA 55771/718A, 484, entry 9), 1.

48. Ibid.

49. Ibid., 2

50. March 14, 1932, letter from Egbert Crossett, Senior Patrol Inspector, Naco, Arizona, to Chief Patrol Inspector, Tucson, Arizona (NARA 55771/718A, entry 9).

51. April 22, 1932, memo from Assistant Attorney General Nugent Dodds to Secretary of Labor (NARA 55771/718A, 484, entry A).

52. For information on the anti-Chinese movement in Mexico, see Grace Delgado, "In the Age of Exclusion: Race, Region, and Chinese Identity in the Making of the Arizona-Sonora Borderlands, 1863–1943" (PhD diss., University of California, Los Angeles, 2000); Evelyn Hu-DeHart, The Chinese Experience in Arizona and Northern Mexico (Tucson: Arizona Historical Society, 1980); and Mishima, Destino México. On the anti-Chinese movement in the United States, see Saxton, Indispensable Enemy.

53. Rak, Border Patrol, 124.

54. Records of District Courts of the U.S.-Southern California Division, vols. 4–7, including dockets no. 1994h to no. 3317 (NARA-Laguna Niguel, RG 21).

55. Gary Charles (pseudonym), notes from talk with Gary Charles, April 24, 1990 (NBPM), 1. See also Rak, Border Patrol, 140.

56. June 7, 1933, letter to U.S. Immigration Service from G. C. Wilmoth, District director, El Paso, Texas (NARA 55494/25A, 3, 58A734),1.

57. Francisco E. Balderrama and Raymond Rodríguez, Decade of Betrayal; Camille Guerin-Gonzales, Mexican Workers and American Dreams: Immigration, Repatriation, and California Farm Labor, 1900–1939 (New Brunswick, NJ: Rutgers University Press, 1994); Abraham Hoffman, Unwanted Mexican Americans in the Great Depression: Repatriation Pressures, 1929–1939 (Tucson: University of Arizona Press, 1974); Reynolds Mackay, "The Federal Deportation Campaign in Texas: Mexican Deportation from the Lower Rio Grande Valley during the Great Depression," Borderlands 5, no. 1 (1981): 95–120. See also George Sánchez's discussion of the Immigration Service's raid at La Placita in , Becoming Mexican American, 214.

58. Sánchez, Becoming Mexican American, 61.

4. MEXICO'S LABOR EMIGRANTS, AMERICA'S ILLEGAL IMMIGRANTS

1. Alan Knight, The Mexican Revolution, vol. 1, Porfirians, Liberals, and Peasants, and vol. 2, Counter-Revolution and Reconstruction (Lincoln: University of Nebraska Press, 1986); Ramon Ruíz, The Great Rebellion: Mexico, 1905–1924 (New York: W. W. Norton, 1980); John Tutino, From Insurrection to Revolution in Mexico: Social Bases of Agrarian Violence, 1750–1940 (Princeton, NJ: Princeton University Press, 1987).

2. Aguila, "Protecting "México de Afuera"; Cardoso, Mexican Emigration, 96–118; Gustavo Durón González, Problemas migratorios de México (Mexico City: Talleres de la Cámara de Diputados, 1925); Alfonso Fábila, El problema de la emigración de obreros y campesinos mexicanos (Mexico City: Talleres Gráficos de la Nación, 1929); David Fitzgerald, A Nation of Emigrants: How Mexico Manages Its Migration (Berkeley and Los Angeles: University of California Press, 2009); Martínez, "Mexican Emigration"; Navarro, Los extranjeros en México, 3:202.

3. Quoted in Martínez, "Mexican Emigration," 76. See also Fitzgerald, Nation of Emigrants.

4. Fernando Saúl Alanís Enciso, "La Constitución de 1917 y la emigración de trabajadores mexicanos a Estados Unidos," *Relaciones* 22, no. 87 (2001): 205–30.

5. For example see, Jorge Durand, "Migration Policy and the Asymmetry of Power: The Mexican Case, 1900–2000," in *Citizenship and Those Who Leave: The Politics of Emigration and Expatriation*, ed. Nancy Green and Francois Weil (Urbana: University of Illinois Press, 2007), 224.

6. Alan Knight, "Popular Culture and the Revolutionary State in Mexico, 1910–1940," *Hispanic American Historical Review* 74, no. 3 (1994): 396. See also Marjorie Becker, *Setting the Virgin on Fire: Lázaro Cárdenas and the Redemption of the Mexican Revolution* (Berkeley and Los Angeles: University of California Press, 1995); Knight, *Mexican Revolution*, vol. 2; Mary Kay Vaughan and Stephen E. Lewis, eds., *The Eagle and the Virgin: National and Cultural Revolution in Mexico, 1920–1940* (Durham, NC: Duke University Press, 2006).

7. Knight, "Popular Culture and the Revolutionary State," 395.

8. Durón González, *Problemas migratorios de México*; Gamio, *Mexican Immigration to the United States: A Study of Human Migration and Adjustment* (Chicago: University of Chicago Press, 1930); Navarro, *Los extranjeros en México*, and Moisés González Navarro, *La colonización en México, 1877–1910* (Mexico City: Talleres de Impresión de Estampillas y Valores, 1960), 193–332; Andrés Molina Enríquez, *Los grandes problemas nacionales* (Mexico City: Ediciones Era, 1981); Enrique Santibáñez, *Ensayo acerca de la inmigración mexicana en los Estados Unidos* (San Antonio, TX: Clegg, 1930).

9. Devra Weber, "Introducción," in *El inmigrante mexicano: La historia de su vida, entrevistas completas, 1926–1927*, ed. Devra Weber, Roberto Melville, and Juan Vicente Palerm, 33–34; see also Arthur Schmidt, "Mexicans, Migrants and Indigenous Peoples: The Work of Manuel Gamio in the United States, 1925–1927" in *Strange Pilgrimages: Travel, Exile, and Foreign Residency in the Creation of Latin American Identity, 1800–1990s*, ed. Ingrid E. Fey and Karine Racine (Wilmington, DE: Scholarly Resources, 2000), 170.

10. Gamio, *Mexican Immigration*, 35–40.

11. Ibid.

12. Ibid., 30.

13. Ibid.

14. 17 de julio de 1928, "Del subsecretario de Relaciones Exteriores al Oficial Mayor de Gobernación," nota 991 (Archivo Histórico de la Secretaría de Relaciones Exteriores, Ciudad de México, México, 21-26-50, ff. 32–33; hereafter cited as AHSRE). See also 14 de septiembre de 1927, "[De la Secretaría de Relaciones Exteriores] a los Secretarías de Gobernación, Agricultura, e Industria, Comercio y Trabajo" (AHSRE 21-26-50, folder 1); 2 de agosto 1928, "Estudio sobre las preguntas hechas por el señor Burton Froom, de la Escuela Superior de South Pasadena de California, E.U.A," por José Inés Pérez, Inspector de Segunda del Departamento de Migración (Archivo Histórico del Instituto Nacional de Migración, Ciudad de México, México, 4-350-383; hereafter cited as AHINM).

15. 2 de agosto 1928, "Estudio sobre las preguntas hechas por el señor Burton Froom" (AHINM 4-350-383), 3.

16. Ibid.

17. Gamio, *Mexican Immigration*, 47.

18. Ibid.

19. Casey Walsh, "Eugenic Acculturation: Manuel Gamio, Migration Studies, and the Anthropology of Development in Mexico, 1910–1940," *Latin American Perspectives* 31, no. 5 (2004): 118–45.

20. Gamio, *Mexican Immigration*, 159–69. See also David Fitzgerald, "State and Emigration: A Century of Emigration Policy in Mexico, working paper 123 (Center for Comparative Immigration Studies, University of California at San Diego, September 2005), 7–9.

21. Gamio, *Mexican Immigration*, 64. See also Manuel Gamio, *Forjando Patria* (Mexico City: Editorial Porrúa, 1960).

22. Gamio, quoted in Cardoso, *Mexican Emigration*, 93.

23. Gamio, *Mexican Immigration*, 67.

24. Ibid., 69

25. Walsh, "Eugenic Acculturation," 132. See also Devra Weber, "Introducción," 33–34; Schmidt, "Mexicans, Migrants and Indigenous Peoples," 170.

26. Fernando Saúl Alanís Enciso, *El primer programa bracero y el gobierno de México* (San Luis Potosí: El Colegio de San Luis, 1999).

27. Gamio, *Mexican Immigration*, 9–12.

28. While U.S. census data indicated that more than five hundred thousand Mexicans entered the U.S. illegally between 1920 and 1930, the U.S. Commissioner General of Immigration noted only two hundred and eighty-nine thousand undocumented immigrants apprehended during this period. See U.S. Department of Labor, *Annual Report of the Secretary of Labor, Fiscal Year 1935* (Washington, DC: GPO, 1936), 35.

29. 12 de mayo de 1926, "Informe dirigido a la Secretaría de Gobernación de la visita practicada a la Oficina de Nuevo Laredo, Tamaulipas," Visitador de Migración Fernando Félix (AHINM 4–161–12).

30. 16 de octubre de 1930, "Visita a la delegación de migración en Matamoros," José Bravo Betancourt, Inspector de Migración (AHINM 4–161–144).

31. Ibid.

32. Ibid.

33. "Paso del norte, qué cerca te vas quedando: Circular número 16 de la Secretaría de Gobernación girada por el Departamento de Migración, 11 de abril de 1924," *Relaciones* 21, no. 83 (2000): 145.

34. 12 de mayo de 1926, "Informe de la visita practicada a la Oficina de Nuevo Laredo, Tamaulipas," 1.

35. Ibid.

36. Monroy, *Rebirth*, 89.

37. Gamio, *Mexican Immigration*, 204–5.

38. "Paso del norte, qué cerca te vas quedando: Circular número 16 de la Secretaría de Gobernación."

39. Ibid.

40. Ibid.

41. 11 de mayo de 1926, "Visita practicada a la Agencia del Servicio en Villa Acuña, Coah.," (AHINM 4–161–13), 2.

42. 5 de febrero de 1931, "Informe del Delegado de Migración en Matamoros, Tamauli-

pas, relativo a los contrabandistas que pasaban a los braceros en gran número violando las leyes del país," José Bravo Betancourt, Inspector de Migración (AHINM 4–013–2), 2.

43. Ibid.

44. 13 de marzo de 1929, "Informe general de la visita practicada a la Delegación de Migración en Piedras Negras," José Inéz Pérez, Inspector de Segunda del Departamento de Migración (AHINM 4–161–52).

45. AHSRE IV-93–32 (Border Patrol).

46. AHSRE IV-87–53 (Brownsville); AHSRE IV-93–32 (Border Patrol).

47. AHSRE IV-87–53 (Brownsville).

48. Ibid.

49. See also Consul Enrique Santibáñez's 1929 reports on south Texas jails (AHSRE 4–87–43 [Brownsville]).

50. Andrés Landa y Piña, El Servicio de Migración en México (Mexico City: Talleres Gráficos, 1930), 11.

51. Ibid. See also Santibáñez, Ensayo acerca de la inmigración mexicana, 68.

52. Creación de Consejo Consultivo Población 1935 (AHINM 4–350–228), 3. For later examples, see Agustín Arroyo a Secretaría de Gobernación, "El éxito de la Convención de Población," 26 de marzo de 1938 (AHINM 4–350–1935–228b [Hora Nacional]).

53. Navarro, Los extranjeros en México, 194. See also 19 de agosto 1937, "Tráfico internacional de personas por la frontera de El Paso, Texas," Ernesto Hidalgo, Oficial Mayor (AHINM 4–350–477).

54. 27 de febrero de 1929, "Informe sobre medidas para impedir la inmigración de mexicanos a los Estados Unidos," Rodolfo S. Rodríguez, Departamento de Migración (AHINM 4–350–405).

55. Ibid.

56. For a list of stations with checkpoints, see José M. Dávila interview, carton 10, folder 5, Mexican Labor in US—Field Notes, box 10, folder 5: Series B, set 1 (Paul Schuster Taylor Collection). See also Martínez, "Mexican Emigration," 79; 12 de mayo de 1926, "Informe de la visita practicada a la Oficina de Nuevo Laredo, Tamaulipas," 9; "Nuevas Restricciones para ir a Estados Unidos," Excelsior, 3 de febrero de 1926, 9.

57. 12 de mayo de 1926, "Informe de la visita practicada a la Oficina de Nuevo Laredo, Tamaulipas," 1.

58. Ibid.

59. Ibid. See also, 5 de septiembre de 1930, "Visita a la Delegación de Migración en Guadalajara," Oscar R. Peralta, Inspector del Servicio de Migración (AHINM 4–161–130); 20 de octubre de 1930, "Informe sobre visita a la Oficina de Monterrey, N.L.," por el Jefe de la Sección Técnica (AHINM 4–161–156); 2 de agosto de 1928, "Estudio sobre las preguntas hechas por el señor Burton Froom, de la Escuela Supérior de South Pasadena de California, E.U.A., por José Inés Pérez, Inspector de Segunda del Departamento de Migración," (AHINM 4–350–383), 6; November 3, 1928 statement of Hermolao Torres, vice consul in Nogales, Arizona, to Paul Schuster Taylor (Paul Schuster Taylor Collection, unpublished notes, carton 10, folder 4.)

60. José M. Dávila, interview. Paul S. Taylor Collection. Carton 10, folder 5, Mexican Labor in US—Field Notes, series B, set 1. See also Martínez, "Mexican Emigration," 79; 12

de mayo de 1926, "Informe de la visita practicada a la Oficina de Nuevo Laredo, Tamaulipas," 9.

61. 12 de mayo de 1926, "Informe de la visita practicada a la Oficina de Nuevo Laredo, Tamaulipas," 9.

62. Ibid.

63. Ibid.; see also 3 de noviembre de 1925, "Oficio dirigido al Secretario de Gobernación en el que se remite copia del oficio dirigido al agente encargado del Servicio General de Migración in Saltillo, Coah., acerca de la vigilancia que debe observar en lo sucesivo abordo de los trenes número 2 y 3 y 1 y 4 para las lineas de Nuevo Laredo y Piedras Negras" (AHINM 4–161–1).

64. Ibid.

65. 11 de mayo de 1926, "Visitas a las oficinas de su jurisdicción," Delegación de Migración en Piedras Negras (AHINM 4–161–13), 2.

66. 16 de octubre de 1930, "Visita al la Delegación de Migración en Matamoros," José Bravo Betancourt, Inspector de (AHINM 4–161–144), 1. See also 5 de febrero de 1931 "Informe del Delegado de Migración en Matamoros, Tamaulipas, relativo a los contrabandistas que pasaban a los braceros en gran número violando las leyes del país," José Bravo Betancourt, Inspector de Migración (AHINM 4–013–2), 1.

67. 24 de diciembre de 1930, "Visita a la Delegación de Migración en Ciudad Juárez," Ramón Tirado, Inspector del Servicio de Migración (AHINM 4–161–159), 1.

68. 5 de febrero 1931, "Informe del Delegado de Migración en Matamoros, Tamaulipas"; 12 de mayo de 1926, "Informe de la visita practicada a la Oficina de Nuevo Laredo, Tamaulipas," 9.

69. 11 de septiembre de 1933, "Informe de que el Sr. José Martínez, pretendió proteger el paso clandestino por el Río Bravo, al citado connacional," Delegado de Migración en Piedras Negras (AHINM 4–013.7–10), 1.

70. Balderrama and Rodríguez, *Decade of Betrayal;* Fernando Saúl Alanís Enciso, "No cuenten conmigo: La política de repatriación del gobierno mexicano y sus nacionales en Estados Unidos, 1910–1928," *Mexican Studies/Estudios Mexicanos* 19, no. 2 (2003): 401–31; Guerin-Gonzales, *Mexican Workers and American Dreams;* Hoffman, *Unwanted Mexican Americans;* Mercedes Carreras de Valesco, *Los Mexicanos que devolvió la crisis, 1929–1932* (Mexico City: Secretaría de Relaciones Exteriores, 1974).

5. A NEW BEGINNING

1. Bob Salinger (pseudonym), interviewed by David Burnett on April 4, 1987, in Harlingen, Texas (NBPM), 3.

2. Emmanuel Avant "Dogie" Wright, oral history (untranscribed), conducted on June 14, 1983, by Jim Cullen in Sierra Blanca, Texas (OH no. 86, Archives of the Big Bend, Sul Ross State University). The INS managed internment camps for "enemy aliens" in Fort Stanton, New Mexico; Fort Missoula, Montana; and Fort Lincoln, North Dakota. For more information on the Border Patrol's role in managing the internment camps and guarding the interned families, see "Administrative History of the Immigration and Naturalization Service during WWII" (CIS/HRL). For information on Border Patrol activities during the riot at the Tule

Lake facility, see "Memo regarding transfer of internees from Tule Lake to Fort Lincoln about February 11, 1945" (NARA 56084/74, 2152, 58A734); J. R. Breechen, interviewed by Terrie. Cornell, February 15, 1988 (Institute of Oral History, University of Texas at El Paso), 3.

3. For additional information on the World War II–related duties of the INS and U.S. Border Patrol, see *Annual Report of Lemuel B. Schofield, Special Assistant to the Attorney General in Charge of the Immigration and Naturalization Service, Fiscal Year 1942* (Washington, DC: GPO, 1943), 22–24.

4. *Annual Report of the Commissioner of Immigration and Naturalization, Fiscal Year 1939* (Washington, DC: GPO, 1939), 100.

5. The U.S. Border Patrol was first placed within the Bureau of Immigration of the Labor Department in 1924. The Bureau of Immigration and the Bureau of Naturalization were consolidated on June 10, 1933, and renamed the Immigration and Naturalization Service (INS). The Border Patrol remained under the secretary of labor within the INS until 1940, when the *Reorganization Act of 1939* went into effect and switched the INS from the Department of Labor to the Justice Department. Therefore, in 1940 the Attorney General took over direct supervision of the U.S. Border Patrol. For more information, see *Annual Report of the Attorney General for the Year 1941* (Washington, DC: GPO, 1941), 226.

6. Burnett, Personal Narrative (NBPM), 19.

7. Harrison H. Merkel, Electronics Engineer, Central Office, "Mobile Operational Communications," *I and N Reporter* 9, no. 3 (1961): 35. See also Burnett, Personal Narrative, 19–21.

8. Burnett, Personal Narrative, 21.

9. Ed Parker, *Prop Cops: The First Quarter Century Aloft* (El Paso, Texas: Border Patrol Foundation, 1983), chap. 4 (NBPM). See also James E. Parker, "Border Patrol Air Operations," in *I and N Reporter* 4, no. 2 (1955): 17–18.

10. Parker, *Prop Cops*, chap. 4. See also Parker, "Border Patrol Air Operations," 17–18.

11. July 21, 1942, "Attention of Chief Supervisor of Border Patrol," memo from W. W. Eyster, District Director, District No. 6, to Commissioner, Immigration and Naturalization Service, Philadelphia, Pennsylvania (NARA 55879/9J, 712, 58A734), 3.

12. Ibid.

13. Salinger interview, 1–2.

14. Ibid., 2

15. Breechen interview, 3.

16. December 8, 1944, memo from G. C. Wilmoth to W. F. Kelly (NARA 55853/317C, 440, 58A734).

17. September 26, 1941, memo from Eddie E. Adcok, District Supervisor in El Paso, Texas, to District Director Wilmoth (NARA 55853/317A, 440, 58A734).

18. August 19, 1942, memo from Carson Morrow to the District Director in El Paso (NARA 55853/317A, 440, 58A734).

19. April 12, 1941, memo from Chief Patrol Inspector Griffith McBee (NARA 55853/317, 440, 58A734).

20. June 1, 1941, memo from Richard H. Wells, Chief Patrol Inspector, El Centro, California, to District Director, Los Angeles (NARA 55853/320, 441, 58A734), 1.

21. Ibid.

22. June 5, 1941, memo from William A. Carmichael, District Director, Los Angeles Dis-

trict, to Lemuel B. Schofield, Special Assistant to the Attorney General (NARA 55853/320, 441, 58A734), 1.

23. Ibid.

24. William Blaise (pseudonym), interviewed by Terrie Cornell, February 18, 1988 (NBPM).

25. "Border Patrol Folklore," untranscribed audiotaped interviews conducted by Jeannie Egbert (NBPM).

26. Burnett, Personal Narrative, 47.

27. Ibid.

28. June 5, 1941, memo from Carmichael to Schofield.

29. The primary provisions of the Bracero labor contract were (1) Mexican contract workers would not engage in U.S. military service; (2) Mexicans entering under the Bracero program would not be subject to discrimination of any kind; (3) braceros were to be guaranteed transportation, living expenses, and repatriation; (4) braceros would not be employed to displace domestic workers or reduce their wages.

30. Calavita, Inside the State; Nelson Gage Copp, "Wetbacks" and Braceros: Mexican Migrant Laborers and American Immigration Policy, 1930–1960 (San Francisco: R and E Research Associates, 1971); Richard B. Craig, The Bracero Program: Interest Groups and Foreign Policy (Austin: University of Texas Press, 1971).

31. Galarza, Merchants of Labor, 16.

32. Gilbert G. González, Guest Workers or Colonized Labor: Mexican Labor Migration to the United States (Boulder, CO: Paradigm, 2006), 2; Gilbert G. González and Raúl A. Fernández, A Century of Chicano History: Empire, Nations, and Migration (New York: Routledge, 2003).

33. Calavita, Inside the State.

34. Deborah Cohen, "From Peasant to Worker: Migration, Masculinity, and the Making of Mexican Workers in the U.S.," International Labor and Working Class History 69 (Spring 2006): 81–103, and "Caught in the Middle: The Mexican State's Relationship with the U.S. and Its Own Citizen-Workers, 1942–1958," Journal of American Ethnic History 20, no. 3 (2001): 110–32. See also Howard Lloyd Campbell, "Bracero Migration and the Mexican Economy, 1951–1964" (PhD diss., The American University, 1972).

35. Deborah Cohen, Transnational Subjects: Braceros, Nation, and Migration (the United States and Mexico, 1942–1964 (Chapel Hill: University of North Carolina Press, 2010), chap. 1.

36. Ana Rosas, "Familias Flexibles (Flexible Families): Bracero Families' Lives across Cultures, Communities, and Countries, 1942–1964" (PhD diss., University of Southern California, 2006), 8.

37. Héctor Aguilar Camín and Lorenzo Meyer, In the Shadow of the Mexican Revolution: Contemporary Mexican History, 1910–1989 (Austin: University of Texas Press, 1993); María Luisa González Marín, La industrialización en México (Mexico City: Instituto de Investigaciones Económicas, Universidad Nacional Autónoma de México; Porrúa, 2002); Elsa M. Gracida, El siglo XX Mexicano: Un capítulo de su historia, 1940–1982 (Mexico City: Universidad Nacional Autónoma de México, 2002); Niblo, War, Diplomacy, and Development, and Impact of War.

38. Jonathan C. Brown, *Oil and Revolution in Mexico* (Berkeley and Los Angeles: University of California Press, 1992).

39. Although the tenor of foreign relations seemed to suggest that the U.S. and Mexican governments could reconcile few of their conflicts, particularly since the ousting of Porfirio Díaz, Alan Knight has argued that similar trends in U.S. and Mexican politics actually built common ground between diplomats of each country despite multiple disagreements; see his *U.S.-Mexican Relations, 1910–1940: An Interpretation* (La Jolla: Center for U.S.-Mexican Studies at the University of California–San Diego, 1987).

40. Niblo, *War, Diplomacy, and Development*, 89–122.

41. Ibid., 112.

42. Ibid., 130.

43. García, *Operation Wetback*, 22–25; Walsh, "Development in the Borderlands," 468–500; Walsh, "Demobilizing the Revolution: Migration, Repatriation, and Colonization in Mexico, 1911–1940," Working Paper no. 26 (La Jolla: Center for Comparative Immigration Studies at the University of California–San Diego, 2000), 23–24.

44. Ibid.

45. 8 de julio de 1943, carta desde C. José Davalos Alvarez y José G. Sánchez Gutiérrez a Manuel Avila Camacho, Presidente de la República (Archivo General de la Nación, Mexico City [hereafter AGN], FMAC, 793, 546.6/120–1).

46. 19 de febrero de 1944, telegrama desde la Asociación Agrícola del Valle de Mexicali a Presidente de la República (AGN, FMAC 793, 546.6/120–2); 20 de febrero de 1944, telegrama desde Algodonera del Valle a Presidente de la República (AGN, FMAC 793, 546.6/120–1); 24 de junio de 1944, telegrama desde silvestre Silva, Regino Aviles, y Bonifacio Aviles a Presidente de la República (AGN, FMAC 803, 548.1/19). For a history of the political economy of cotton farming in the Matamoros region, see Tomás Martínez Saldaña, *El costo social de un éxito político* (Chapingo, México: Colegio de Postgraduados, 1980), 15–43; Fernando Saúl Alanís Enciso, *El valle bajo del Río Bravo, Tamaulipas, en la década de 1930: El desarrollo regional en la posrevolución a partir de la irrigación, la migración interna y los repatriados de Estados Unidos* (Ciudad Victoria, Tamaulipas, México: El Colegio de Tamaulipas y El Colegio de San Luis, A. C., 2004); and Walsh, "Development in the Borderlands."

47. 13 de octubre de 1942, "MEMORANDUM," desde Confederación de Obreros y Campesinos de México a Presidente de la República (AGN, FMAC 803, 548.1/19–1); 29 de marzo de 1943, "MEMORANDUM" (AGN, FMAC 803, 548.1/19–3); 24 de mayo de 1943, "Contratación de trabajadores mexicanos para los Estados Unidos," desde Ezequiel Padilla, el Secretario de Relaciones Exteriores, a J. Jesús Gonzáles Gallo, Secretario Particular del C. Presidente de la República (AGN, FMAC 803, 548.1/19–3).

48. Copp, *"Wetbacks" and Braceros;* David Richard Lessard, "Agrarianism and Nationalism: Mexico and the Bracero Program, 1942—1947" (PhD diss., Tulane University, 1984); Johnny MacCain, "Contract Labor as a Factor in United States-Mexican Relations, 1942–1947" (PhD diss., University of Texas at Austin, 1970).

49. September 16, 1942, memo from Griffith McBee, Chief Patrol Inspector, El Paso, Texas, to the District Director of the Immigration and Naturalization Service, El Paso, Texas (NARA 55853/317A, 440, 58A734).

50. Otey M. Scruggs, "Texas and the Bracero Program, 1942–1947," *Pacific Historical Review* 32, no. 3 (1963): 251–64.

51. May 29, 1943, memo from Griffith McBee, Chief Patrol Inspector, El Paso, Texas, to District Director, El Paso, Texas (NARA 55853/317B, 440, 58A734).

52. *Principal Activities of the U.S. Border Patrol, Fiscal Year 1943* (CIR/HRL).

53. May 29, 1943, memo from Chief Patrol Inspector Griffith McBee.

54. Ibid.

55. Ibid.

56. See also December 22, 1943, letter from J. F. McGurk, Assistant Chief, Division of the American Republics, to Mr. Earl G. Harrison, Commissioner, Immigration and Naturalization Service (NARA 56161/109, 2662, 58A734); and "Salaries and Expenses 1946," 139 (CIS/HRL).

57. Ibid.

58. Jarnagin, "The Effect of Increased Illegal Mexican Migration," 91–92.

59. *Annual Report of the Secretary of Labor, Fiscal Year 1940* (Washington, DC: GPO, 1941), 111.

60. December 11, 1943, memo no. 9956, from the Mexican Embassy in Washington, D.C. (NARA 56161/109, 2662, 58A734).

61. June 9, 1944, memo from Andrew Jordan, District Director, Chicago, to Commissioner General of INS regarding "Mexican Aliens" (NARA 55853/313A, 439, 58A734).

62. July 15, 1944, "Border Patrol Operations in McAllen Sector," from H. P. Brady, District Alien Control Division, to W. F. Kelly, Assistant Commissioner for Alien Control, Philadelphia (NARA 55853/314B, 439, 58A734).

63. Memo from J. W. Nelson, Chief of the Border Patrol Section, to W. F. Kelly, Asst. Commissioner for Alien Control, n.d. (NARA 56195/713, 2848, 58A734).

64. October 16, 1944, "Mexican Border Situation," from Albert Del Guercio, District Director, Los Angeles, to Joseph Savoretti, Acting Commissioner (NARA 56195/713, 2848, 58A734), 2.

65. November 2, 1944, memo from W. F. Kelly, Asst. Commissioner, Enforcement Division, to G. C. Wilmoth (NARA 55853/317C, 440, 58A734).

66. January 2, 1945, memo from Earl Fallis to G. C. Wilmoth (NARA 56364/43 sw, pt. 1, 91, 59A2038).

67. Ibid.

68. Ibid.

69. November 2, 1944, memo from W. F. Kelly to G. C. Wilmoth.

70. *The Other Side of the Story* (NBPM). All names provided are pseudonyms.

71. Ibid.

72. John Rosier, interview responses by Jesse T. Rose, September 16, 1986 (D96.68.2, NBPM), 2.

73. Ibid.

74. *The Other Side of the Story.*

75. Ibid.

76. Galarza, *Merchants of Labor*, 58–71; Copp, *"Wetbacks" and Braceros*, 78–99. For analyses of the risks of using Border Patrol apprehension statistics to measure undocumented

immigration, see Jorge Bustamante, "Measuring the Flow of Undocumented Immigrants," in *Mexican Migration to the United States: Origins, Consequences, and Policy Options*, ed. Wayne Cornelius and Jorge Bustamante, (La Jolla: Center for U.S.-Mexican Studies at the University of California–San Diego, 1989), 95–106; Thomas J. Espenshade, "Using INS Border Apprehension Data to Measure the Flow of Undocumented Migrants Crossing the U.S.-Mexico Frontier," *International Migration Review* 29, no. 2 (1995): 545–65. For more general examinations of crime statistics, see Eric H. Monkkonen, "The Quantitative Historical Study of Crime and Criminal Justice," in *History and Crime: Implications for Criminal Justice Policy*, ed. J. A. Inciardi and C. E. Faupel (Beverly Hills, CA: Sage, 1980), 53–73; Mark L. Dantzker, Arthur J. Lurigio, Magnus J. Seng, and James M. Sinacore, *Practical Applications for Criminal Justice Statistics* (Boston. MA: Butterworth-Heinemann, 1998).

6. THE CORRIDORS OF MIGRATION CONTROL

1. January 17, 1948, letter from M.K. Fritz of Fritz Funeral Home (Chicago) to Pres. of México (AGN, FMAV, 587, 545.3/98).

2. Ibid.

3. Ibid.

4. Ibid.

5. Dudziak, *Cold War Civil Rights;* Borstlemann, *The Cold War and the Color Line.*

6. Lizabeth Cohen, *Making a New Deal: Industrial Workers in Chicago, 1919–1939* (New York: Cambridge University Press, 1990), 324–60. See also Gerald Horne, *Black and Brown: Africans and the Mexican Revolution, 1910–1920* (New York: New York University Press, 2005); Johnson, *Revolution in Texas;* Sandos, *Rebellion in the Borderlands;* Daniel Widener and Luis Alvarez, "Chicana/o–African American Cultural and Political Relations," *Aztlan: A Journal of Chicano Studies* 33, no. 1 (2008): 143–96.

7. Thomas A. Guglielmo, "Fighting for Caucasian Rights."

8. Foley, "Partly Colored or Other White," 341–55.

9. Guglielmo, *White on Arrival: Italians, Race, Color, and Power in Chicago, 1890–1945* (New York: Oxford University Press, 2003); Roediger, *Wages of Whiteness.*

10. November 27, 1945, memo from Joseph Savoretti to Grover C. Wilmoth, District Director of El Paso, "Removal of Mexican nationals apprehended in the Los Angeles District through El Paso and Nogales" (NARA 55853/300D, 437, 58A734).

11. For a discussion of the airlifts, see the testimony by Argyle R. Mackey, commissioner of the Immigration and Naturalization Service, and Willard F. Kelly, Assistant Commissioner, Enforcement Division, Immigration and Naturalization Service, in Senate Subcommittee on Labor and Labor-Management Relations of the Committee on Labor and Public Welfare, *Migratory Labor Hearings*, 82nd Cong., 2nd sess. on migratory labor, pt. 1, 1952, 735–47.

12. September 20, 1956, memo from Marcus Neely, District Director, El Paso, to E. D. Kelliher, Chief, Detention, Deportation and Parole, El Paso (National Archives and Records Administration, College Park, MD, RG 85, Acc 67A2033, box 13, file 659.4, pt. 1; hereafter cited as NARA 2). For a similar scenario with the airlifts, see November 5, 1957, memo, "AIRLIFT—Reynosa to León, Guanajuato," from John P. Swanson, Assistant Regional

Commissioner for Enforcement, Southwest Region, to All Chief Patrol Inspectors, Southwest Region (NARA 2, RG 85, Acc 67A0233, box 13, file 659.4, pt. 1). See also Ben A. Parker, interviewed by Douglas V. Meed, July 25, 1984 (Interview no. 661, Institute of Oral History, University of Texas at El Paso), 8–10.

13. Ibid.

14. Ibid.

15. June 27, 1957, memo, "Movement of Buslifted Aliens," from P. A. Reyes, Patrol Inspector, El Paso, to Chief Patrol Inspector, El Paso (NARA 2, RG 85, Acc 67A0233, box 13, file 659.4, pt. 1).

16. "Desordenes públicos entre braceros que conducía el Barco Platanero citato en el Río Pánuco" (AHINM 4-009-1); 10 de septiembre de 1956, "Informe relacionado con la arribada forzosa del vapor mercante nacional MERCURIO,"carta desde Francisco Rabatte, el Jefe del Servicio, Oficina de Población en Tampico, Tamaulipas, al Secretario de Gobernación (AHINM 4-009-1).

17. Letter from the Commissioner to Honorable Jon Phillips on January 19, 1948 (NARA 56084/946, 9, 59A2034).

18. July 1, 1949, report, "Preliminary Estimate for Lighting of Boundary Fence, Installing Protective Devices, and Erection of Observation Towers at Calexico, San Ysidro, and Nogales" (NARA 56084/946A, 9, 59A2034), 1.

19. June 27, 1949, memo from Nick Collaer to W. F. Kelly, "Guarding of the International Fence, Calexico" (NARA 56364/43 sw, pt. 1, 93, 59A2038); July 12, 1949, memo from H. R. Landon to M. H. A. Lindsay, Chief Engineer, ADT Co. (NARA 56084/946A, 9, 59A2038).

20. July 1, 1949, report, "Preliminary Estimate for Lighting of Boundary Fence," 1; see also November 28, 1952, memo from R. L. Williams to H. Landon, "International Fence at Calexico" (NARA 56084/946A, 9, 59A2034).

21. July 9, 1951, memo from Chief Patrol Inspector, El Centro, to District Enforcement Officer in Los Angeles (NARA 56084/946A, 9, 59A2034).

22. Arthur Adams, interviewed by Jim Marchant and Oscar J. Martínez, August 10, 1977 (Interview no. 646, Institute of Oral History, University of Texas at El Paso), 19.

23. Ben A. Parker interview, 7–8.

24. "Mexican Workers Flood Across Line," Los Angeles Times, May 2, 1950.

25. "Bodies of Five Men Believed to Be Wetbacks Found in Desert," Imperial Valley Press, February 4, 1952. Such newspaper reports would become common in the 1990s after the United States implemented Operation Hold the Line in El Paso and Operation Gatekeeper in San Diego, California, which forced undocumented migrants to cross through the desert. For example, see "Bodies of Two Men Found in Imperial Valley Desert," San Diego Union-Tribune, September 8, 1999.

26. Brawley News, May 26, 1952, "Wetback Drowns Near Calexico" (Ernesto Galarza Papers, box 50, folder 6).

27. Imperial Valley Press, June 1, 1952 "Body Is Found in All American" (Ernesto Galarza Papers, box 50, folder 6).

28. "Bodies of Five Men Believed to be Wetbacks found in Desert," Imperial Valley Press, February 4, 1952,

29. See Michel Foucault, *The History of Sexuality: An Introduction* (New York: Vintage Books, 1990), 137. For a discussion of the many dimensions of state power and violence at the contemporary U.S.-Mexico border, see the following: Wayne Cornelius, "Death at the Border: Efficacy and Unintended Consequences of U.S. Immigration Control Policy, "*Population and Development Review* 27, no. 4 (2001): 661–85; Jonathan Xavier Inda, "Border Prophylaxis: Technology, Illegality, and the Government of Immigration," *Cultural Dynamics* 18, no. 2 (2006): 115–38; and Gilberto Rosas, "The Thickening of the Borderlands: Diffused Exceptionality and 'Immigrant Struggles' during the 'War on Terror,'" *Cultural Dynamics* 18, no. 3 (2006): 335–49.

30. June 4, 1953, "Reports and Excerpts from Patrol Inspectors in Charge of Border Patrol Units in the McAllen Sector of the San Antonio District" (NARA 56364/43 sw, pt. 3, 91, 59A2038).

31. March 17, 1953, memo from Owen T. Miller to Acting Collector of Customs (NARA 56364/43 sw, pt. 3, 91, 59A2038).

32. July 15, 1953, memo from Richard Wischkaemper to Chief Patrol Inspector, Sacramento (NARA 56364/43 sw, pt. 3, 91, 59A2038).

33. March 10, 1953, memo from District Director, El Paso, to Commissioner of Immigration, "The Escape of Detainees at Indio, CA" (NARA 56364/43 sw, pt. 3, 91, 59A2038).

34. "Reports and Excerpts from Patrol Inspectors in Charge of Border Patrol Units," 3.

35. Ibid., 2

36. Ibid., 4

37. Ibid., 3

38. Ibid.

39. Ibid.

40. Ibid.

41. See Dougal Massey et al., *Return to Aztlan: The Social Process of International Migration from Western Mexico* (Berkeley and Los Angeles: University of California Press, 1987).

42. David Burnett, Personal Narrative (NBPM), 14.

43. Ibid.

44. 13 de marzo de 1953, Carta de Celestino Alemán Carvajal, Jefe del Servicio de Población, a C. Arcadio Ojeda García, Jefe de Migración (AHINM 4-357.1-1380, tomo 5, 2).

45. 17 de agosto de 1945, "Asesinatos en la zona del Bravo," por el Cónsul General de México, El Paso, Texas (AHINM 4-357.1-295).

46. Cohen, "From Peasant to Worker"; Ana Rosas, "Flexible Families."

47. April 3, 1953, memo from Samuel McKone to Chief Patrol Inspector (NARA 56364/43 sw, pt. 3); January 19, 1956, letter from the Attorney General to John Foster Dulles (NARA 56364/44.14, 102, 59A2038).

48. "Un mexicano por día se ahoga en el Bravo," *Excelsior,* July 21, 1949.

49. 12 de noviembre de 1946, "Comunicación de identidad de los trabajadores que salieron de los EEUU," Trabajadores Agrícolas Mexicanos (AHINM 4-357.1-295, tomo 60); 14 de diciembre de 1946, "Informe medidas tomadas para evitar explotación trabajadores mexicanos regrasan al país" (AHINM 4-357.1-295, tomo 61); 2 de julio de 1946, "Informe de coyotaje" (AHINM 4-357.1-295).

50. 3 de mayo, 1948, "Remitiendo documentos que se indican," Andrés Guerra, Jefe de Servicio de Población (AHINM 4-357.1-6339), 2.

51. 22 de febrero de 1950, "Informe sobre muerte accidental," Secretaría de Relaciones Exteriores (AHINM 4-357.1-7527).

52. Ibid.

53. April 3, 1953, memo from Samuel McKone to Chief Patrol Inspector; January 19, 1956, letter from the Attorney General to John Foster Dulles.

54. The early release of women, children, and family groups from Border Patrol custody meant that the rising numbers of women and children engaged in unsanctioned migration were not entered into the official digests of Border Patrol apprehension statistics. This offers another example of the incomplete picture that Border Patrol statistics provide of the dynamics of unsanctioned Mexican immigration, which is often assumed to be an almost entirely male migration.

55. March 20, 1953, memo from David Snow, Patrol Inspector in Charge, Brownsville, Texas to Fletcher Rawls, Chief Patrol Inspector, McAllen, Texas, "Need for construction of boundary fence and observation towers in vicinity of Brownsville, Texas-Matamoros, Mexico to control illegal traffic," (NARA 56084/946A, 9, 59A2034), 7.

56. "Reports and Excerpts from Patrol Inspectors in Charge of Border Patrol Units," 11.

57. March 20, 1953, memo from David Snow, 14.

58. Ibid.

59. Ibid.

60. Ibid.

61. Ibid.

62. Ibid.

63. 14 de abril de 1946,"Relacionado con la internación ilegal a Estados Unidos de braceros mexicanos," Cipriano Villanueva Garza, Mexicali, B. C., Oficina De Población (AHINM 4-357.1-295).

64. 10 de octubre de 1946, "Informando falta personal," Andrés Guerra, Jefe de Servicio de Población (AHINM 4-357.1-295, 2-3).

65. Dana Markiewicz, The Mexican Revolution and the Limits of Reform, 1915-1946, 134. See also Historia de la cuestión agraria Mexicana, coordinación general, Carlota Botey y Everardo Escárcega, vols. 6-8 (Mexico City: Siglo XXI Editores–Centro de Estudios Históricos del Agrarismo Mexicano, 1989); and William Whitney Hicks, The Agricultural Development of Mexico, 1940-1960 (Ann Arbor: University of Michigan Microfilms, 1974).

66. 19 de febrero de 1944, telegrama desde la Asociación Agrícola del Valle de Mexicali a Presidente de la República; 20 de febrero de 1944, telegrama desde Algodonera del Valle a Presidente de la República; 24 de junio de 1944, telegrama desde Silvestre Silva, Regino Aviles, y Bonifacio Aviles a Presidente de la República. For a history of the political economy of cotton farming in the Matamoros region, see Saldaña, El costo social de un éxito político, 15-43; Enciso, El valle bajo del Río Bravo; and Walsh, "Development in the Borderlands," 468-500. For a history of agriculture in Mexicali, see Adalberto Walter Meade, El valle de Mexicali (Mexicali: Universidad Autónoma de Baja California, 1996).

67. 21 de febrero de 1944, Extracto de Corl. Rodolfo Sánchez Taboada, Gobernador Territorio Norte, Mexicali, B.C., a Presidente de la República (AGN, FMAC 793, 546.6/120-

1). See also David Richard Lessard, "Agrarianism and Nationalism: Mexico and the Bracero Program, 1942–1947" (PhD diss., Tulane University, 1984), 157.

68. Brad Thomas (pseudonym), interviewed December 27, 1989 (NBPM; untranscribed); Jack Chamberlain (pseudonym), interviewed by Terri Cornell, January 24, 1990 (NBPM; untranscribed); and, Henry Laughlin (pseudonym), interviewed by Terri Cornell, February 14, 1989 (NBPM; untranscribed).

69. Ernesto Julio Teissier, "Lluvia tempranera dañó las plantas que no se pizcaron: Gestiones ante la presidencia para que se tomen medidas que impidan la ruina de la región," *Novedades* (Mexico City), 25 de julio de 1949.

70. Refugio Vargas Castillo, "Impotencia para evitar que se mate a braceros: Precauciones nuevos para evitar que se repitan los crímenes," *Novedades* (Mexico City), 10 de julio de 1949. See also 16 de junio de 1951, "Tráfico ilegal de trabajadores para pasarlos a EEUU" (AHINM 4-350-295, tomo 2); and "Contrabandistas de braceros en Reynosa, Tamaulipas," informes sobre este motivo, 1948–1952 (AHINM 4-013.7-34).

71. Rodolfo F. Guzmán, "Que las autoridades municipales los venden como si fueran esclavos," *Novedades* (Mexico City), 20 de julio de 1949.

72. Navarro, *Los extranjeros en México*, 46.

73. 30 de diciembre de 1948, "Informe sobre contrabandistas de braceros en Reynosa," Andrés Guerra, Jefe de Servicio de Población (AHINM 4-013.7-34); 31 de enero de 1949, "Informe que el citado fué consignado por presunto enganchador," Andrés Guerra, Jefe de Servicio de Población (AHINM 4-357.1-7007).

74. Andrés G. Guerra, Jefe de Servicio de Población, "Reunión de la Conferencia Internacional del Trabajo," (AHINM 4-350-295).

75. "Evita el ejército el éxodo ilegal de los braceros a EE. UU.," *Novedades* (Mexico City), 26 de julio de 1949; "Se ha contenido el éxodo de braceros: Vigilancia militar, pero sin la menor molestia para los fugitivos," *Novedades* (Mexico City), 27 de julio de 1949.

76. 1 de agosto de 1949, "Pidiendo que se trasladen inmediatamente las oficinas de contratación . . . a esta ciudad de Matamoros" (AGN, FMAV 594, 546.6/1–27), 3.

77. "Protección para el bracero deportado: El gobierno de México tomó ayer radicales medidas de emergencia," *Novedades* (Mexico City), 25 de julio de 1952; "Mexico Launches Own Round Up of Wetbacks," *Valley Evening Monitor*, July 20, 1952.

78. "El ejercito de México evitará la entrada a EU de braceros ilegales," *La Opinion*, 24 de agosto de 1953; "México estrecha su vigilancia de los ilegales," *La Opinion*, 20 de agosto de 1953.

79. October 16, 1953, letter from W. F. Kelly, Assistant Commissioner of the Immigration and Naturalization Service, to William Belton, Officer in Charge, Mexican Affairs Division, Department of State, including enclosed articles, "Captain Alberto Moreno Works with a Hand of Steel with His Patrol Agents on Those Who Commit Any Irregularity," and "Two More Boatmen Are Apprehended" (NARA 2, RG 59, 811.06/Mexico/12–453, box 4407).

80. Nadelmann, *Cops across Borders*, xiv.

81. *Annual Report of the Immigration and Naturalization Service for Fiscal Year Ending June 30, 1948* (Washington, DC: GPO, 1948), 24.

82. Bob Salinger (pseudonym), interviewed by David Burnett (pseudonym), April 4, 1987 (NBPM), 11.

83. Ibid.

84. Ibid.

85. Ibid.

86. Ibid.

87. Henry Wallave Pope, "U.S. Concentration Camp: Shaved Heads for Mexicans—Are Tattoos Next?" *National Guardian,* August 1, 1949 (Ernesto Galarza Papers, box 50, folder 3).

88. September 20, 1953, memo from Chief Patrol Inspector Fletcher Rawls (NARA 56364/43 sw, pt. 3, 91, 59A2038).

89. January 30, 1958, untitled memo from Regional Commissioner, San Pedro, California (NARA 2, RG 85, Acc 67A0233, box 13, file 659.4, pt. 1).

90. September 20, 1953, memo from Chief Patrol Inspector Fletcher Rawls (NARA 56364/43 sw, pt. 3, 91, 59A2038). See also May 4, 1950, interview with Francisco Wallis-Diaz (NARA 56084/74A, 2152, 58A734); April 26, 1950, "Our Consul Sleeps and Becomes Humble to the Laborer," translated article from Mexican newspaper, *Baja California,* (NARA 56084/74A, 2152, 58A734); March 12, 1957, memo from Frank Partridge to David Carnahan, "Parasitic Infestation—Detention Facilities" (NARA 56364/43.39, 98, 59A2038); May 4, 1950, "Immigrant examination at camp Elliott, San Diego, California" (NARA 56084/74A, 2152, 58A734), 4; May 7, 1953, memo from W. F. Kelly (NARA 56364/43 sw, pt. 3, 91, 59A2038); and June 12, 1950, memo from Albert del Guercio to Commissioner of INS, "Newspaper article alleging mistreatment of Mexican aliens" (NARA 56084/74A, 2152, 58A734). See also Michael Ignatieff *A Just Measure of Pain: The Penitentiary in the Industrial Revolution, 1750–1850* (New York: Pantheon, 1978), 100.

91. July 9, 1951, memo from Chief Patrol Inspector of El Centro, California, to District Enforcement Officer, Los Angeles, "Mexican Airlift" (NARA 56084/946A, 9, 59A2034).

92. James C. Scott, *Weapons of the Weak: Everyday Forms of Peasant Resistance* (New Haven, CT: Yale University Press, 1985)

93. "Reports and Excerpts from Patrol Inspectors in Charge of Border Patrol Units."

94. "Bentsen Raps Airlift as Useless Waste: Wetback Plane Tours, Detention Camps Blasted," *Valley Evening Monitor,* June 10, 1952.

95. *Annual Report of the Immigration and Naturalization Service for Fiscal Year Ending June 30, 1949* (Washington, DC: GPO, 1949), 23–26. See also *Annual Report of the Immigration and Naturalization Service for Fiscal Year Ending June 30, 1947* (Washington, DC: GPO, 1947), 28.

96. Ibid.

97. Ibid.

98. "General Swing's Little Mexican Girl," *Valley Evening Monitor,* June 3, 1956.

99. "Five Drown in Jump from Wetback Ship *Mercurio,*" *Valley Evening Monitor,* August 27, 1956; "Full-Dress Congress Investigation of 'Hell Ship' *Mercurio* Shapes Up," *Valley Evening Monitor,* August 28, 1956.

100. "Que son tratados como bestias los braceros deportados," *El Heraldo de Chihuahua,* 7 de Mayo de 1956 (AGN, FARC 883, 546.6/55).

101. American G.I. Forum, *What Price Wetback?* (Austin, TX: American G.I. Forum, 1953), 17.

102. Ibid., 19.

103. September 20, 1953, memo from Fletcher Rawls.

104. Ibid.

105. Ibid.

106. Paul Schuster Taylor, *An American-Mexican Frontier*, 85.

107. Timothy M. Chambless, "Pro-Defense, Pro-Growth, and Anti-Communism," in *The Cold War American West*, ed. Kevin J. Fernlund, (Albuquerque: University of New Mexico Press, 1998), 101–17; Foley, *From Peones to Politicos*; Gerald D. Nash, *World War II and the West: Reshaping the Economy* (Lincoln: University of Nebraska Press, 1990).

108. Montejano, *Anglos and Mexicans in the Making of Texas*, 263.

109. Foley, *From Peones to Politicos*, 105–34.

110. Stanley Childs (pseudonym), interviewed by Terri Cornell, December 8, 1986 (NBPM), 5.

111. Ibid.

7. UPRISING

1. Jeff Milton biography file (Center for American History, University of Texas, Austin).

2. Ibid.

3. Jeff Milton personnel file (NBPM).

4. Egbert Crossett personnel file (NBPM).

5. September 25, 1947, memo from Nick Collaer, Acting Assistant Commissioner for Alien Control, to T. B. Shoemaker, Acting Commissioner (NARA 56364/43 sw, pt. 1, 91, 59A2038).

6. Bob Salinger interview, April 4, 1987 (NBPM), 13.

7. Ibid.

8. *The Other Side of the Story* (NBPM).

9. Ibid.

10. August 11, 1941, letter from J. M. Whipff, Commissioner, addressed "To Whom It May Concern" (NARA 56084/74, 2152, 58A734).

11. February 27, 1950, memo from Fletcher Rawls to "Jefe Brady" (NARA 56364/43 sw pt. 2, 93, 59A2038), 2.

12. Ibid.

13. November 4, 1947, "Apprehension of Aliens on the Fletcher Farm Near Las Cruces, New Mexico," from Bruce L. Long, Patrol Inspector, Las Cruces, New Mexico, to G. J. McBee, Chief Patrol Inspector, El Paso, Texas (NARA 56192/582A, 2839, 58A734), 1. See also July 27, 1948, memo from District Director of El Paso to Central Office, "Criminal Proceedings against L. S. and Leigh Fletcher" (NARA 56192/582A, 2839, 58A734); July 27, 1948, memo from Taylor C. Carpenter, District Adjudications Officer, to District Director, El Paso, Texas (NARA 56192/582A, 2839, 58A734); and June 28, 1948, memo from Taylor C. Carpenter to District Director, El Paso, Texas (NARA 56192/582A, 2839, 58A734).

14. November 5, 1947, "Report Concerning the Circumstances of the Serving of Warrants of Arrest on the C. S. Fletcher Farm in Las Cruces, New Mexico," from Robert W. Brew-

ster, Patrol Inspector, to G. J. McBee, Chief Patrol Inspector, El Paso, Texas (NARA 56192/582A, 2839, 58A734), 2.

15. Ibid.

16. Ibid., 3

17. *Act of August 7, 1946*, 79th Cong., 2nd sess. (60 *Stat.* 865; 8 *U.S.C.* 110).

18. June 28, 1948, memo, "Ten-Dollar Club," from Earl Fallis, Chief Patrol Inspector, Alpine, Texas, to District Director, El Paso, Texas (NARA 56364/43 sw, pt. 1, 91, 59A2038).

19. July 27, 1948, memo from District Director, El Paso, "Criminal Proceedings against L. S. and Leigh Fletcher."

20. Letter to District Director of the INS, Walter Sahli, from the editor of the *Brownsville Herald* (NARA 56364/43.3sw, 94, 59A2038).

21. March 30, 1953, memo from Patrol Inspector Edward Hensley to Fletcher Rawls (NARA 56364/43 sw, pt. 3, 91, 59A2038); June 4, 1953, "Reports and Excerpts from Patrol Inspectors in Charge of Border Patrol Units," (NARA 56364/43 sw, pt. 3, 91, 59A2038), 3.

22. September 30, 1953, memo from Griffith McBee, Chief Patrol Inspector, El Paso, Texas (NARA 56084/74, 2152, 58A734).

23. Brad Thomas (pseudonym), interview conducted December 27, 1989, untranscribed (NBPM).

24. Ibid.

25. Ibid.

26. February 11, 1950, memo from Albert Quillin, Patrol Inspector in Charge, San Benito, Texas, to Fletcher Rawls, Chief Patrol Inspector, McAllen, Texas, "Activities of this Station, February 7 through February 10" (NARA 56364/43 sw, pt. 2, 93, 59A2038).

27. Ibid.

28. February 27, 1950, Fletcher Rawls memo to "Jefe Brady," 1.

29. David Burnett, Personal Narrative, 20–22.

30. July 16, 1952, memo from J. W. Holland to Congressman Rooney (NARA 56364/43 sw, pt. 2, 93, 59A2038).

31. "Wetbacks Warned to Stay in Mexico," *Caller-Times News Service,* n.d. Scrapbook (NBPM). See also February 10, 1952, letter from Luis Cortez to Department of Immigration of the United States of North America, El Centro, California (NARA 56364/43 sw, pt. 2, 93, 59A2038).

32. Ibid.

33. Ibid.

34. September 11, 1950, Report from H. H. Tannahill, Investigator, San Antonio, Texas, to Wm. A. Whalen, District Director, San Antonio, Texas, "Patrol Inspector in Charge, Thomas J. Karnes, El Indio, Texas; Investigation of Complaint Dated August 15, 1950" (NARA 56084/74B, 2152, 58A734).

35. Ibid.

36. Ibid.

37. Ibid.

38. August 18, 1954, letter from L. C. Martindale to Griffith McBee (NARA 56364/41.11 pt. 1, 83, 59A2038).

39. January 19, 1951, "Complaint against Patrol Inspector Harold Bassham, Marfa,

Texas, alleging he was abusive and used profane language against and to Mr. W. M. Allison, Marfa, Texas," memo from Taylor C. Carpenter, District Adjudications Officer, El Paso, Texas, to District Director, El Paso (NARA 56084/74B, 2152, 58A734),2.

40. Ibid.
41. Ibid.
42. Ibid.
43. Ibid., 1.
44. Ibid., 2.
45. Ibid., 4.
46. Ibid.
47. September 30, 1943, memo from Griffith McBee; June 4, 1953, "Reports and Excerpts from Patrol Inspectors in Charge of Border Patrol Units."
48. D. C. Newton, oral history, interviewed by Oscar J. Martínez and Virgilio H. Sánchez, October 9, 1978 (Interview no. 721, Institute of Oral History, University of Texas at El Paso).
49. Ibid., 22.
50. Ibid., 23.
51. Ibid., 24.
52. Ibid.
53. Ibid.
54. Ibid., 25.
55. Ibid.
56. Ibid., 23.
57. Ibid., 25–26.
58. Dudziak, Cold War Civil Rights; Borstlemann, The Cold War and the Color Line.
59. Foley, From Peones to Politicos, 105–34.
60. "Why the Mexicans?" El Paso Times, August 19, 1953.
61. "Alliance against the Valley," El Paso Herald, October 5, 1953.
62. "Wetback Airlift Held Cruel By Hidalgo Grand Jurors: Responsible Parties Should Be Censured, Probers Declare in Written Report," Edinburg, United Press, n.d. (LBJ Senate Papers, container 232, Leg. Alien Labor [3rd folder of three], Lyndon Baines Johnson Library, University of Texas at Austin; hereafter cited as LBJ Library).
63. March 18, 1952, letter from Mrs. Robert J. Potts to Hon. Tom Connally (NARA 56364/41.11 pt. 1, 83, 59A2038).
64. August 24, 1951, letter from S. A. Gill to Connally and Senator Lyndon Johnson (LBJ Senate Papers, container 232, Leg. Alien Labor [3rd folder of three]. LBJ Library).
65. June 6, 1951, letter against the U.S. Border Patrol from W. A. Mitchell to Senator Lyndon Johnson (LBJ Senate Papers, container 232, Leg. Alien Labor [3rd folder of three], LBJ Library).
66. May 21, 1952, letter from C. B. Ray to Commissioner Mackay (NARA 56364/41.11, pt. 1, 83, 59A2038).
67. Ibid.
68. Ibid., 2
69. Ibid.

70. Ibid.

71. Ibid., 1

72. June 4, 1953, "Reports and Excerpts from Patrol Inspectors in Charge of Border Patrol Units," 13.

73. January 21, 1952, "'Wetback' or Migrant Labor Control" (LBJ Senate Papers, container 232, Leg. Alien Labor [3rd folder of three], LBJ Library).

74. June 13, 1952, letter from Ed Brindson to Lyndon Johnson (LBJ Senate Papers, container 232, Leg. Alien Labor [3rd folder of three], LBJ Library).

75. "Brownsville CC Scores Plans for Wetback Stockade," *Harlingen Texas Star,* June 4, 1952.

76. "Valley Resentment at Alien Airlift Says It with Names," *Valley Evening Monitor,* June 13, 1952.

77. "Civet Center Also on Way Out as Solons Fail to Vote Funds," *Valley Morning Star,* June 27, 1952.

78. *Act of March 20, 1952,* 82nd Cong., 1st sess (66 *Stat.* 26). This act amended section 8 of the *Immigration Act of 1917* (chap. 29, 64th Cong., 2nd sess.) and Title IV of the *Act of February 27, 1925* (chap. 364, 68th Cong., 2nd sess.). The changes were as follows: (1) transportation within the United States of known illegal entrants was, for the first time, made an offense; (2) employment and normal practices incident to employment did not constitute harboring illegal aliens; (3) arrests for harboring, smuggling, and transporting illegals was restricted to designated officers and employees of the INS, and all other officers whose duties were to enforce criminal law; (4) provision was made for officers to have access to private lands, but not dwellings, within twenty-five miles of any external border, for the purposes of patrolling that border to prevent illegal entry of aliens.

79. September 15, 1950, memo from Wm. A. Whalen, District Director, to Edward A. Loughran, Assistant Commissioner, Administrative Division, Central Office, regarding complaint of a group of residents of El Indio, Texas, dated August 15, 1950, against Patrol Inspector in Charge Thomas J. Carnes (NARA 56084/74B, 2152, 58A734).

80. "May Be Like Old Times: Border Patrol's Withdrawal to Bring Influx of Wetbacks," *Corpus Christi Caller-Times* July 1, 1952.

81. Ibid.

82. "Farmers Agree to Renew Hiring of Braceros," *El Paso Herald-Post,* October 6, 1953.

83. "Upper Valley Farmers Blast at Border Patrol," *Brownsville Herald,* July 3, 1952.

84. "May Be Like Old Times," *Corpus Christi Caller-Times.*

85. July 2, 1951, letter from C. E. Blodget to Senator Lyndon Johnson (LBJ Senate Papers, container 232, Leg. Alien Labor [3rd folder of three], LBJ Library).

86. Foley, *From Peones to Politicos,* 18.

8. THE TRIUMPHS OF '54

1. See incomplete memo from D. R. Kelley, n.d. (NARA 56364/50, 104,. 59A2038).

2. August 13, 1954, memo from H. R. Landon, District Director of Los Angeles, to Com-

missioner of the INS, "Memorandum by Los Angeles District on Plans and Estimates for Control of the Mexican Border" (NARA 56364/44.15, 102, 59A2038), 10.

3. García, *Operation Wetback*, 227–28.

4. August 13, 1954, memo from H. R. Landon, District Director of Los Angeles, to Commissioner of the INS, "Memorandum by Los Angeles District," 10. Between June 10 and October 25, 1954, the Border Patrol deported 117,709 immigrants from California and Texas. They deported another 1,157 from the Chicago area, for a total of 118,866. See October 8, 1954, memo from Commissioner of the Immigration and Naturalization Service (NARA 56364/45.2, 103, 59A2038); "Memo to Mr. Carter (to October 4th)," n.d. (NARA 56364/45.2, 103, 59A2038); and July 29, 1954, press release (NARA 56364/45.6, vol. 9, 104, 59A2038).

5. Foley, *From Peones to Politicos*, 105–34.

6. Senate Subcommittee on Labor and Labor-Management Relations of the Committee on Labor and Public Welfare, *Migratory Labor Hearings*, testimony of Gus García, General Counsel, American G. I. Forum of Texas, and Ed Idar, State Chairman, American G. I. Forum of Texas, 82nd Cong., 2nd sess., pt. 1, 1952, 131; hereafter cited as U.S. Senate, *Migratory Labor Hearings*. See also, Marquez, *LULAC*, 16.

7. Ibid.

8. March 10, 1952, letter from Mr. Drineo González, Mission, Texas (LBJ Senate Papers, container 232, Leg. Alien Labor [3rd folder of three], LBJ Library).

9. U.S. Senate, *Migratory Labor Hearings*, testimony of Juanita García, 230. See also, Galarza, *Merchants of Labor*, 216–17.

10. National Farm Labor Union—Wetback Strike (Paul Schuster Taylor Collection, carton 46, folder 53).

11. Letter from Ernesto Galarza to Eugenio Pesqueira, Mexican Consul in Calexico, California (Ernesto Galarza Papers, box 50, folder 3).

12. Ed Idar Jr. and Andrew C. McClellan for the American G. I. Forum and the Texas State Federation of Labor (AFL), *What Price Wetbacks?* (Austin, TX: The Forum, 1953), 41.

13. July 7, 1954, memo from J. W. Holland, District Director, San Antonio, Texas, to Commissioner Joseph Swing (NARA 56364/50, 104, 59A2038).

14. June 27, 1951, "Special Mobile Force," memo from H. B. Carter to W. F. Kelly (NARA 55853/314B, 439, 58A734).

15. Ibid.

16. Idar and McClellan, *What Price Wetbacks?* For a similar study, see Lyle Saunders and Olen Leonard, *The Wetback in the Lower Rio Grande Valley of Texas* (Austin: University of Texas, 1951).

17. Idar and McClellan, *What Price Wetbacks?* 5.

18. Ibid., 54.

19. David Burnett, Personal Narrative (NBPM), 10.

20. Ibid., 10–11.

21. Ibid., 11.

22. Ibid.

23. Ibid.

24. Untitled press release, D87.136.33 (NBPM).

25. Ibid.
26. Ibid.
27. Ibid.
28. Ibid.
29. Ibid.
30. Ibid.
31. Ibid.
32. Ibid.
33. Reports and Excerpts from Patrol Inspectors in Charge of Border Patrol Units in the McAllen Sector of the San Antonio District (NARA 56364/43 sw, pt. 3, 91, 59A2038), 12.
34. Ibid.
35. August 27, 1953, "Wetback Mexican Problems in California," memorandum to the honorable Herbert Brownell Jr., Attorney General of the United States, from Don C. Bitler, District Attorney, Imperial County, California (NARA 56364/45.7, 104, 59A2038), 2. See also, April 30, 1953, excerpt of report from El Centro, California, station (NARA 56364/43 sw, pt. 3, 91, 59A2038).
36. Ibid.
37. August 27, 1953, "Wetback Mexican Problems in California," memorandum to the honorable Herbert Brownell Jr., Attorney General of the United States, 2.
38. Ibid.
39. Ibid., 3.
40. Saunders and Leonard, Wetback, 26–41.
41. Bill Toney, "Remembering 'Gizmo' Garrison," The Border Line: A Publication of the Fraternal Order of Retired Border Patrol Officers 20, no. 2 (1997): 17. Many of Garrison's cartoons were either saved by officers and archived at the Border Patrol Museum in El Paso, Texas, or were reproduced in The Border Line.
42. Earl Garrison, Illustrated Version of the Wetback in the Lower Rio Grande (NBPM).
43. November 23, 1955, "Survey of Conditions," memo from Ford B. Rackley and John Hensley, Patrol Inspectors, El Paso, Texas, to Regional Commissioner, Southwest Region, San Pedro, California (NARA 56364/42.2, 104, 59A2038), 2.
44. August 28, 1953, "Mexican Border Control and the Removal of Mexican Illegal Entrants," memo from W. F. Kelly, Assistant Commissioner, Immigration and Natural-ization Service, to J. Lee Rankin, Assistant Attorney General (NARA 56056/600, 1947, 58A734).
45. Ibid., 1–3.
46. July 16, 1953, "California-Mexican Border Situation," from W. F. Kelly, Assistant Commissioner, Border Patrol, to U.S. Attorney General regarding a meeting between H. B. Carter, Herman Landon, Ralph Holton, General Swing, and General Jones (NARA 56364/42.18, 84, 59A2038), 1–2.
47. Ibid., 2
48. July 30, 1953, "Memorandum for file," from Harlon B. Carter (NARA 56364/42.18, 82, 59A2038).
49. A copy of the letter was placed in the personnel file of each of the officers that par-ticipated in the operation (NARA 56364/45.2, 103, 59A2038).

50. June 29, 1954, press release (NARA 56364/45.6, vol. 9, 104, 59A2038).

51. "Highlights of Operation Wetback," n.d. (NARA 56364/43.3, 94, 59A2038).

52. May 20, 1954, telegram from Dulles to American Embassy, Mexico, D.F. (NARA 2, RG 59, 811.06[M], 2–354, 4408).

53. May 22, 1954, telegram from White to Secretary of State (NARA 2, RG 59, 811.06[M], 2–354, 4408).

54. May 24, 1954, memo, "Special Border Patrol Force" from A. C. Devaney, Assistant Commissioner, Inspections and Examinations Division (NARA 56364/45.6 vol. 1, 104, 59A2038).

55. August 13, 1954, "Plans and Estimates for Control of Mexican Border," memo from H. R. Langdon, District Director, Los Angeles, to Commissioner Swing (NARA 56364/44.15, 102, 59A2038), 10.

56. July 29, 1954, "Mexican Aliens Illegally in the United States Employed by Industry," from Investigator Special Detail, Los Angeles, California, to District Director, Los Angeles (NARA 56364/45.6, vol. 9, 104, 59A2038), 5.

57. Ibid., 4

58. Ibid., 4–5.

59. July 8, 1954, "Memorandum on Observations in the Lower Rio Grande Valley," Louis Blanchard (NARA 2, RG 59, 811.06[M] 2–354, box 4408), 6.

60. Calavita, *Inside the State,* 85–95.

61. December 7, 1954, memo and copy of "the pledge" sent from Harlon Carter to General Partridge (NARA 56364/43, 91, 59A2038).

62. July 29, 1954, "Mexican Aliens Illegally in the United States Employed by Industry."

63. February 10, 1956, "Supplement to Survey of Conditions Report of November 15, 1955," from Oran G, Pugh, Patrol Inspector, McAllen, Texas, to Regional Commissioner, Southwest Region, San Pedro, California (NARA 56364/42.2, 104, 59A2038), 15. For a discussion of Schuster's earlier activities against the Border Patrol, see Idar and McClellan, *What Price Wetbacks?* 12.

64. Ibid.

65. November 23, 1955, "Survey of Conditions," memo from Ford B. Rackley and John Hensley, 2.

66. Burnett, Personal Narrative (NBPM), 24.

67. General Swing, "Highlights of Fiscal Year 1959," *I and N Reporter* 8, no. 3 (1960): 30.

68. March 3, 1955, "Special Mobile Force," from Regional Commissioner, Southwest Region, to District Directors, San Francisco, El Paso, and San Antonio (NARA 56364/41.23, 84, 59A2038). See also Burnett, Personal Narrative, 27–28 (NBPM).

69. U.S. Senate Committee on Departments of State, Justice, Commerce, and the Judiciary Appropriations for Fiscal Year 1953, *Hearings before the Subcommittee of the Committee on Appropriations,* testimony of A. R. Mackey, Immigration Commissioner, 82nd Cong., 2nd sess. (Washington, DC: GPO, 1952), 196.

70. Interview with Mario Chamberlain, conducted by Oscar J. Martínez, June 18, 1979 (Interview no. 608, Institute of Oral History, University of Texas at El Paso), 7.

71. Interview with Arthur Adams, conducted by Jim Marchant and Oscar J. Martínez, August 10, 1977 (Interview no. 646 Institute of Oral History, University of Texas at El Paso), 22.

72. Interview with Mario Chamberlain, 7.

73. William T. Toney, *A Descriptive Study of the Control of Illegal Mexican Immigration in the Southwestern U.S.* (San Francisco: R & E Associates, 1977), 44.

74. U.S. Senate, Committee on Departments of State, Justice, and Commerce Appropriations for Fiscal Year 1961, *Hearings before the Subcommittee of the Committee on Appropriations*, 86th Cong., 2nd sess. on H. R. 11666 (Washington: GPO, 1960), 450.

75. Burnett, Personal Narrative (NBPM), 27–28..

76. August 14, 1953, telegram from David Moreno, Chairman, American G. I. Forum, Elsa, Texas, to Herbert Brownell, U.S. Attorney General (NARA 56364/45.7, 104, 59A2038).

77. July 7, 1954, memo from J. W. Holland, District Director, San Antonio, to Commissioner Joseph Swing (NARA 56364/50, 104, 59A2038).

78. Ibid.

79. Ibid.

80. July 7, 1954, letter from J. W. Holland, District Director, San Antonio District, to Chris Aldrete, President of the American G. I. Forum, Del Rio, Texas (NARA 56364/50, 104, 59A2038).

81. Ibid.

82. July 7, 1954, memo from J. W. Holland to Commissioner Joseph Swing.

83. July 7, 1954, letter from J. W. Holland to Chris Aldrete.

84. July 8, 1954, "Houston Convention and Wetback Drive," from Ed Idar, Executive Secretary, American G. I. Forum, to all state officers of the American G. I. Forum (NARA 56364/50, 104, 59A2038).

85. Ibid.

86. Ibid.

87. July 22, 1954, memo from J. W. Holland, District Director, San Antonio, to Commissioner Joseph Swing (NARA 56364/50, 104, 59A2038).

88. August 14, 1954, letter from Ed Idar Jr. to Hon. Joseph M. Swing (NARA 56357/466, 3402, 58A734).

89. November 17, 1954, letter from J. W. Holland to Frank Partridge (NARA 56364/43.3, 94, 59A2038).

90. August 2, 1954, memo from J. W. Holland to Frank Piñedo, President of LULAC (NARA 56357/466, 3402, 58A734).

91. March 21, 1955, letter from Ed Idar to Walter Sahli, District Director, San Antonio (NARA 56364/43.48, pt. 1, 98, 59A2038). See also Ed Idar Jr., "Parole—1955 Style," *Bulletin*, February 1955 (published by the American G. I. Forum).

92. Quoted in Calavita, *Inside the State*, 29.

93. Manuel García y Griego, *The Importation of Mexican Contract Laborers to the United States, 1942–1964: Antecedents, Operation, and Legacy.* Working Papers in U.S.-Mexican Studies, no. 11 (La Jolla: University of California–San Diego, 1980), 50.

94. March 21, 1955, letter from Ed Idar Jr. to Mr. Walter Sahli, District Director of the INS, San Antonio (NARA 56364/43.38, pt. 1, 98, 59A2038).

95. December 2, 1955, letter from Hector P. García, M. D., to Mr. Walter Sahli of the INS, San Antonio (NARA 56364/43.38, pt. 1, 98, 59A2038).

96. December 29, 1955, untitled memo from Harlon B. Carter; December 30, 1955, letter from DeWitt Marshall (NARA 56364/43.38, pt. 1, 98, 59A2038).

9. "THE DAY OF THE WETBACK IS OVER"

1. Gertrude D. Krichefsky, "Importation of Alien Laborers," *I and N Reporter* 5, no. 1 (July 1956): 4. See also *Annual Report of the Immigration and Naturalization Service for Fiscal Year Ending June 30, 1955* (Washington, DC: GPO, 1955), 15.

2. "Canadian Border Operations" (NARA 56364/43, 91, 59A2038). See also U.S. Senate, Committee on Departments of State, Justice, the Judiciary, and Related Agencies Appropriations, *Hearings before the Subcommittee of the Committee on Appropriations*, 86th Cong., 2nd sess., on H.R. 11666,1961, 450.

3. *Annual Report of the Immigration and Naturalization Service for Fiscal Year Ending June 30, 1956* (Washington, DC: GPO, 1956), 9; *Annual Report of the Immigration and Naturalization Service for Fiscal Year 1957* (Washington, DC: GPO, 1957), 11–14.

4. U.S. Senate Committee on Appropriations, *Second Supplemental Appropriation Bill for 1960: Supplemental Hearings before the Committee on Appropriations on H.R. 10743*, 86th Cong., 2nd sess., 1959, 19.

5. Bob Salinger, interview, April 4, 1987 (NBPM).

6. Ibid., 9.

7. Ibid.

8. Parker, *Prop Cops*, n.p.

9. House Committee on Appropriations, *Departments of State, Justice, and Commerce Appropriations for 1958: Hearings before the Subcommittee of the Committee on Appropriations*, 85th Cong., 2nd sess., 1957, 20.

10. Sector Activity Report, August 1960 (NARA 2, RG 85, Acc 64A1851, box 161, file 660.4, pt. 22).

11. "Border Patrol Memories," 1998 (NBPM), 14.

12. Ibid.

13. U.S. Senate, *Hearings before the Subcommittee of the Committee on Appropriations*, 86th Cong., 2nd sess. on H. R. 11666, 1961, 450.

14. Ralph Williams (pseudonym), oral history (untranscribed; NBPM).

15. March 28, 1929, memo from Acting Chief Patrol Inspector Chester C. Courtney to U.S. Immigration Service District Director, El Paso (NARA 55606/670, 4, 58A734).

16. Joe Aubin, interviewed by Leslie J. Pyatt, February 21, 1978 (Interview no. 700, Institute of Oral History, University of Texas at El Paso), 5.

17. *Annual Report of the Immigration and Naturalization Service for Fiscal Year Ending June 30, 1964* (Washington, DC: GPO, 1964), 8.

18. Untitled statistical summary of interior removal operations (NARA 2, RG 85, Acc 71A2917, box 319, file 1168, pt. 1). See also August 6 and 7, 1963, call reports from Coppock to Gilman (NARA 2, RG 85, Acc 67A3254, box 9, file 659, pt. 2).

19. January 22, 1959, incomplete memo from H.C. Hardin, Assistant Commissioner, Special Projects Division (NARA 2, RG 85, Acc 67A2033, box 13, file 659.4, pt, 1).

20. "Sacramento Memories" (NBPM), 3.

21. May 17, 1956, "Increase in Apprehension of Women and Children—El Paso Sector," from John P. Swanson, Chief Enforcement Officer, to Frank H. Partridge, Assistant Commissioner, Enforcement Division, Central Office, (NARA 56364/42.1 sw, 87, 59A2038).

22. Monthly Sector Activity Report—March 1957—El Paso, Texas (NARA 2, RG 85, Acc 67A0233, confidential—box 13, 660.4, pt. 2, section 3), 1.

23. March 28, 1957, "Women and Children, Your SW 40/300B2 dated March 22, 1957," from D.L. McClaren, Chief Patrol Inspector, El Paso, Texas, to Regional Commissioner, Southwest Region (NARA 2, RG 60, Acc 67A0233, box 13, file 659.4, pt. 1).

24. January 27, 1961, "Memo for the File," from James F. Greene, Assistant Commissioner of Enforcement (NARA 2, RG 60, Acc 67A0233, box 13, file 659.4, pt. 1).

25. July 27, 1954, "Contract Laborers' Wives and Children," from John P. Swanson, Chief Patrol Inspector, El Centro, California, to District Director of Los Angeles (NARA 56364/45.6, vol. 9, 104, 59A2038).

26. October 6, 1954, memo from Investigator Earnest McFadden, Los Angeles, to District Director, Los Angeles (NARA 56364/45.2, 103, 59A2038).

27. There were many types of fraudulent documents. See Julian Samora, *Los Mojados: The Wetback Story* (Notre Dame, IN: University of Notre Dame Press, 1971), 20–24, 76–78.

28. Edgar C. Niebuhr, Assistant Chief of Border Patrol, Central Office, "False Claims to United States Citizenship by Mexican Aliens," *I and N Reporter* 9, no. 1 (1960): 1–3.

29. "Monthly Activity Report Resume–Southwest Region–April 1957, Section 3" (NARA 2, RG 85, Acc 67A2033, box 13, file 660.4, pt. 2).

30. Senate Committee on Appropriations, *State, Justice, Commerce, the Judiciary, and Related Agencies Appropriations: Hearings before the Committee on Appropriations on H.R. 15404*, 93rd Cong., 2nd sess., 1975, 613.

31. November 2, 1956, "Nomenclature with Respect to Aliens," from Chief Enforcement Officer, Southwest Region, San Pedro, California, to Assistant Commissioner, Enforcement Division, Washington, DC; and November 15, 1956, "Nomenclature with Respect to Aliens," from E.J. Wildblood to General Partridge (NARA 56364/43.3, 94, 59A2038).

32. October 20, 1955, "Border Patrol Publicity" (NARA 56364/43.3, 94, 59A2038).

33. Ibid.

34. January 13, 1956, "Border Patrol Publicity," from Richard A. Golling, Regional Commissioner, St. Paul, Minnesota, to Commissioner, Washington, DC (NARA 56364/43.3, 94, 59A2038).

35. Undated report, "The United States Border Patrol" (NARA 56364/43.3, 94, 59A2038).

36. November 3, 1958, "Re: Criminal—Immoral—Narcotic Border Program at El Paso, Texas," from Assistant Regional Commissioner for Investigations Oshwaldt, Southwest Region, to District Directors, Officers in Charge, Chief Patrol Inspectors of the Southwest Region (NARA 2, RG 60, Acc 67A0233, box 13, file 659.4, pt. 1).

37. "Investigations Division, Southern Border Criminal—Immoral—Narcotic Program, Justification for Program" (NARA 2, RG 60, Acc 67A0233, box 13, file 659.4, pt. 1).

38. November 3, 1958, "Criminal—Immoral—Narcotic Border Program at El Paso, Texas," 4.

39. "CIN Program, Douglas, Arizona," n.d. (NARA 2, RG 60, Acc 67A3254, box 9, file 659, pt. 2).

40. November 3, 1958, "Criminal—Immoral—Narcotic Border Program at El Paso, Texas," 1.

41. April 23, 1956, "Searching of Aliens," from Don Coppock, Acting Chief of Border Patrol (NARA 56364/43.39, 98, 59A2038).

42. April 1961 memo from L. W. Gilman, Assoc. Deputy Regional Commissioner, Operations, Southwest Region, to Asst. Commissioner, Enforcement, Central Office (NARA 2, RG 85, Acc 67A2033, box 13, file 659.4, pt. 1). See also March 1961 memo from Del Rio Office (NARA 2, RG 85, Acc 67A2033, box 13, file 659.4, pt. 1).

43. January 22, 1965, "Prosecution of Illegal Entrants," from L. W. Gilman, Associate Deputy Regional Commissioner, Operations, Southwest Region, to District Director, El Paso (NARA 2, RG 85, Acc 71A2917, box 296, file 809, pt. 2).

44. August 18, 1955, memo from Commissioner Swing to Mr. Rutherford (NARA 56364/43, 91, 59A2038).

45. House Committee on Appropriations, *Departments of State, Justice, and Commerce Appropriations for 1958: Hearings before the Subcommittee of the Committee of Appropriations*, testimony of Commissioner Joseph Swing, 85th Cong., 1st sess., 1957, 170.

46. January 9, 1957, memo to E. DeWitt Marshall, "Prosecutions" (NARA 2, RG 85, Acc 71A2917, box 296, file 809, pt. 2).

47. Aubin interview, 19.

48. Ibid., 11.

49. Ibid., 8.

50. Walter Bradley (pseudonym), interview, May 1988 (NBPM), 14.

51. Aubin interview, 8.

52. Friedman, *Crime and Punishment in American History*, 273–76; Christian Parenti, *Lockdown America: Police and Prisons in the Age of Crisis* (New York: Verso, 1999), 3–28; Jonathan Simon, *Governing Through Crime: How the War on Crime Transformed American Democracy and Created a Culture of Fear* (Oxford: Oxford University Press, 2007).

53. McWilliams, *The Protectors*, 127–48.

54. Musto, *American Disease*, 231.

55. Rufus King, "Narcotic Drug Laws and Enforcement Policies," *Law and Contemporary Problems* 22, no. 1 (1957): 113–31; Musto, *American Disease*, 245–47.

56. *Annual Report of the Immigration and Naturalization Service for Fiscal Year Ending June 30, 1956* (Washington, DC: GPO, 1956), 9; Prince and Keller, *U.S. Customs Service*, 229–33. See also Earl Fallis oral history, taken by Teresa Whittington on August 27, 1976, in Alpine, Texas (Interview no. 11, Archives of the Big Bend, Sul Ross State University), 11.

57. Charles W. Mapel, Deputy Chief, Border Patrol Central Office, "INS Efforts in Narcotics Enforcement," *I and N Reporter* 24, no. 2 (1975): 23–26.

58. Guadalupe González and Marta Tienda, eds., *The Drug Connection in U.S.-Mexican Relations* (La Jolla: Center for U.S.-Mexican Studies at the University of California–San Diego, 1989); María Celia Toro, *Mexico's "War" on Drugs: Causes and Consequences* (Boul-

der, CO: Rienner, 1995); Peter Smith, ed., *Drug Policy in the Americas* (Boulder, CO: Westview Press, 1992).

59. "Report of the Commissioner of Immigration and Naturalization," in *Annual Report of the Immigration and Naturalization Service for Fiscal Year Ending June 30, 1970* (Washington, DC: GPO, 1970), 16.

60. Mario Chamberlain, interviewed by Oscar J. Martínez, June 18, 1979 (Interview no. 608, Institute of Oral History, University of Texas at El Paso), 7.

61. Ibid.

62. Ibid.

63. February 11, 1965, "Political Report for January 1965," memo from American Consulate, Mexicali, to Department of State (NARA 2, RG 59, Pol-Mexico, box 2470).

64. Camín and Meyer, *Shadow of the Mexican Revolution*, 162.

65. Ibid., 164.

66. Ibid., 203.

67. Ibid., 162.

68. De Genova, "Legal Production of Mexican/Migrant 'Illegality,'" 169–70.

69. *Annual Report of the Immigration and Naturalization Service for Fiscal Year Ending June 30, 1967* (Washington, DC: GPO, 1967), 11.

70. "Report of the Commissioner of Immigration and Naturalization," in *Annual Report of the Immigration and Naturalization Service for Fiscal Year Ending June 30, 1968* (Washington, DC: GPO, 1968), 14. See also *Annual Report of the Immigration and Naturalization Service for Fiscal Year Ending June 30, 1955* (Washington, DC: GPO, 1955), 18–20.

71. "Report of the Commissioner of Immigration and Naturalization," in *Annual Report of the Immigration and Naturalization Service for Fiscal Year Ending June 30, 1969* (Washington, DC: GPO, 1969), 12. See also Samora, *Los Mojados* (55, note) regarding campaigns against unsanctioned Mexican immigrants.

72. "Report of the Commissioner of Immigration and Naturalization," in *Annual Report of the Immigration and Naturalization Service for Fiscal Year Ending June 30, 1973* (Washington, DC: GPO, 1973), 9.

73. Ibid. See also Mike Castro, "Dispute Ebbs over Alien Pursuit around Church," *Los Angeles Times*, October 5, 1975.

74. Frank del Olmo, "600 Arrested in Roundup of Illegal Aliens," *Los Angeles Times*, May 24, 1973, and "Alien Roundup Continues; 600 More Arrested," *Los Angeles Times*, May 30, 1973; Reverend Mark Day, "Dragnet Raids" (editorial), *Los Angeles Times*, June 11, 1973.

75. "Report of the Commissioner of Immigration and Naturalization," in *Annual Report of the Immigration and Naturalization Service for Fiscal Year Ending June 30, 1974* (Washington, DC: GPO, 1974), 9. See also Commissioner Leonard F. Chapman, "Illegal Aliens—A Growing Problem," *I and N Reporter* 24, no. 2 (1975): 15–18.

76. Donnel Nunes, "U.S. Puts Number of Illegal Aliens Under 5 Million," *Washington Post*, January 31, 1980.

77. Such claims sharply contrasted with studies such as that of Vic Villapando, *A Study of the Impact of Illegal Aliens on the County of San Diego on Specific Socioeconomic Areas*

(San Diego, CA: San Diego County Human Resources Agency, 1975). Villapando found that during a twenty-month study of the bookings by the San Diego Sheriffs at the San Diego County jail, only 0.005 percent were undocumented immigrants.

EPILOGUE

1. "Fifty Years on the Line," paper by Samuel Tidwell, Border Patrol Agent/Public Information Officer of the Marfa Sector (NBPM).
2. "First Fifty Years," *I and N Reporter* 23, no. 1 (1974): 2–17, at 9.
3. *Immigration and Nationality Act* (66 *Stat.* 228, Section 274 [a] [2]; 8 *U.S.C.* 1324 [a] [2]).
4. *United States v. Brignoni-Ponce* (422 *U.S.* 873, 1975).
5. Donald J. Mabry and Robert J. Shafer, *Neighbors, Mexico, and the United States: Wetbacks and Oil* (Chicago: Nelson-Hall, 1981), 108.
6. Reverend Mark Day, "Dragnet Raids" (letter to the editor), *Los Angeles Times,* June 11, 1973.
7. *Annual Report of the Immigration and Naturalization Service, Fiscal Year 1974* (Washington, DC: GPO, 1974), 12.
8. U.S. Commission on Civil Rights, *The Tarnished Golden Door: Civil Rights Issues in Immigration; A Report of the United States Commission on Civil Rights* (Washington, DC: GPO, 1980).
9. David Gutiérrez, *Walls and Mirrors,* 177–87; Ian Haney Lopez, *Racism on Trial: The Chicano Fight for Justice* (Cambridge, MA: Harvard University Press, 2003); and Ernesto Chávez, *Mi Raza Primero!: Nationalism, Identity, and Insurgency in the Chicano Movement in Los Angeles, 1966–1978* (Berkeley and Los Angeles: University of California Press, 2002). See also, American Friends Service Committee, "Human and Civil Rights Violations on the U.S. Mexico Border, 1995–1997, San Diego, California," a publication of the American Friends Service Committee—U.S. Mexico Border Program, Immigration Law Enforcement Monitoring Project; and Stanley Bailey, "Migrant Deaths at the Texas-Mexico Border, 1985–1994: A Preliminary Report" (Houston, TX: Center for Immigration Research, University of Houston, February 1996).
10. Aubin, oral history interview, 4. See also "The New Wetback Infiltration: A Preliminary Report" (Paul Schuster Taylor Collection, carton 44, folder 14, "Wetback PROBLEM."
11. "Human Rights at the Mexico-U.S. Border: Second Annual Report" (Houston, TX: Immigration Law and Enforcement Monitoring Project, American Friends Service Committee, 1990).
12. House Committee on Foreign Affairs, *Allegations of Violence along the United States-Mexico Border: Hearing before the Subcommittee on Human Rights and International Organizations of the Committee on Foreign Affairs,* 101st Cong., 2nd sess., April 18, 1990, 15.
13. "The Militarization of the U.S.-Mexico Border: Border Communities Respond to Militarization from Slave Patrol to Border Patrol: An Interview with María Jiménez," *In Motion Magazine,* February 2, 1998, available online at www.inmotionmagazine.ca/mjl.html; María Jiménez, "War in the Borderlands," *Report on the Americas* 26, no. 1 (1992): 29–33.

282 NOTES TO PAGES 224–227

14. David Montejano, "On the Future of Anglo-Mexican Relations in the United States," in *Chicano Politics and Society in the Late Twentieth Century*, ed. David Montejano (Austin: University of Texas Press, 1999), 234–57. See also Rosas, "Thickening Borderlands."

15. James D. Cockroft, *Outlaws in the Promised Land: Mexican Immigrant Workers and America's Future* (New York: Grove Press, 1986).

16. "Meet Leonel J. Castillo: Our New Commissioner," *INS Reporter* 26, no. 1 (1977): 1–2; "President's Proposal on Undocumented Aliens," *INS Reporter* 26, no. 2 (1977): 24–27.

17. Thank you to Timothy Waller of the National Association of Former Border Patrol Officers, who offered a definition of the "mandatory exodus" via e-mail on April 11, 2008.

18. Mission Statement of the Fraternal Order of Retired Border Patrol Officers, available online at http://www.forbpo.org/id3.html (accessed on April 9, 2008).

19. Mission Statement of the Fraternal Order of Retired Border Patrol Officers.

20. Buck Brandemuhl, *The Border Line* 16 (Spring 1992): 21.

21. David Burnett, Personal Narrative, submitted on May 16, 1987 (NBPM), 53.

22. Ibid.

23. Ibid.

24. "Women in Law Enforcement," *Women in Action: An Information Summary for Federal Women's Program* 9, no. 2 (1979): 2. See also "Minorities and Women in INS," *INS Reporter* 26, no. 7 (1977): 2–6.

25. Earl Fallis, oral history, taken by Teresa Whittington on August 27, 1976, in Alpine, Texas (Interview no. 11, Archives of the Big Bend, Sul Ross State University), 13.

26. Quoted in Robert Lee Maril, *Patrolling Chaos: The U.S. Border Patrol in Deep South Texas* (Lubbock: Texas Tech University Press, 2006), 71.

27. Elizabeth Newell, "Border Patrol Looks to Hire More Women, Minorities," available online at the Government Executive.com Web site (June 27, 2007), http://www.govexec.com/dailyfed/0607/062707e1.htm (accessed on April 8, 2008).

28. Eric Lynden (pseudonym), interviewed by Bonnie Quint, February 1989 (NBPM), 5–6.

29. Ibid., 5

30. Ibid., 6

31. "Borders and Barriers—A Special Report; Black Officers in I.N.S. Push Racial Boundaries," *New York Times*, October 30, 1994.

32. Ibid.

33. "Minorities and Women in INS"; "Borders and Barriers."

34. Hernán Rozemberg, "Border Patrol Sets Out to Recruit More Blacks," *Express-News*, January 10, 2008. See also "A Busy School for Border Patrol in New Mexico," *New York Times*, June 24, 2006. Sixty-two percent of new recruits are Latino, 35 percent are white, and blacks and Asians account for less than 1 percent, respectively.

35. Josiah C. Heyman, "U.S. Immigration Officers of Mexican Ancestry as Mexican Americans, Citizens, and Immigration Police," *Current Anthropology* 43, no. 3 (2002): 479–507.

36. "Congressman Biography—Joined Immigration and Naturalization Service, Elected to Congress, Became Chair of the Congressional Hispanic Caucus." Available online at

http://biography.jrank.org/pages/3435/Reyes-Silvestre-1944-Congressman.html (accessed on April 7, 2008).

37. Suzanne Gamboa, "Rep. Reyes: 1st Hispanic Intel. Chairman," *Washington Post*, December 2, 2006.

38. Biography of Congressman Silvestre Reyes (online; see n. 39 above).

39. Cornelius, "Death at the Border," 662.

40. Reyes received the El Paso Hispanic Chamber of Commerce's "Moving Forward Award" (1997).

41. Cornelius, "Death at the Border," 662.

42. Andreas, *Border Games;* Nevins, *Operation Gatekeeper.*

43. Andreas, *Border Games;* Cornelius, "Death at the Border"; Nevins, *Operation Gatekeeper;* Karl Eschbach, Jacqueline Hagan, and Nestor Rodríguez, "Causes and Trends in Migrant Deaths along the U.S.-Mexico Border, 1985–1998" (Houston, TX: Center for Immigration Research, University of Houston, 2001).

44. Cornelius, "Death at the Border," 671.

45. Meisner, quoted in Mike Davis and Justin Akers Chacon, *No One Is Illegal: Fighting Racism and State Violence on the U.S.-Mexico Border* (Chicago: Haymarket Books, 2006), 208.

46. Maril, *Patrolling Chaos,* 31.

47. Ibid., 22.

48. Dunn, *Militarization of the U.S.-Mexico Border,* 87.

49. Federal and local agencies have become increasingly involved in immigration law enforcement. See Lisa M. Seghetti, Stephen R. Viña, and Karma Ester, "Enforcing Immigration Law: The Role of State and Local Law Enforcement," *CRS Report for Congress* on March 11, 2004.

50. Dannielle Blumenthal, Public Affairs Specialist, Office of Public Affairs, "Border Patrol to Accelerate Border Patrol Strategy with National Guard," in *Customs and Border Protection Today,* May 2006. available online at http://www.cbp.gov/xp/CustomsToday/2006/may/president_bush.xml (accessed April 2008).

51. Edgar Wideman, "The Politics of Prison: Doing Time, Marking Race," *Nation,* October 30, 1995, 503.

52. See Marc Mauer, *Race to Incarcerate* (New York: New Press, 1999); Don Sabo, Terry A. Kupers, and Willie London, eds., *Prison Masculinities* (Philadelphia, PA: Temple University Press, 2001); and Michael Tonry and Joan Petersilia, eds., *Prisons* (Chicago: University of Chicago Press, 1999).

53. Marc Mauer and Meda Chesney-Lind, *Invisible Punishment;* Joan Petersilia, *When Prisoners Come Home: Parole and Prisoner Reentry* (Oxford: Oxford University Press, 2003).

54. Ibid.

55. Western, *Punishment and Inequality in America;* Mauer and Chesney-Lind, *Invisible Punishment.*

56. Loïc Wacquant, "From Slavery to Mass Incarceration: Rethinking the 'Race Question' in the U.S.," *New Left Review* 13 (January–February 2002): 41–60. See also Loïc Wacquant, "Race as Civic Felony," *International Social Science Journal* 57, no. 183 (2005): 127–42, and Jeff Manza and Christopher Uggen, "The Civic Reintegration of Criminal Offenders," *Annals of the American Academy of Political and Social Science,* 605, no. 1 (2006): 281–310.

57. Exceptions include Mark Dow, *American Gulag: Inside U.S. Immigration Prisons* (Berkeley and Los Angeles: University of California Press, 2004); Hernández, "Undue Process"; Robert S. Kahn, *Other People's Blood: U.S. Immigration Prisons in the Reagan Decade* (Boulder, CO: Westview Press, 1996); Jonathan Simon, "Refugees in a Carceral Age: The Rebirth of Immigration Prisons in the United States," *Public Culture* 10, no. 3 (1998): 577-606.

58. Scalia and Litras, "Immigration Offenders in the Federal Criminal Justice System." See also Siskin and Lee, *Detention of Noncitizens in the United States.*

59. Gramsci, *Selections from Prison Notebooks,* 324.

60. Scott Reynolds Nelson, *Steel Drivin' Man—John Henry—The Untold Story of an American Legend* (Oxford: Oxford University Press, 2007), 161.

SELECTED BIBLIOGRAPHY

ARCHIVAL COLLECTIONS
United States

American Friends Service Committee, United States-Mexico Border Program Records, Mandeville Special Collections Library, Geisel Library, University of California at San Diego

Archives of the Big Bend, Bryan Wildenthal Memorial Library, Sul Ross State University, Alpine, Texas

Border Patrol Scrapbooks and Oral Histories, National Border Patrol Museum (NBPM), El Paso, Texas

Center for American History, University of Texas at Austin (Cited as CAH)

Citizen and Immigration Services, Historical Reference Library, Washington, DC (Cited as CIS/HRL)

Ernesto Galarza Papers, Green Library Special Collections, Stanford University, Palo Alto, California

Institute of Oral History, University of Texas at El Paso

Lyndon Baines Johnson Memorial Library, University of Texas at Austin

National Archives and Records Administration, Washington, DC (cited as NARA)
    Records of the U.S. Immigration and Naturalization Service, Record Group 85.

National Archives and Records Administration, College Park, Maryland (cited as NARA 2)
    Records of the U.S. Department of State Records, Record Group 59.
    Records of the Department of Justice, Record Group 60.
    Records of the U.S. Immigration and Naturalization Service, Record Group 85.

National Archives and Records Administration, Fort Worth, Texas (cited as NARA–Fort Worth)
    Records of the U.S. District Court, Southern District of Texas, Laredo Division, Record Group 21.

National Archives and Records Administration, Laguna Niguel, California (cited as NARA–Laguna Niguel)
  Records of District Courts of the U.S.-Southern California Division, Record Group 21.
Oral History Collection, Southwest Collection, Texas Tech University, Lubbock, Texas
Paul Schuster Taylor Collection, Bancroft Library, University of California at Berkeley
San Diego Historical Society, San Diego, California

Mexico

Archivo General de la Nación, Mexico City, Mexico (Cited as AGN)
  Ramo Manuel Ávila Camacho (FMAC)
  Ramo Miguel Alemán (FMAV)
  Ramo Adolfo Ruiz Cortines (FARC)
  Ramo Adolfo López Mateos (FALM)
Archivo Histórico de la Secretaría de Relaciónes Exteriores, Mexico City, Mexico
  Archivo de Concentraciones (Cited as AHSRE)
Archivo Histórico del Instituto Nacional de Migración, Mexico City, Mexico (Cited as AHINM)

ARTICLES, BOOKS, AND DISSERTATIONS

Aguila, Jaime. "Protecting 'México de Afuera': Mexican Emigration Policy, 1876–1928." PhD diss., Arizona State University, 2000.
Aleinikoff, T. Alexander. *Semblances of Sovereignty: The Constitution, the State, and American Citizenship.* Cambridge, MA: Harvard University Press, 2002.
American G. I. Forum. *What Price Wetback?.* Austin, TX: American G. I. Forum, 1953.
Anderson, Malcolm. *Policing the World: Interpol and the Politics of International Police Cooperation.* New York: Oxford University Press, 1989.
Andreas, Peter. *Border Games: Policing the U.S.-Mexico Divide.* Ithaca, NY: Cornell University Press, 2000.
Andres, Benny Joseph, Jr. "Power and Control in Imperial Valley, California: Nature, Agribusiness, Labor, and Race Relations, 1900–1940." PhD diss., University of New Mexico, 2003.
Askins, Charles. *Unrepentant Sinner: The Autobiography of Colonel Charles Askins.* Boulder, CO: Paladin Press, 1984.
Bailey, Stanley, with Karl Eschbach, Jaqueline Hagan, and Nestor Rodríguez. "Migrant Deaths at the Texas-Mexico Border, 1985–1994: A Preliminary Report." Houston, TX: Center for Immigration Research, University of Houston, February 1996.
Balderrama, Francisco E., and Raymond Rodríguez. *Decade of Betrayal: Mexican Repatriation in the 1930s.* Albuquerque: University of New Mexico Press, 1995.
Barrett, James, and David Roediger. "Inbetween Peoples: Race, Nationality, and the New Immigrant Working Class." *Journal of American Ethnic History* 16 (Spring 1997): 3–44.
Barry, Tom, with Harry Browne and Beth Sims. *Crossing the Line: Immigrants, Economic Integration, and Drug Enforcement on the U.S.-Mexico Border.* Albuquerque, NM: Resource Center Press, 1994.

Bayley, David. *Patterns of Policing: A Comparative International Analysis*. New Brunswick, NJ: Rutgers University Press, 1985.

Bender, Thomas, ed. *Rethinking American History in a Global Age*. Berkeley and Los Angeles: University of California Press, 2002.

Bibler Coutin, Susan. *Legalizing Moves: Salvadoran Immigrants' Struggle for U.S. Residency*. Ann Arbor: University of Michigan Press, 2000.

Bittner, Egon. "Florence Nightingale in Pursuit of Willie Sutton: A Theory of the Police." In *The Potential for Reform of Criminal Justice*, edited by Herbert Jacob, 17–44. Beverly Hills, CA: Sage, 1974.

———. *The Functions of Police in Modern Society*. Washington, DC: GPO, 1970.

Borstelmann, Thomas. *The Cold War and the Color Line: American Race Relations in the Global Arena*. Cambridge, MA: Harvard University Press, 2001.

Bustamante, Jorge. "Commodity Migrants: Structural Analysis of Mexican Immigration to the United States." In *Views across the Border: The United States and Mexico*, edited by Stanley P. Ross, 183–203. Albuquerque: University of New Mexico Press, 1978.

———. "Measuring the Flow of Undocumented Immigrants." In *Mexican Migration to the United States: Origins, Consequences, and Policy Options*, edited by Wayne Cornelius and Jorge Bustamante, 95–108. La Jolla: Center for U.S. Mexican Studies at the University of California–San Diego, 1989.

Calavita, Kitty. *Inside the State: The Bracero Program, Immigration, and the I. N. S*. New York: Routledge, 1992.

———. *U.S. Immigration Law and the Control of Labor, 1820–1924*. London: Academic Press, 1984.

Camín, Héctor Aguilar, and Lorenzo Meyer. *In the Shadow of the Mexican Revolution: Contemporary Mexican History, 1910–1989*. Austin: University of Texas Press, 1993.

Cardoso, Lawrence. *Mexican Emigration to the United States: 1897–1931*. Tucson: University of Arizona Press, 1980.

Chan, Sucheng. *This Bittersweet Soil: The Chinese in California Agriculture, 1860–1910*. Berkeley and Los Angeles: University of California Press, 1986.

Chavez, Leo. *Shadowed Lives: Undocumented Immigrants in American society*. Fort Worth, TX: Harcourt Brace College Publishers, 1998.

Cleveland, Jeffrey Kirk. "Fight Like a Devil: Images of the Texas Rangers and the Strange Career of Jesse Perez." Master's thesis, University of Texas, 1992.

Coatsworth, John. *Growth against Development: The Economic Impact of Railroads in Porfirian Mexico*. DeKalb: Northern Illinois University Press, 1981.

Cockroft, James D. *Outlaws in the Promised Land: Mexican Immigrant Workers and America's Future*. New York: Grove Press, 1986.

Cohen, Deborah. "Caught in the Middle: The Mexican State's Relationship with the U.S. and Its Own Citizen-Workers, 1942–1958." *Journal of American Ethnic History* 20, no. 3 (2001): 110–32.

———. "From Peasant to Worker: Migration, Masculinity, and the Making of Mexican Workers in the U.S." *International Labor and Working Class History* 69 (March 2006): 81–103.

Cohen, Lizabeth. *Making a New Deal: Industrial Workers in Chicago, 1919–1939*. New York: Cambridge University Press, 1996.

Copp, Nelson Gage. *"Wetbacks" and Braceros: Mexican Migrant Laborers and American Immigration Policy, 1930–1960*. San Francisco: R and E Research Associates, 1971.

Cornelius, Wayne A. "Death at the Border: Efficacy and Unintended Consequences of U.S. Immigration Control Policy." *Population and Development Review* 27, no. 4 (2001): 661–89.

———. *Mexican Migration to the United States: Causes, Consequences, and U.S. Responses*. Cambridge: Migration and Development Study Group, Center for International Studies, Massachusetts Institute of Technology, 1978.

Craig, Richard B. *The Bracero Program: Interest Groups and Foreign Policy*. Austin: University of Texas Press, 1971.

Cresswell, Stephen. *Mormons and Cowboys, Moonshiners and Klansmen*. Tuscaloosa: University of Alabama Press, 1991.

Daniel, Cletus E. *Bitter Harvest: A History of California Farm Workers, 1870–1941*. Ithaca, NY: Cornell University Press, 1981.

Daniels, Roger. *Coming to America: A History of Immigration and Ethnicity in American Life*. 2nd ed. New York: Perennial, 2002.

———. *Guarding the Golden Door: American Immigration Policy and Immigrants since 1882*. New York: Hill and Wang, 2004.

———. *The Politics of Prejudice: The Anti-Japanese Movement in California and the Struggle for Japanese Exclusion*. Berkeley and Los Angeles: University of California Press, 1977.

Davis, Mike, and Justin Akers Chacon. *No One Is Illegal: Fighting Violence and State Repression on the U.S.-Mexico Border*. Chicago: Haymarket Books, 2006.

De Genova, Nicholas. "The Legal Production of Mexican/Migrant "Illegality." *Latino Studies* 2, no. 2 (July 2004): 160–85.

———. "Migrant 'Illegality' and Deportability in Everyday Life." *Annual Review of Anthropology* 31 (October 2002): 419–47.

———. *Working the Boundaries: Race, Space, and "Illegality" in Mexican Chicago*. Durham, NC: Duke University Press, 2005.

Delgado, Grace. "In the Age of Exclusion: Race, Region, and Chinese Identity in the Making of the Arizona-Sonora Borderlands, 1863–1943." PhD diss., University of California, Los Angeles, 2000.

Dow, Mark. *American Gulag: Inside U.S. Immigration Prisons*. Berkeley and Los Angeles: University of California Press, 2004.

Dudziak, Mary. *Cold War Civil Rights: Race and the Image of American Democracy*. Princeton, NJ: Princeton University Press, 2000.

Dunn, Timothy. *The Militarization of the U.S.-Mexico Border, 1978–1992: Low Intensity Conflict Doctrine Comes Home*. Austin: Center for Mexican American Studies, University of Texas at Austin, 1996.

Enciso, Fernando Saúl Alanís. "La Constitución de 1917 y la emigración de trabajadores mexicanos a Estados Unidos." *Relaciones* 22, no. 87 (2001): 205–30.

———. *El primer programa bracero y el Gobierno de México*. San Luís Potosí: El Colegio de San Luis, 1999.

—. *El valle bajo del Río Bravo, Tamaulipas, en la década de 1930: El desarrollo regional en la posrevolución a partir de la irrigación, la migración interna y los repatriados de Estados Unidos.* Mexico City: El Colegio de Tamaulipas y El Colegio de San Luis, A. C., 2003.

Escobar, Edward J. *Race, Police, and the Making of a Political Identity: Mexican Americans and the Los Angeles Police Department, 1900—1945.* Berkeley and Los Angeles: University of California Press, 1999.

Espenshade, Thomas J. "Using INS Border Apprehension Data to Measure the Flow of Undocumented Migrants Crossing the U.S.-Mexico Frontier." *International Migration Review* 29, no. 2 (1995): 545–65.

Fellner, Jamie. *Losing the Vote: The Impact of Felony Disenfranchisement Law in the United States.* Washington, DC: Sentencing Project, 1998.

Fields, Barbara J. "Ideology and Race in American History." In *Region, Race, and Reconstruction: Essays in Honor of C. Vann Woodward,* edited by J. Morgan Kousser and James M. McPherson, 143–77. Oxford: Oxford University Press, 1982.

Fitzgerald, David. *A Nation of Emigrants: How Mexico Manages Its Emigrants.* Berkeley and Los Angeles: University of California Press, 2009.

Foley, Douglas, with Clarice Mota, Donald E. Post, and Ignacio Lozano. *From Peones to Politicos: Class and Ethnicity in a South Texas Town, 1900-1987.* Austin: University of Texas Press, 1988.

Foley, Neil. "Becoming Hispanic: Mexican Americans and the Faustian Pact with Whiteness." In *Reflexiones 1997,* ed. Neil Foley, 53–70. Austin: University of Texas Press, 1998.

—. "Partly Colored or Other White: Mexican Americans and Their Problem with the Color Line." In *American Dreaming, Global Realities: Rethinking U.S. Immigration History,* edited by Vicki L. Ruíz and Donna R. Gabaccia, 361–78. Champaign: University of Illinois Press, 2006.

—. *The White Scourge: Mexicans, Blacks, and Poor Whites in Texas Cotton Culture.* Berkeley and Los Angeles: University of California Press, 1997.

Friedman, Lawrence M. *Crime and Punishment in American History.* New York: Basic Books, 1993.

Galarza, Ernesto. *Merchants of Labor: The Mexican Bracero Story, An Account of the Managed Migration of Mexican Farm Workers in California, 1942-1960.* Santa Barbara, CA: McNally and Loftin, 1964.

Gamio, Manuel. *The Life Story of the Mexican Immigrant: Autobiographical Documents.* New York: Dover, 1971.

—. *Mexican Immigration to the United States: A Study of Human Migration and Adjustment.* Chicago: University of Chicago Press, 1930.

García, Juan Ramón. *Operation Wetback: The Mass Deportation of Mexican Undocumented Workers in 1954.* Westport, CT: Greenwood Press, 1980.

García y Griego, Manuel. *The Importation of Mexican Contract Laborers to the United States, 1942-1964: Antecedents, Operation, and Legacy.* Working Papers in U.S.-Mexican Studies, no. 11. La Jolla: University of California–San Diego, 1980.

García, Mario T. *Desert Immigrants: The Mexicans of El Paso, 1880-1920.* New Haven, CT: Yale University Press, 1981.

García, Matt. *A World of Its Own: Race, Labor, and Citrus in the Making of Greater Los Angeles, 1900–1970.* Chapel Hill: University of North Carolina Press, 2001.

Garland, David. *The Culture of Control: Crime and Social Order in a Contemporary Society.* Chicago: University of Chicago Press, 2001.

———, ed. *Mass Imprisonment: Social Causes and Consequences.* New York: Russell Sage Foundation, 2001.

———. *Punishment and Modern Society: A Study in Social Theory.* Chicago: University of Chicago Press, 1990.

Gilliland, Maude T. *Horsebackers of the Brushcountry: A Story of the Texas Rangers and Mexican Liquor Smugglers.* Brownsville, TX: Springman-King, 1968.

Gilmore, Ruth Wilson. *Golden Gulag: Prisons, Surplus, Crisis, and Opposition in Globalizing California.* Berkeley and Los Angeles: University of California Press, 2006.

González, Gilbert. *Guest Workers or Colonized Labor: Mexican Labor Migration to the United States.* Boulder, CO: Paradigm, 2006.

———. *Mexican Consuls and Labor Organizing: Imperial Politics in the American Southwest.* Austin: University of Texas Press, 1999.

———, and Raúl Fernández. *A Century of Chicano History: Empire, Nations, and Migration.* New York: Routledge, 2003.

González, Guadalupe, and Marta Tienda, eds. *The Drug Connection in U.S.-Mexican Relations.* La Jolla: Center for U.S.-Mexican Studies at the University of California–San Diego, 1989.

Gottschalk, Marie. *The Prison and the Gallows: The Politics of Mass Incarceration in America.* Cambridge: Cambridge University Press, 2006.

Gramsci, Antonio. *Selections from Prison Notebooks.* Edited by Quinten Hoare and Geoffrey Nowell Smith. New York: International Publishers, 1985.

Guerin-Gonzales, Camille. *Mexican Workers and American Dreams: Immigration, Repatriation, and California Farm Labor, 1900–1939.* New Brunswick, NJ: Rutgers University Press, 1994.

Guglielmo, Thomas A. "Fighting for Caucasian Rights: Mexicans, Mexican-Americans, and the Transnational Fight for Civil Rights in World War II Texas." *Journal of American History* 92, no. 4 (2006): 1212–37.

———. *White on Arrival: Italians, Race, Color, and Power in Chicago, 1890–1945.* New York: Oxford University Press, 2003.

Gutiérrez, David. *Walls and Mirrors: Mexican Americans, Mexican Immigrants, and the Politics of Ethnicity.* Berkeley and Los Angeles: University of California Press, 1995.

Hadden, Sally. *Slave Patrols: Law and Violence in Virginia and the Carolinas.* Cambridge, MA: Harvard University Press, 2001.

Hall, Stuart, Charles Critcher, Tony Jefferson, John Clarke, and Brian Robert. *Policing the Crisis: Mugging, the State, and Law and Order.* London: Macmillan, 1978.

Harring, Sidney L. *Policing a Class Society: The Experience of American Cities, 1865–1915.* New Brunswick, NJ: Rutgers University Press, 1983.

Hart, John Mason. *Empire and Revolution: The Americans in Mexico since the Civil War.* Berkeley and Los Angeles: University of California Press, 2002.

———. *Revolutionary Mexico: The Coming and Process of the Mexican Revolution.* Berkeley and Los Angeles: University of California Press, 1997.

Hellyer, Clement David. *The U.S. Border Patrol.* New York: Random House, 1963.

Hernández, David. "Pursuant to Deportation: Latinos and Immigrant Detention." *Latino Studies* 6, nos. 1–2 (2008): 35–63.

———. "Undue Process: Immigrant Detention, Due Process, and Lesser Citizenship." ISSC Fellows Working Papers, ISSC_WP_06. Institute for the Study of Social Change, University of California at Berkeley, November 3, 2005.

Hester, Torrie. "Deportation: Origins of a National and International Power." PhD diss., University of Oregon, 2008.

Heyman, Josiah. "State Effects on Labor Exploitation: The INS and Undocumented Immigrants at the U.S.-Mexico Border." *Critique of Anthropology* 18, no. 2 (1998): 161–80.

———. "U.S. Immigration Officers of Mexican Ancestry as Mexican Americans, Citizens, and Immigration Police." *Current Anthropology* 43, no. 3 (2002): 479–507.

Higham, John. *Strangers in the Land: Patterns of American Nativism, 1860–1925.* Rev. ed. New York: Rutgers University Press, 2002.

Hoffman, Abraham. *Unwanted Mexican Americans in the Great Depression: Repatriation Pressures, 1929–1939.* Tucson: University of Arizona Press, 1974.

Horne, Gerald. *Black and Brown: Africans and the Mexican Revolution, 1910–1920.* New York: New York University Press, 2005.

Horsman, Reginald. *Race and Manifest Destiny: The Origins of American Racial Anglo-Saxonism.* Cambridge, MA: Harvard University Press, 1981.

Hu-DeHart, Evelyn. *The Chinese Experience in Arizona and Northern Mexico.* Tucson: Arizona Historical Society, 1980.

———. "Immigrants to a Developing Society: The Chinese in Northern Mexico, 1875–1932." *Journal of Arizona History* 21 (Autumn 1980): 49–86.

Jacobson, Matthew Frye. *Whiteness of a Different Color: European Immigrants and the Alchemy of Race.* Cambridge, MA: Harvard University Press, 1998.

James, Joy, ed. *States of Confinement: Policing, Detention, and Prisons.* New York: Palgrave, 2000.

Jarnagin, Richard Tait. "The Effect of Increased Illegal Mexican Migration upon the Organization and Operations of the United States Immigration Border Patrol, Southwest Region." Master's thesis, University of Southern California, 1957.

Jelinek, Lawrence J. *Harvest Empire: A History of California Agriculture.* 2nd ed. San Francisco: Boyd and Frasur, 1982.

Johnson, Benjamin Heber. *Rebellion in Texas: How a Forgotten Rebellion and Its Bloody Suppression Turned Mexicans into Americans.* New Haven, CT: Yale University Press, 2003.

Johnson, David K. *The Lavender Scare: The Cold War Persecution of Gays and Lesbians in the Federal Government.* Chicago: University of Chicago Press, 2004.

Johnson, David R. *American Law Enforcement: A History.* St. Louis: Forum Press, 1981.

———. *Illegal Tender: Counterfeiting and the Secret Service in Nineteenth-Century America.* Washington, DC: Smithsonian Institution, 1995.

Johnson, Kevin R. "The Case against Race Profiling in Immigration Enforcement." *Washington University Law Quarterly* 78, no. 3 (2000): 675–736.

———. "The End of 'Civil Rights' as We Know It? Immigration and the New Civil Rights Law." 49 *UCLA Law Review* 1481 (2002).

———. *The "Huddled Masses" Myth: Immigration and Civil Rights.* Philadelphia, PA: Temple University Press, 2004.

Jordan, Bill. *Tales of the Rio Grande.* El Paso, TX: National Border Patrol Museum, 1995.

Jung, Moon-Ho. *Coolies and Cane: Race, Labor, and Sugar in the Age of Emancipation.* Baltimore, MD: Johns Hopkins University Press, 2006.

Kahn, Robert S. *Other People's Blood: U.S. Immigration Prisons in the Reagan Decade.* Boulder, CO: Westview Press, 1996.

Kanstroom, Daniel. *Deportation Nation: Outsiders in American History.* Cambridge, MA: Harvard University Press, 2007.

King, Desmond. *Making Americans: Immigration, Race, and the Origins of the Diverse Democracy.* Cambridge, MA: Harvard University Press, 2000.

Klockars, Carl B. *The Idea of Police.* Beverly Hills, CA: Sage, 1985.

Knight, Alan. *The Mexican Revolution.* 2 vols. Lincoln: University of Nebraska Press, 1986.

———. *U.S.-Mexican Relations, 1910–1940: An Interpretation.* La Jolla: Center for U.S.-Mexican Studies, University of California–San Diego, 1987.

Krauss, Erich, and Alex Pacheco. *On the Line: Inside the U.S. Border Patrol—Doing the Most Dangerous Job in America.* New York: Citadel Press Books, 2004.

Kraut, Alan M. *The Huddled Masses: The Immigrant in American Society, 1880–1921.* Wheeling, WV: Harlan Davidson, 2001.

Landa y Piña, Andrés. *El Servicio de Migración en México.* Mexico City: Talleres Gráficos, 1930.

Lane, Roger. *Policing the City: Boston, 1822–1885.* Cambridge, MA: Harvard University Press, 1971.

Lee, Erika. *At America's Gates: Chinese Immigration during the Exclusion Era, 1882–1943.* Chapel Hill: University of North Carolina Press. 2004.

———. "Enforcing the Borders: Chinese Exclusion along the U.S. Borders with Canada and Mexico, 1882—1924." *Journal of American History* 89, no. 1 (2002): 54–86.

LeMay, Michael. *From Open Door to Dutch Door: An Analysis of U.S. Immigration Policy Since 1920.* New York: Praeger, 1987.

Lessard, David Richard. "Agrarianism and Nationalism: Mexico and the Bracero Program." PhD diss., Tulane University, 1984.

Luibhéid, Eithne. *Entry Denied: Controlling Sexuality at the Border.* Minneapolis: University of Minnesota Press, 2002.

Mabry, Donald J., and Robert J. Shafer. *Neighbors, Mexico, and the United States: Wetbacks and Oil.* Chicago: Nelson-Hall, 1981.

MacCain, Johnny. "Contract Labor as a Factor in United States-Mexican Relations, 1942—1947." PhD diss., University of Texas at Austin, 1970.

Mackay, Reynolds. "The Federal Deportation Campaign in Texas: Mexican Deportation from the Lower Rio Grande Valley during the Great Depression." *Borderlands* 5, no. 1 (1981): 95–120.

Manza, Jeff, and Christopher Uggen. *Locked Out: Felon Disenfranchisement and American Democracy.* Oxford: Oxford University Press, 2006.

Maril, Robert Lee. *Patrolling Chaos: The U.S. Border Patrol in Deep South Texas.* Lubbock: Texas Tech University Press, 2006.

Marín, María Luisa González. *La Industrialización en México.* Mexico City: Instituto de Investigaciónes Económicas, Universidad Nacional Autónoma de México: 2002.

Markiewicz, Dana. *The Mexican Revolution and the Limits of Agrarian Reform, 1915-1946.* Boulder, CO: Lynne Rienner, 1993.

Márquez, Benjamin. *LULAC: The Evolution of a Mexican American Political Organization.* Austin: University of Texas Press, 1993.

Martínez, John. "Mexican Emigration to the United States, 1910–1930." PhD diss., University of California, 1957.

Massey, Douglas S., Jorge Durand, and Nolan J. Malone. *Beyond Smoke and Mirrors: Mexican Immigration in an Era of Economic Integration.* New York: Russell Sage Foundation, 2002.

———, Rafael Alarcón, Jorge Durand, and Humberto González. *Return to Aztlan: The Social Process of International Migration from Western Mexico.* Berkeley and Los Angeles: University of California Press, 1987.

Mauer, Marc. *Race to Incarcerate.* New York: New Press, 1999.

———, and Meda Chesney-Lind, eds. *Invisible Punishment: The Collateral Consequences of Mass Imprisonment.* New York: Free Press, 2002.

McWilliams, Carey. *Factories in the Field: The Story of Migratory Farm Labor in California.* 1939; reprint, Santa Barbara, CA: Peregrine, 1971.

McWilliams, John C. *The Protectors: Harry J. Anslinger and the Federal Bureau of Narcotics, 1930–1962.* Newark, DE: University of Delaware Press, 1990.

Meade, Adalberto Walter. *El valle de Mexicali.* Mexicali, Mexico: Universidad Autónoma de Baja California, 1996.

Menchaca, Martha. "Chicano Indianism: A Historical Account of Racial Repression in the United States." *American Ethnologist* 20, no. 3 (1993): 583—604.

———. *Recovering History, Constructing Race: the Indian, Black, and White Roots of Mexican Americans.* Austin: University of Texas Press, 2001.

Miller, Wilbur R. *Cops and Bobbies: Police Authority in New York and London, 1830-1870.* Columbus: Ohio State University Press, 1999.

———. *Revenuers and Moonshiners: Enforcing Federal Liquor Law in the Mountain South, 1865-1900.* Chapel Hill: University of North Carolina Press, 1991.

Mishima, María Elena Ota, ed. *Destino México: Un estudio de las migraciones asiáticas a México, siglos XIX y XX.* Mexico City: El Colegio de México, 1997.

Monkkonen, Eric H. *Police in Urban America, 1860–1920.* New York: Cambridge University Press, 2004.

Monroy, Douglas. *Rebirth: Mexican Los Angeles from the Great Migration to the Great Depression.* Berkeley and Los Angeles: University of California Press, 1999.

———. *Thrown among Strangers: The Making of Mexican Culture in Frontier California.* Berkeley and Los Angeles: University of California Press, 1990.

Montejano, David. *Anglos and Mexicans in the Making of Texas, 1836-1986.* Austin: University of Texas Press, 1987.

Moore, Alvin Edward. *The Border Patrol.* Santa Fe, NM: Sunstone Press, 1988.

Motomura, Hiroshi. *Americans in Waiting: The Lost Story of Immigration and Citizenship in the United States.* New York: Oxford University Press, 2006.

Musto, David F. *The American Disease: Origins of Narcotics Control.* 3rd ed. New York: Oxford University Press, 1999.

Myers, John Myers. *The Border Wardens.* Englewood Cliffs, NJ: Prentice-Hall, 1971.

Nadelmann, Ethan A. *Cops across Borders: The Internationalization of U.S. Criminal Law Enforcement.* University Park: Pennsylvania State University Press, 1993.

Nash, Gerald D. *World War II and the West: Reshaping the Economy.* Lincoln: University of Nebraska Press, 1990.

Navarro, Moisés González. *La colonización en México, 1877-1910.* Mexico City: Talleres de Impresión de Estampillas y Valores, 1960.

———. *Los extranjeros en México y los mexicanos en el extranjero, 1821-1970.* Vol. 3 of 3. Mexico City: El Colegio de México, 1994.

———. *Sociedad y cultura en el Porfiriato.* Mexico City: Consejo Nacional para la Cultura y las Artes, 1994.

Nelson, Scott Reynolds. *Steel Drivin' Man—John Henry: The Untold Story of An American Legend.* Oxford: Oxford University Press, 2007.

Neuman, Gerald L. *Strangers to the Constitution: Immigrants, Borders, and Fundamental Law.* Princeton, NJ: Princeton University Press, 1996.

Nevins, Joseph. *Operation Gatekeeper: The Rise of the "Illegal Alien" and the Making of the U.S.-Mexico Boundary.* New York: Routledge, 2002.

Ngai, Mae. *Impossible Subjects: Illegal Aliens and the Making of Modern America.* Princeton, NJ: Princeton University Press, 2004.

Niblo, Stephen. *The Impact of War: Mexico and World War II.* Melbourne, Australia: La Trobe University Institute of Latin American Studies, Occasional Paper No. 10, 1988.

———. *War, Diplomacy, and Development: The United States and Mexico, 1938-1954.* Wilmington, DE: Scholarly Resources, 1995.

Odens, Peter. *The Desert Trackers: Men of the Border Patrol.* Arizona: privately printed, 1975.

Omi, Michael, and Howard Winant. *Racial Formation in the United States: From the 1960s to the 1990s.* 2nd ed. New York: Routledge, 1994.

Paredes, Américo. *"With His Pistol in His Hand": A Border Ballad and Its Hero.* Austin: University of Texas Press, 1958.

Parenti, Christian. *Lockdown America: Police and Prisons in the Age of Crisis.* New York: Verso, 1999.

Parker, Ed. *Prop Cops: The First Quarter Century Aloft.* El Paso, TX: Border Patrol Foundation, 1983.

Perkins, Clifford Alan. *Border Patrol: With the U.S. Immigration Service on the Mexican Boundary, 1910-1954.* El Paso: Texas Western Press, 1978.

Petersilia, Joan. *When Prisoners Come Home: Parole and Prisoner Reentry.* Oxford: Oxford University Press, 2003.

Pisani, Donald J. *From the Family Farm to Agribusiness: The Irrigation Crusade in California and the West, 1850-1931.* Berkeley and Los Angeles: University of California Press, 1984.

Pitt, Leonard. *The Decline of the Californios: A Social History of the Spanish-Speaking Californians, 1846-1890.* Berkeley and Los Angeles: University of California Press, 1998.

Prince, Carl E., and Mollie Keller. *The U.S. Customs Service: A Bicentennial History*. Washington, DC: Department of Treasury, 1989.

Raat, Dirk W. *Mexico and the United States: Ambivalent Vistas*. Athens: University of Georgia Press, 2004.

Rak, Mary Kidder. *The Border Patrol*. Boston, MA: Houghton Mifflin, 1938.

Reiner, Robert. *The Politics of the Police*. New York: St. Martin's Press, 1985.

Reisler, Mark. *By the Sweat of Their Brow: Mexican Immigrant Labor in the United States, 1900—1940*. Westport, CT: Greenwood, Press, 1976.

Richardson, James F. *The New York Police, Colonial times to 1901*. New York: Oxford University Press, 1970.

Roediger, David. *The Wages of Whiteness: Race and the Making of the American Working Class*. New York: Verso, 2007.

———. *Working toward Whiteness: How America's Immigrants Became White: The Strange Journey from Ellis Island to the Suburbs*. New York: Basic Books, 2005.

Romero, Robert Chao. "Transnational Chinese Immigrant Smuggling to the United States via Mexico and Cuba, 1882–1916," *Amerasia Journal* 30, no. 3 (2004/2005): 1–16.

Rosas, Ana. "Familias Flexibles (Flexible Families): Bracero Families' Lives across Cultures, Communities, and Countries, 1942–1964." PhD diss., University of Southern California, 2006.

Rosas, Gilberto. "The Thickening of the Borderlands: Diffused Exceptionality and 'Immigrant Struggles' during the 'War on Terror.'" *Cultural Dynamics* 18, no. 3 (2006): 335–49.

Rousey, Dennis. *Policing the Southern City: New Orleans, 1805–1889*. Baton Rouge: Louisiana State University Press, 1996.

Sabo, Don, Terry A. Kupers, and Willie London, eds. *Prison Masculinities*. Philadelphia, PA: Temple University Press, 2001.

Sackman, Douglas. *Orange Empire: California and the Fruits of Eden*. Berkeley and Los Angeles: University of California Press, 2005.

Saldaña Martínez, Tomás. *El costo social de un éxito político*. Chapingo, México: Colegio de Postgraduados, 1980.

Salyer, Lucy E. *Laws Harsh as Tigers: Chinese Immigrants and the Shaping of Modern Immigration Law*. Chapel Hill: University of North Carolina Press, 1995.

Samora, Julian. *Los Mojados: The Wetback Story*. Notre Dame, IN: University of Notre Dame Press, 1971.

———, with Joe Bernal and Albert Peña. *Gunpowder Justice: A Reassessment of the Texas Rangers*. Notre Dame, IN: University of Notre Dame Press, 1979.

Sánchez, George. *Becoming Mexican American: Ethnicity, Culture, and Identity in Chicano Los Angeles, 1900-1945*. New York: Oxford University Press, 1993.

———. "Face the Nation: Race, Immigration, and the Rise of Nativism in Late Twentieth-Century America." *International Migration Review* 31, no. 4 (1997): 1009–30.

Sandos, James A. *Rebellion in the Borderlands: Anarchism and the Plan of San Diego, 1904–1923*. Norman: University of Oklahoma Press, 1992.

Santibáñez, Enrique. *Ensayo acerca de la inmigración mexicana en los Estados Unidos*. San Antonio, TX: Clegg, 1930.

Saunders, Lyle, and Olen Leonard. *The Wetback in the Lower Rio Grande Valley of Texas.* Austin: University of Texas, 1951.

Saxton, Alexander. *The Indispensable Enemy: Labor and the Anti-Chinese Movement in California.* Berkeley and Los Angeles: University of California Press, 1971.

Scalia, John, and Marika Litras. "Immigration Offenders in the Federal Criminal Justice System, 2000." Bureau of Justice Statistics: Special Report (August 2002). Washington, DC: U.S. Department of Justice, Office of Justice Programs, 2002.

Schmidt, Arthur. "Mexicans, Migrants and Indigenous Peoples: The Work of Manuel Gamio in the United status, 1925–1927." In *Strange Pilgrimages: Exile, Travel, and National Identity in Latin America, 1800–1990s,* edited by Ingrid E. Fey and Karine Racine, 163–78. Wilmington, DE: Scholarly Resources, 2000.

Schuck, Peter H. *Citizens, Strangers, and In-Betweens: Essays on Immigration and Citizenship.* Boulder, CO: Westview Press, 1998.

Secretaría de Gobernación. *Compilación histórica de la legislación migratoria en México: 1821–2000.* Mexico City: Secretaría de Gobernación/Instituto Nacional de Migración, 2000.

Sheptycki, J. W. *In Search of Transnational Policing: Toward a Sociology of Global Policing.* Aldershot, U.K.: Ashgate, 2003.

———. *Issues in Transnational Policing.* New York: Routledge, 2000.

———. "Transnational Policing and the Makings of a Postmodern State." *British Journal of Criminology* 35, no. 4 (1995): 613–35.

Simon, Jonathan. *Governing Through Crime: How the War on Crime Transformed American Democracy and Created a Culture of Fear.* Oxford: Oxford University Press, 2007.

———. "Refugees in a Carceral Age: The Rebirth of Immigration Prisons in the United States." *Public Culture* 10, no. 3 (1998): 577–606.

Siskin, Alison, and Margaret Mikyung Lee. *Detention of Noncitizens in the United States.* Report RL31606. Washington, DC: Congressional Research Service, October 15, 2003.

Smith, Peter, ed. *Drug Policy in the Americas.* Boulder, CO: Westview Press, 1992.

Steen, Murphy F. *Twenty-Five Years a U.S. Border Patrolman.* Dallas: Royal Publishing, 1958.

Stern, Alexandra Minna. "Buildings, Boundaries, and Blood." *Hispanic American Historical Review* 79, no. 1 (1999): 41–81.

———. "Nationalism on the Line: Masculinity, Race, and the Creation of the U.S. Border Patrol, 1910–1940." In Truett and Young, *Continental Crossroads.*

Stolberg, Mary M. "Policing the Twilight Zone: Federalizing Crime Fighting during the New Deal." *Journal of Policy History* 7, no. 4 (1995): 393–415.

Taylor, Lawrence Douglas. "El contrabando de chinos a lo largo de la frontera entre México y Estados Unidos, 1882—1931." *Frontera Norte* 6, no. 11 (1994): 41–55.

Taylor, Paul Schuster. *An American-Mexican Frontier: Nueces County, Texas.* New York: Russell and Russell, 1934.

———. *Mexican Labor in the United States: Dimmit County, Winter Garden District, South Texas.* Berkeley and Los Angeles: University of California Press, 1930.

———. *Mexican Labor in the United States: Imperial Valley.* Berkeley and Los Angeles: University of California Press, 1930.

Thelen, David. "Rethinking History and the Nation-State: Mexico and the United States." Special issue, *Journal of American History* 86, no. 2 (1999): 439–53.

Tichenor, Daniel J. *Dividing Lines: The Politics of Immigration Control in America*. Princeton, NJ: Princeton University Press, 2002.

Tonry, Michael, and Joan Petersilia, eds. *Prisons*. Chicago: University of Chicago Press, 1999.

Toro, María Celia. *Mexico's "War" on Drugs: Causes and Consequences*. Boulder, CO: Rienner, 1995.

Truett, Samuel, and Elliott Young. *Continental Crossroads: Remapping U.S.-Mexico Borderlands History*. Durham, NC: Duke University Press, 2004.

Tumlinson, John, with Robert Kuykendall, Nicholas Clopper, and Moses Morrison. *Manuscripts, Documents, and Letters of Early Texans*. Austin, TX: The Steck Company, 1937.

Utley, Robert M. *Lone Star Justice: The First Century of the Texas Rangers*. Oxford: Oxford University Press, 2002.

———. *Lone Star Lawmen: The Second Century of the Texas Rangers*. Oxford: Oxford University Press, 2007.

Valesco, Mercedes Carreras de. *Los mexicanos que devolvió la crisis, 1929–1932*. Mexico City: Secretaría de Relaciones Exteriores, 1974.

Vargas, Zaragosa. *Labor Rights Are Civil Rights: Mexican American Workers in Twentieth-Century America*. Princeton, NJ: Princeton University Press, 2005.

Velkamp, Theresa, A. *So Far from Allah, So Close to Mexico: Middle Eastern Immigrants in Modern Mexico*. Austin: University of Texas Press, 2007.

Von Eschen, Penny. *Race against Empire: Black Americans and Anticolonialism, 1937–1957*. Ithaca, NY: Cornell University Press, 1997.

———. *Race and Empire During the Cold War*. Cambridge, MA: Harvard University Press, 2004.

Wacquant, Loïc. "From Slavery to Mass Incarceration: Rethinking the 'Race Question' in the U.S." *New Left Review* 13 (January–February 2002): 41–60.

———. "Race as Civic Felony." *International Social Science Journal* 57, no. 183 (2005): 127–42.

Walker, Neil. "The Pattern of Transnational Policing." In *Handbook of Policing*, edited by Tim Newburn, 111–35. Cullompton, U.K.: Willan Publishing, 2003.

Walker, Samuel. *Popular Justice: A History of American Criminal Justice*. Oxford: Oxford University Press, 1997.

Walker, William O. *Drug Control in the Americas*. Albuquerque: University of New Mexico Press, 1989.

Walsh, Casey. "Demobilizing the Revolution: Migration, Repatriation, and Colonization in Mexico, 1911–1940." Working Paper no. 26. La Jolla: Center for Comparative Immigration Studies at the University of California–San Diego, 2000.

———. "Development in the Borderlands: Cotton Capitalism, State Formation, and Regional Political Culture in Northern Mexico." PhD diss., New School University, 2001.

———. "Eugenic Acculturation: Manuel Gamio, Migration Studies, and the Anthropology of Development in Mexico, 1910–1940." *Latin American Perspectives* 31, no. 5 (2004): 118–45.

Webb, Walter Prescott. *The Texas Rangers: A Century of Frontier Defense*. Austin: University of Texas Press, 1965.

Weber, Devra. *Dark Sweat, White Gold: California Farm Workers, Cotton, and the New Deal*. Berkeley and Los Angeles: University of California Press, 1994.

———, Roberto Melville, and Juan Vicente Palerm, eds. *El inmigrante mexicano: La historia de su vida, entrevistas completas, 1926–1927: Manuel Gamio.* Mexico City: University of California, Institute for Mexico and the United States; CIESAS, 2002.

Western, Bruce. *Punishment and Inequality in America.* New York: Russell Sage Foundation, 2006.

Westley, William. *Violence and the Police: A Sociological Study of Law, Custom, and Morality.* Cambridge, MA: MIT Press, 1970.

Wideman, John Edgar. "The Politics of Prison: Doing Time, Marking Race." *Nation,* October 30, 1995.

INDEX

Page references given in italics indicate illustrations or material contained in their captions.

AMERICAN CROSSROADS

Edited by Earl Lewis, George Lipsitz, Peggy Pascoe, George Sánchez, and Dana Takagi

TEXT
10/12.5 Minion Pro

DISPLAY
Minion Pro

COMPOSITOR
Integrated Composition Systems

INDEXER
Kevin Millham

CARTOGRAPHER
Bill Nelson

PRINTER AND BINDER
Maple-Vail Book Manufacturing Group